Say I Love You.

11

by
Kanae
Hazuki

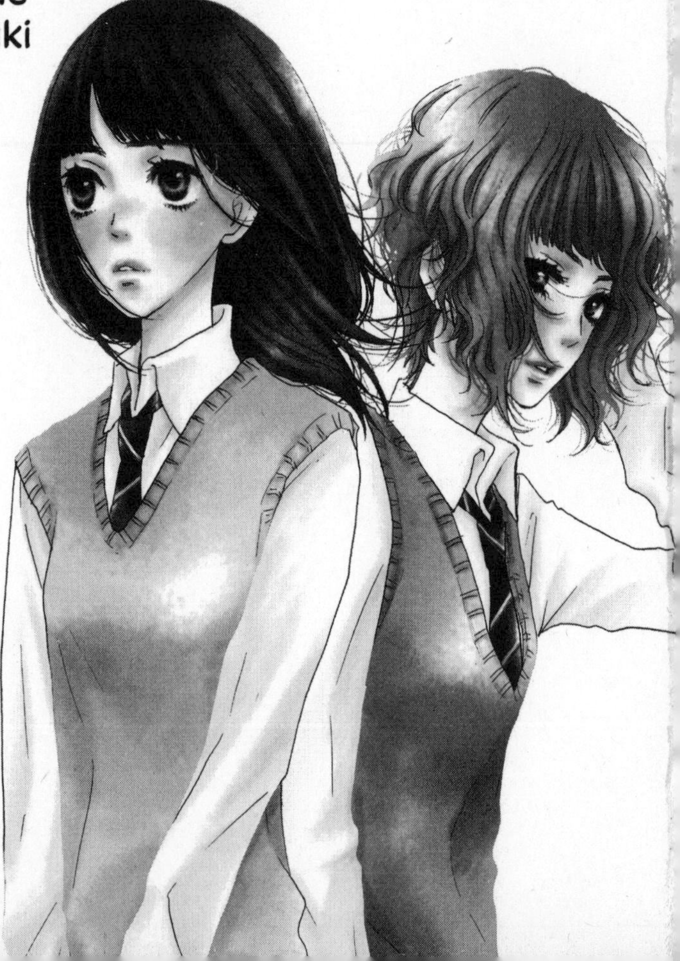

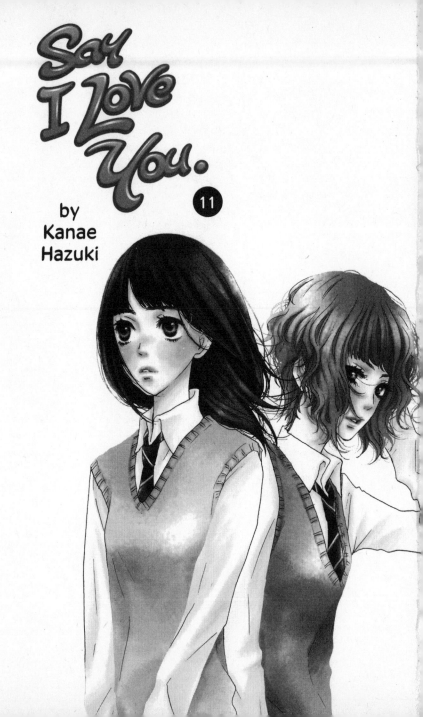

Kanae Hazuki
presents

Chapter 41

Chapter 42

Chapter 43

Chapter 44

CHARACTERS

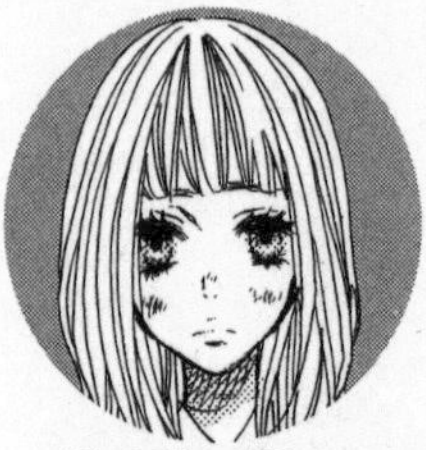

Mei Tachibana

A girl who hasn't had a single friend, let alone a boyfriend, in sixteen years and has lived her life trusting no one. She finds herself attracted to Yamato, who, for some reason, just won't leave her alone, and they start dating.

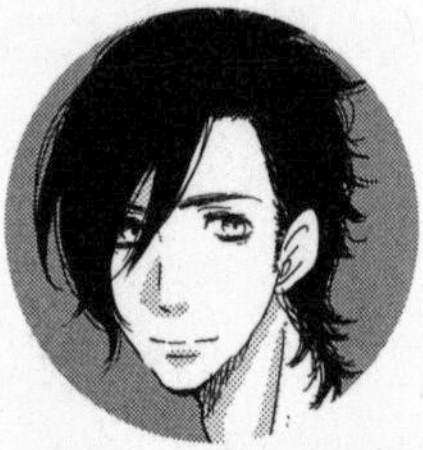

Yamato Kurosawa

The most popular boy at Mei's school. He has the love of many girls, yet for some reason, he is obsessed with Mei, the brooding weirdo girl from another class.

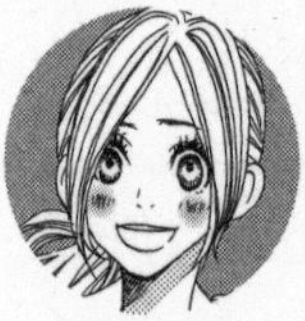

Mei's first friend. Unlike the other kids, she treats Mei like a normal person. She had a thing for Yamato, but now she is head over heels for his friend Nakanishi.

Asami

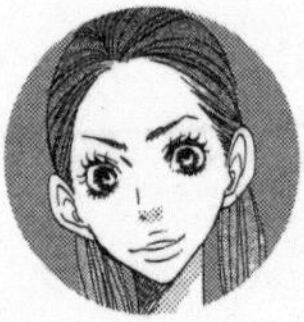

Mei's first rival. She had a crush on Yamato and was jealous of Mei, but now they are close friends. She is currently dating Masashi, who always loved her.

Aiko

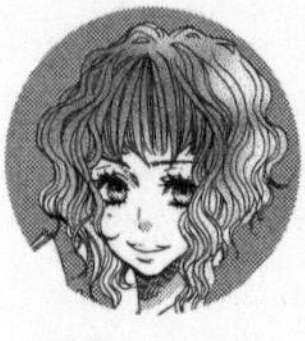

An amateur model who has her sights set on Yamato. She transferred to his school and got him a modeling job, and the two gradually grew closer. In the end, Yamato rejected her, but now she has moved on and is going forward with a positive outlook.

Megumi

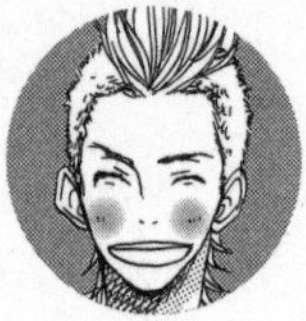

Yamato's classmate from middle school who had been the victim of bullying. For his own reasons, he started high school a year late. He likes Mei and told her so, but...?

Kai

STORY

Mei Tachibana spent sixteen years without a single friend or boyfriend, but then, for some reason, Yamato Kurosawa, the most popular boy in school, took a liking to her. Mei was drawn in by Yamato's kindness and sincerity, and now they have entered the second year of their relationship. That Christmas, Mei went to a party with Asami, Aiko, and the others at Yamato's house, and when her friends learned it was also her birthday, they gave her a warm celebration. Then, thanks to the scheming of their friends, Mei and Yamato were left alone, and they finally joined in heart and body—it was a day she'll never forget, but...?!

Chapter
41

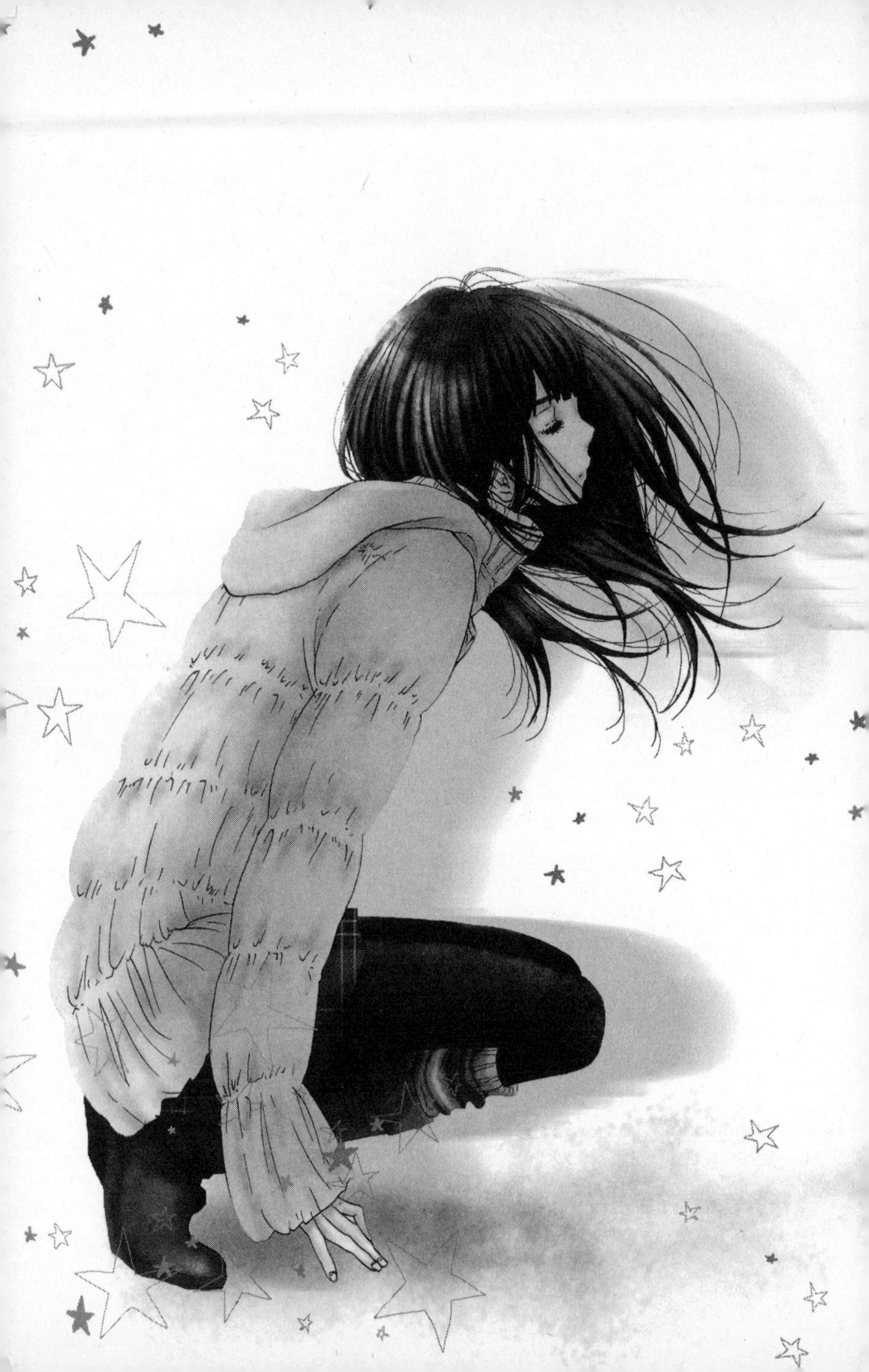

Say "I love you".

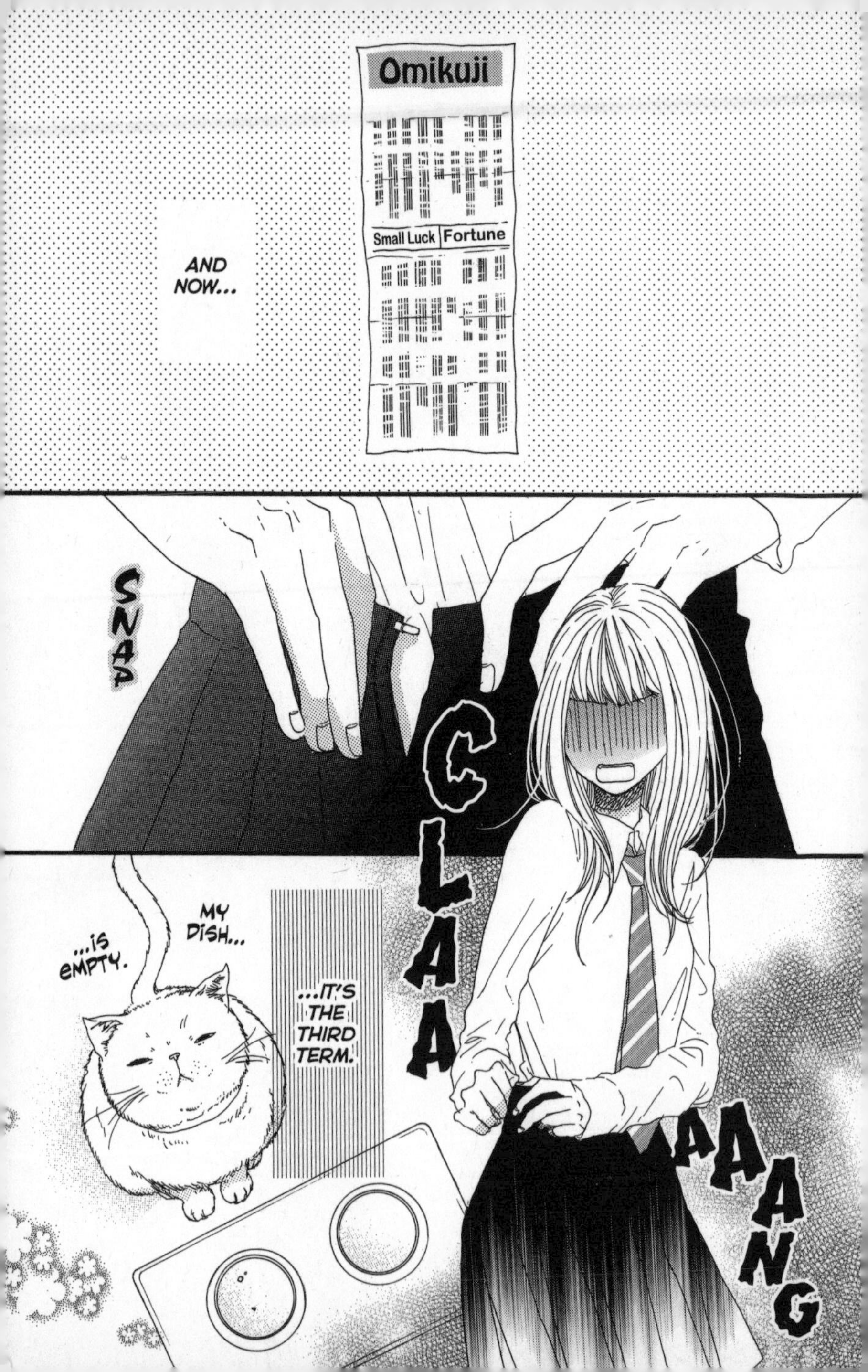
Omikuji
Small Luck
Fortune
AND NOW...
CLAAAAAAANG
SNAP
...IT'S THE THIRD TERM.
MY DISH...
...is empty.

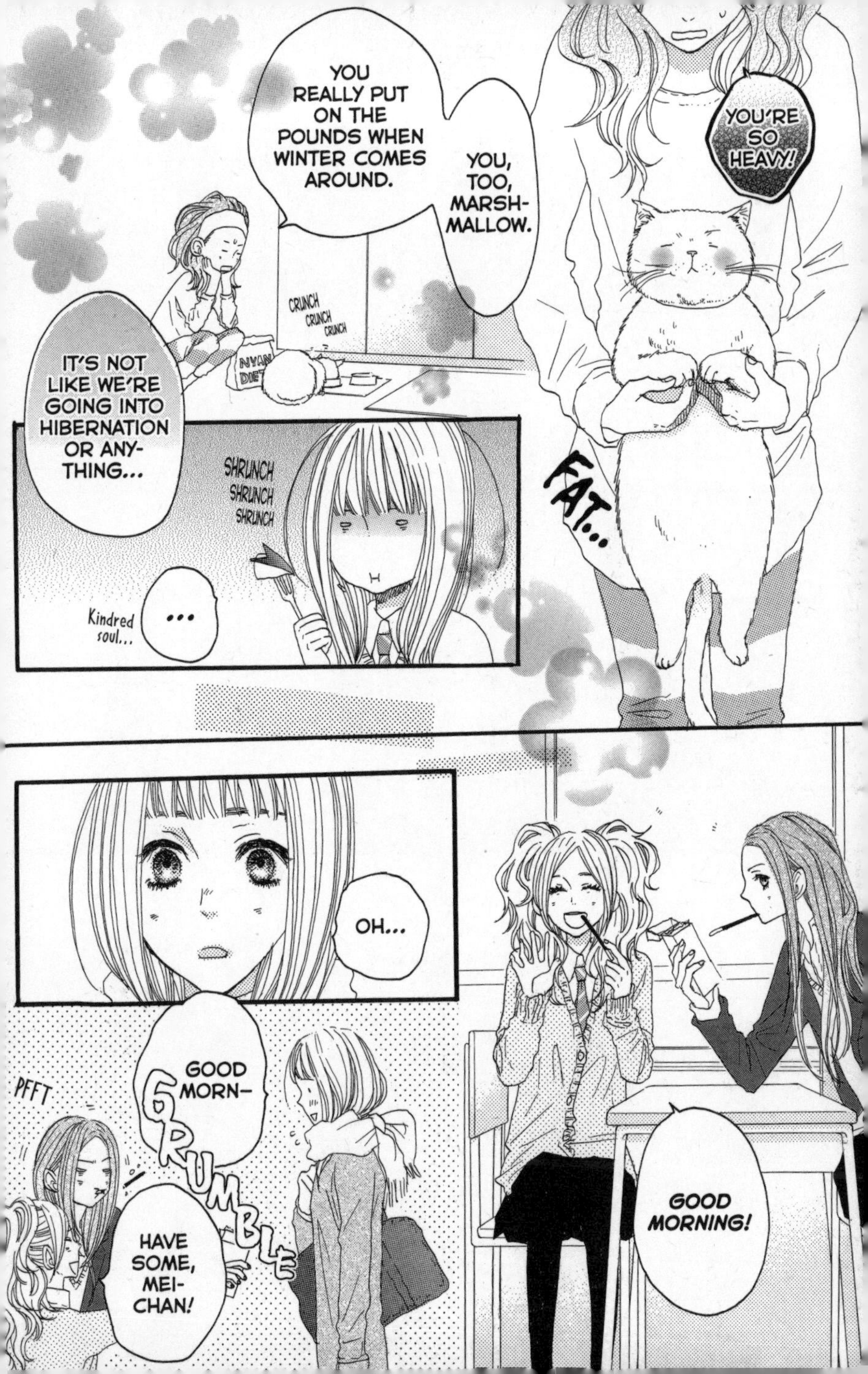
YOU'RE SO HEAVY!
FAT...
YOU REALLY PUT ON THE POUNDS WHEN WINTER COMES AROUND.
YOU, TOO, MARSHMALLOW.
CRUNCH CRUNCH CRUNCH
NYAN DIET
IT'S NOT LIKE WE'RE GOING INTO HIBERNATION OR ANY-THING...
SHRUNCH SHRUNCH SHRUNCH
...
Kindred soul...
GOOD MORNING!
OH...
GOOD MORN—
GRUMBLE
HAVE SOME, MEI-CHAN!
PFFT

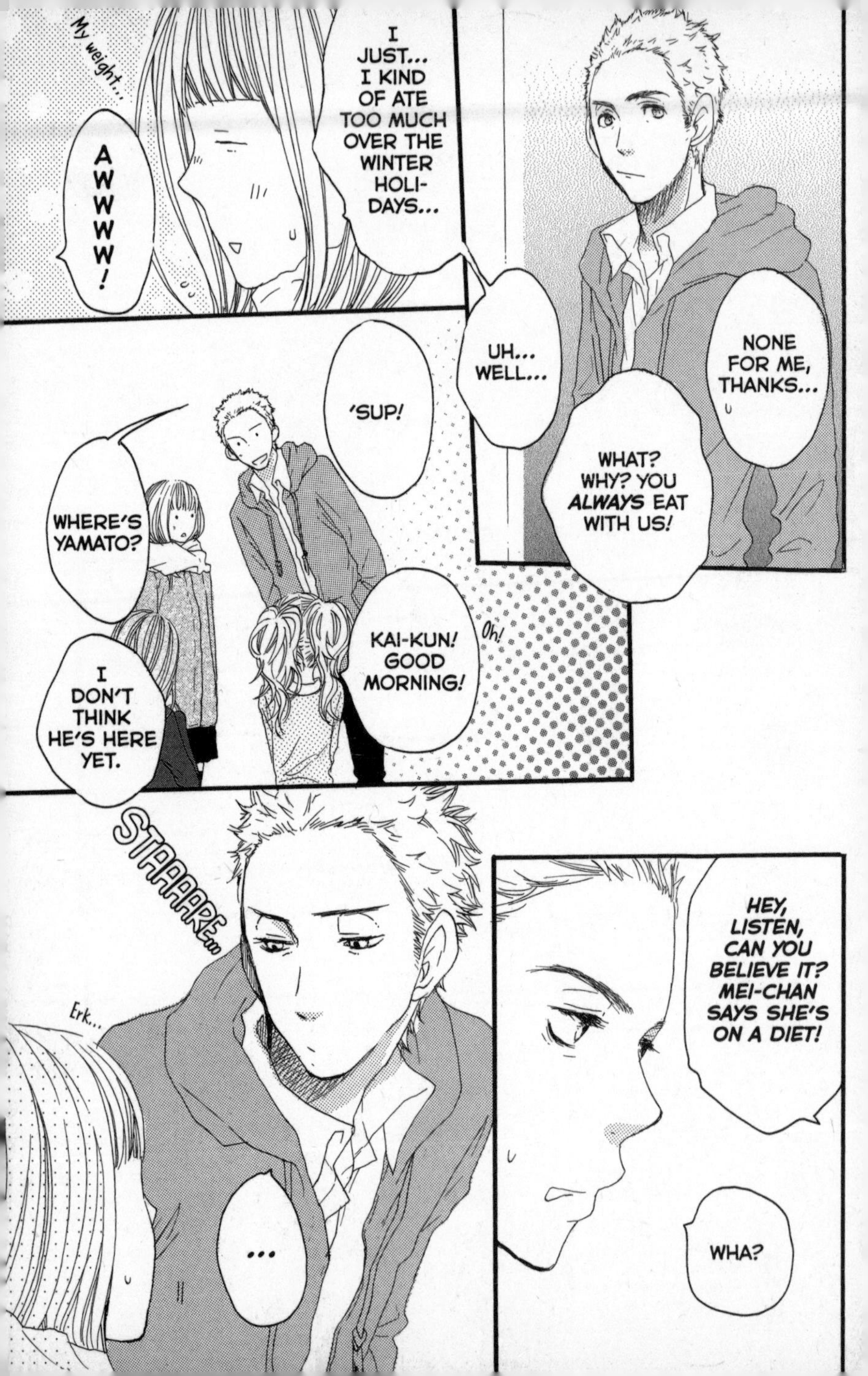
NONE FOR ME, THANKS...
WHAT? WHY? YOU *ALWAYS* EAT WITH US!
UH... WELL...
I JUST... I KIND OF ATE TOO MUCH OVER THE WINTER HOLI-DAYS...
AWWWWW!
My weight...
KAI-KUN! GOOD MORNING!
Oh!
'SUP!
WHERE'S YAMATO?
I DON'T THINK HE'S HERE YET.
HEY, LISTEN, CAN YOU BELIEVE IT? MEI-CHAN SAYS SHE'S ON A DIET!
WHA?
STAAARE...
...
Erk...

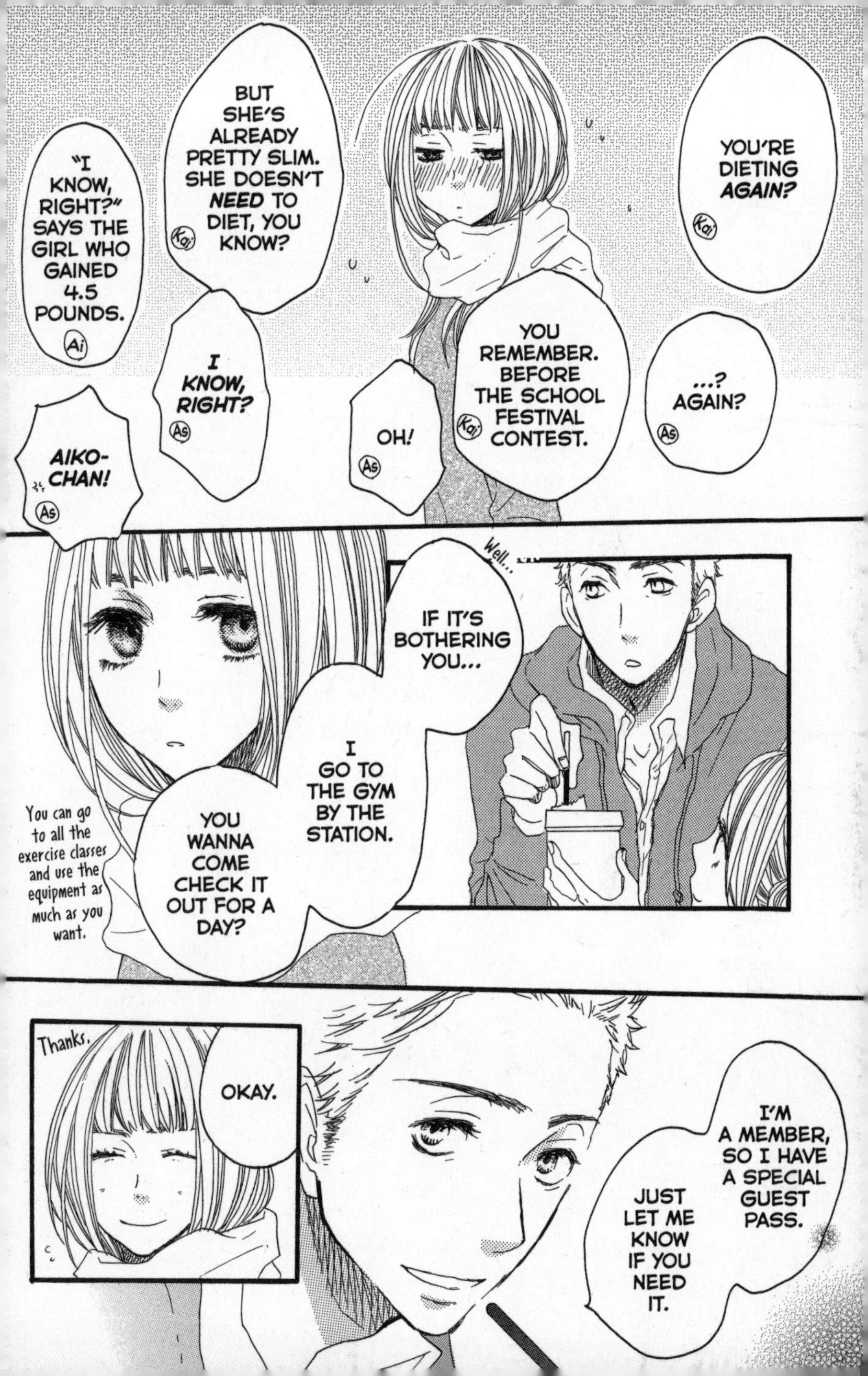
YOU'RE DIETING AGAIN?
...? AGAIN?
YOU REMEMBER. BEFORE THE SCHOOL FESTIVAL CONTEST.
OH!
BUT SHE'S ALREADY PRETTY SLIM. SHE DOESN'T NEED TO DIET, YOU KNOW?
I KNOW, RIGHT?
"I KNOW, RIGHT?" SAYS THE GIRL WHO GAINED 4.5 POUNDS.
AIKO-CHAN!
Well...
IF IT'S BOTHERING YOU...
I GO TO THE GYM BY THE STATION.
YOU WANNA COME CHECK IT OUT FOR A DAY?
You can go to all the exercise classes and use the equipment as much as you want.
I'M A MEMBER, SO I HAVE A SPECIAL GUEST PASS.
JUST LET ME KNOW IF YOU NEED IT.
Thanks.
OKAY.

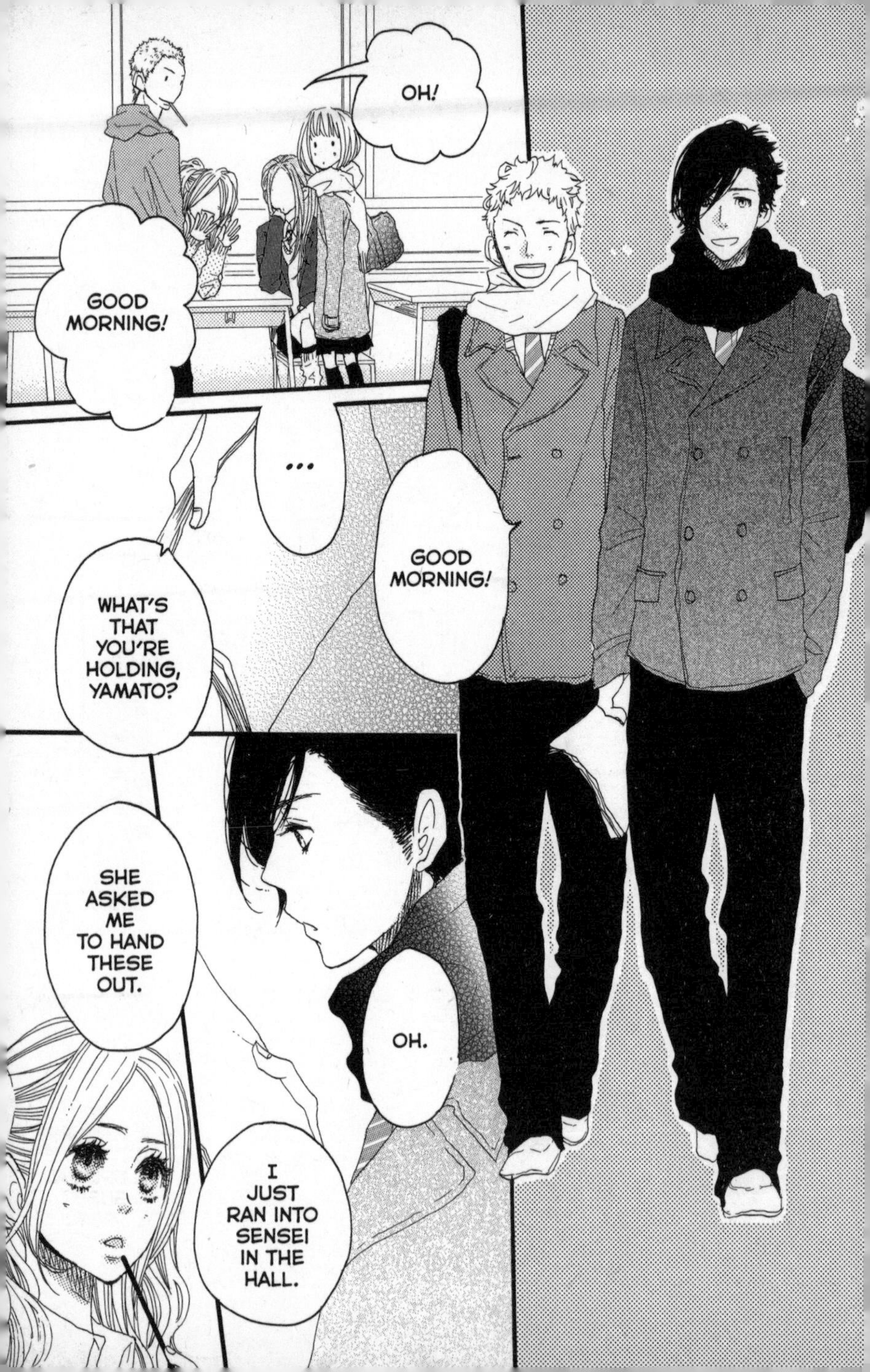
GOOD MORNING!
OH!
GOOD MORNING!
...
WHAT'S THAT YOU'RE HOLDING, YAMATO?
OH.
I JUST RAN INTO SENSEI IN THE HALL.
SHE ASKED ME TO HAND THESE OUT.

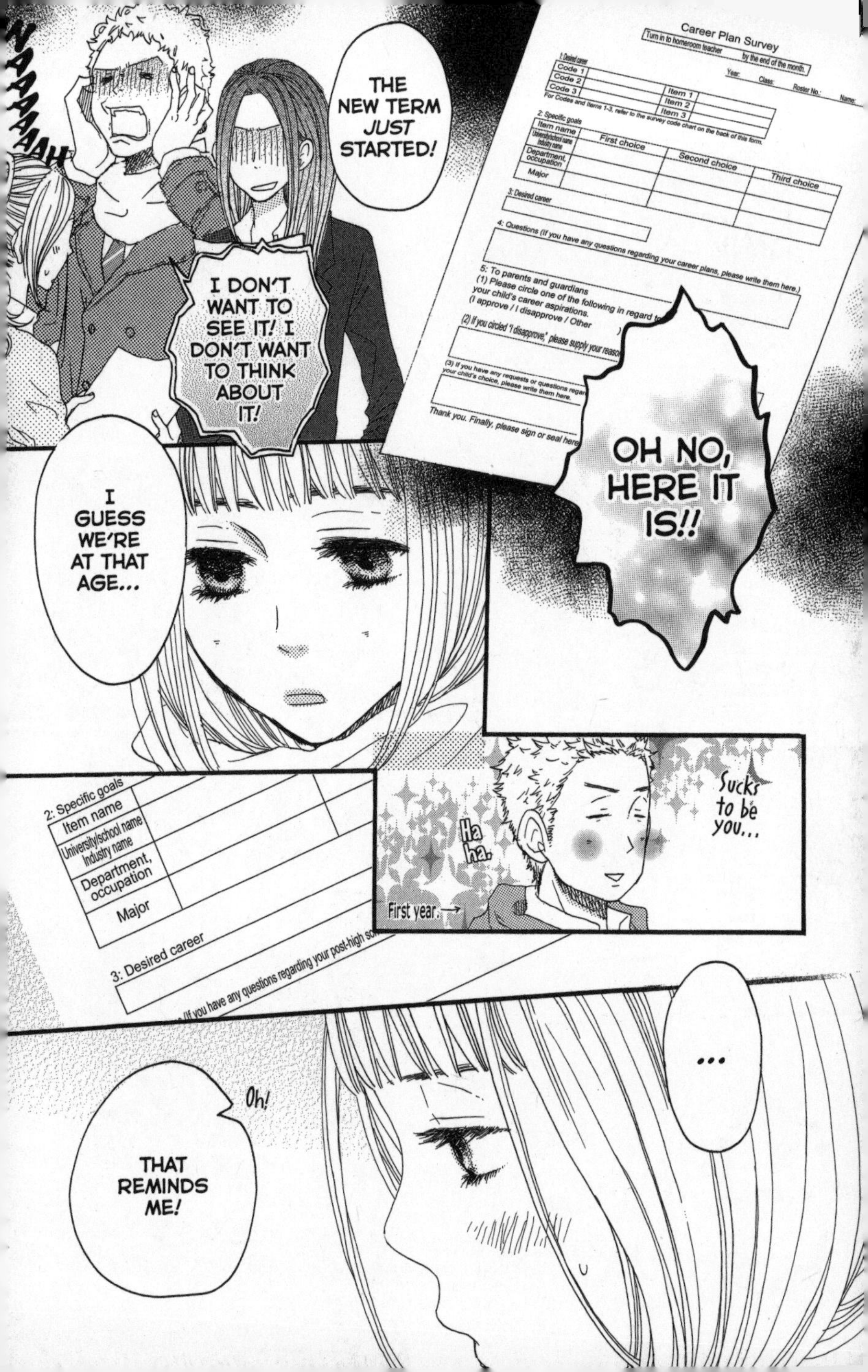
Career Plan Survey
Turn in to homeroom teacher by the end of the month.
1: Desired career
Year: Class: Roster No.: Name:
Code 1
Code 2
Code 3
Item 1
Item 2
Item 3
For Codes and Items 1-3, refer to the survey code chart on the back of this form.
2: Specific goals
Item name
University/school name Industry name
Department, occupation
Major
First choice
Second choice
Third choice
3: Desired career
4: Questions (If you have any questions regarding your career plans, please write them here.)
5: To parents and guardians
(1) Please circle one of the following in regard to your child's career aspirations.
(I approve / I disapprove / Other)
(2) If you circled "I disapprove," please supply your reason
(3) If you have any requests or questions regar your child's choice, please write them here.
Thank you. Finally, please sign or seal here
OH NO, HERE IT IS!!
THE NEW TERM JUST STARTED!
WAAAAAAAH
I DON'T WANT TO SEE IT! I DON'T WANT TO THINK ABOUT IT!
I GUESS WE'RE AT THAT AGE...
Sucks to be you...
Ha ha.
First year. →
2: Specific goals
Item name
University/school name Industry name
Department, occupation
Major
3: Desired career
(If you have any questions regarding your post-high sc
...
Oh!
THAT REMINDS ME!

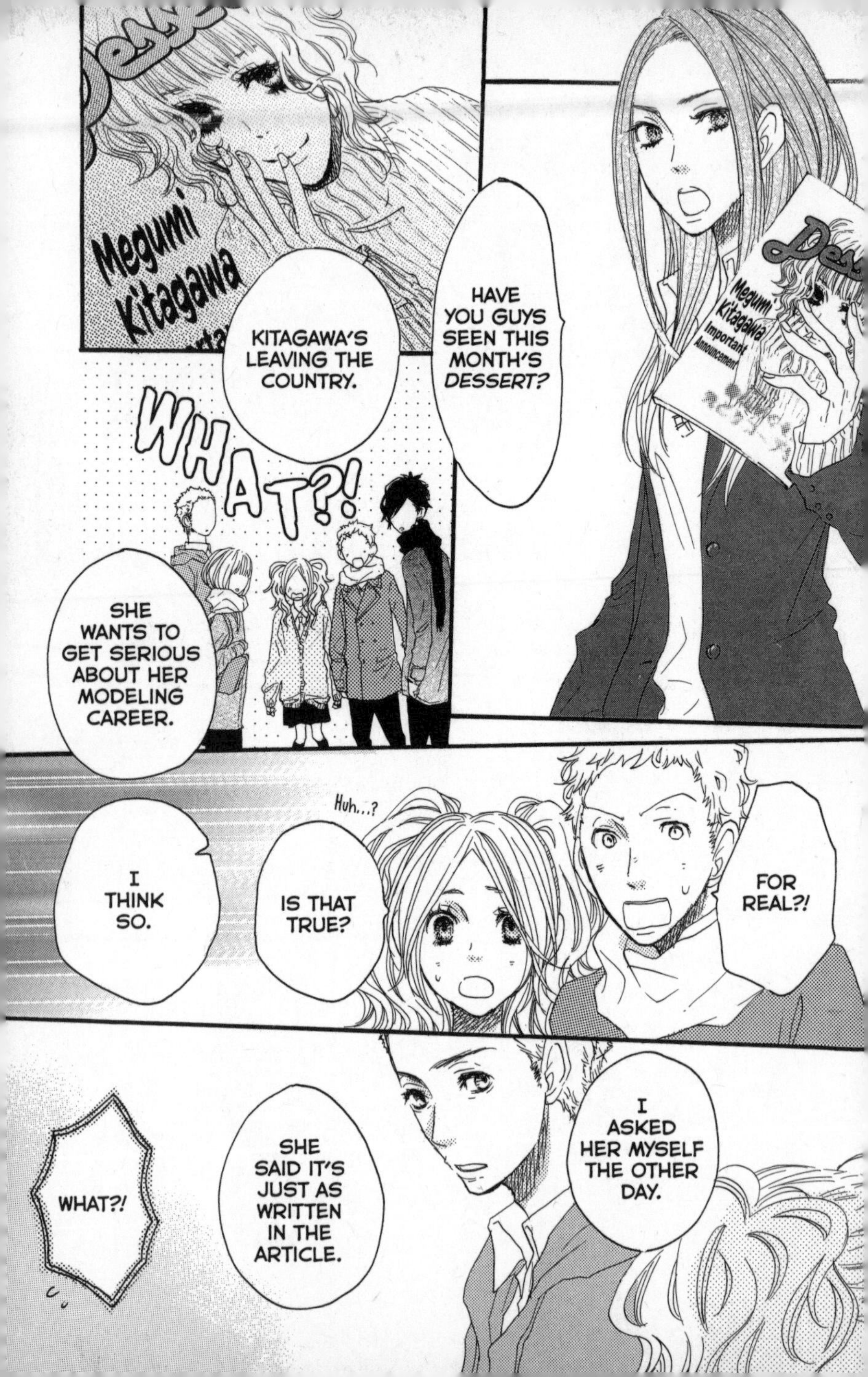
HAVE YOU GUYS SEEN THIS MONTH'S DESSERT?
Megumi Kitagawa Important Announcement
Megumi Kitagawa
KITAGAWA'S LEAVING THE COUNTRY.
WHAT?!
SHE WANTS TO GET SERIOUS ABOUT HER MODELING CAREER.
FOR REAL?!
Huh...?
IS THAT TRUE?
I THINK SO.
I ASKED HER MYSELF THE OTHER DAY.
SHE SAID IT'S JUST AS WRITTEN IN THE ARTICLE.
WHAT?!

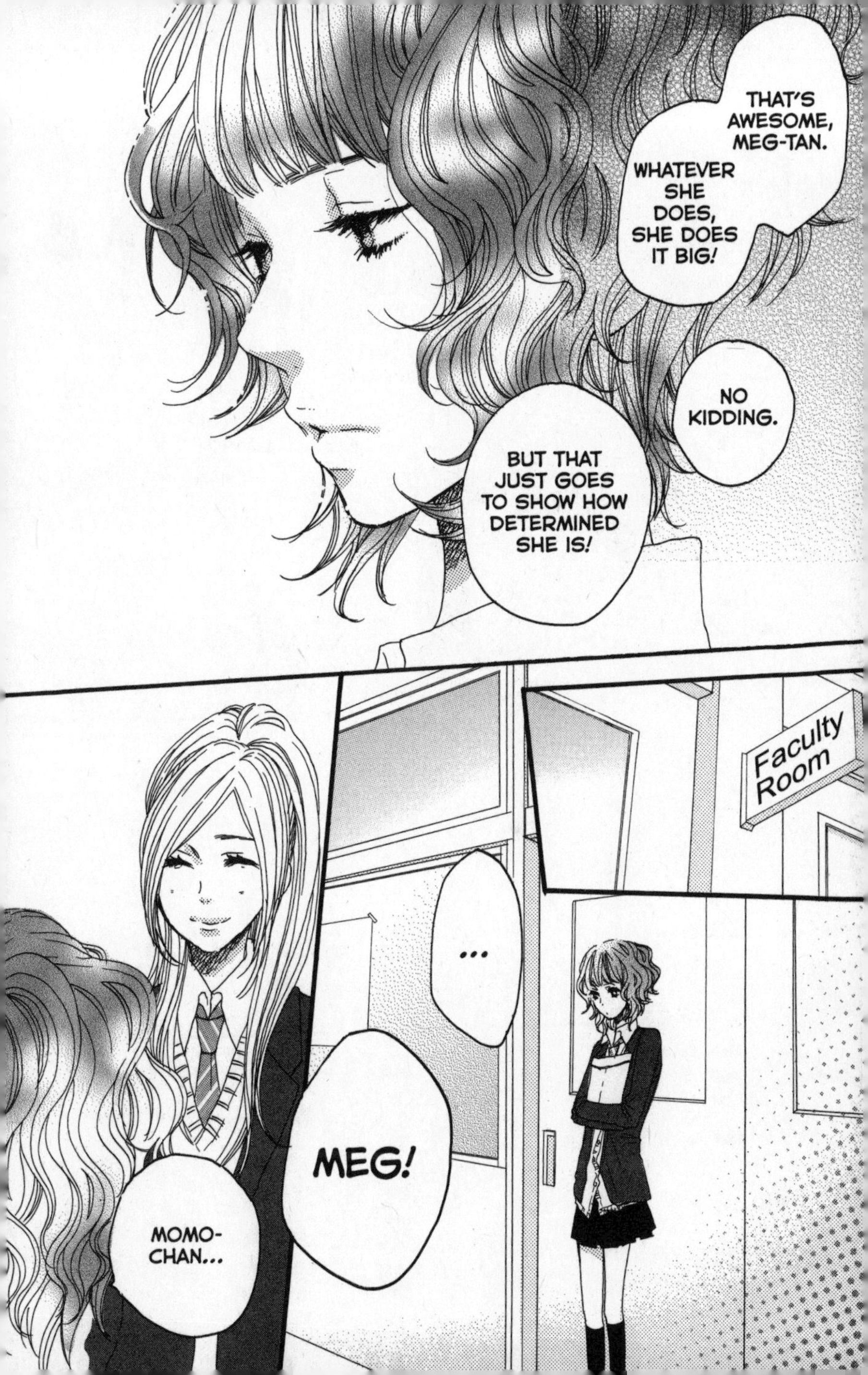
THAT'S AWESOME, MEG-TAN. WHATEVER SHE DOES, SHE DOES IT BIG!
NO KIDDING.
BUT THAT JUST GOES TO SHOW HOW DETERMINED SHE IS!
Faculty Room
...
MEG!
MOMO-CHAN...

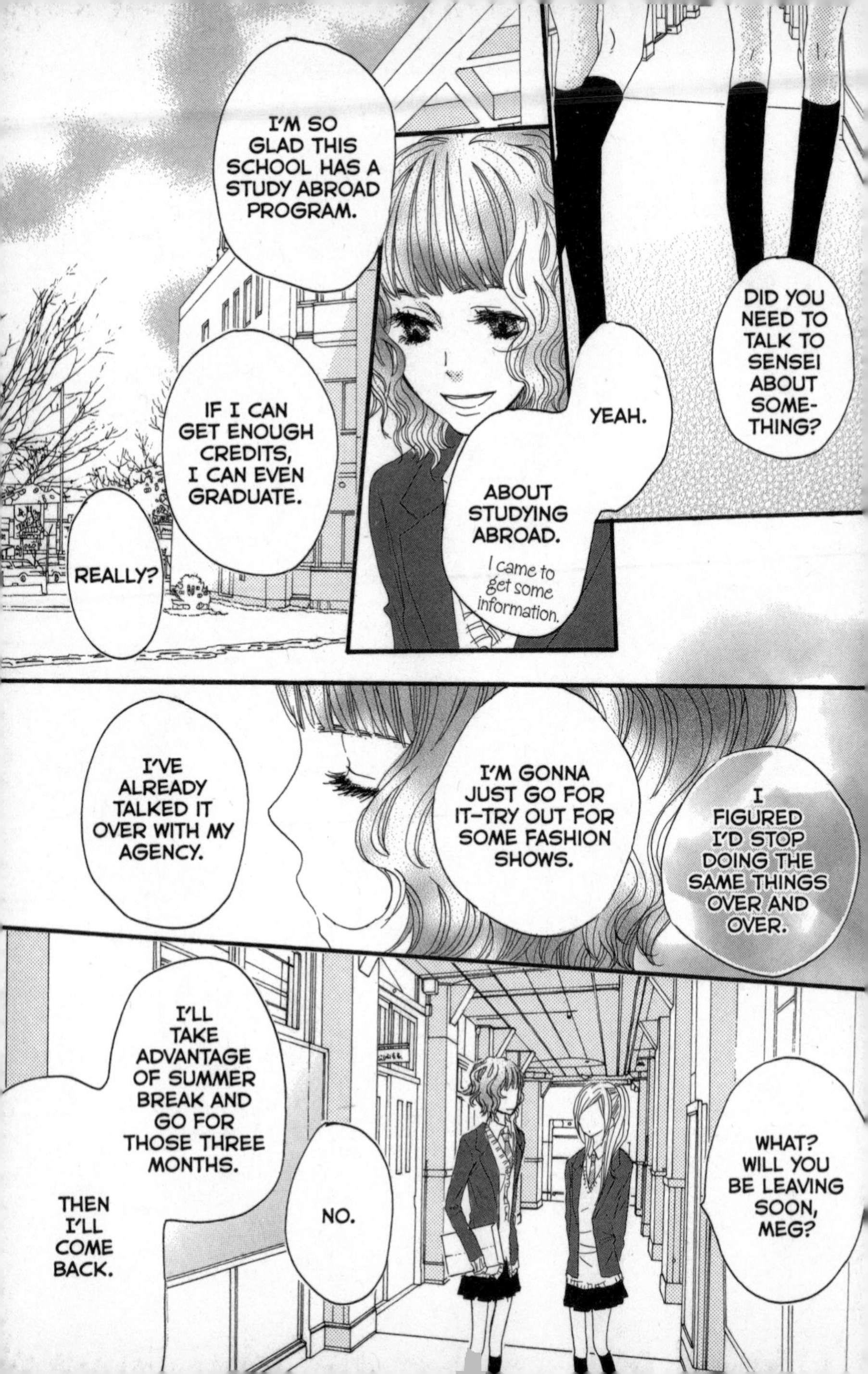
DID YOU NEED TO TALK TO SENSEI ABOUT SOME-THING?
YEAH.
ABOUT STUDYING ABROAD.
I came to get some information.
I'M SO GLAD THIS SCHOOL HAS A STUDY ABROAD PROGRAM.
IF I CAN GET ENOUGH CREDITS, I CAN EVEN GRADUATE.
REALLY?
I FIGURED I'D STOP DOING THE SAME THINGS OVER AND OVER.
I'M GONNA JUST GO FOR IT—TRY OUT FOR SOME FASHION SHOWS.
I'VE ALREADY TALKED IT OVER WITH MY AGENCY.
WHAT? WILL YOU BE LEAVING SOON, MEG?
NO.
I'LL TAKE ADVANTAGE OF SUMMER BREAK AND GO FOR THOSE THREE MONTHS.
THEN I'LL COME BACK.

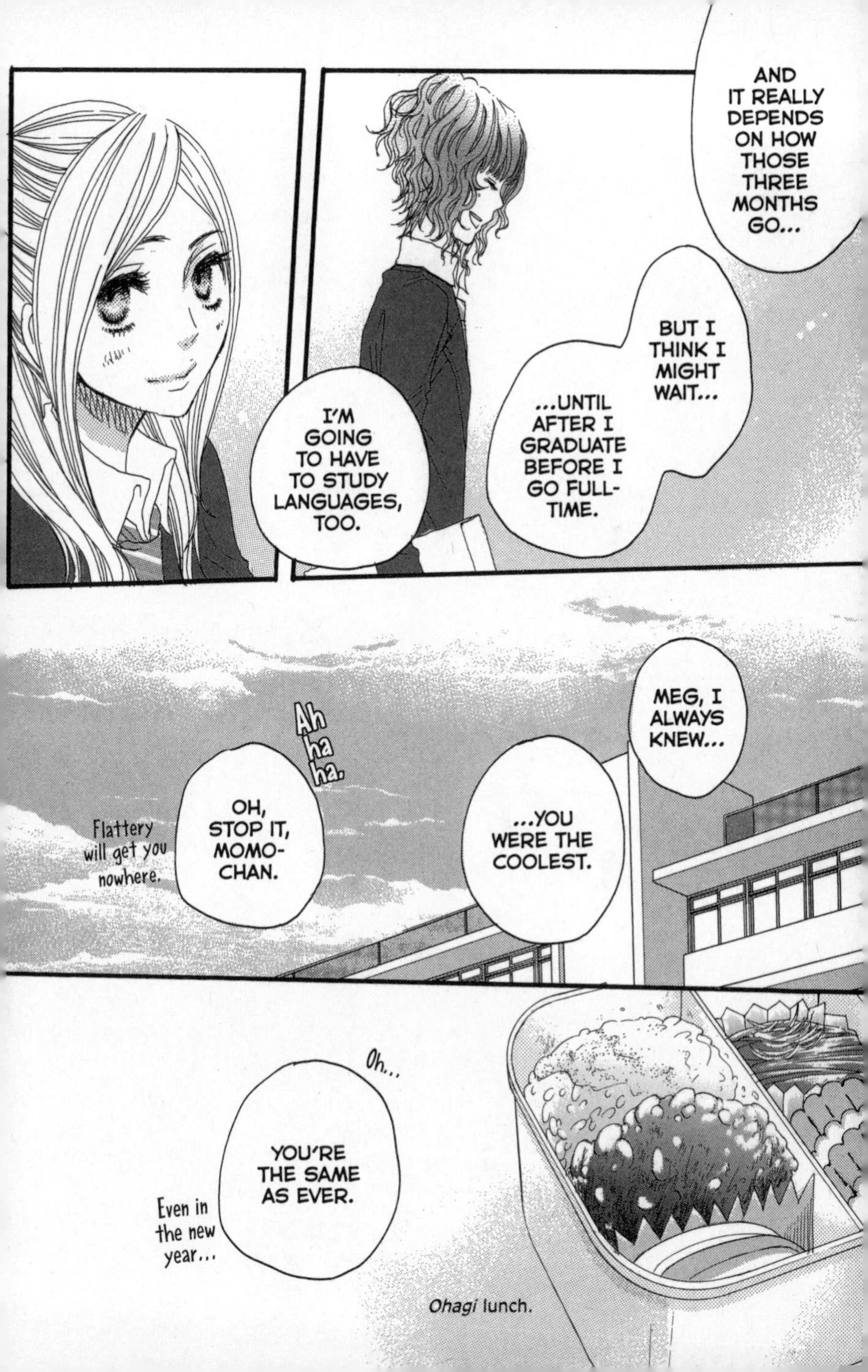
AND IT REALLY DEPENDS ON HOW THOSE THREE MONTHS GO...
BUT I THINK I MIGHT WAIT...
...UNTIL AFTER I GRADUATE BEFORE I GO FULL-TIME.
I'M GOING TO HAVE TO STUDY LANGUAGES, TOO.
MEG, I ALWAYS KNEW...
...YOU WERE THE COOLEST.
Ah ha ha.
OH, STOP IT, MOMO-CHAN.
Flattery will get you nowhere.
Oh...
YOU'RE THE SAME AS EVER.
Even in the new year...
Ohagi lunch.

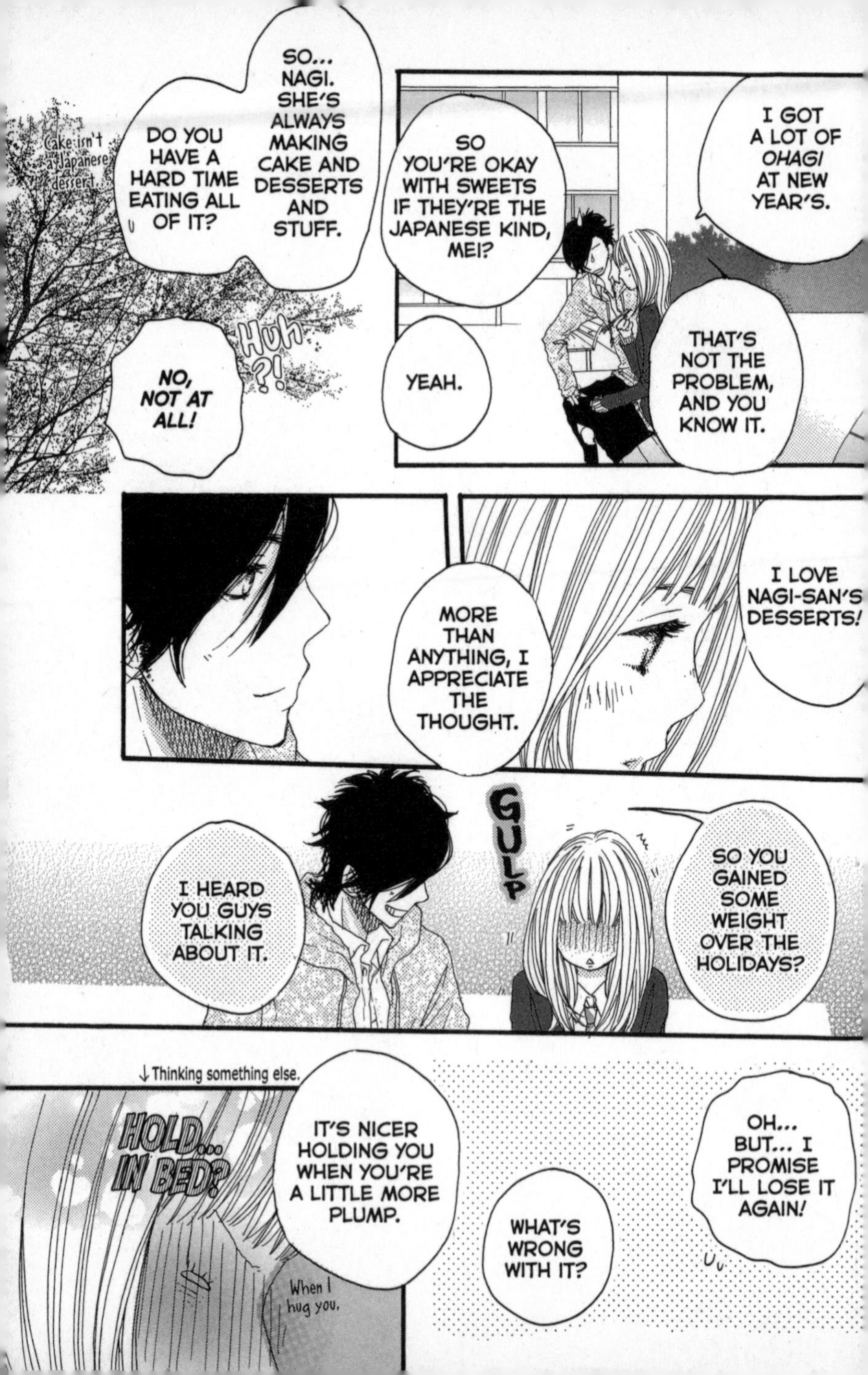
I GOT A LOT OF *OHAGI* AT NEW YEAR'S.
SO YOU'RE OKAY WITH SWEETS IF THEY'RE THE JAPANESE KIND, MEI?
THAT'S NOT THE PROBLEM, AND YOU KNOW IT.
YEAH.
SO... NAGI. SHE'S ALWAYS MAKING CAKE AND DESSERTS AND STUFF.
DO YOU HAVE A HARD TIME EATING ALL OF IT?
Cake isn't a Japanese dessert...
HUH ?!
NO, NOT AT ALL!
I LOVE NAGI-SAN'S DESSERTS!
MORE THAN ANYTHING, I APPRECIATE THE THOUGHT.
SO YOU GAINED SOME WEIGHT OVER THE HOLIDAYS?
GULP
I HEARD YOU GUYS TALKING ABOUT IT.
OH... BUT... I PROMISE I'LL LOSE IT AGAIN!
WHAT'S WRONG WITH IT?
IT'S NICER HOLDING YOU WHEN YOU'RE A LITTLE MORE PLUMP.
↓Thinking something else.
HOLD... IN BED?
When I hug you.

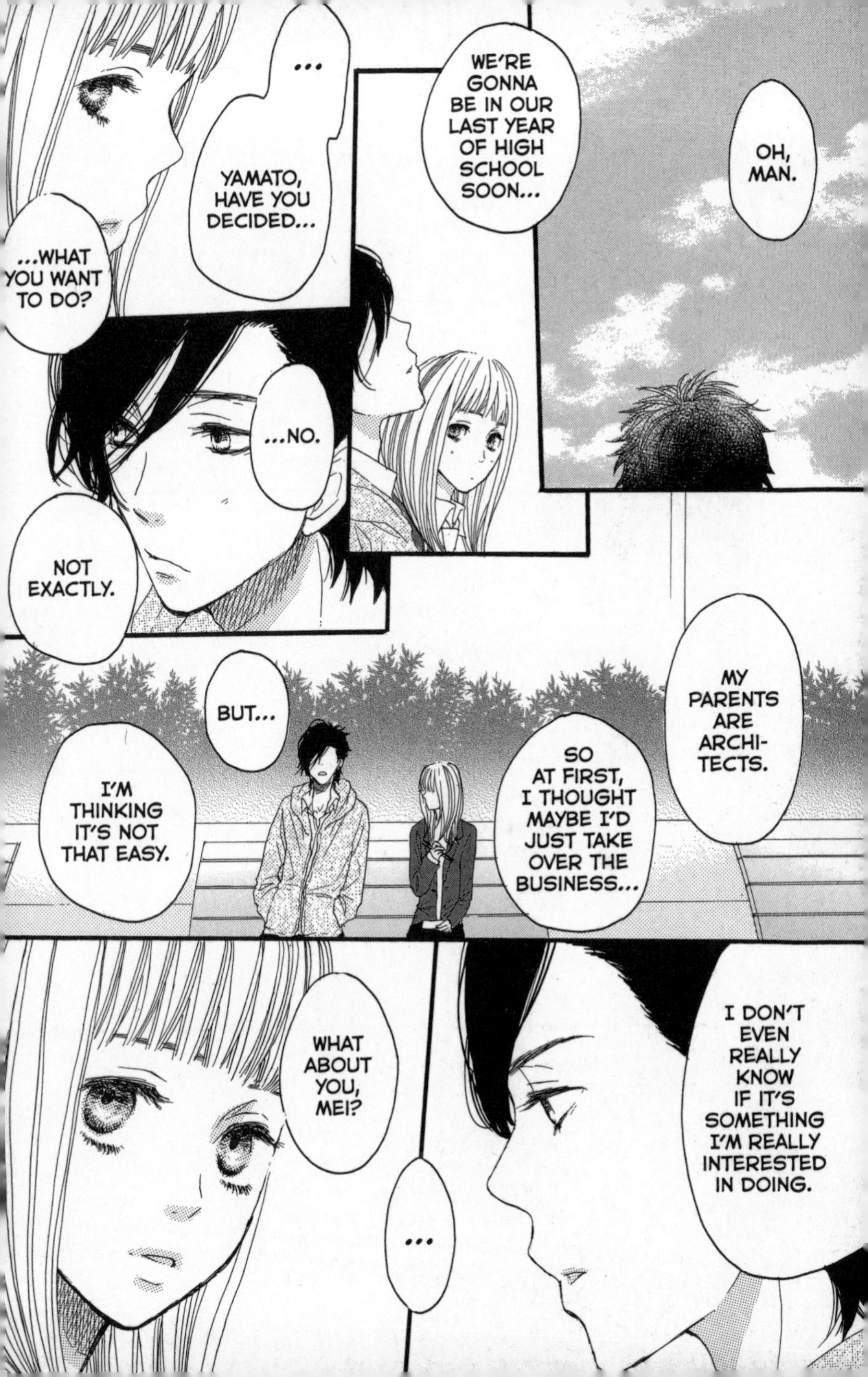
OH, MAN.
WE'RE GONNA BE IN OUR LAST YEAR OF HIGH SCHOOL SOON...
...
YAMATO, HAVE YOU DECIDED...
...WHAT YOU WANT TO DO?
...NO.
NOT EXACTLY.
MY PARENTS ARE ARCHITECTS.
SO AT FIRST, I THOUGHT MAYBE I'D JUST TAKE OVER THE BUSINESS...
BUT...
I'M THINKING IT'S NOT THAT EASY.
I DON'T EVEN REALLY KNOW IF IT'S SOMETHING I'M REALLY INTERESTED IN DOING.
...
WHAT ABOUT YOU, MEI?

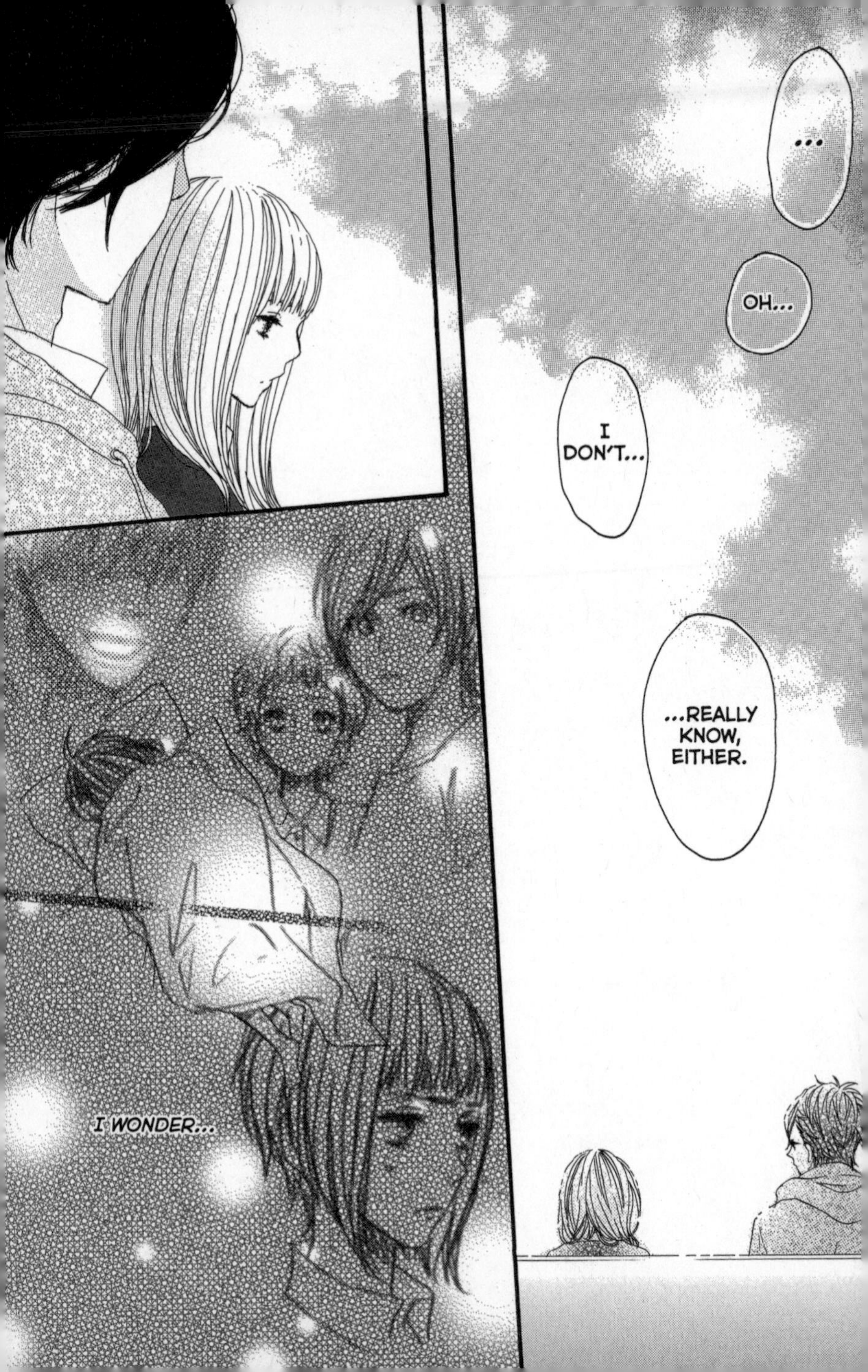
...
OH...
I DON'T...
...REALLY KNOW, EITHER.
I WONDER...

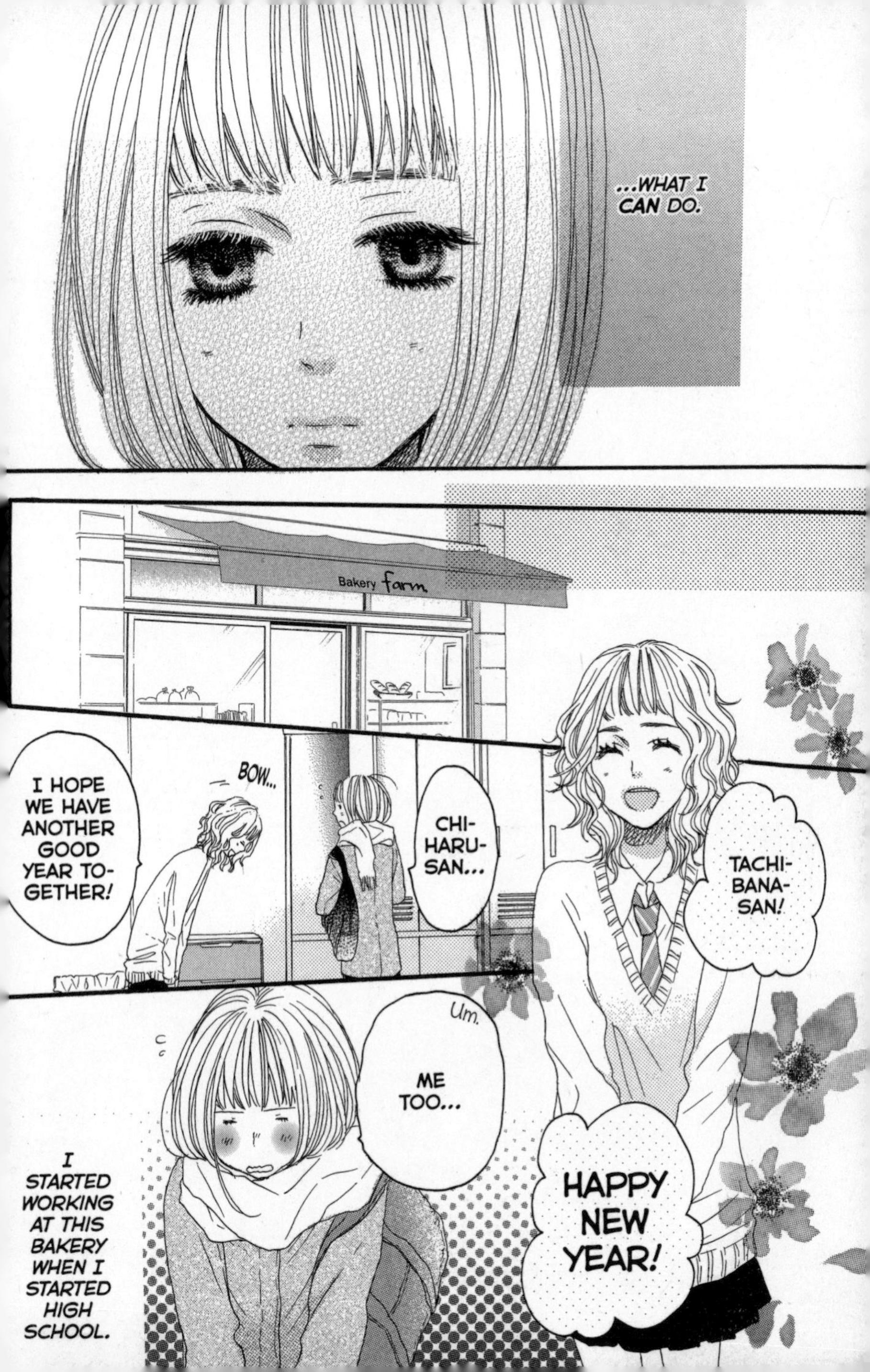
...WHAT I CAN DO.
Bakery farm
TACHI-BANA-SAN!
HAPPY NEW YEAR!
CHI-HARU-SAN...
BOW...
I HOPE WE HAVE ANOTHER GOOD YEAR TO-GETHER!
Um.
ME TOO...
I STARTED WORKING AT THIS BAKERY WHEN I STARTED HIGH SCHOOL.

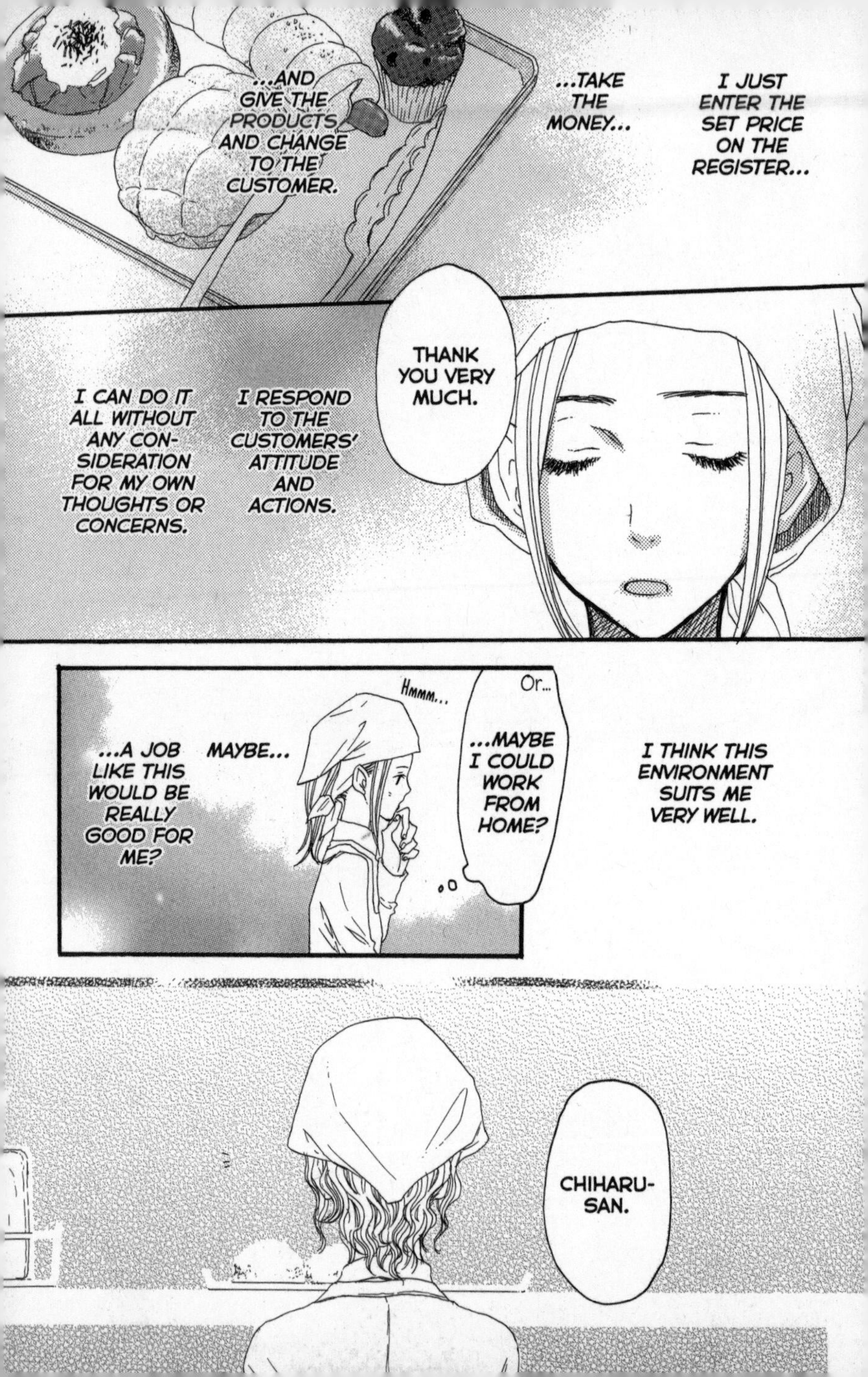
I JUST ENTER THE SET PRICE ON THE REGISTER...
...TAKE THE MONEY...
...AND GIVE THE PRODUCTS AND CHANGE TO THE CUSTOMER.
THANK YOU VERY MUCH.
I RESPOND TO THE CUSTOMERS' ATTITUDE AND ACTIONS.
I CAN DO IT ALL WITHOUT ANY CON-SIDERATION FOR MY OWN THOUGHTS OR CONCERNS.
I THINK THIS ENVIRONMENT SUITS ME VERY WELL.
Or...
...MAYBE I COULD WORK FROM HOME?
Hmmm...
MAYBE...
...A JOB LIKE THIS WOULD BE REALLY GOOD FOR ME?
CHIHARU-SAN.

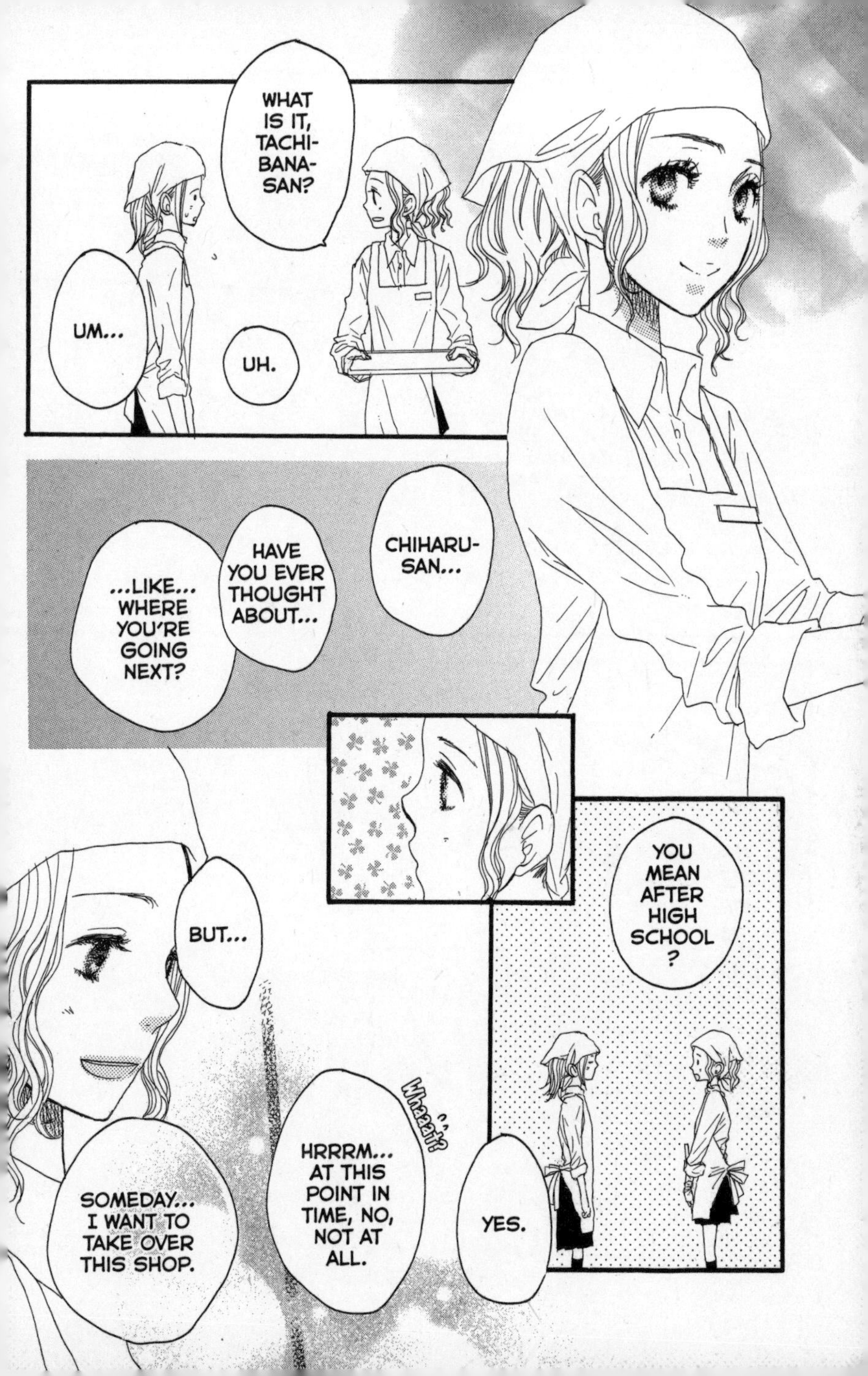
WHAT IS IT, TACHIBANA-SAN?
UH.
UM...
CHIHARU-SAN...
HAVE YOU EVER THOUGHT ABOUT...
...LIKE... WHERE YOU'RE GOING NEXT?
YOU MEAN AFTER HIGH SCHOOL?
YES.
HRRRM... AT THIS POINT IN TIME, NO, NOT AT ALL.
Whaaat!?
BUT...
SOMEDAY... I WANT TO TAKE OVER THIS SHOP.

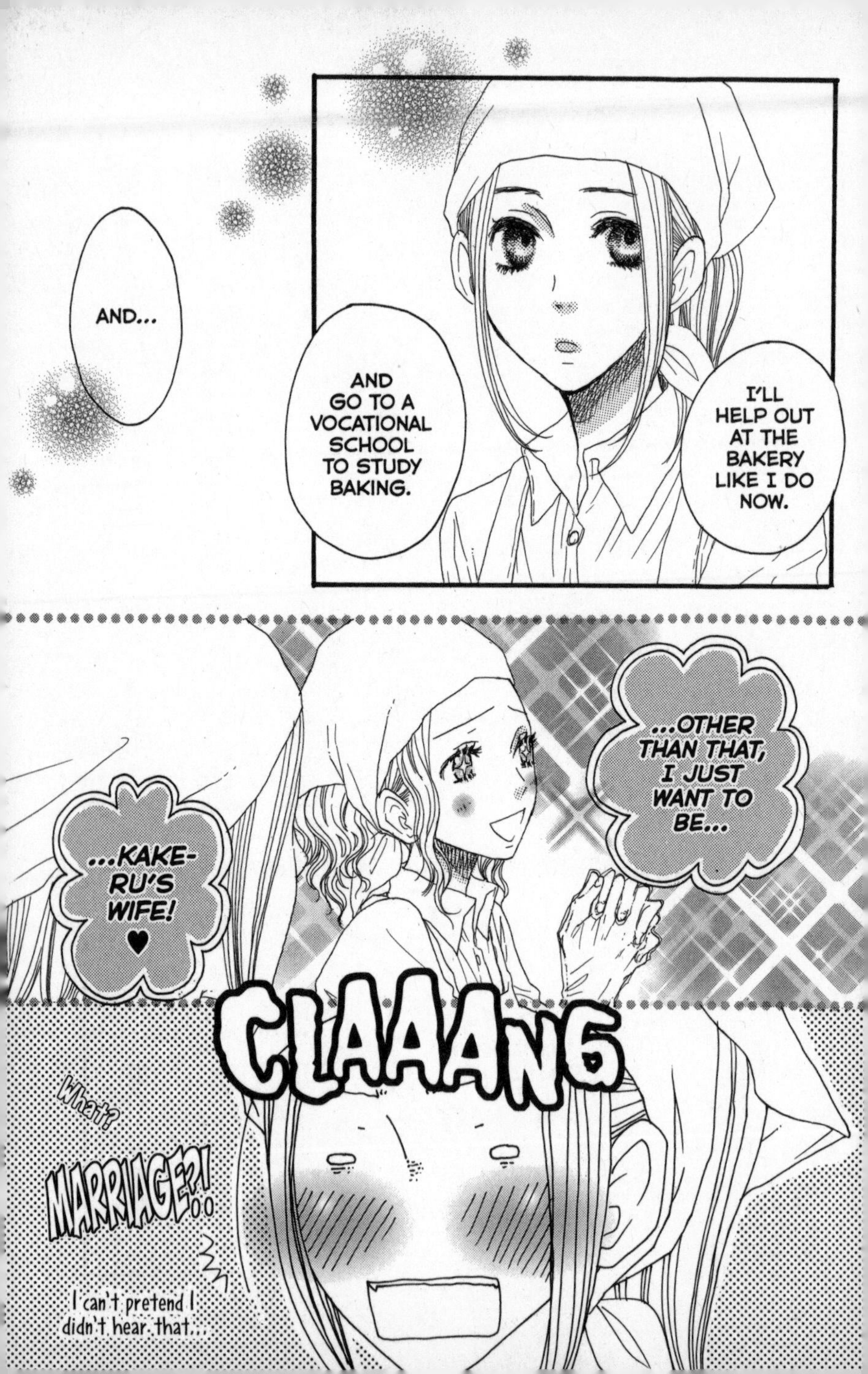
I'LL HELP OUT AT THE BAKERY LIKE I DO NOW.
AND GO TO A VOCATIONAL SCHOOL TO STUDY BAKING.
AND...
...OTHER THAN THAT, I JUST WANT TO BE...
...KAKE-RU'S WIFE! ♥
CLAAANG
What?
MARRIAGE?!
I can't pretend I didn't hear that...

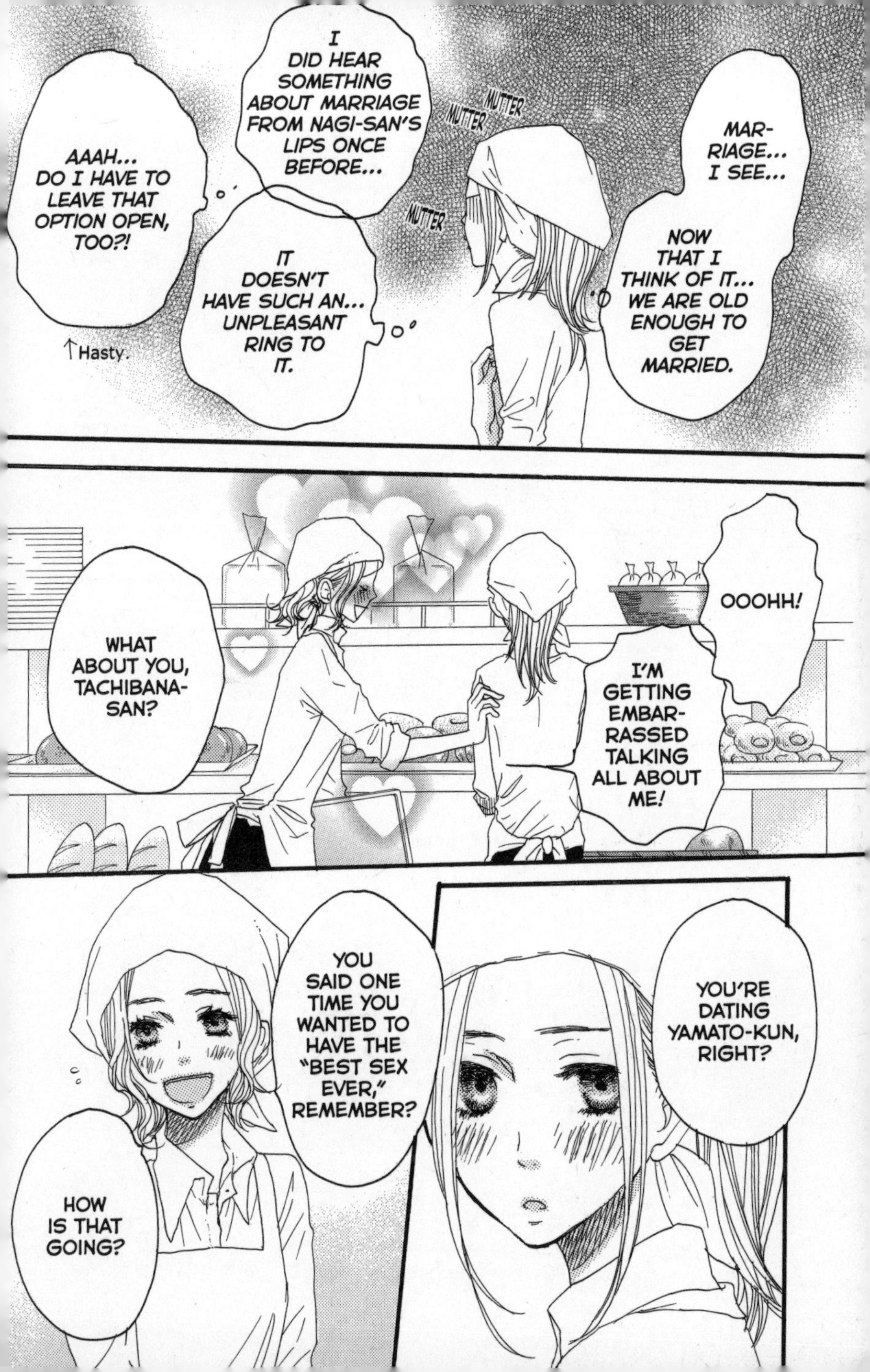
MAR-RIAGE... I SEE...
NOW THAT I THINK OF IT... WE ARE OLD ENOUGH TO GET MARRIED.
MUTTER
MUTTER
MUTTER
I DID HEAR SOMETHING ABOUT MARRIAGE FROM NAGI-SAN'S LIPS ONCE BEFORE...
IT DOESN'T HAVE SUCH AN... UNPLEASANT RING TO IT.
AAAH... DO I HAVE TO LEAVE THAT OPTION OPEN, TOO?!
↑Hasty.
OOOHH!
I'M GETTING EMBAR-RASSED TALKING ALL ABOUT ME!
WHAT ABOUT YOU, TACHIBANA-SAN?
YOU'RE DATING YAMATO-KUN, RIGHT?
YOU SAID ONE TIME YOU WANTED TO HAVE THE "BEST SEX EVER," REMEMBER?
HOW IS THAT GOING?

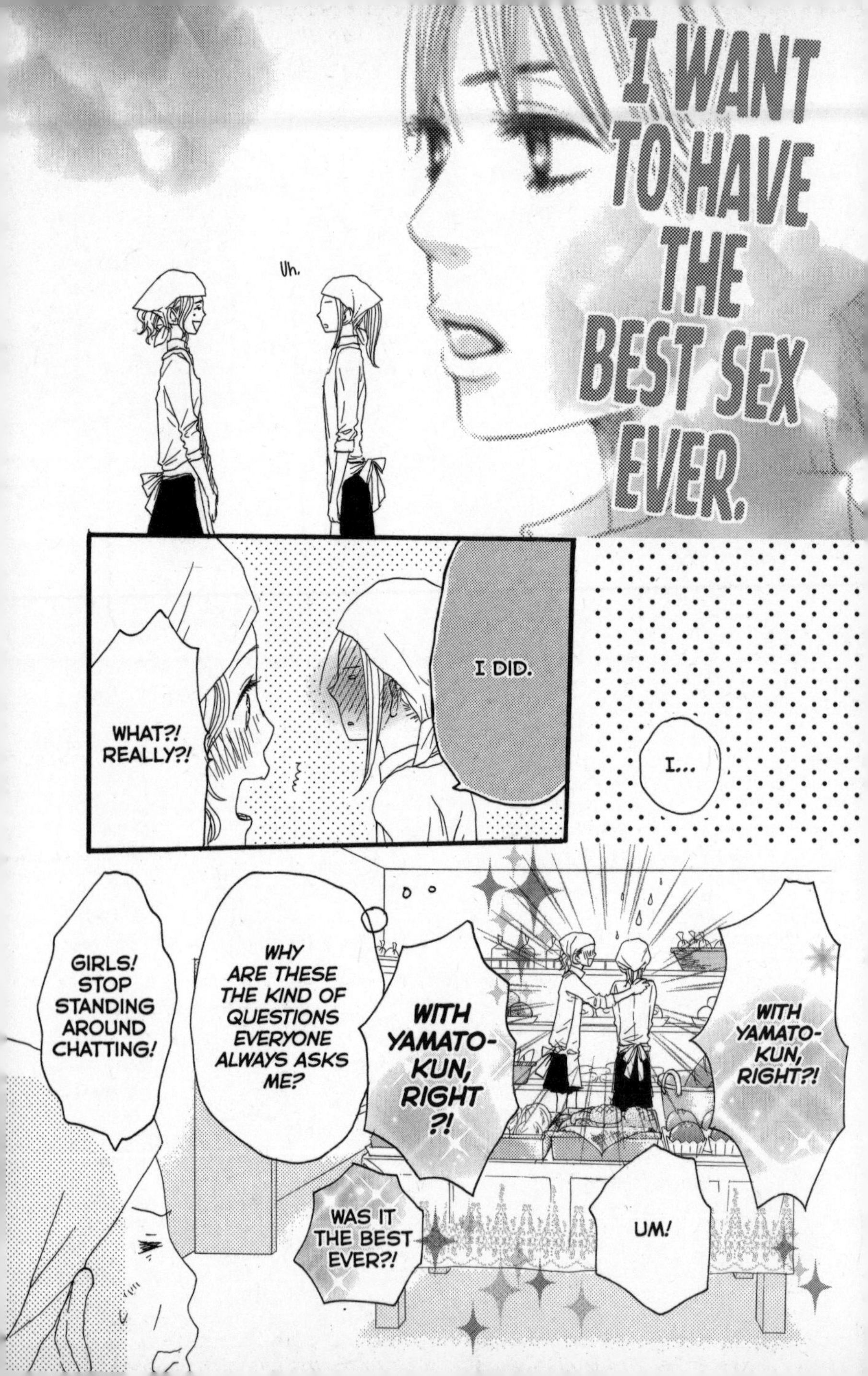
I WANT TO HAVE THE BEST SEX EVER.
Uh.
I...
I DID.
WHAT?! REALLY?!
WITH YAMATO-KUN, RIGHT?!
WITH YAMATO-KUN, RIGHT ?!
UM!
WAS IT THE BEST EVER?!
WHY ARE THESE THE KIND OF QUESTIONS EVERYONE ALWAYS ASKS ME?
GIRLS! STOP STANDING AROUND CHATTING!

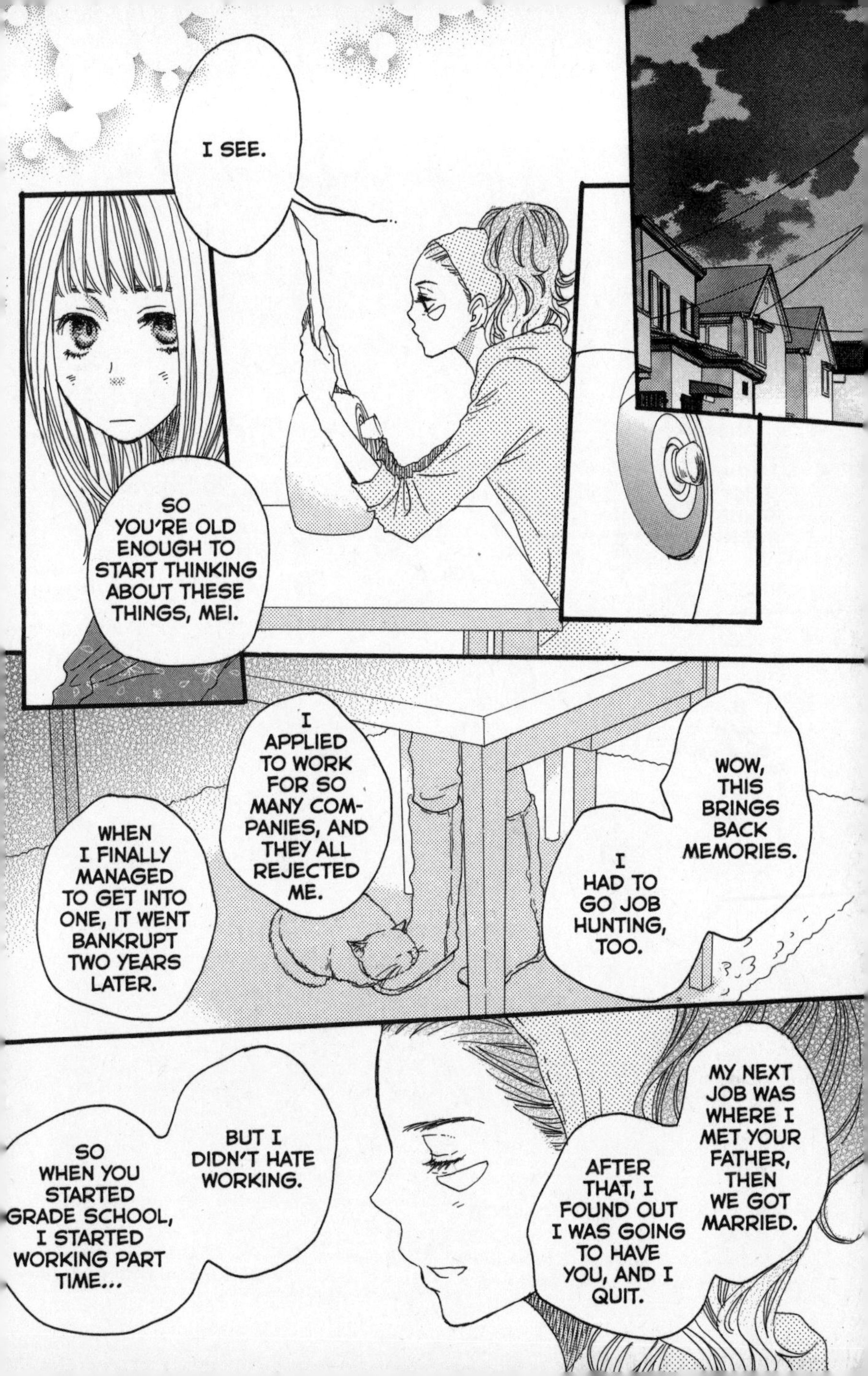
I SEE.
SO YOU'RE OLD ENOUGH TO START THINKING ABOUT THESE THINGS, MEI.
WOW, THIS BRINGS BACK MEMORIES.
I HAD TO GO JOB HUNTING, TOO.
I APPLIED TO WORK FOR SO MANY COM-PANIES, AND THEY ALL REJECTED ME.
WHEN I FINALLY MANAGED TO GET INTO ONE, IT WENT BANKRUPT TWO YEARS LATER.
MY NEXT JOB WAS WHERE I MET YOUR FATHER, THEN WE GOT MARRIED.
AFTER THAT, I FOUND OUT I WAS GOING TO HAVE YOU, AND I QUIT.
BUT I DIDN'T HATE WORKING.
SO WHEN YOU STARTED GRADE SCHOOL, I STARTED WORKING PART TIME...

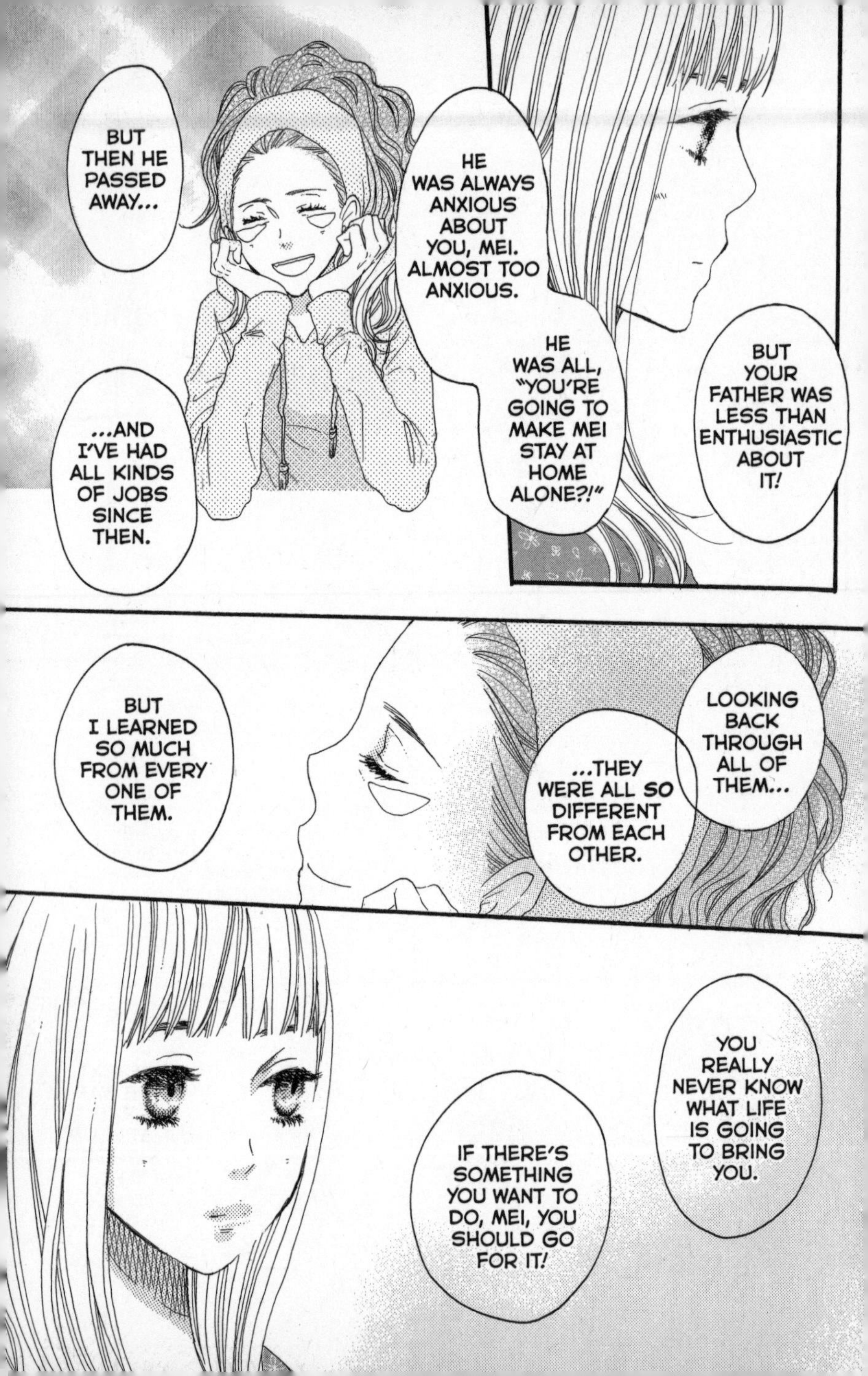
BUT YOUR FATHER WAS LESS THAN ENTHUSIASTIC ABOUT IT!
HE WAS ALWAYS ANXIOUS ABOUT YOU, MEI. ALMOST TOO ANXIOUS.
HE WAS ALL, "YOU'RE GOING TO MAKE MEI STAY AT HOME ALONE?!"
BUT THEN HE PASSED AWAY...
...AND I'VE HAD ALL KINDS OF JOBS SINCE THEN.
LOOKING BACK THROUGH ALL OF THEM...
...THEY WERE ALL SO DIFFERENT FROM EACH OTHER.
BUT I LEARNED SO MUCH FROM EVERY ONE OF THEM.
YOU REALLY NEVER KNOW WHAT LIFE IS GOING TO BRING YOU.
IF THERE'S SOMETHING YOU WANT TO DO, MEI, YOU SHOULD GO FOR IT!

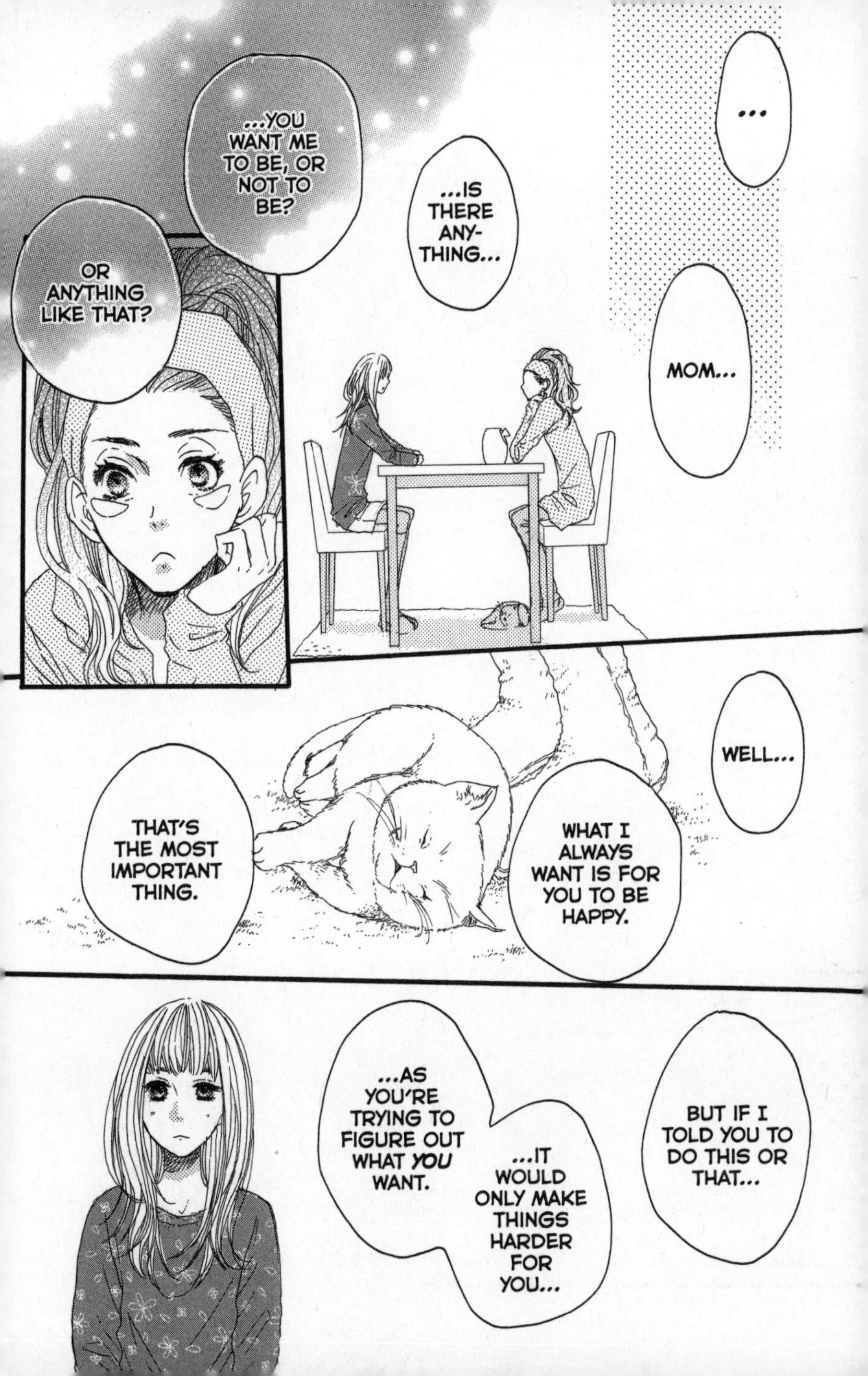
...
MOM...
...IS THERE ANYTHING...
...YOU WANT ME TO BE, OR NOT TO BE?
OR ANYTHING LIKE THAT?
WELL...
WHAT I ALWAYS WANT IS FOR YOU TO BE HAPPY.
THAT'S THE MOST IMPORTANT THING.
BUT IF I TOLD YOU TO DO THIS OR THAT...
...IT WOULD ONLY MAKE THINGS HARDER FOR YOU...
...AS YOU'RE TRYING TO FIGURE OUT WHAT *YOU* WANT.

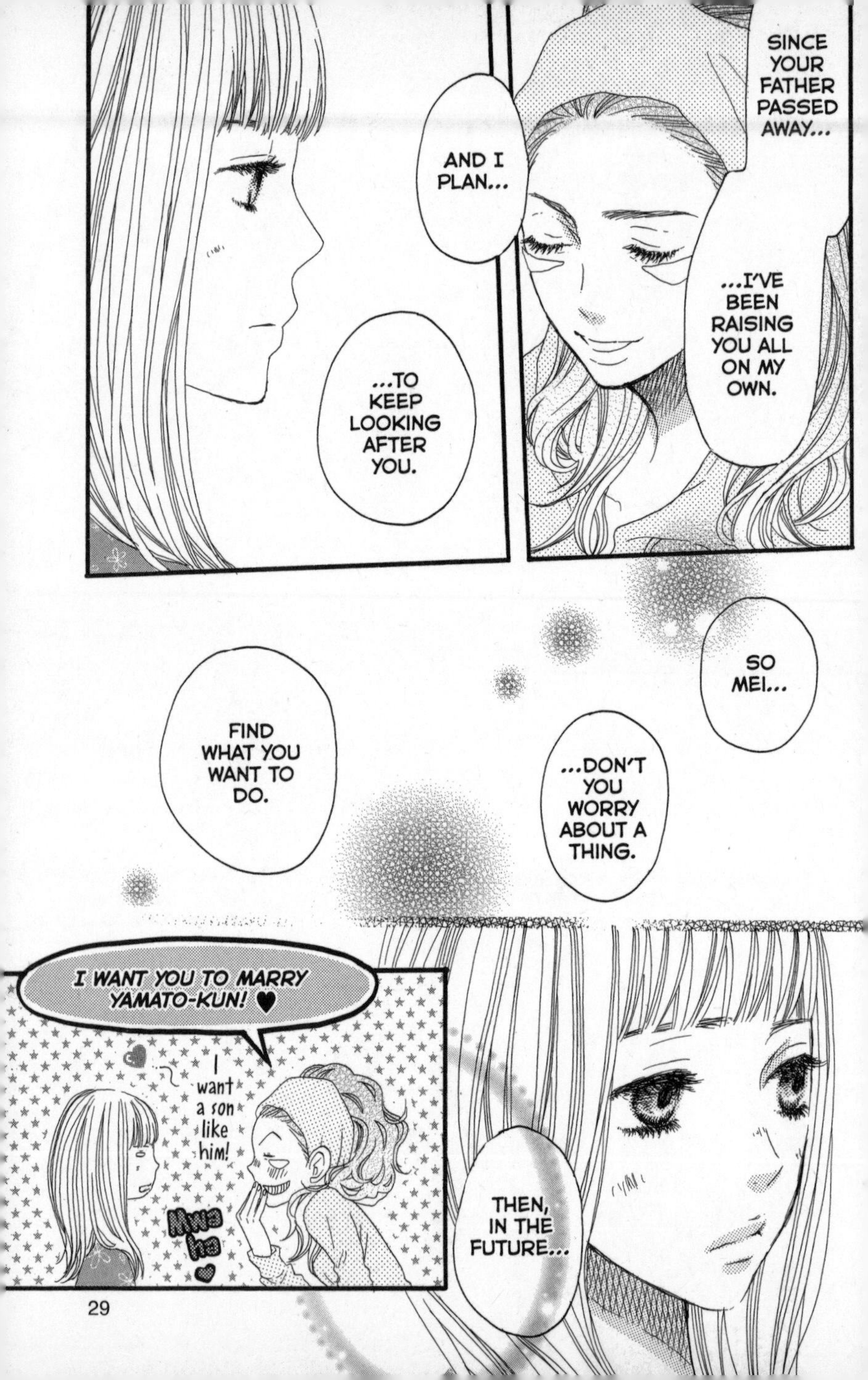
SINCE YOUR FATHER PASSED AWAY...
...I'VE BEEN RAISING YOU ALL ON MY OWN.
AND I PLAN...
...TO KEEP LOOKING AFTER YOU.
SO MEI...
...DON'T YOU WORRY ABOUT A THING.
FIND WHAT YOU WANT TO DO.
THEN, IN THE FUTURE...
I WANT YOU TO MARRY YAMATO-KUN! ♥
I want a son like him!
Mwa ha ♥

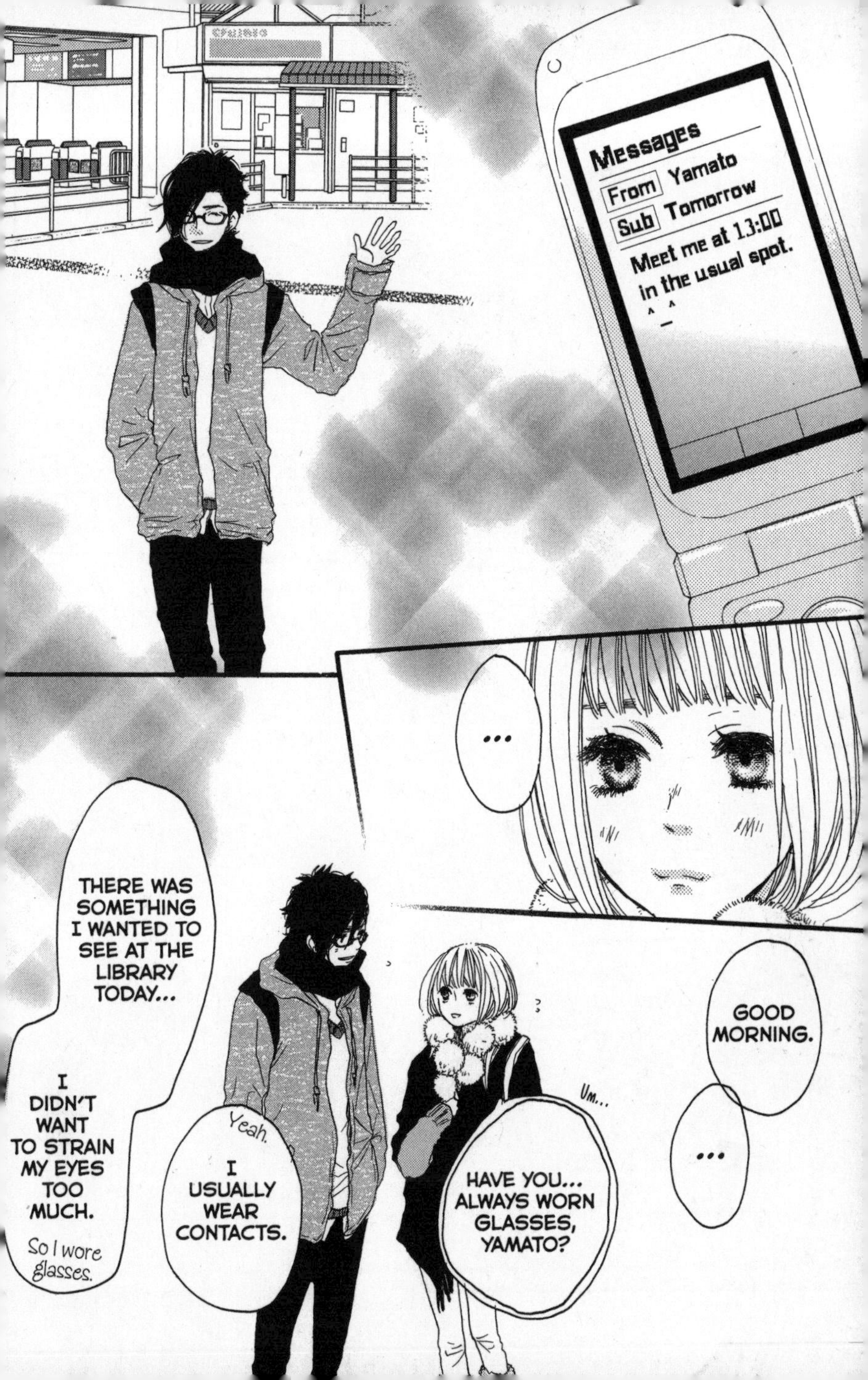
Messages
From Yamato
Sub Tomorrow
Meet me at 13:00 in the usual spot. ^_^
...
GOOD MORNING.
...
Um...
HAVE YOU... ALWAYS WORN GLASSES, YAMATO?
Yeah.
I USUALLY WEAR CONTACTS.
THERE WAS SOMETHING I WANTED TO SEE AT THE LIBRARY TODAY...
I DIDN'T WANT TO STRAIN MY EYES TOO MUCH.
So I wore glasses.

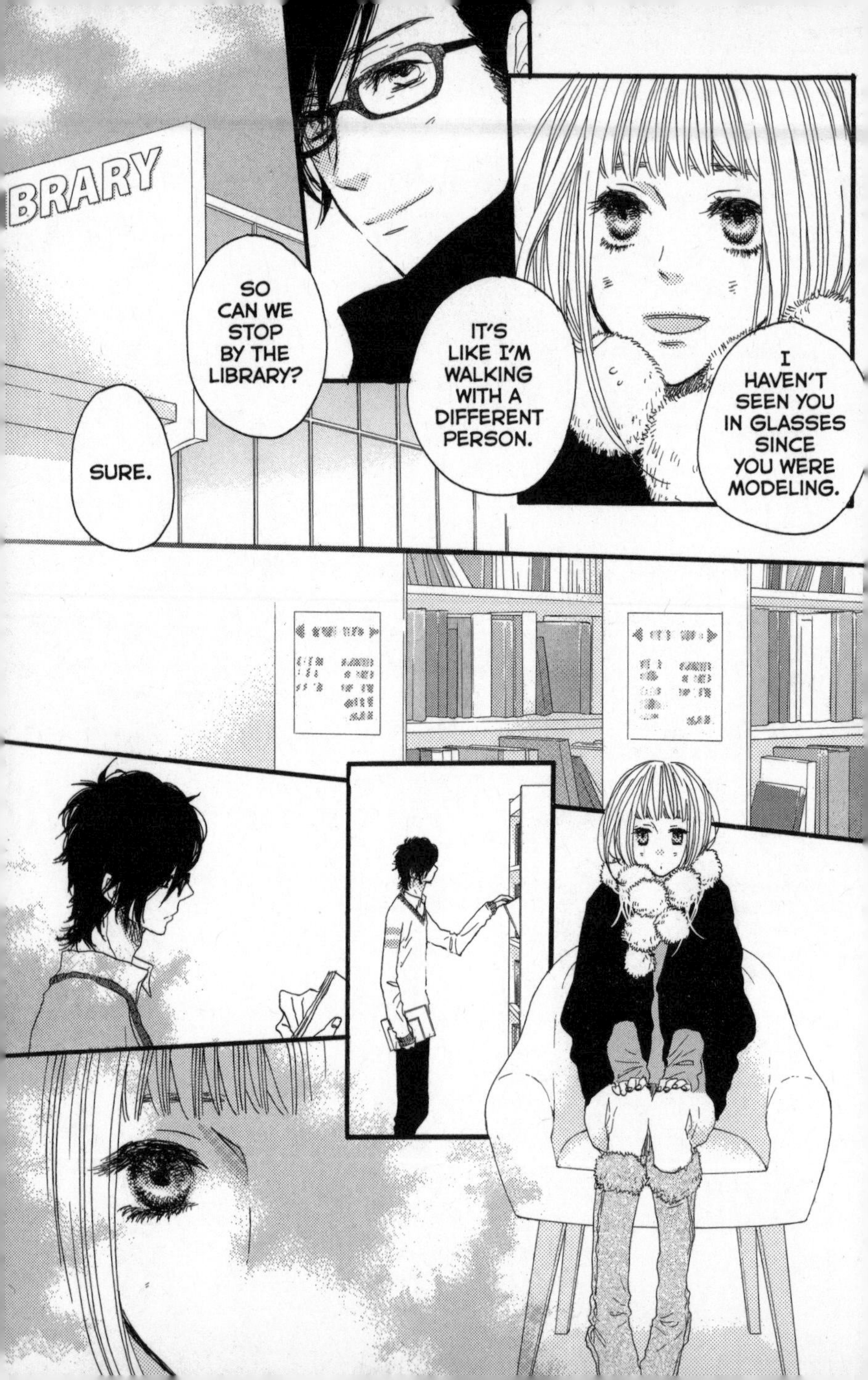
I HAVEN'T SEEN YOU IN GLASSES SINCE YOU WERE MODELING.
IT'S LIKE I'M WALKING WITH A DIFFERENT PERSON.
SO CAN WE STOP BY THE LIBRARY?
BRARY
SURE.

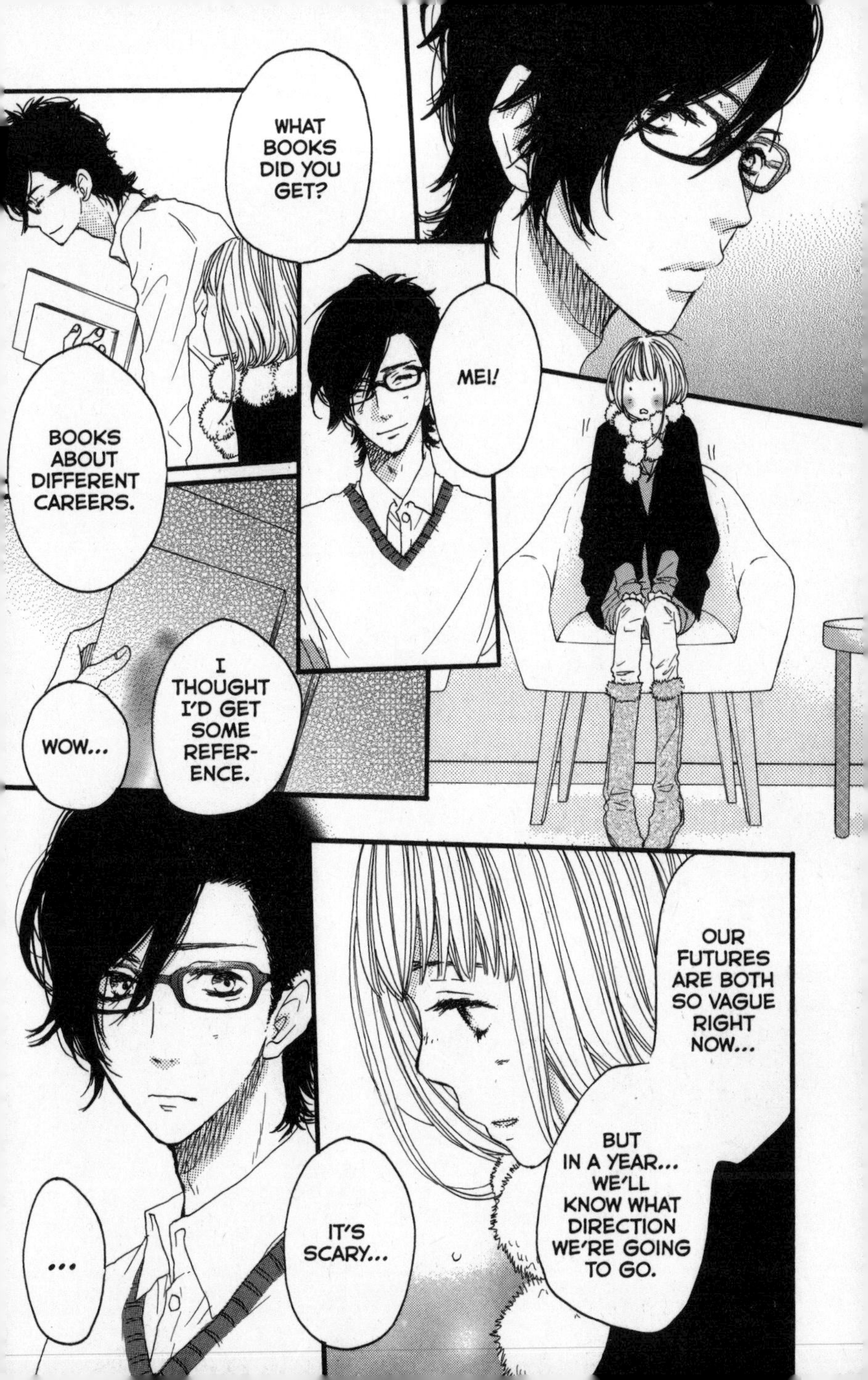
MEI!
WHAT BOOKS DID YOU GET?
BOOKS ABOUT DIFFERENT CAREERS.
I THOUGHT I'D GET SOME REFERENCE.
WOW...
OUR FUTURES ARE BOTH SO VAGUE RIGHT NOW...
BUT IN A YEAR... WE'LL KNOW WHAT DIRECTION WE'RE GOING TO GO.
IT'S SCARY...
...

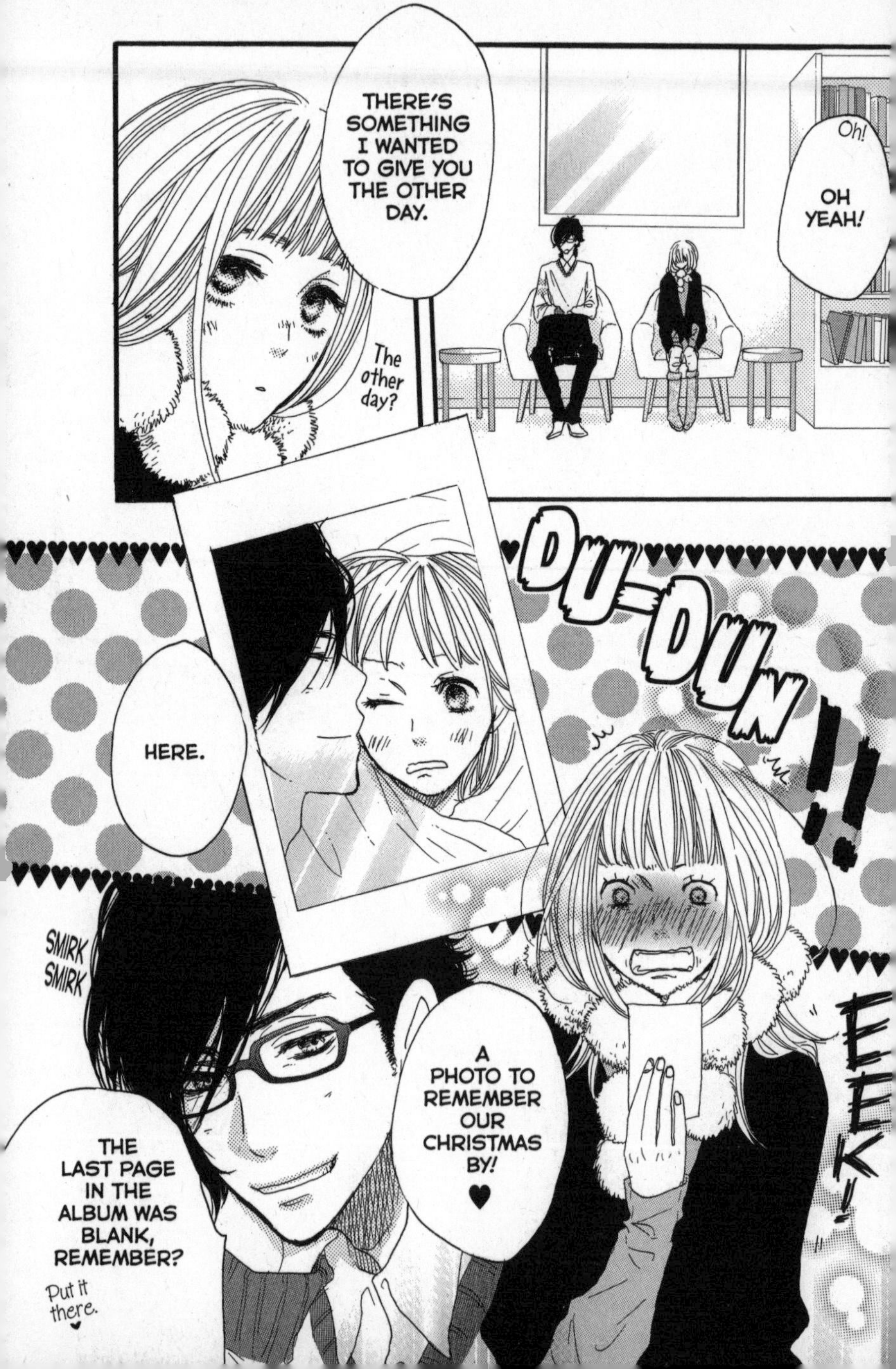
Oh!
OH YEAH!
THERE'S SOMETHING I WANTED TO GIVE YOU THE OTHER DAY.
The other day?
DU-DUN!!
HERE.
EEEK!!
A PHOTO TO REMEMBER OUR CHRISTMAS BY! ♥
SMIRK SMIRK
THE LAST PAGE IN THE ALBUM WAS BLANK, REMEMBER?
Put it there. ♥

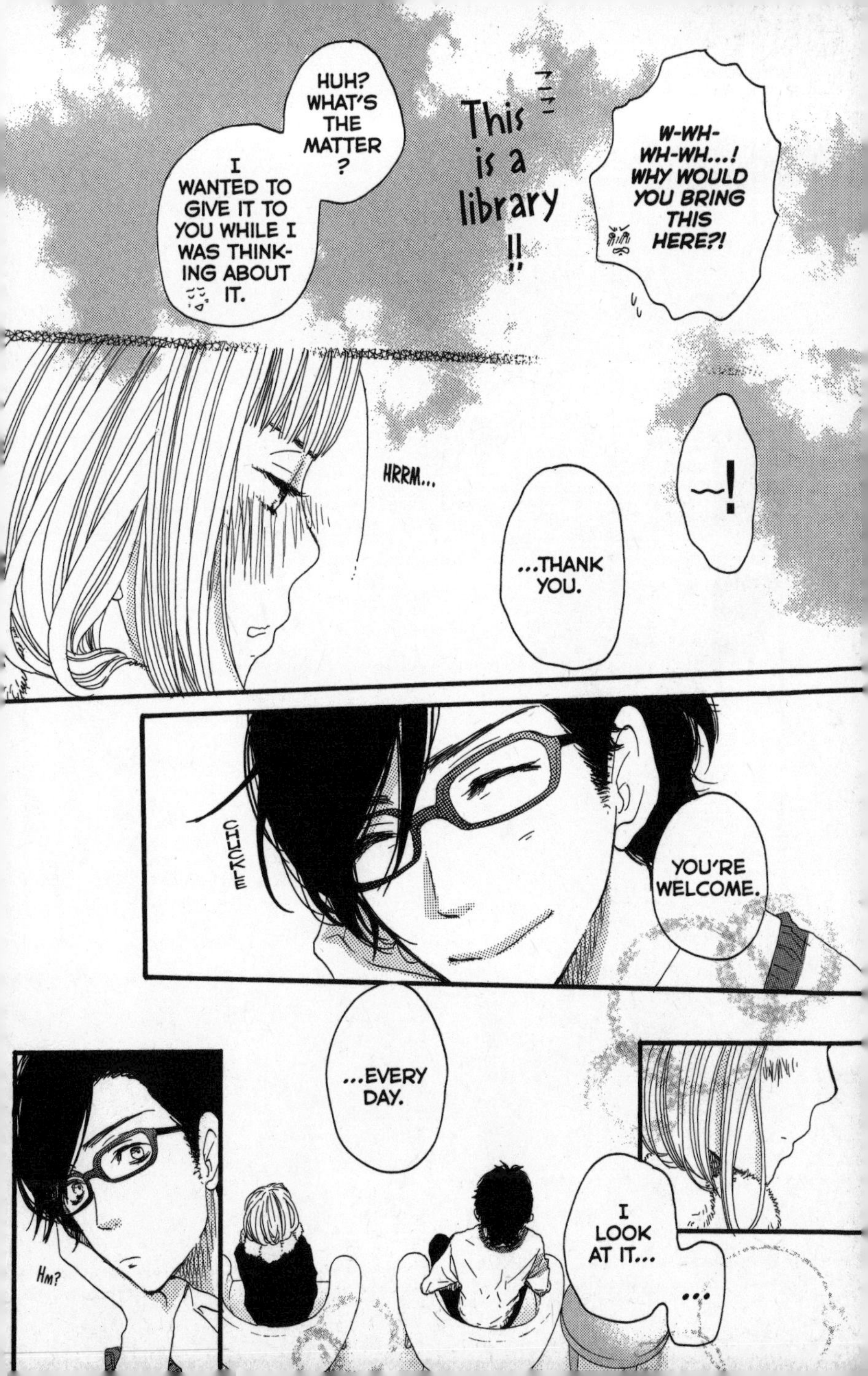
W-WH-WH-WH...! WHY WOULD YOU BRING THIS HERE?!
This is a library!!
HUH? WHAT'S THE MATTER?
I WANTED TO GIVE IT TO YOU WHILE I WAS THINKING ABOUT IT.
~!
...THANK YOU.
HRRM...
YOU'RE WELCOME.
CHUCKLE
I LOOK AT IT...
...EVERY DAY.
...
Hm?

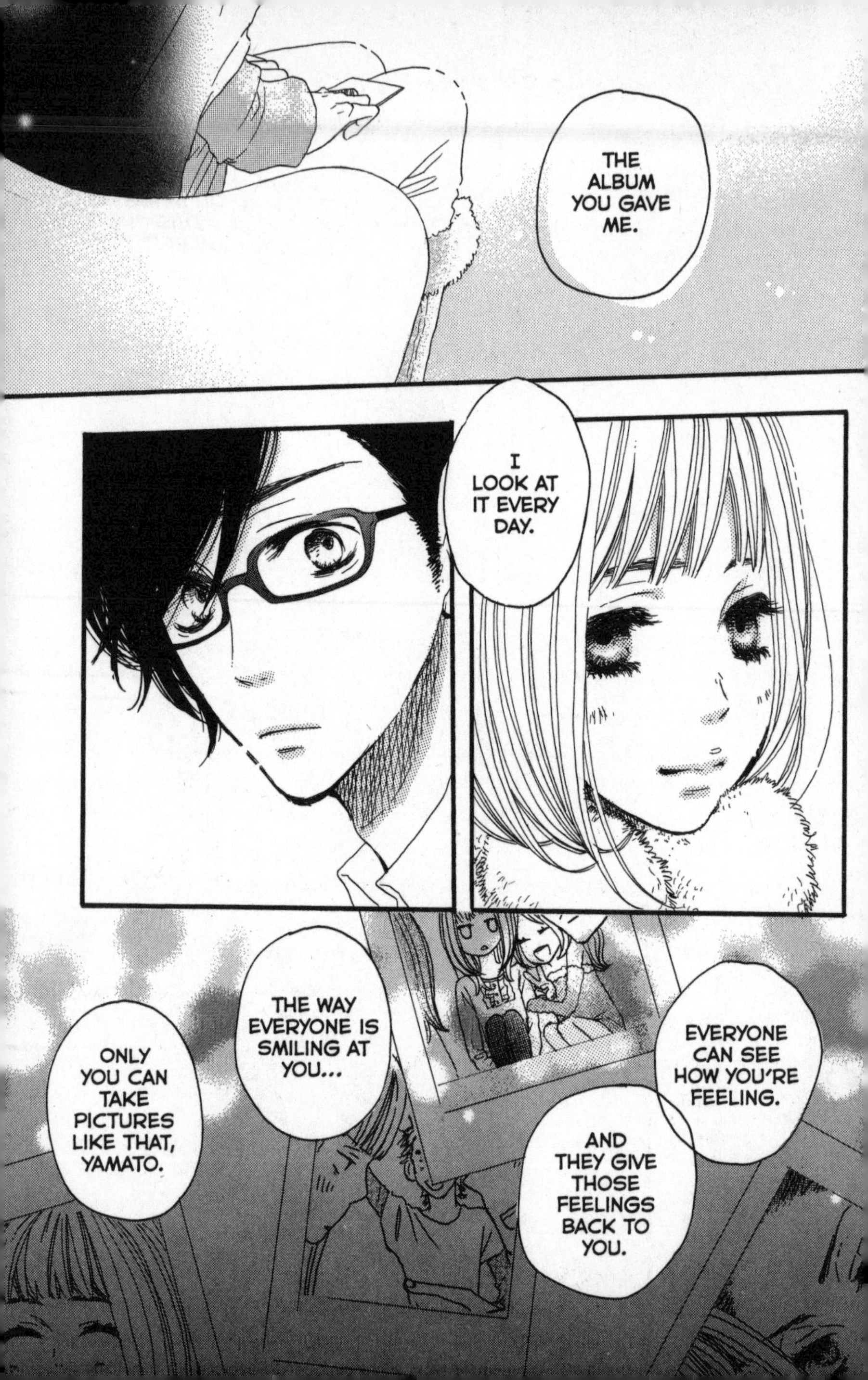
THE ALBUM YOU GAVE ME.
I LOOK AT IT EVERY DAY.
EVERYONE CAN SEE HOW YOU'RE FEELING.
AND THEY GIVE THOSE FEELINGS BACK TO YOU.
THE WAY EVERYONE IS SMILING AT YOU...
ONLY YOU CAN TAKE PICTURES LIKE THAT, YAMATO.

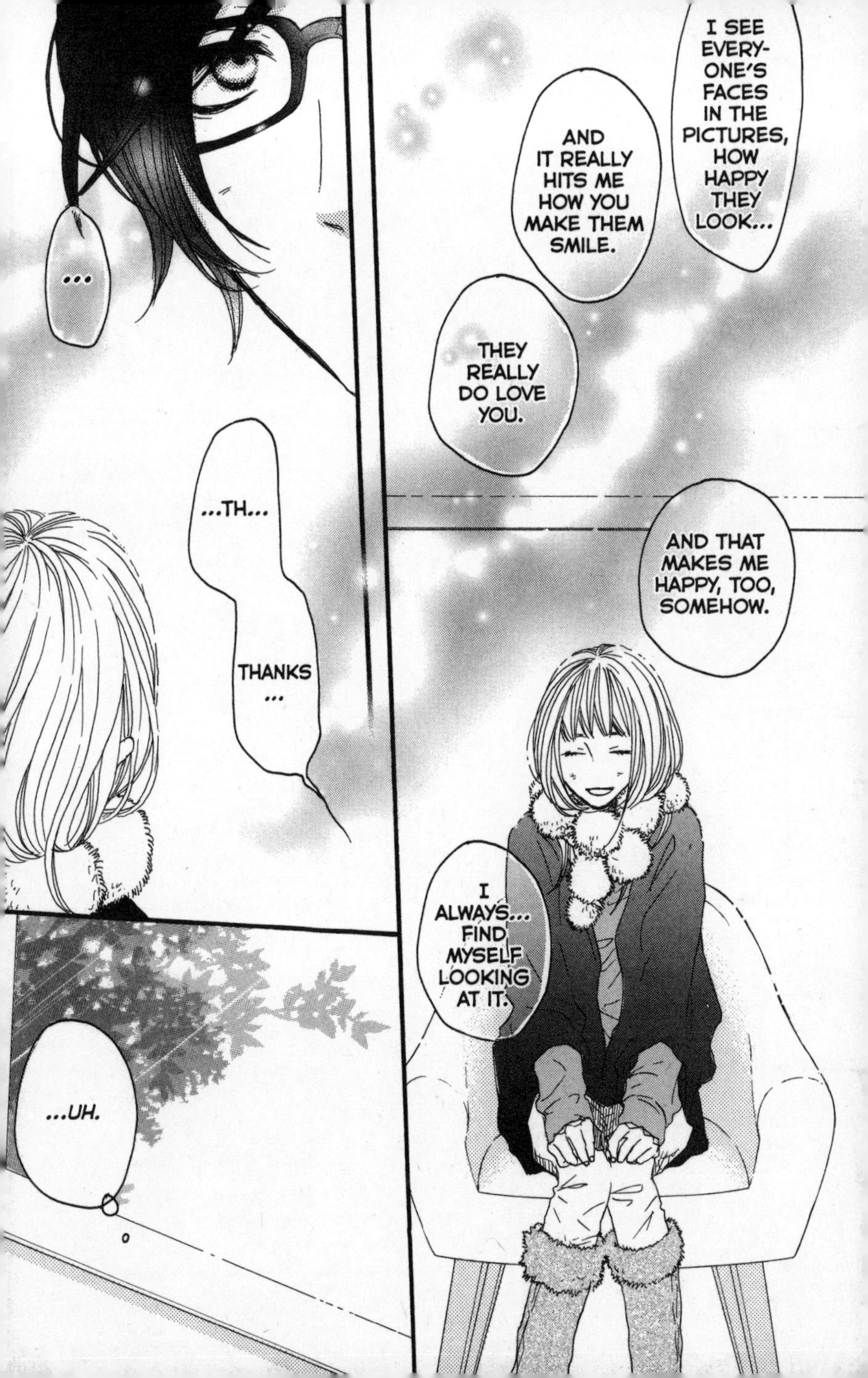
I SEE EVERYONE'S FACES IN THE PICTURES, HOW HAPPY THEY LOOK...
AND IT REALLY HITS ME HOW YOU MAKE THEM SMILE.
THEY REALLY DO LOVE YOU.
AND THAT MAKES ME HAPPY, TOO, SOMEHOW.
I ALWAYS... FIND MYSELF LOOKING AT IT.
...
...TH...
THANKS...
...UH.

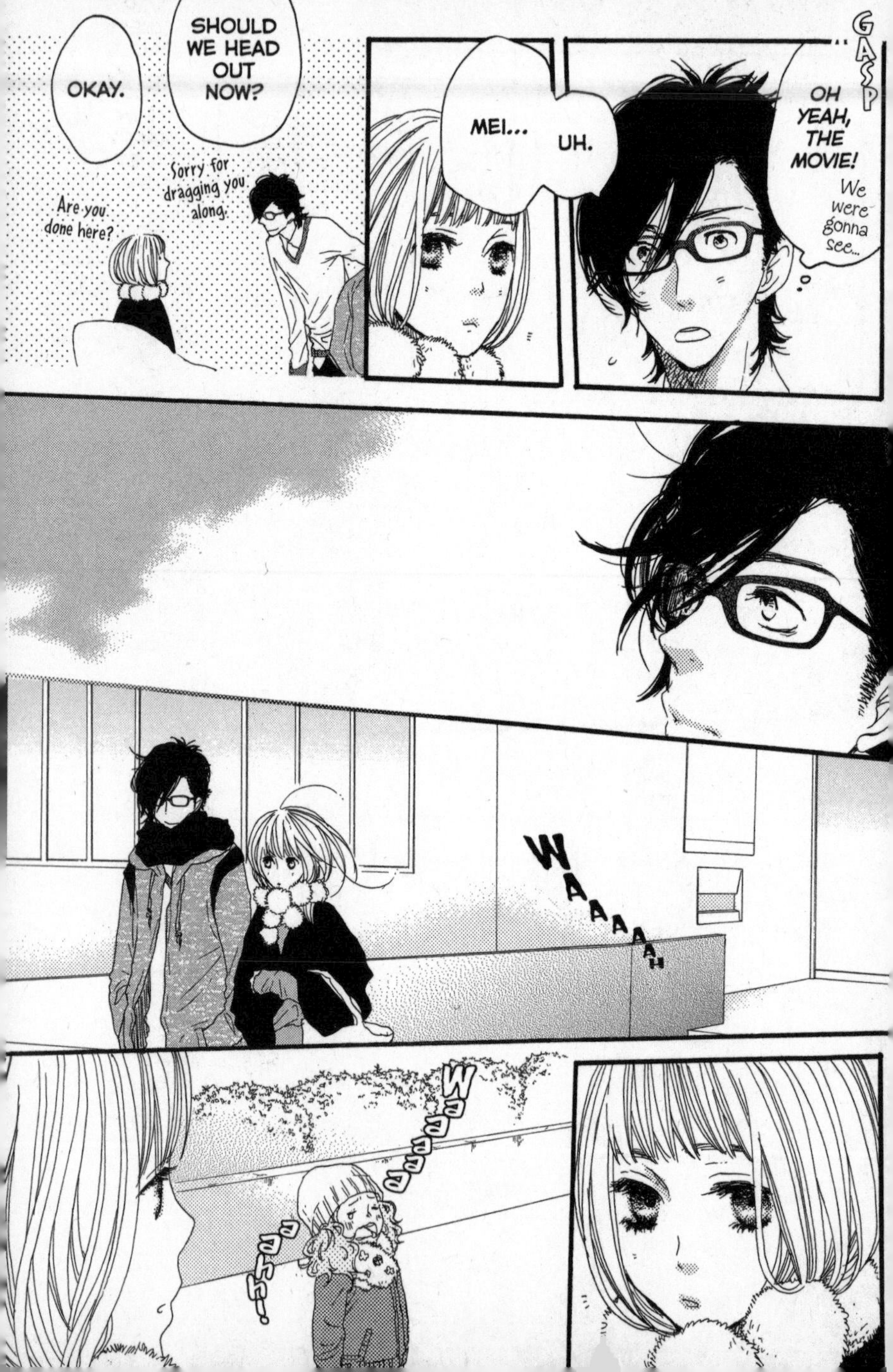
GASP
OH YEAH, THE MOVIE!
We were gonna see...
MEI...
UH.
SHOULD WE HEAD OUT NOW?
OKAY.
Sorry for dragging you along.
Are you done here?
WAAAAAH
Waaaaaa
aahh...!

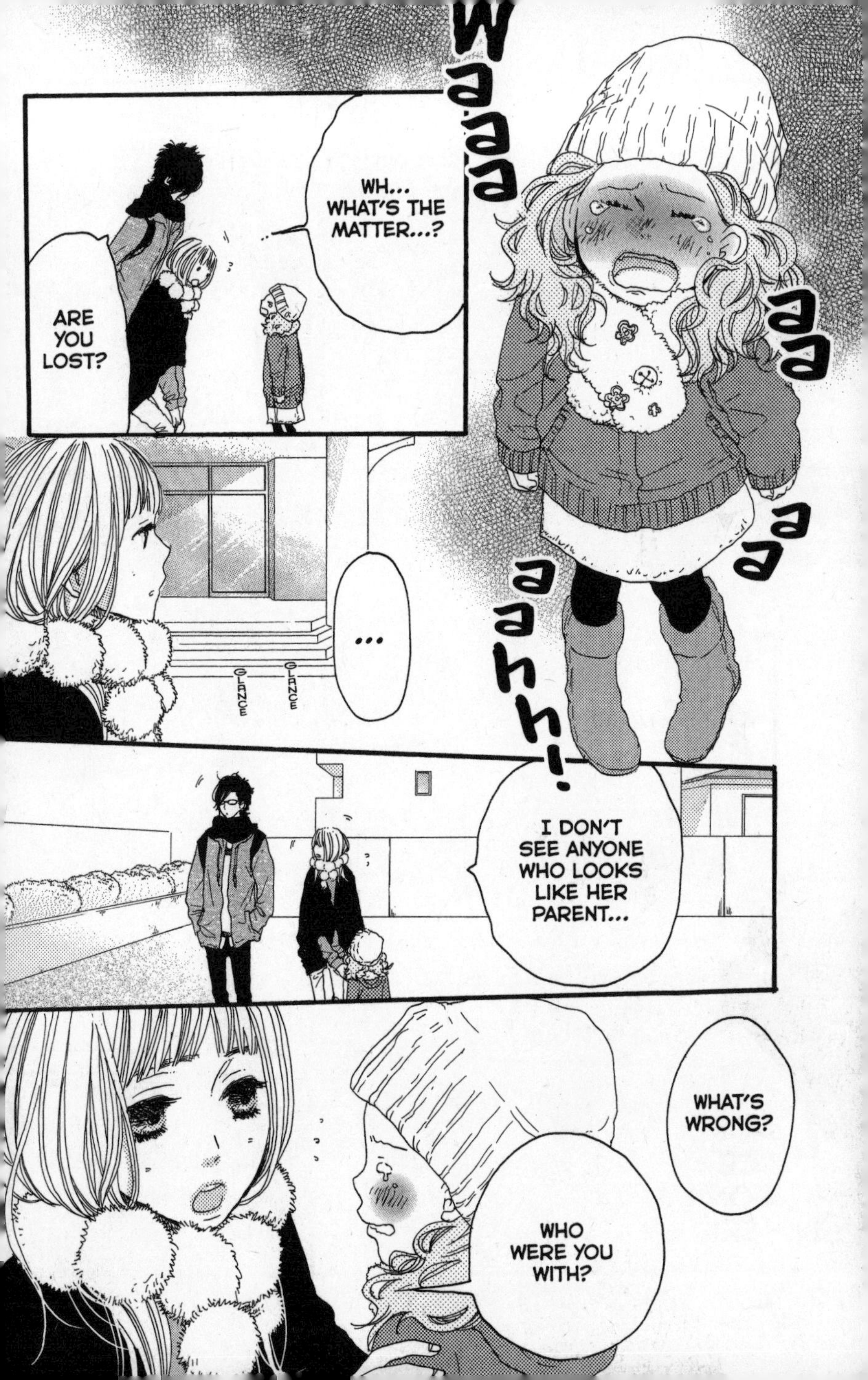
Waaaaaaaaaaahh!
WH... WHAT'S THE MATTER...?
ARE YOU LOST?
...
GLANCE
GLANCE
I DON'T SEE ANYONE WHO LOOKS LIKE HER PARENT...
WHAT'S WRONG?
WHO WERE YOU WITH?

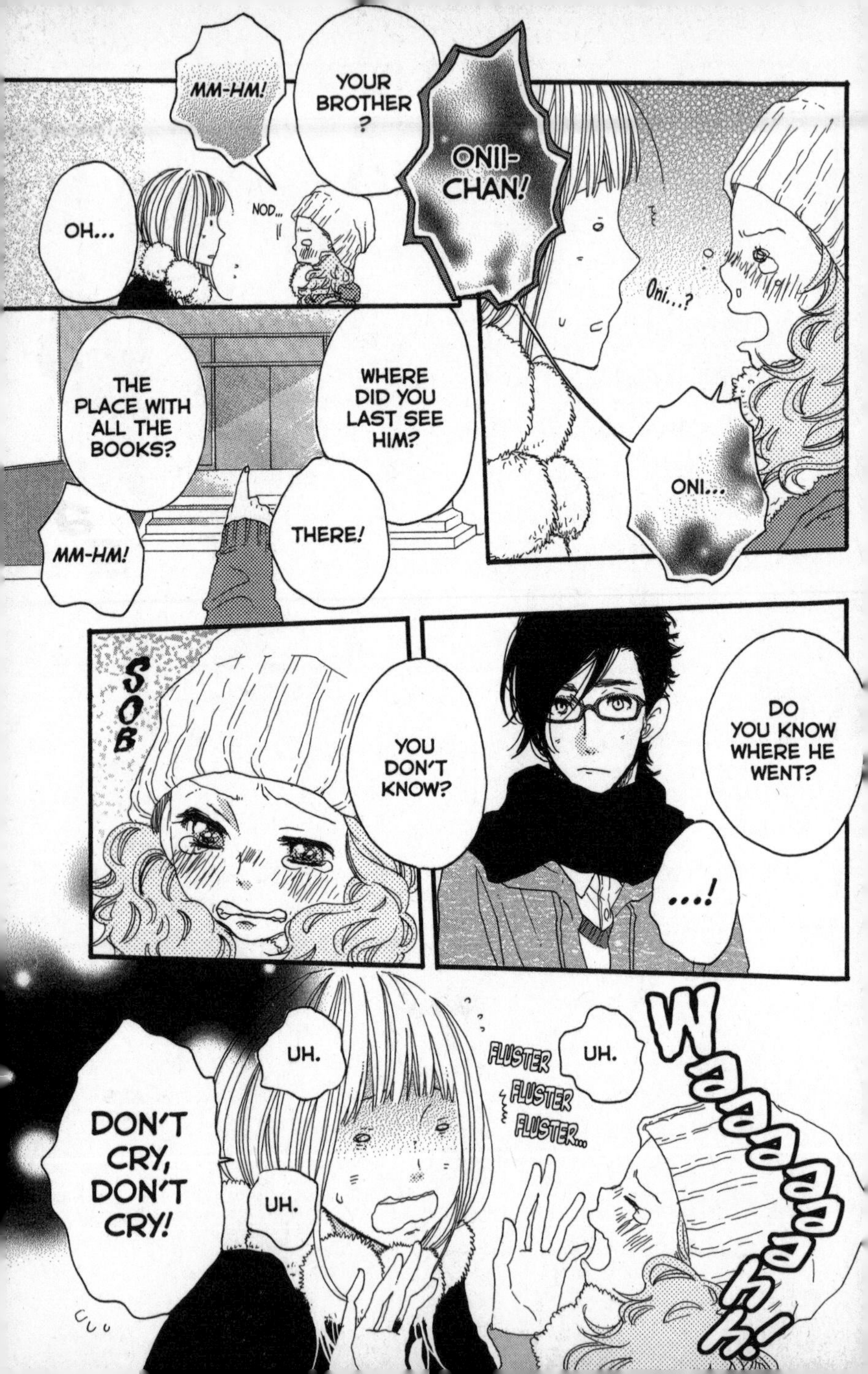
ONII-CHAN!
Oni...?
ONI...
YOUR BROTHER?
MM-HM!
NOD...
OH...
WHERE DID YOU LAST SEE HIM?
THE PLACE WITH ALL THE BOOKS?
THERE!
MM-HM!
DO YOU KNOW WHERE HE WENT?
...!
YOU DON'T KNOW?
SOB
Waaaaaaaahh!
UH.
FLUSTER FLUSTER FLUSTER...
UH.
DON'T CRY, DON'T CRY!
UH.

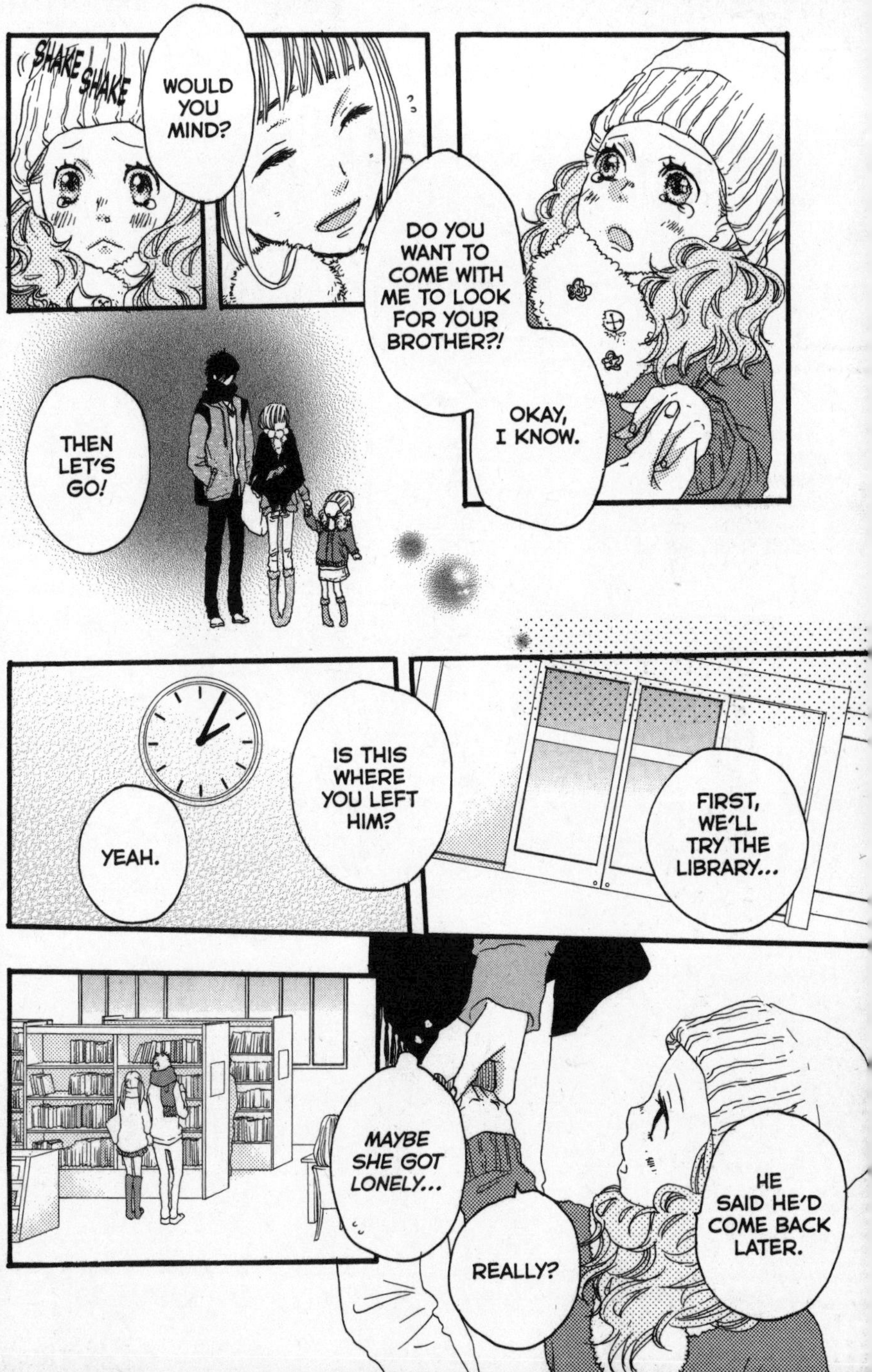
DO YOU WANT TO COME WITH ME TO LOOK FOR YOUR BROTHER?!
OKAY, I KNOW.
WOULD YOU MIND?
SHAKE SHAKE
THEN LET'S GO!
FIRST, WE'LL TRY THE LIBRARY...
IS THIS WHERE YOU LEFT HIM?
YEAH.
HE SAID HE'D COME BACK LATER.
REALLY?
MAYBE SHE GOT LONELY...

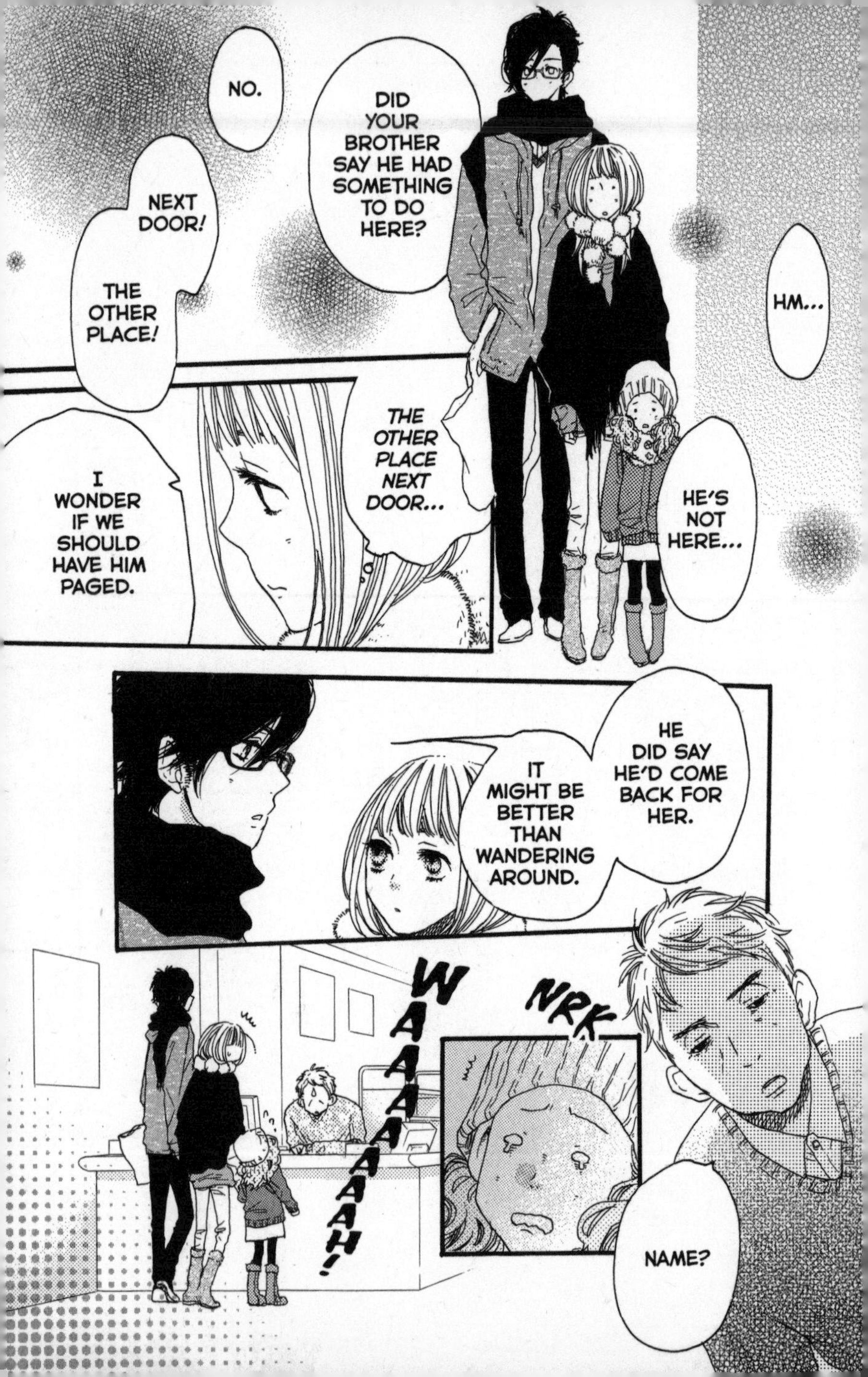
HM...
HE'S NOT HERE...
DID YOUR BROTHER SAY HE HAD SOMETHING TO DO HERE?
NO.
NEXT DOOR!
THE OTHER PLACE!
THE OTHER PLACE NEXT DOOR...
I WONDER IF WE SHOULD HAVE HIM PAGED.
HE DID SAY HE'D COME BACK FOR HER.
IT MIGHT BE BETTER THAN WANDERING AROUND.
NAME?
NRK
WAAAAAAAH!

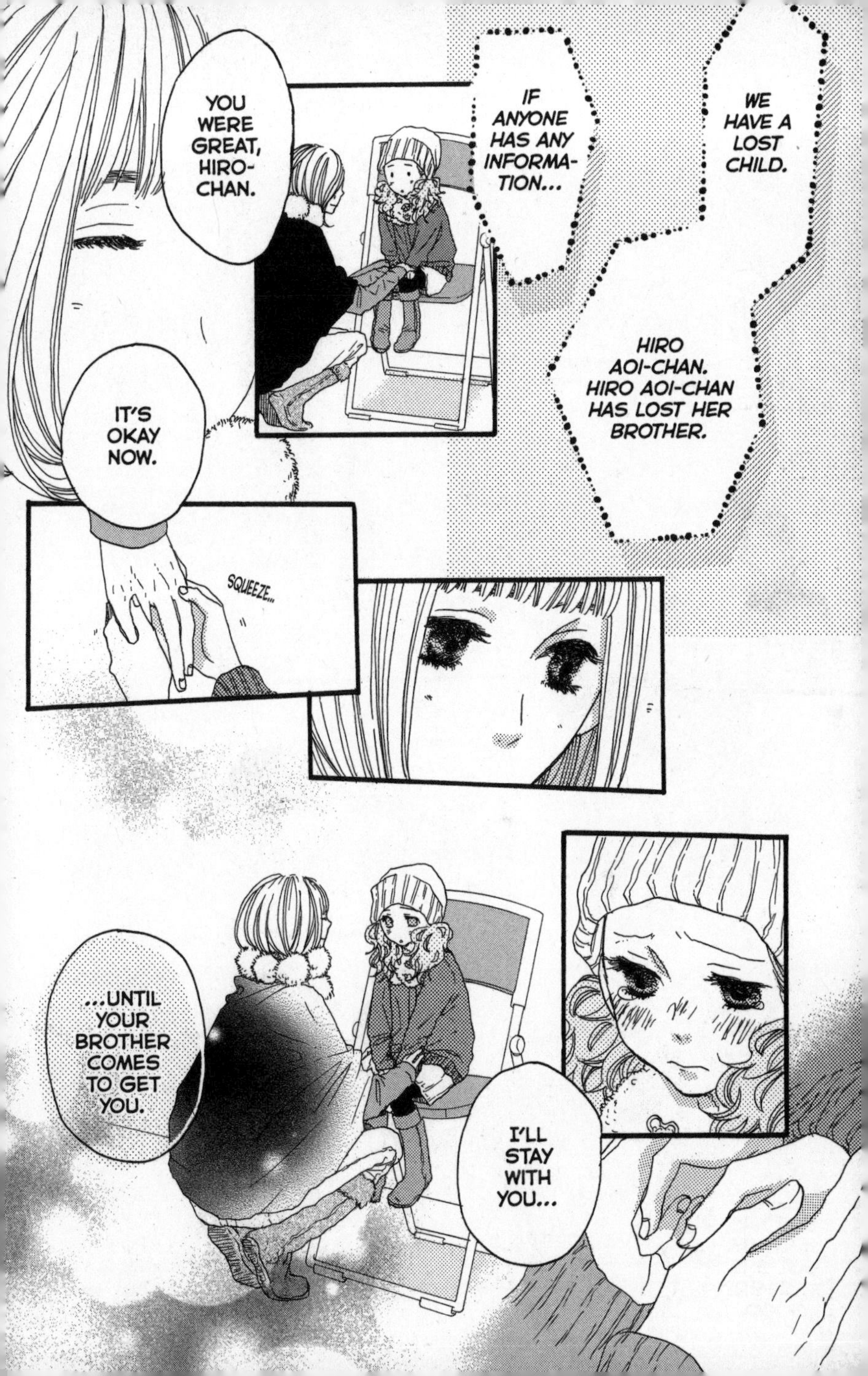
WE HAVE A LOST CHILD.
IF ANYONE HAS ANY INFORMATION...
HIRO AOI-CHAN. HIRO AOI-CHAN HAS LOST HER BROTHER.
YOU WERE GREAT, HIRO-CHAN.
IT'S OKAY NOW.
SQUEEZE...
I'LL STAY WITH YOU...
...UNTIL YOUR BROTHER COMES TO GET YOU.

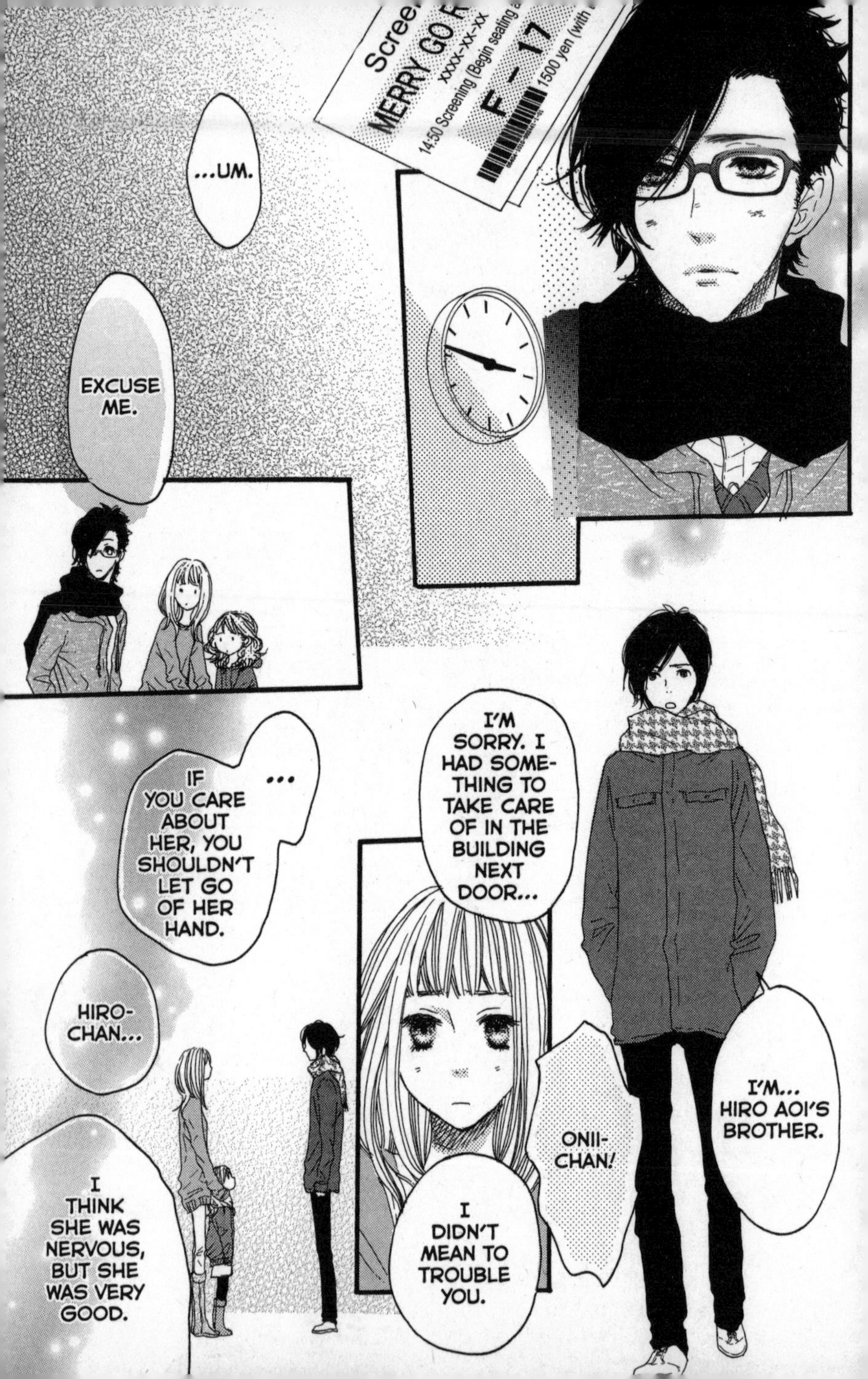
MERRY GO
xxxx-xx-xx
14:50 Screening (Begin seating
F-17
1500 yen (with
...UM.
EXCUSE ME.
I'M SORRY. I HAD SOME-THING TO TAKE CARE OF IN THE BUILDING NEXT DOOR...
I'M... HIRO AOI'S BROTHER.
ONII-CHAN!
I DIDN'T MEAN TO TROUBLE YOU.
...
IF YOU CARE ABOUT HER, YOU SHOULDN'T LET GO OF HER HAND.
HIRO-CHAN...
I THINK SHE WAS NERVOUS, BUT SHE WAS VERY GOOD.

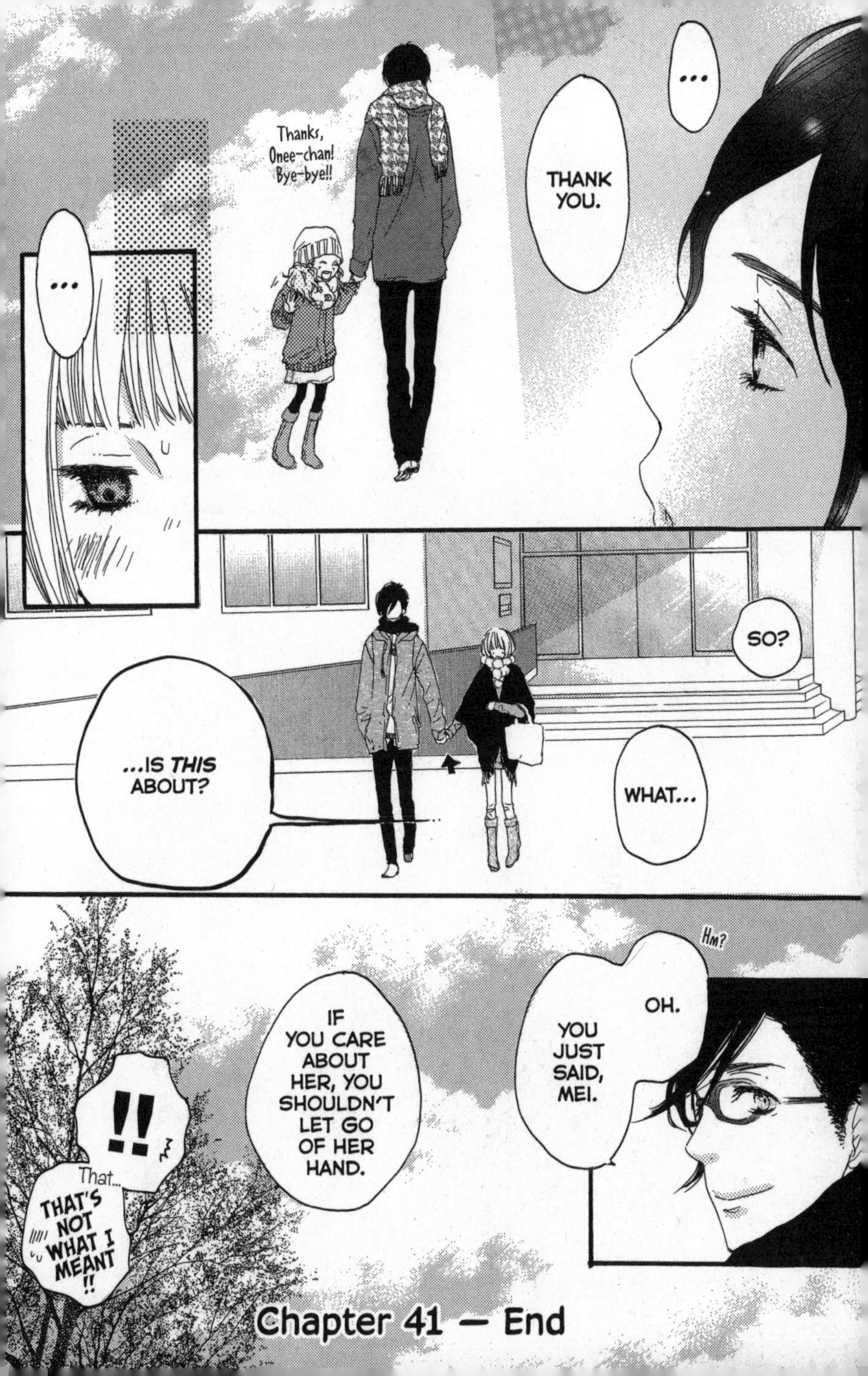
...
THANK YOU.
Thanks, Onee-chan! Bye-bye!!
...
SO?
WHAT...
...IS THIS ABOUT?
Hm?
OH.
YOU JUST SAID, MEI.
IF YOU CARE ABOUT HER, YOU SHOULDN'T LET GO OF HER HAND.
!!
That...
THAT'S NOT WHAT I MEANT!!
Chapter 41 — End

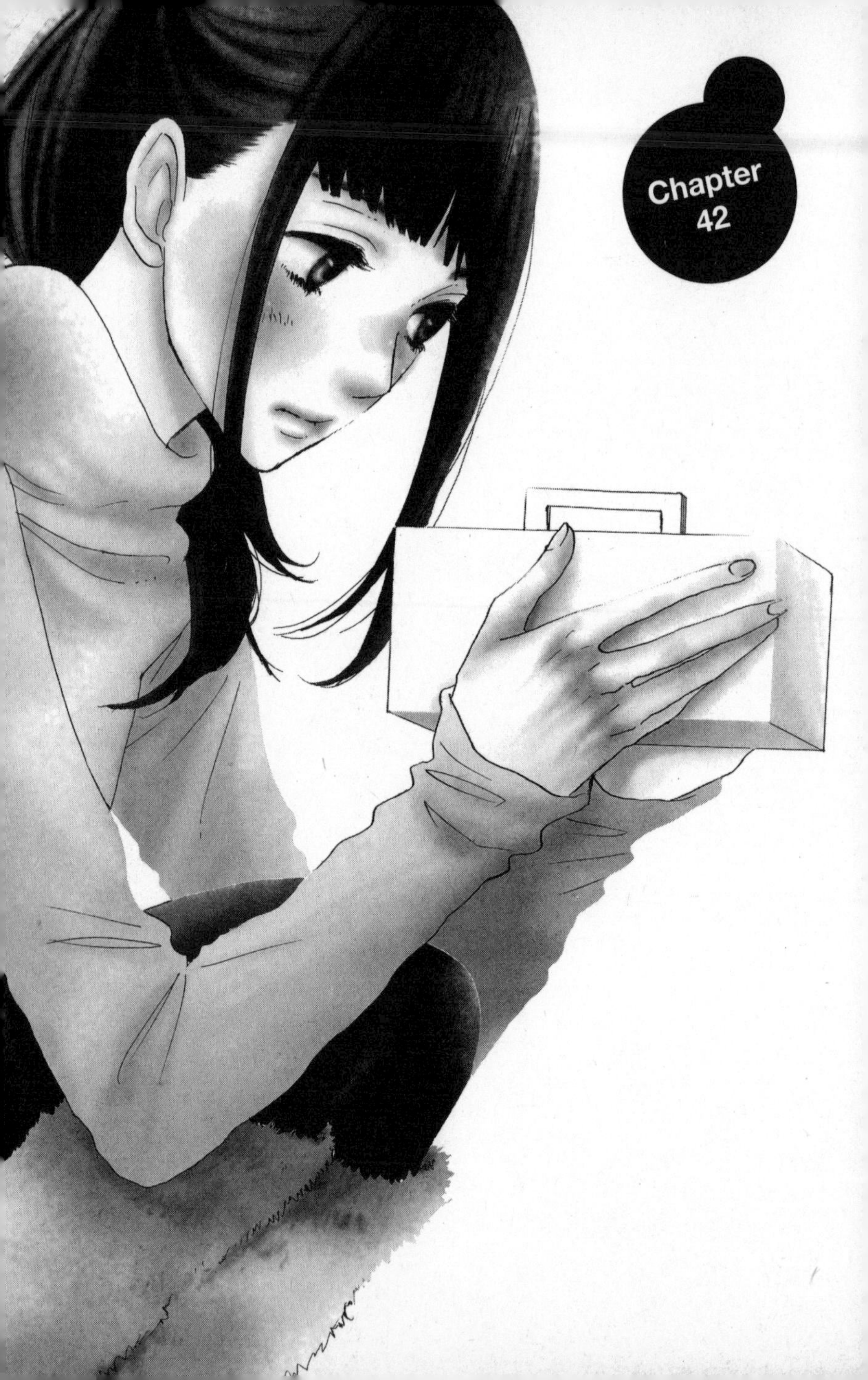
Chapter
42

Say "I love you".

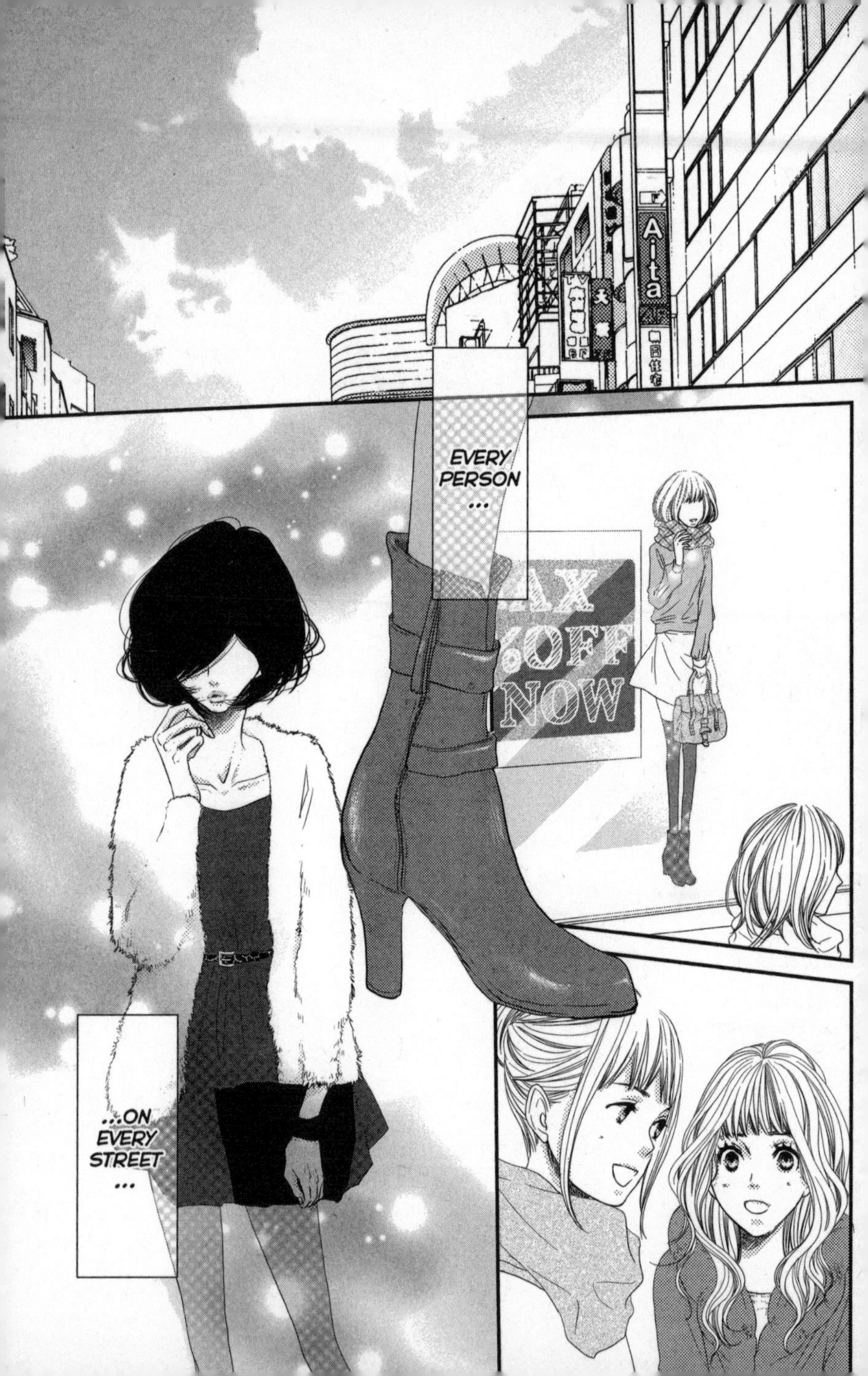
Aita
EVERY PERSON ...
...ON EVERY STREET ...

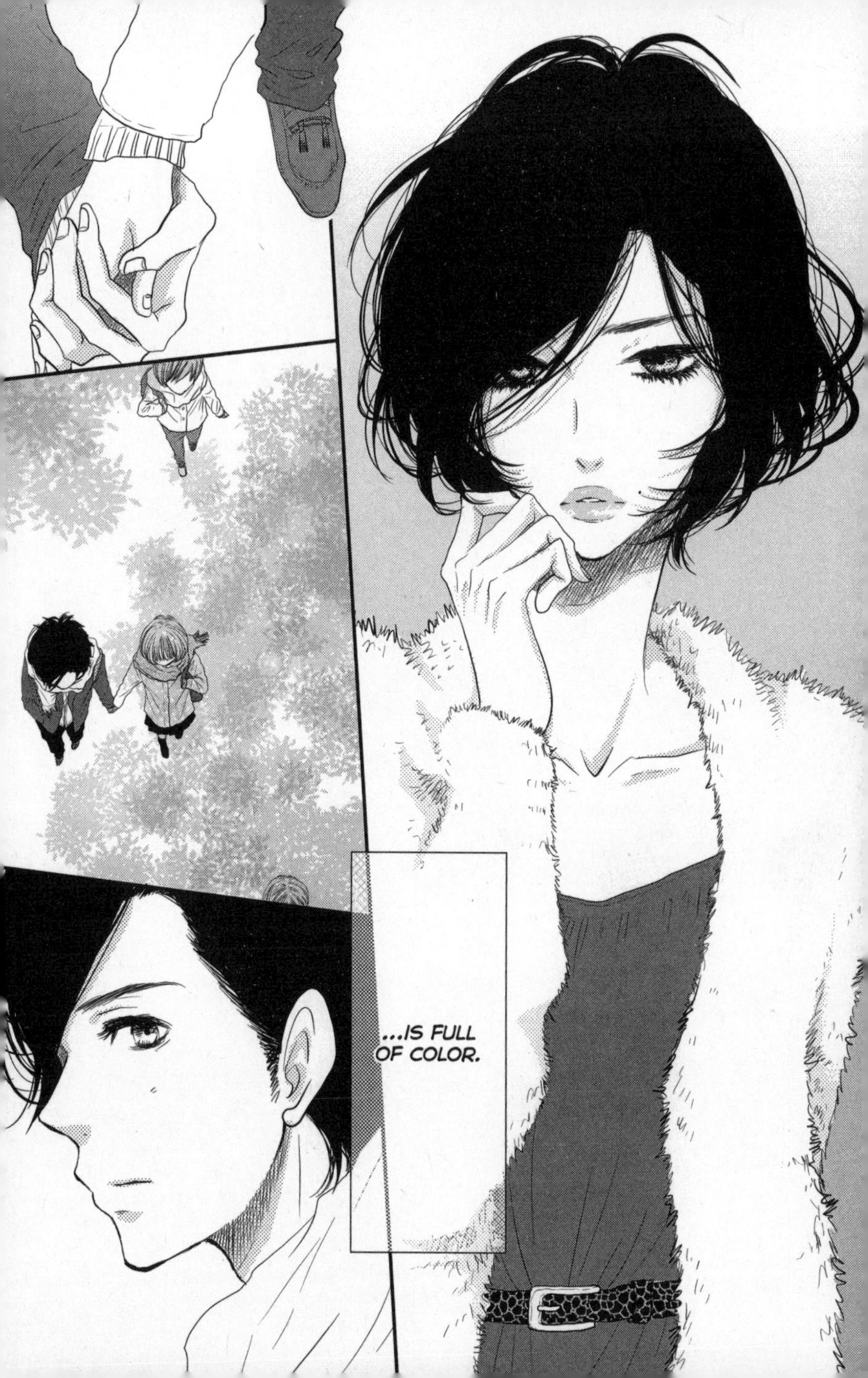
...IS FULL OF COLOR.

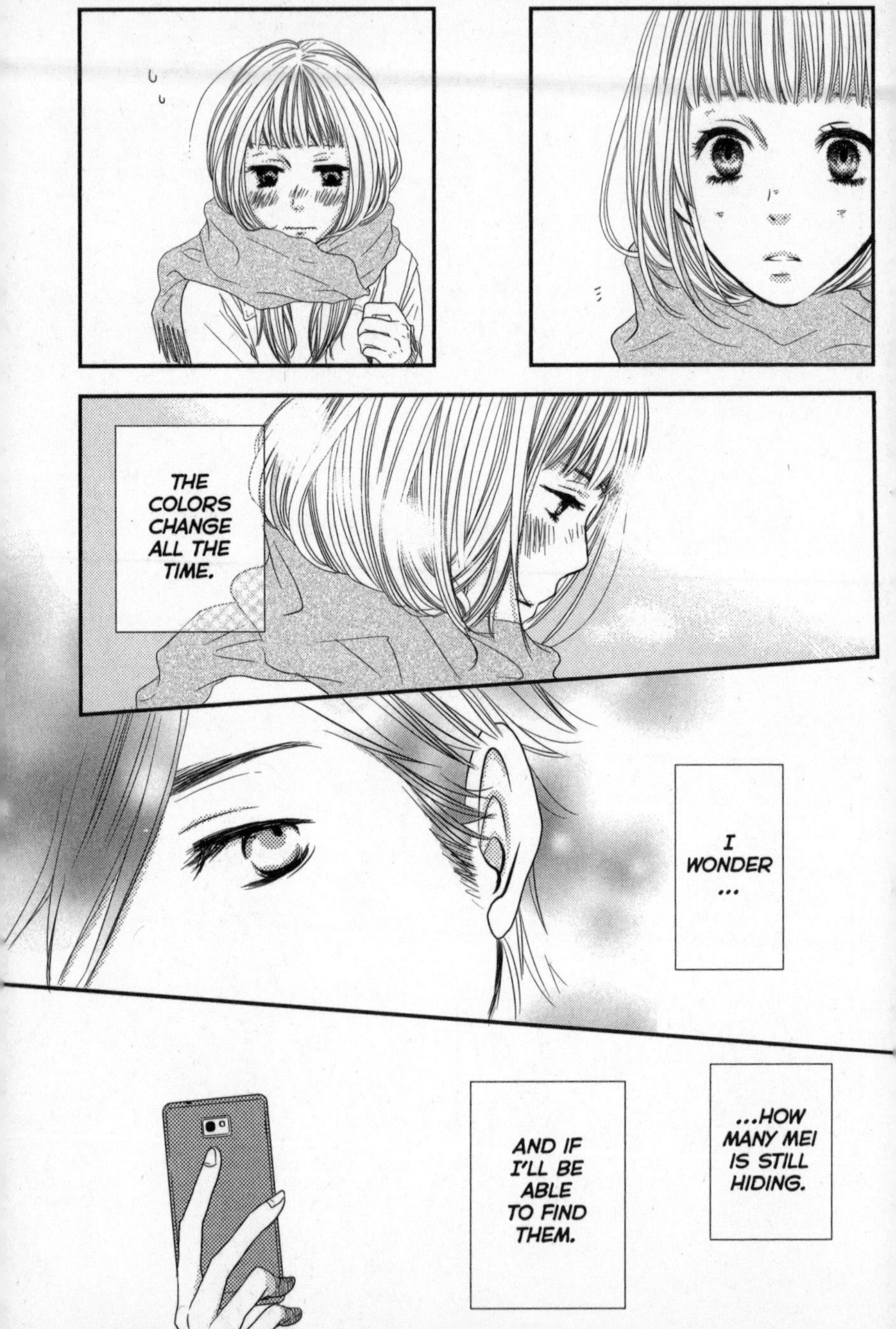
THE COLORS CHANGE ALL THE TIME.
I WONDER ...
...HOW MANY MEI IS STILL HIDING.
AND IF I'LL BE ABLE TO FIND THEM.

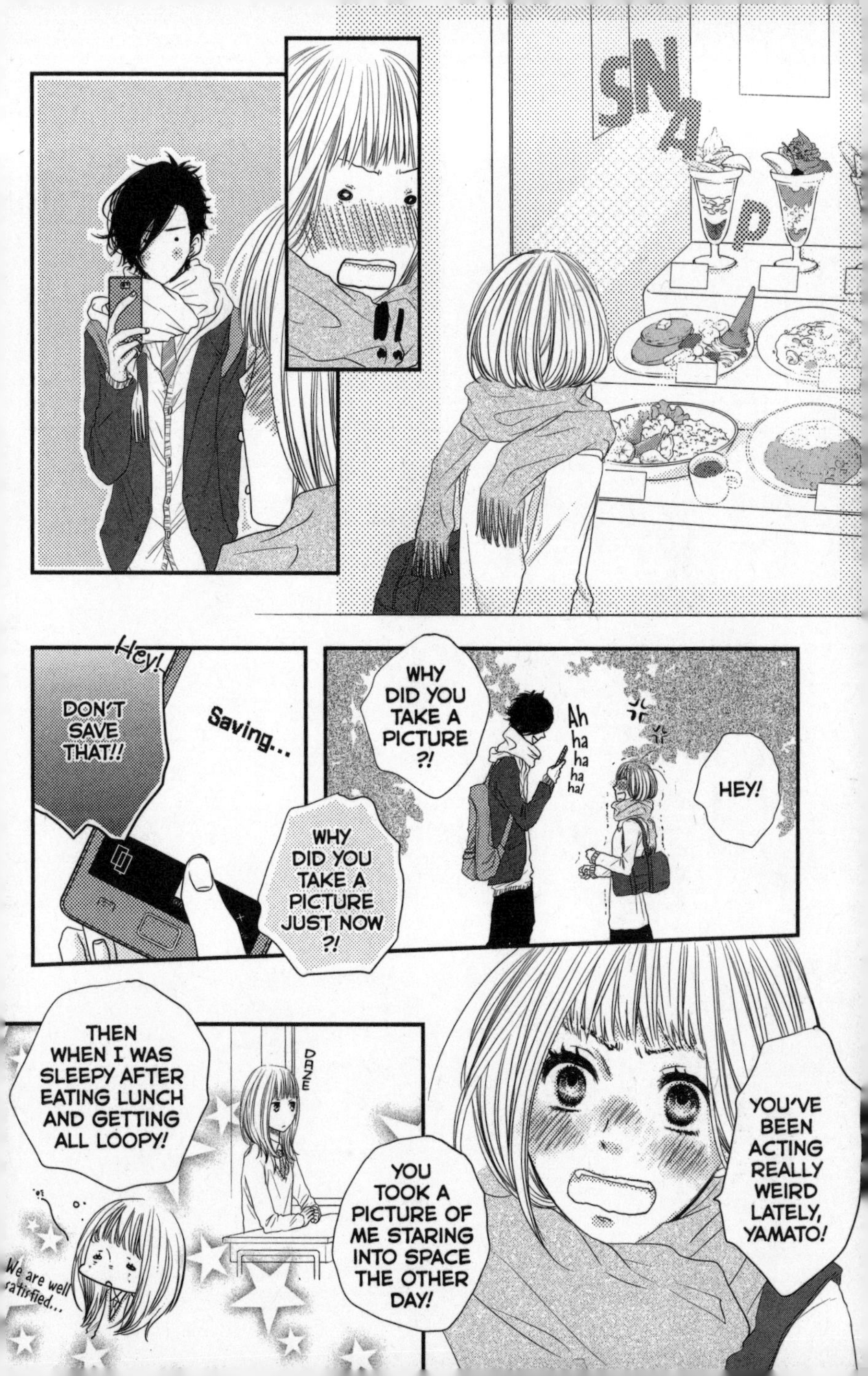
SNAP
!!
HEY!
WHY DID YOU TAKE A PICTURE ?!
Ah ha ha ha ha!
WHY DID YOU TAKE A PICTURE JUST NOW ?!
Saving...
Hey!
DON'T SAVE THAT!!
YOU'VE BEEN ACTING REALLY WEIRD LATELY, YAMATO!
YOU TOOK A PICTURE OF ME STARING INTO SPACE THE OTHER DAY!
THEN WHEN I WAS SLEEPY AFTER EATING LUNCH AND GETTING ALL LOOPY!
DAZE
We are well satisfied...

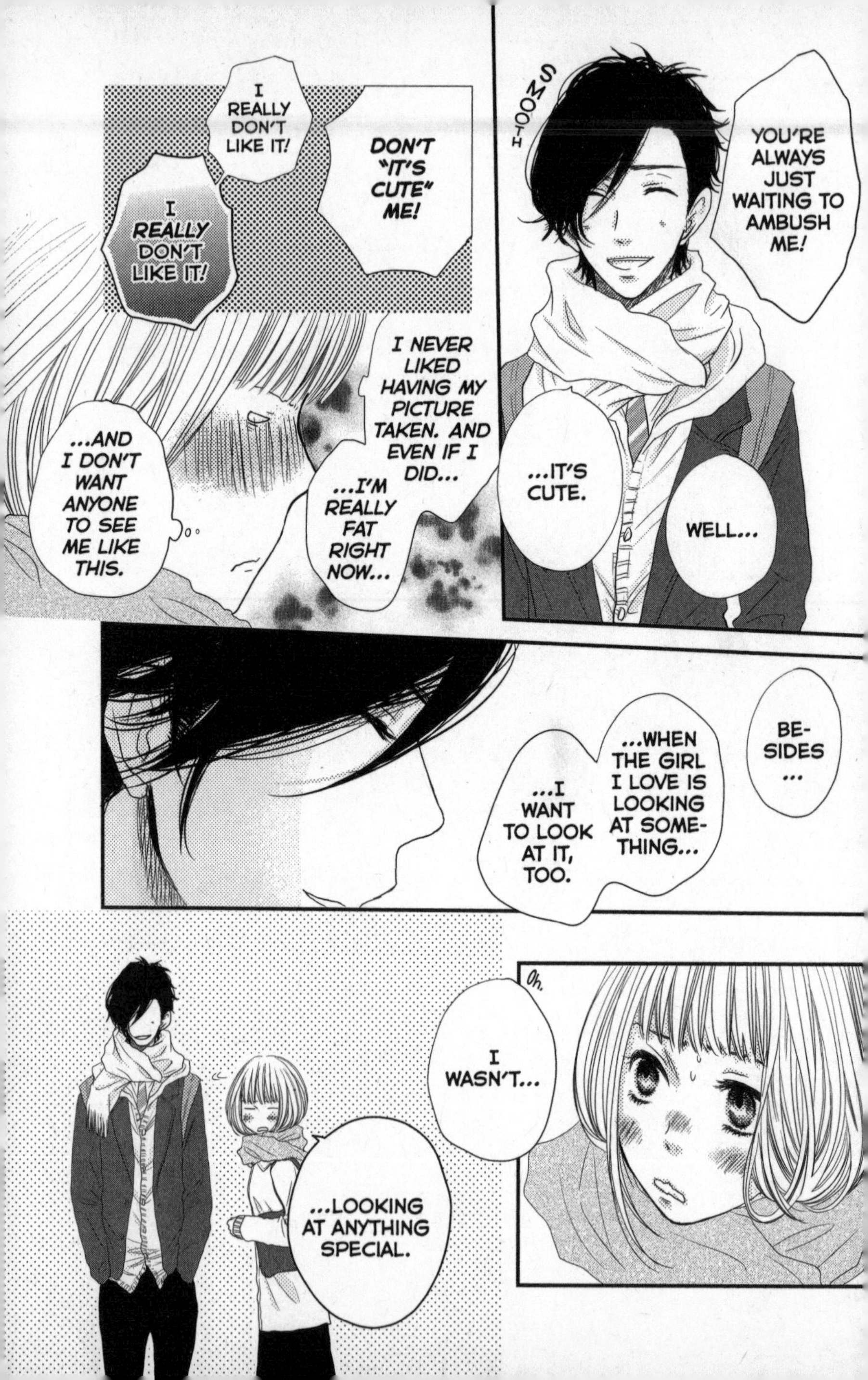
SMOOTH
YOU'RE ALWAYS JUST WAITING TO AMBUSH ME!
WELL...
...IT'S CUTE.
DON'T "IT'S CUTE" ME!
I REALLY DON'T LIKE IT!
I REALLY DON'T LIKE IT!
I NEVER LIKED HAVING MY PICTURE TAKEN. AND EVEN IF I DID...
...I'M REALLY FAT RIGHT NOW...
...AND I DON'T WANT ANYONE TO SEE ME LIKE THIS.
BE-SIDES...
...WHEN THE GIRL I LOVE IS LOOKING AT SOME-THING...
...I WANT TO LOOK AT IT, TOO.
Oh.
I WASN'T...
...LOOKING AT ANYTHING SPECIAL.

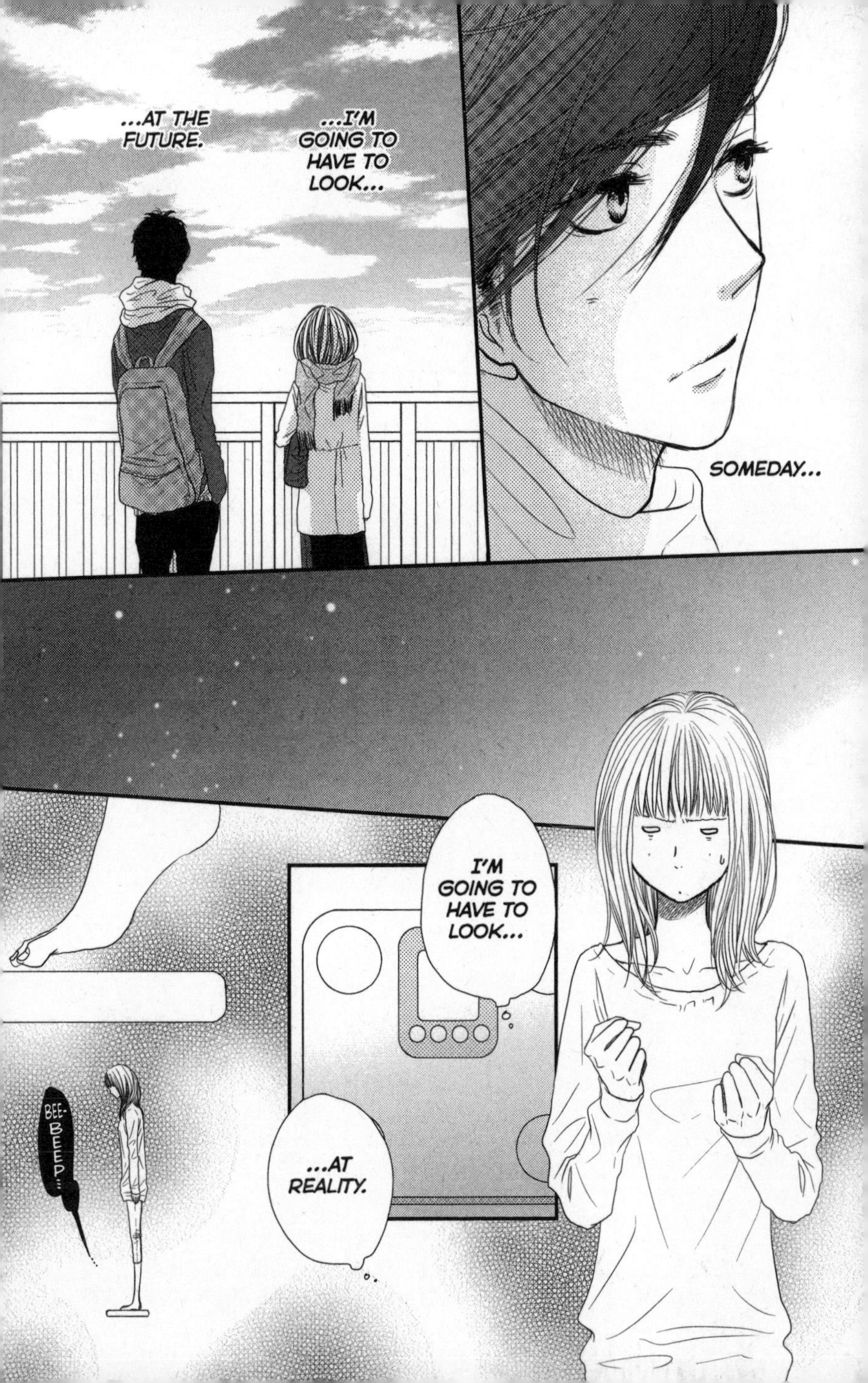

SOMEDAY...
...I'M GOING TO HAVE TO LOOK...
...AT THE FUTURE.
I'M GOING TO HAVE TO LOOK...
...AT REALITY.
BEE-BEEP...

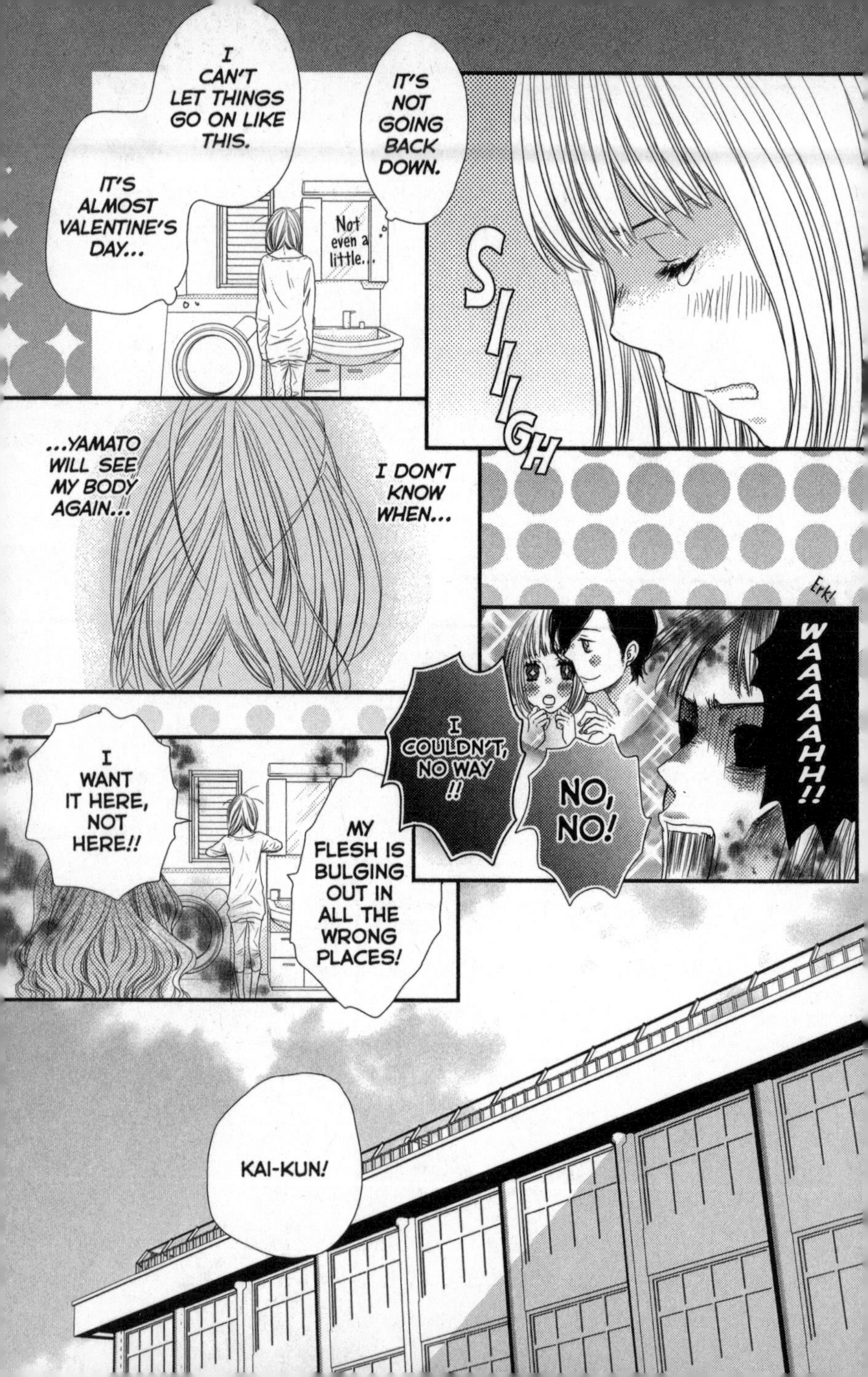
SIIIGH
IT'S NOT GOING BACK DOWN.
Not even a little...
I CAN'T LET THINGS GO ON LIKE THIS.
IT'S ALMOST VALENTINE'S DAY...
Erk!
WAAAAAAH!!
NO, NO!
I COULDN'T, NO WAY!!
I DON'T KNOW WHEN...
...YAMATO WILL SEE MY BODY AGAIN...
MY FLESH IS BULGING OUT IN ALL THE WRONG PLACES!
I WANT IT HERE, NOT HERE!!
KAI-KUN!

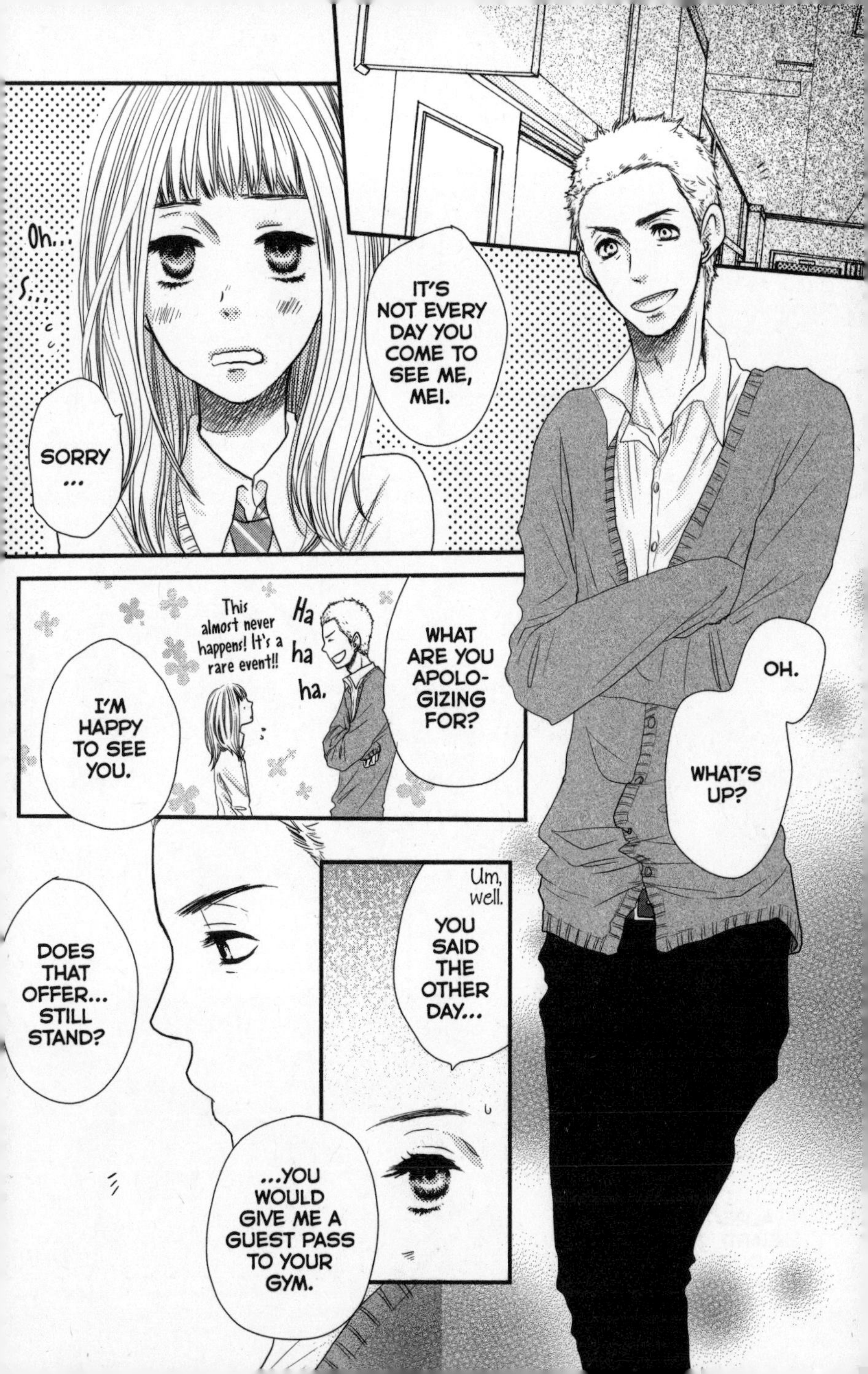
IT'S NOT EVERY DAY YOU COME TO SEE ME, MEI.
Oh... S...
SORRY...
WHAT ARE YOU APOLO-GIZING FOR?
Ha ha ha.
This almost never happens! It's a rare event!!
I'M HAPPY TO SEE YOU.
OH.
WHAT'S UP?
Um, well.
YOU SAID THE OTHER DAY...
...YOU WOULD GIVE ME A GUEST PASS TO YOUR GYM.
DOES THAT OFFER... STILL STAND?

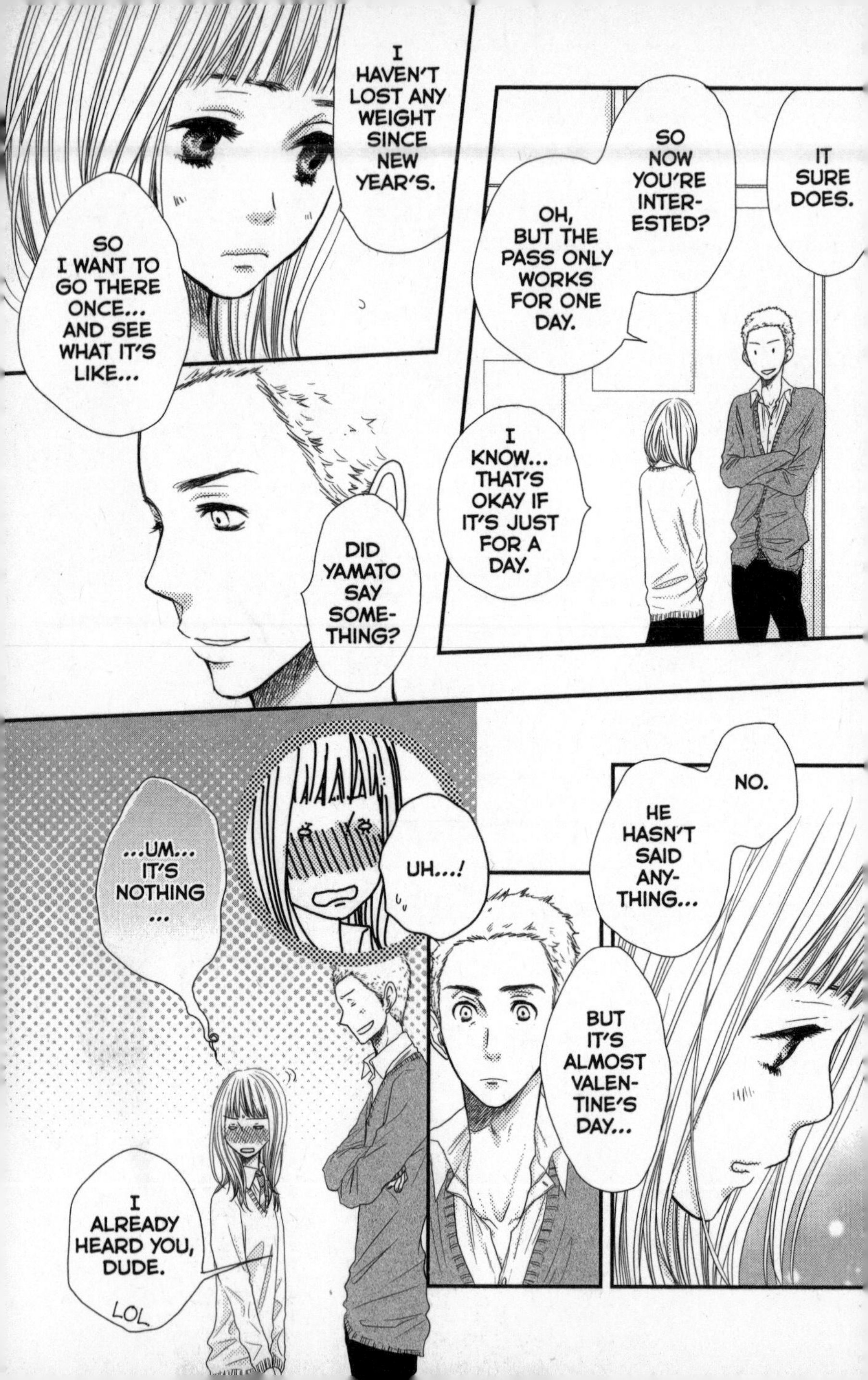
IT SURE DOES.
SO NOW YOU'RE INTER-ESTED?
OH, BUT THE PASS ONLY WORKS FOR ONE DAY.
I KNOW... THAT'S OKAY IF IT'S JUST FOR A DAY.
I HAVEN'T LOST ANY WEIGHT SINCE NEW YEAR'S.
SO I WANT TO GO THERE ONCE... AND SEE WHAT IT'S LIKE...
DID YAMATO SAY SOME-THING?
NO.
HE HASN'T SAID ANY-THING...
BUT IT'S ALMOST VALEN-TINE'S DAY...
UH...!
...UM... IT'S NOTHING ...
I ALREADY HEARD YOU, DUDE.
LOL

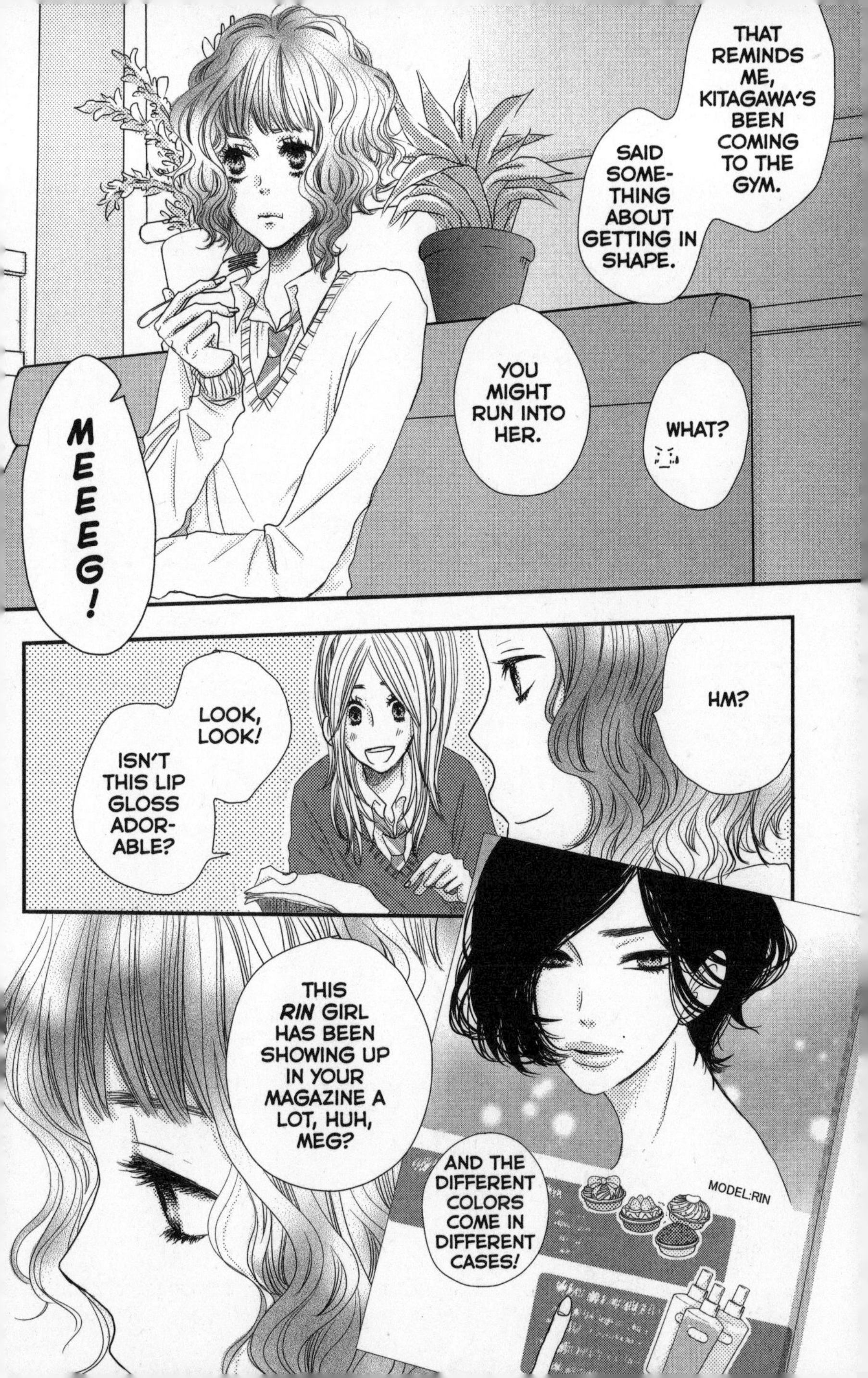
THAT REMINDS ME, KITAGAWA'S BEEN COMING TO THE GYM.
SAID SOMETHING ABOUT GETTING IN SHAPE.
WHAT?
YOU MIGHT RUN INTO HER.
MEEEG!
HM?
LOOK, LOOK!
ISN'T THIS LIP GLOSS ADORABLE?
MODEL:RIN
AND THE DIFFERENT COLORS COME IN DIFFERENT CASES!
THIS *RIN* GIRL HAS BEEN SHOWING UP IN YOUR MAGAZINE A LOT, HUH, MEG?

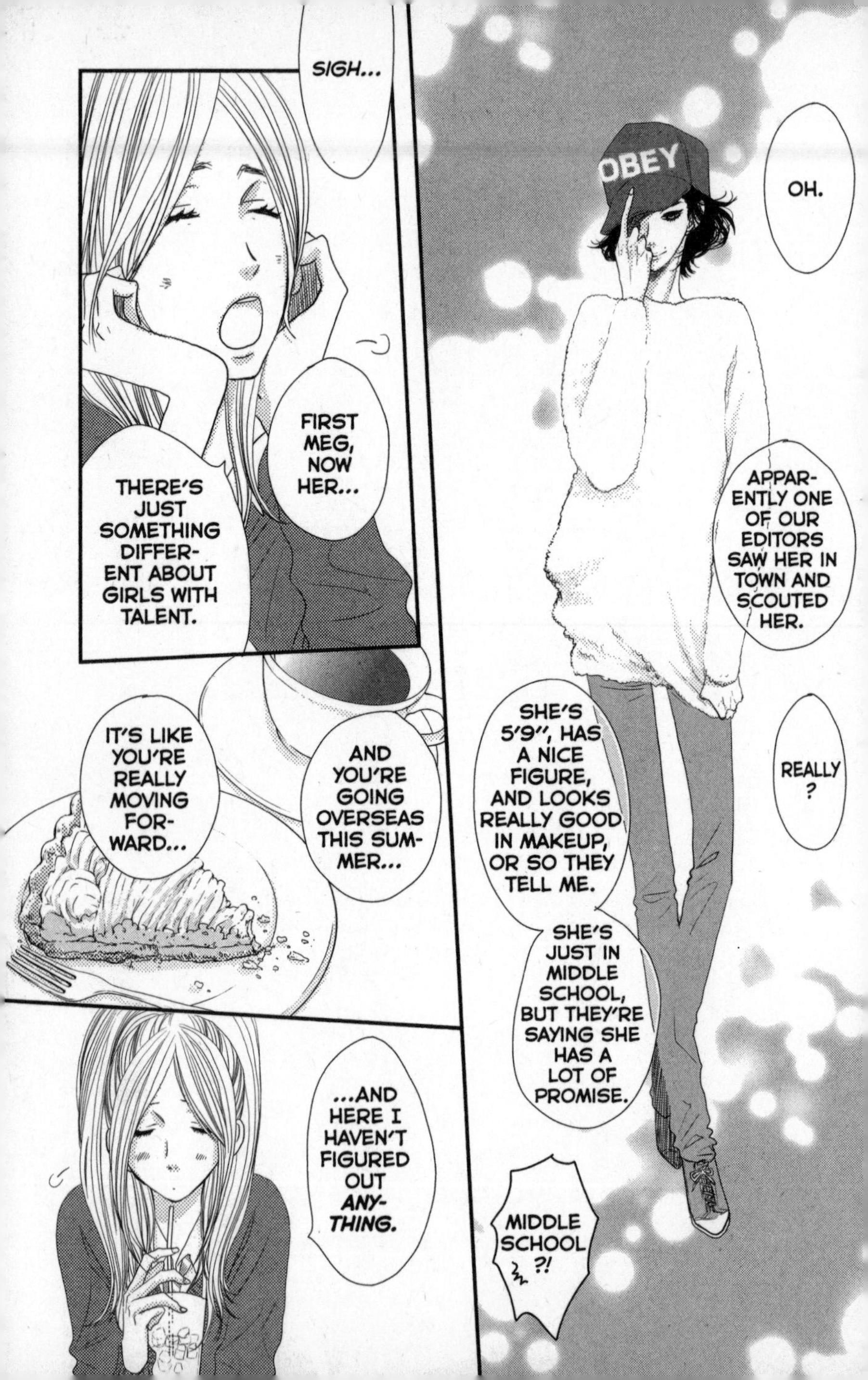
OH.
APPARENTLY ONE OF OUR EDITORS SAW HER IN TOWN AND SCOUTED HER.
REALLY?
SHE'S 5'9", HAS A NICE FIGURE, AND LOOKS REALLY GOOD IN MAKEUP, OR SO THEY TELL ME.
SHE'S JUST IN MIDDLE SCHOOL, BUT THEY'RE SAYING SHE HAS A LOT OF PROMISE.
MIDDLE SCHOOL?!
SIGH...
FIRST MEG, NOW HER...
THERE'S JUST SOMETHING DIFFERENT ABOUT GIRLS WITH TALENT.
AND YOU'RE GOING OVERSEAS THIS SUMMER...
IT'S LIKE YOU'RE REALLY MOVING FORWARD...
...AND HERE I HAVEN'T FIGURED OUT *ANYTHING*.

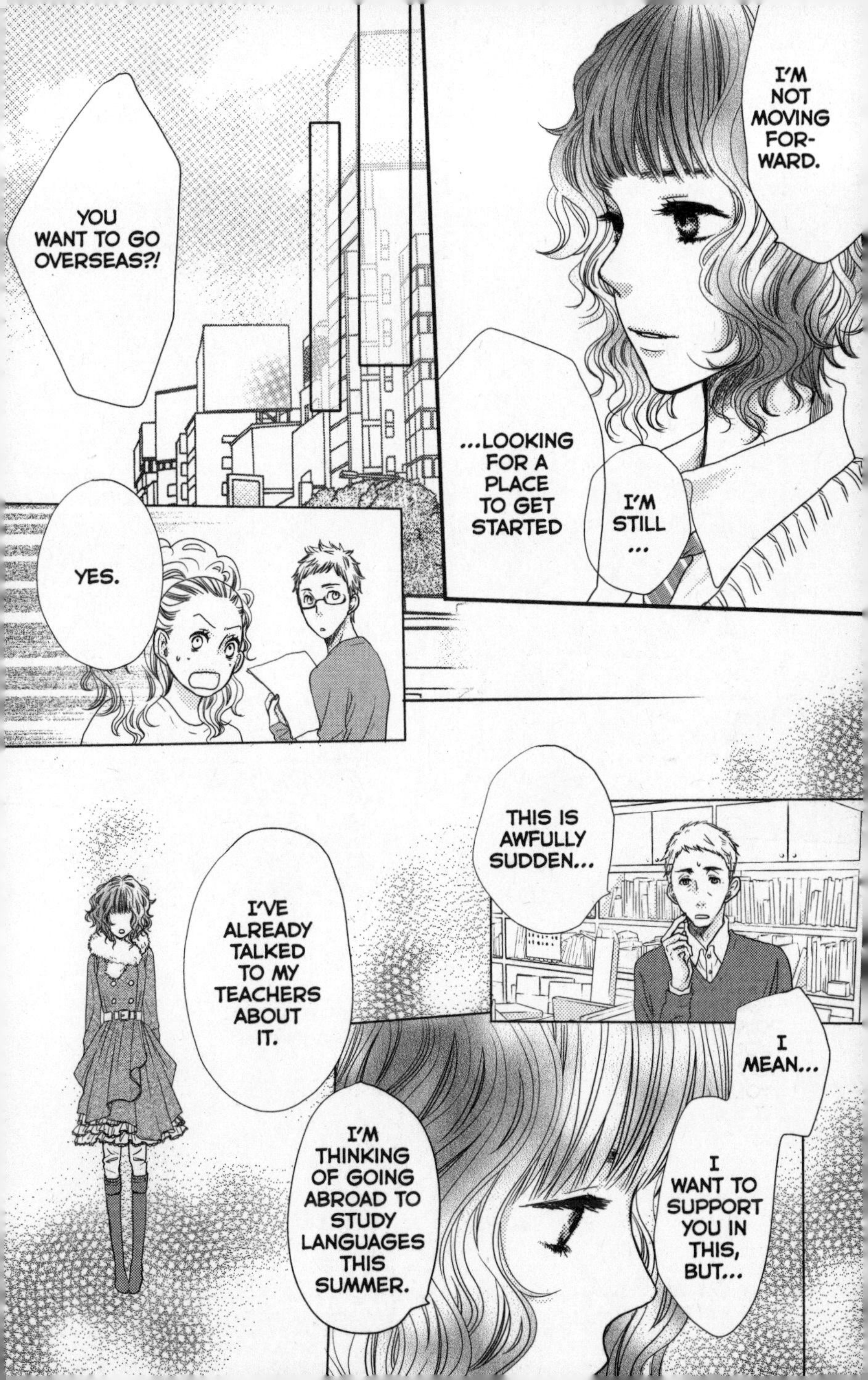
I'M NOT MOVING FOR-WARD.
I'M STILL ...
...LOOKING FOR A PLACE TO GET STARTED
YOU WANT TO GO OVERSEAS?!
YES.
THIS IS AWFULLY SUDDEN...
I MEAN...
I WANT TO SUPPORT YOU IN THIS, BUT...
I'M THINKING OF GOING ABROAD TO STUDY LANGUAGES THIS SUMMER.
I'VE ALREADY TALKED TO MY TEACHERS ABOUT IT.

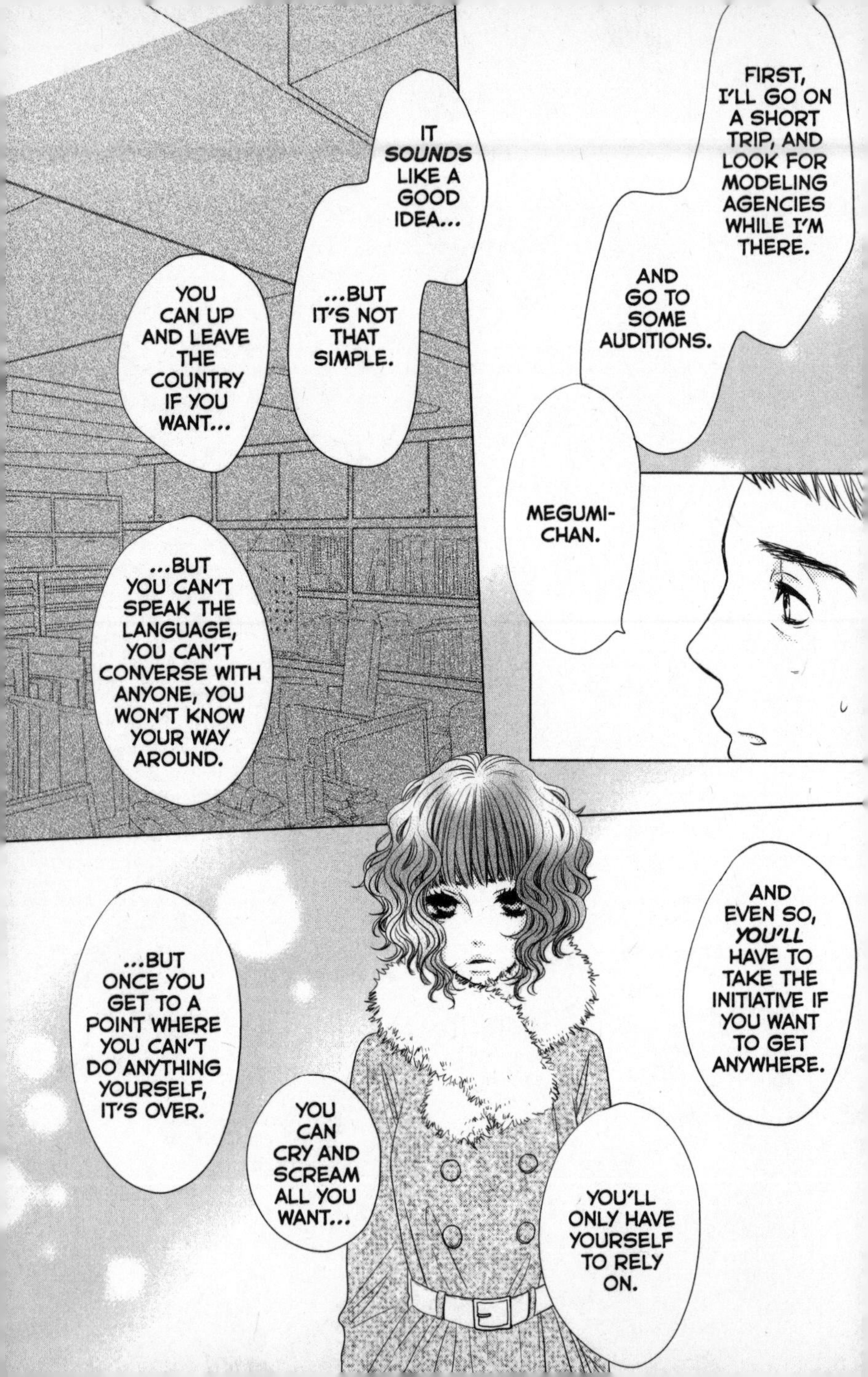
FIRST, I'LL GO ON A SHORT TRIP, AND LOOK FOR MODELING AGENCIES WHILE I'M THERE.
AND GO TO SOME AUDITIONS.
MEGUMI-CHAN.
IT *SOUNDS* LIKE A GOOD IDEA...
...BUT IT'S NOT THAT SIMPLE.
YOU CAN UP AND LEAVE THE COUNTRY IF YOU WANT...
...BUT YOU CAN'T SPEAK THE LANGUAGE, YOU CAN'T CONVERSE WITH ANYONE, YOU WON'T KNOW YOUR WAY AROUND.
...BUT ONCE YOU GET TO A POINT WHERE YOU CAN'T DO ANYTHING YOURSELF, IT'S OVER.
YOU CAN CRY AND SCREAM ALL YOU WANT...
AND EVEN SO, *YOU'LL* HAVE TO TAKE THE INITIATIVE IF YOU WANT TO GET ANYWHERE.
YOU'LL ONLY HAVE YOURSELF TO RELY ON.

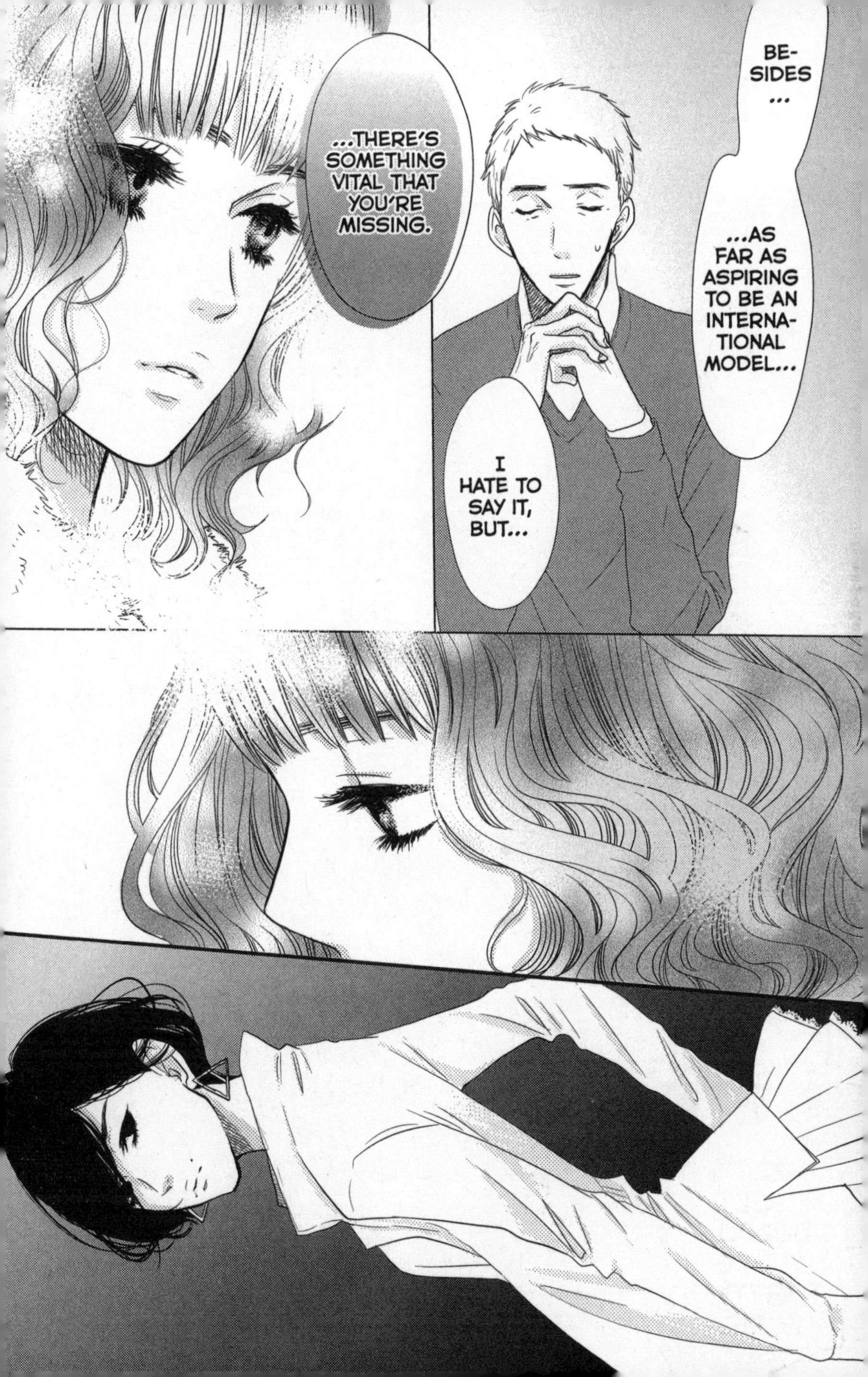
BE-SIDES...
...AS FAR AS ASPIRING TO BE AN INTERNATIONAL MODEL...
I HATE TO SAY IT, BUT...
...THERE'S SOMETHING VITAL THAT YOU'RE MISSING.

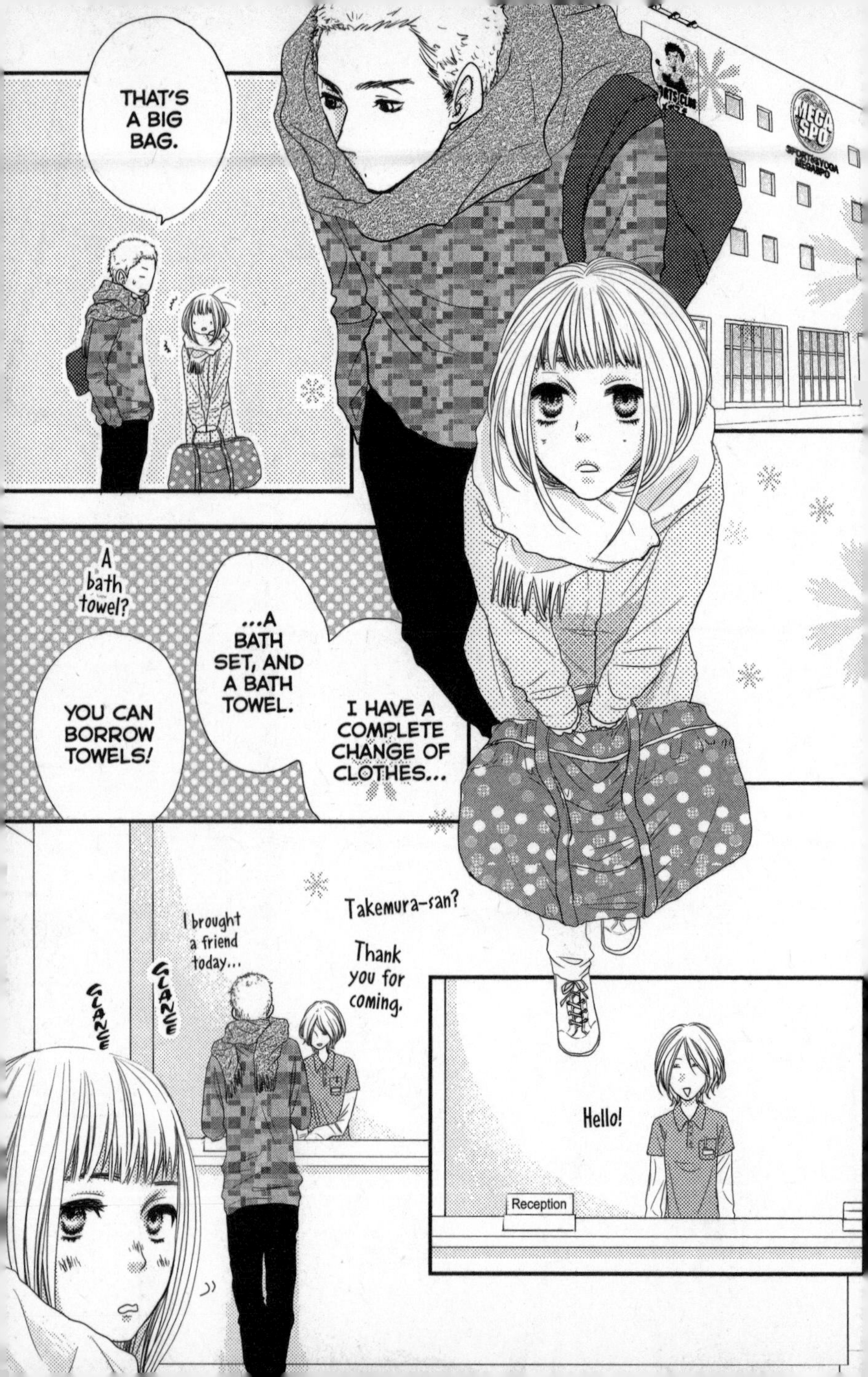
MEGA SPO
THAT'S A BIG BAG.
I HAVE A COMPLETE CHANGE OF CLOTHES...
...A BATH SET, AND A BATH TOWEL.
A bath towel?
YOU CAN BORROW TOWELS!
Reception
Hello!
Takemura-san?
Thank you for coming.
I brought a friend today...
GLANCE
GLANCE

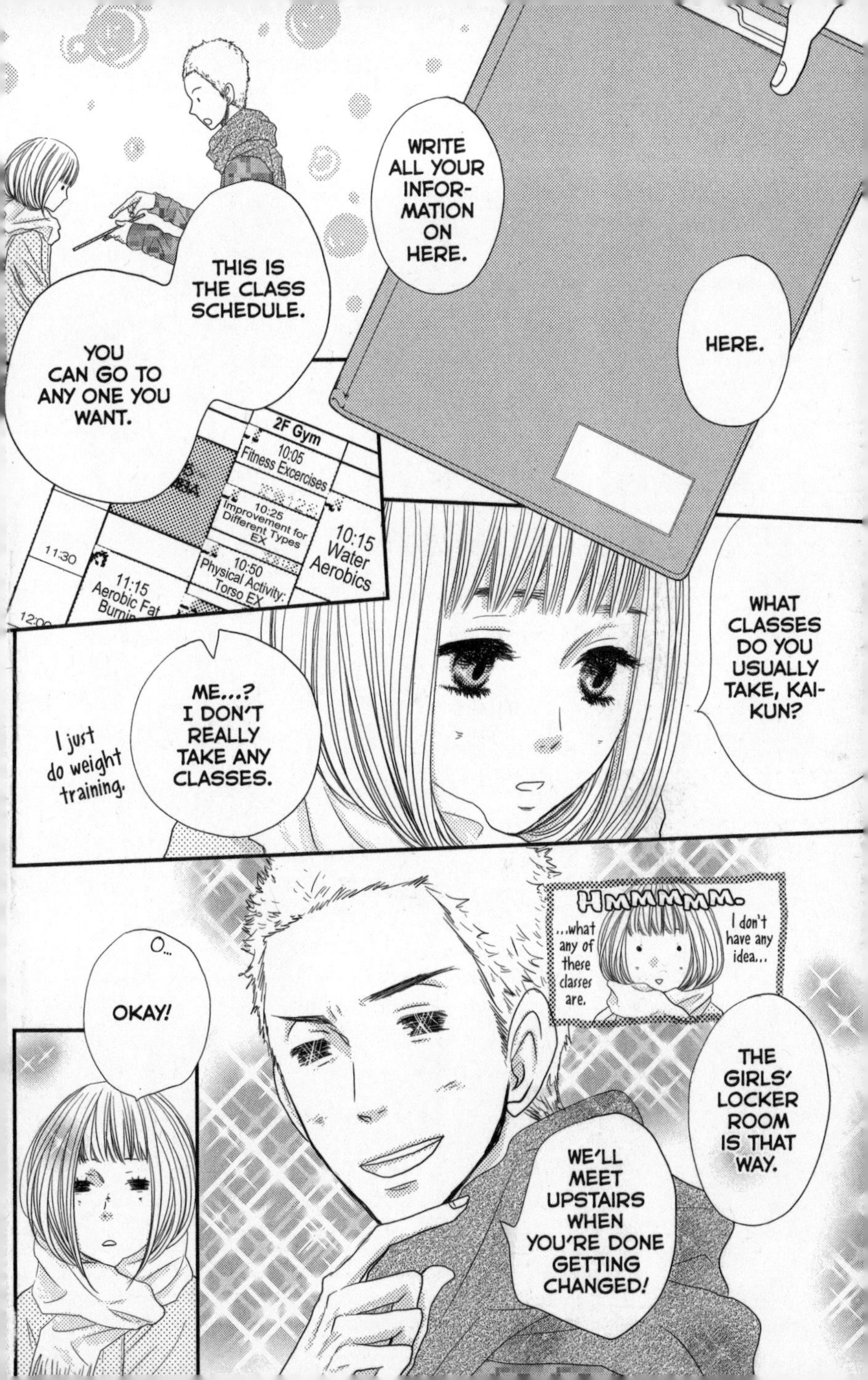
HERE.
WRITE ALL YOUR INFORMATION ON HERE.
THIS IS THE CLASS SCHEDULE.
YOU CAN GO TO ANY ONE YOU WANT.
2F Gym
10:05 Fitness Excercises
10:15 Water Aerobics
10:25 Improvement for Different Types EX
10:50 Physical Activity: Torso EX
11:30
11:15 Aerobic Fat Burnin
WHAT CLASSES DO YOU USUALLY TAKE, KAI-KUN?
ME...? I DON'T REALLY TAKE ANY CLASSES.
I just do weight training.
HMMMMM.
I don't have any idea...
...what any of these classes are.
THE GIRLS' LOCKER ROOM IS THAT WAY.
WE'LL MEET UPSTAIRS WHEN YOU'RE DONE GETTING CHANGED!
O...
OKAY!

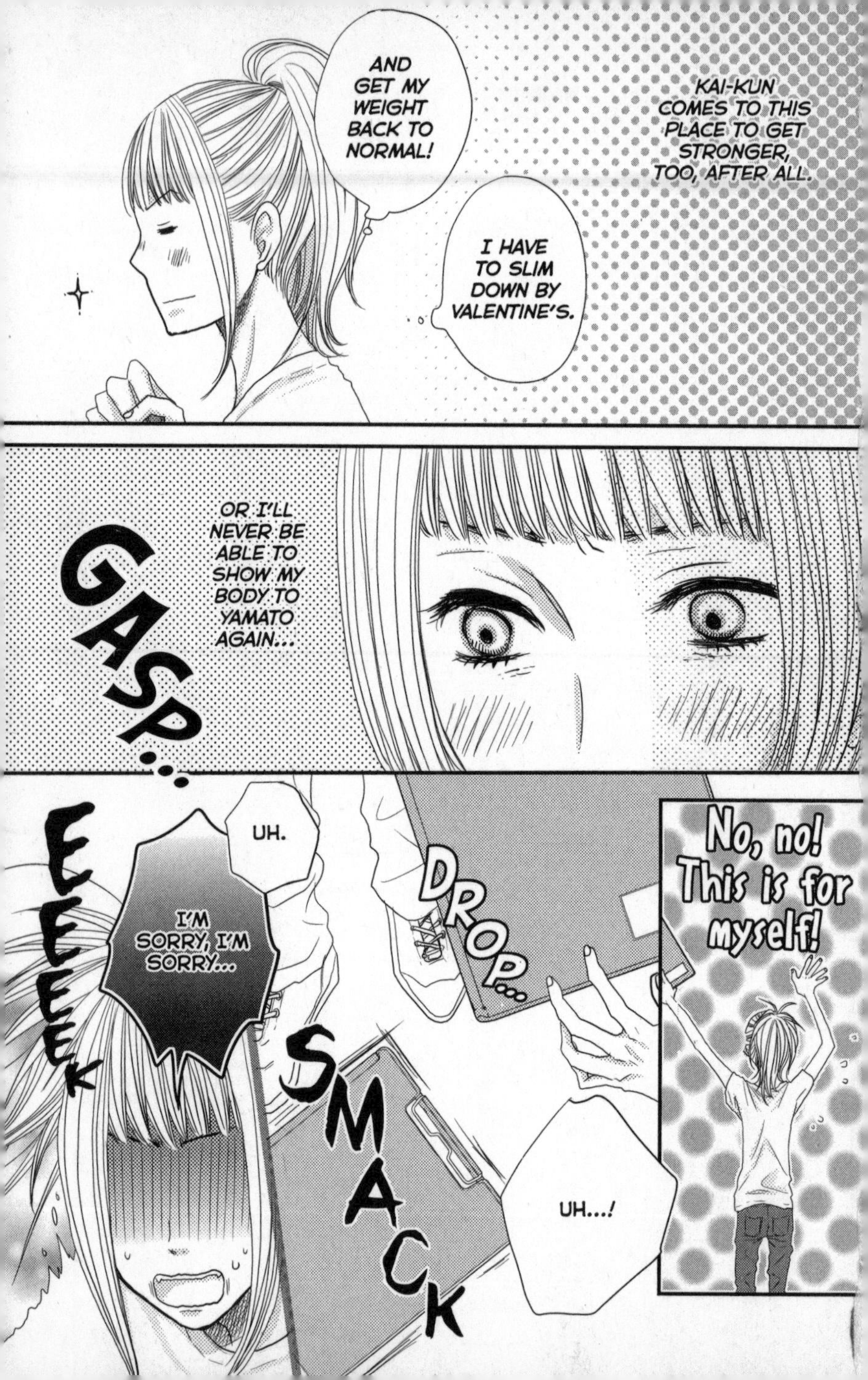
KAI-KUN COMES TO THIS PLACE TO GET STRONGER, TOO, AFTER ALL.
I HAVE TO SLIM DOWN BY VALENTINE'S.
AND GET MY WEIGHT BACK TO NORMAL!
OR I'LL NEVER BE ABLE TO SHOW MY BODY TO YAMATO AGAIN...
GASP...
No, no! This is for myself!
UH.
DROP...
I'M SORRY, I'M SORRY...
EEEEEK
SMACK
UH...!

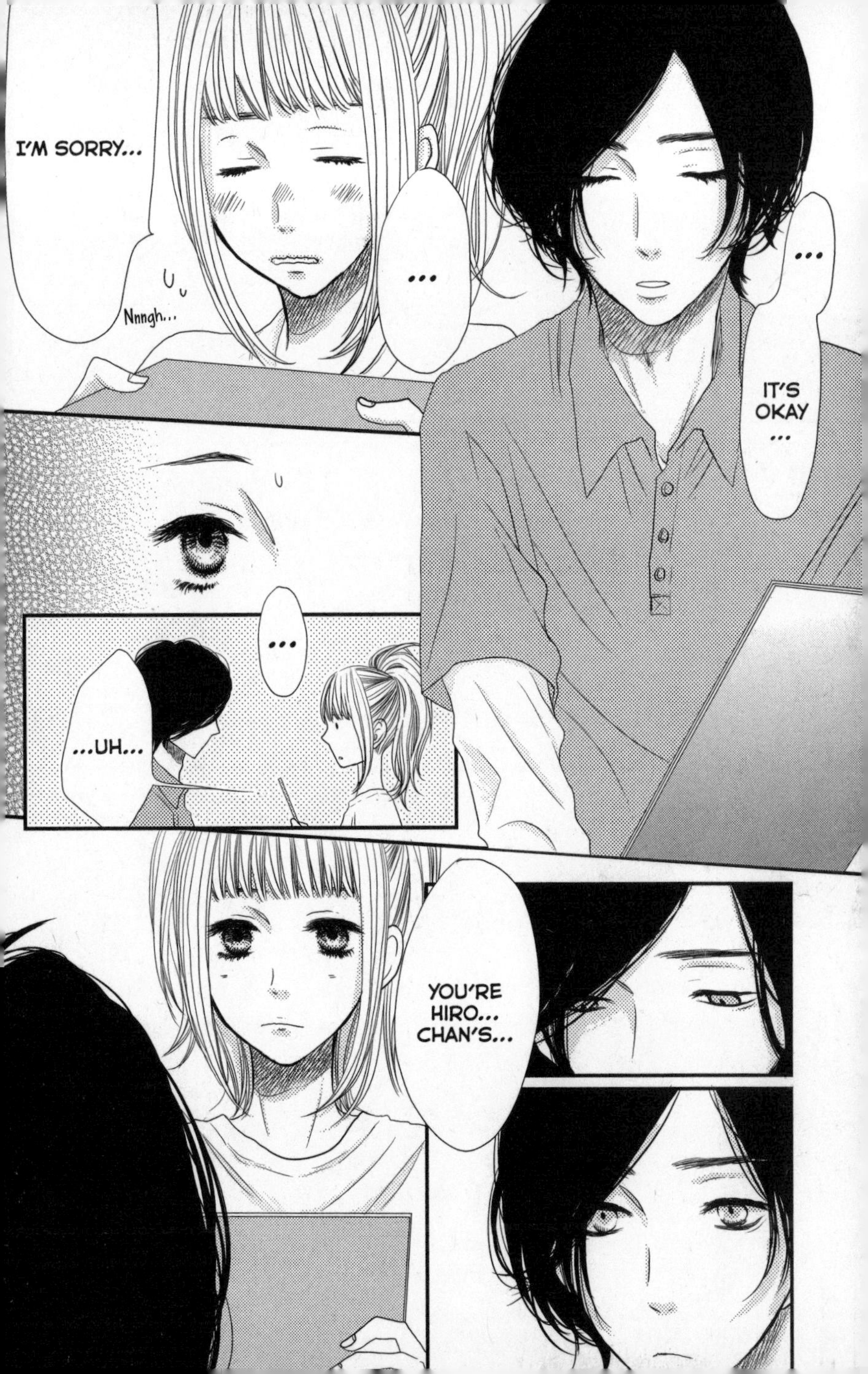
...
IT'S OKAY ...
...
I'M SORRY...
Nnngh...
...
...UH...
YOU'RE HIRO... CHAN'S...

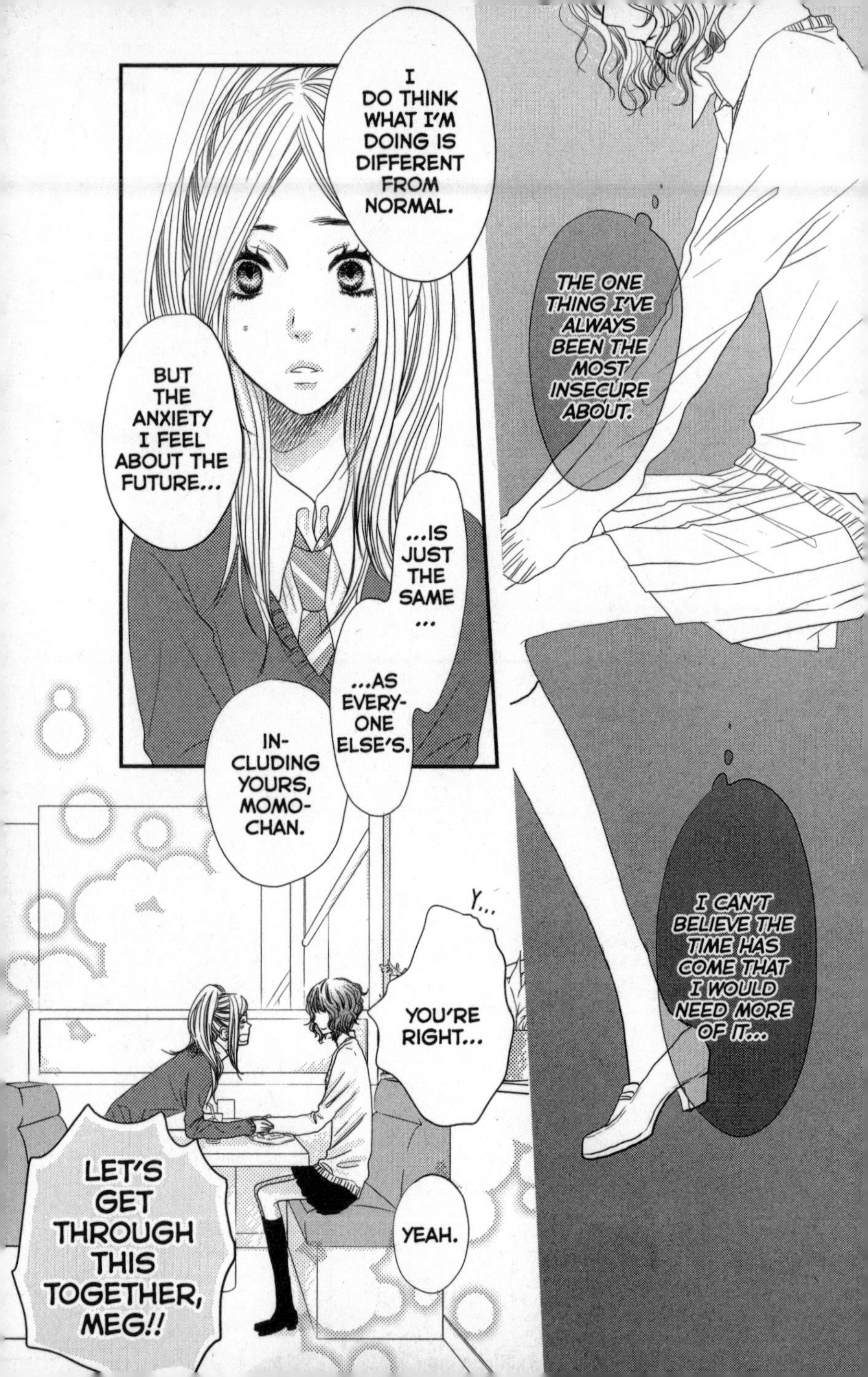
THE ONE THING I'VE ALWAYS BEEN THE MOST INSECURE ABOUT.
I CAN'T BELIEVE THE TIME HAS COME THAT I WOULD NEED MORE OF IT...
I DO THINK WHAT I'M DOING IS DIFFERENT FROM NORMAL.
BUT THE ANXIETY I FEEL ABOUT THE FUTURE...
...IS JUST THE SAME...
...AS EVERY-ONE ELSE'S.
IN-CLUDING YOURS, MOMO-CHAN.
Y...
YOU'RE RIGHT...
YEAH.
LET'S GET THROUGH THIS TOGETHER, MEG!!

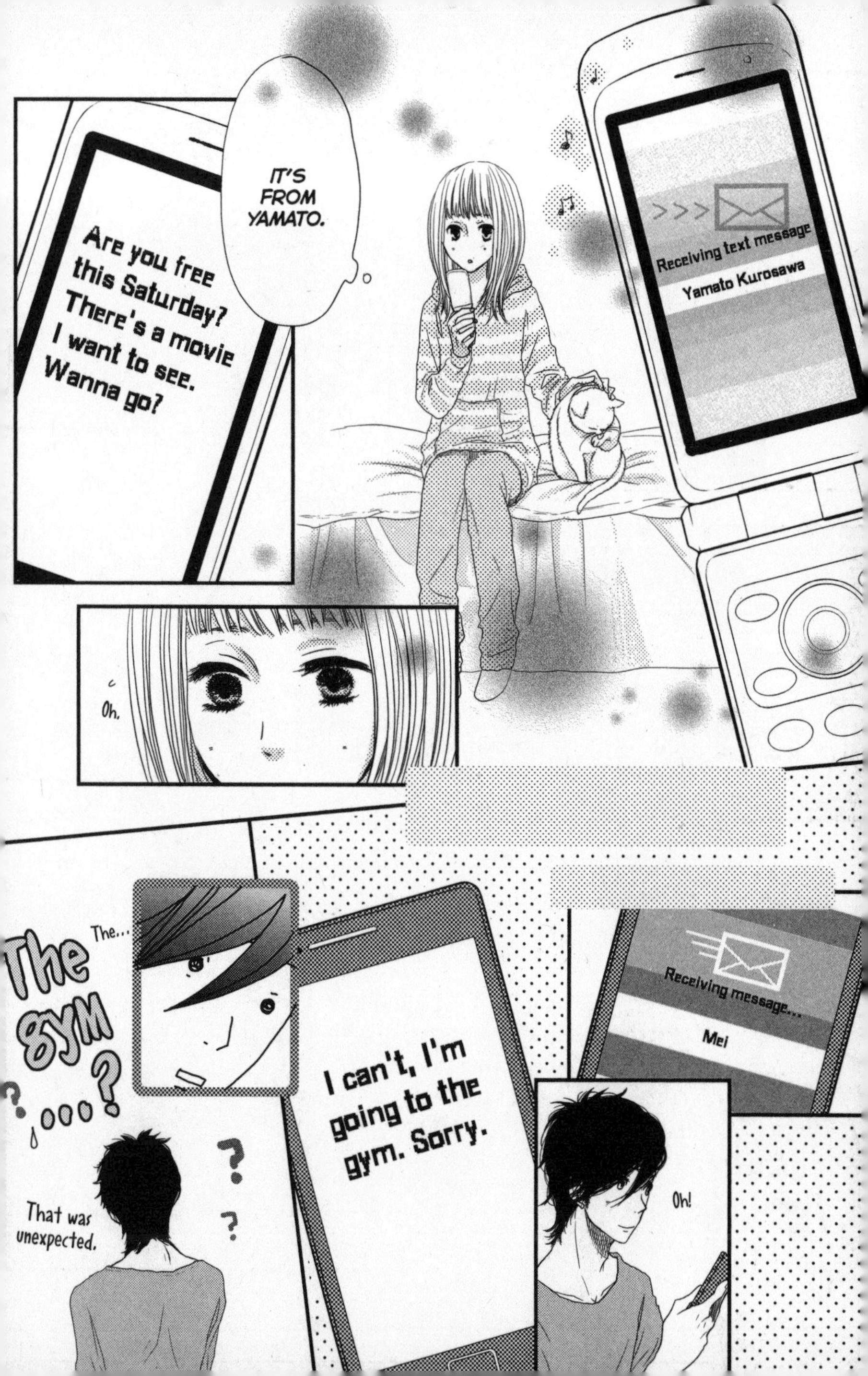
Receiving text message
Yamato Kurosawa
IT'S FROM YAMATO.
Are you free this Saturday? There's a movie I want to see. Wanna go?
Oh.
Receiving message...
Mei
Oh!
I can't, I'm going to the gym. Sorry.
The...
The gym?
That was unexpected.

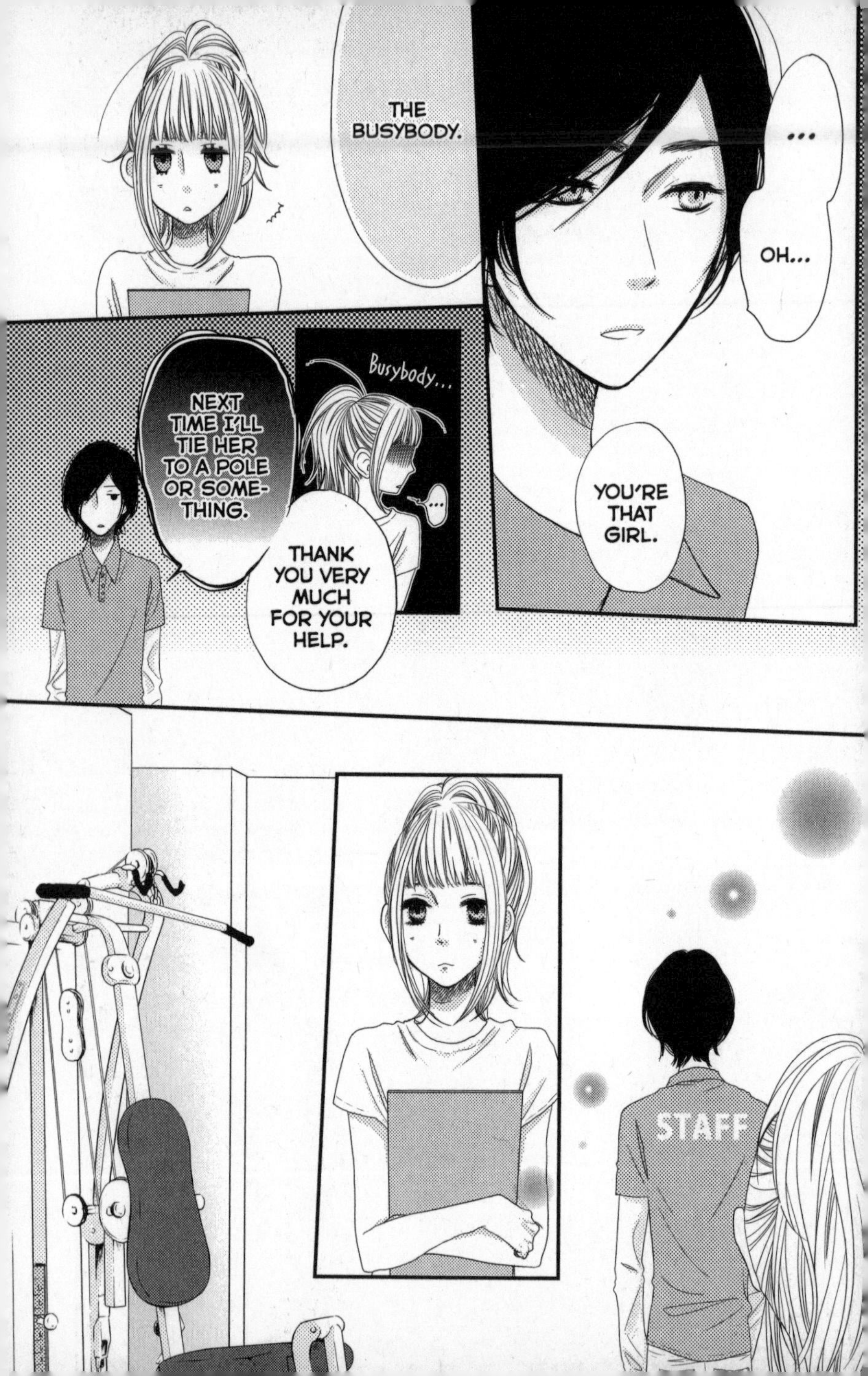
...
OH...
YOU'RE THAT GIRL.
THE BUSYBODY.
Busybody...
...
THANK YOU VERY MUCH FOR YOUR HELP.
NEXT TIME I'LL TIE HER TO A POLE OR SOME-THING.
STAFF

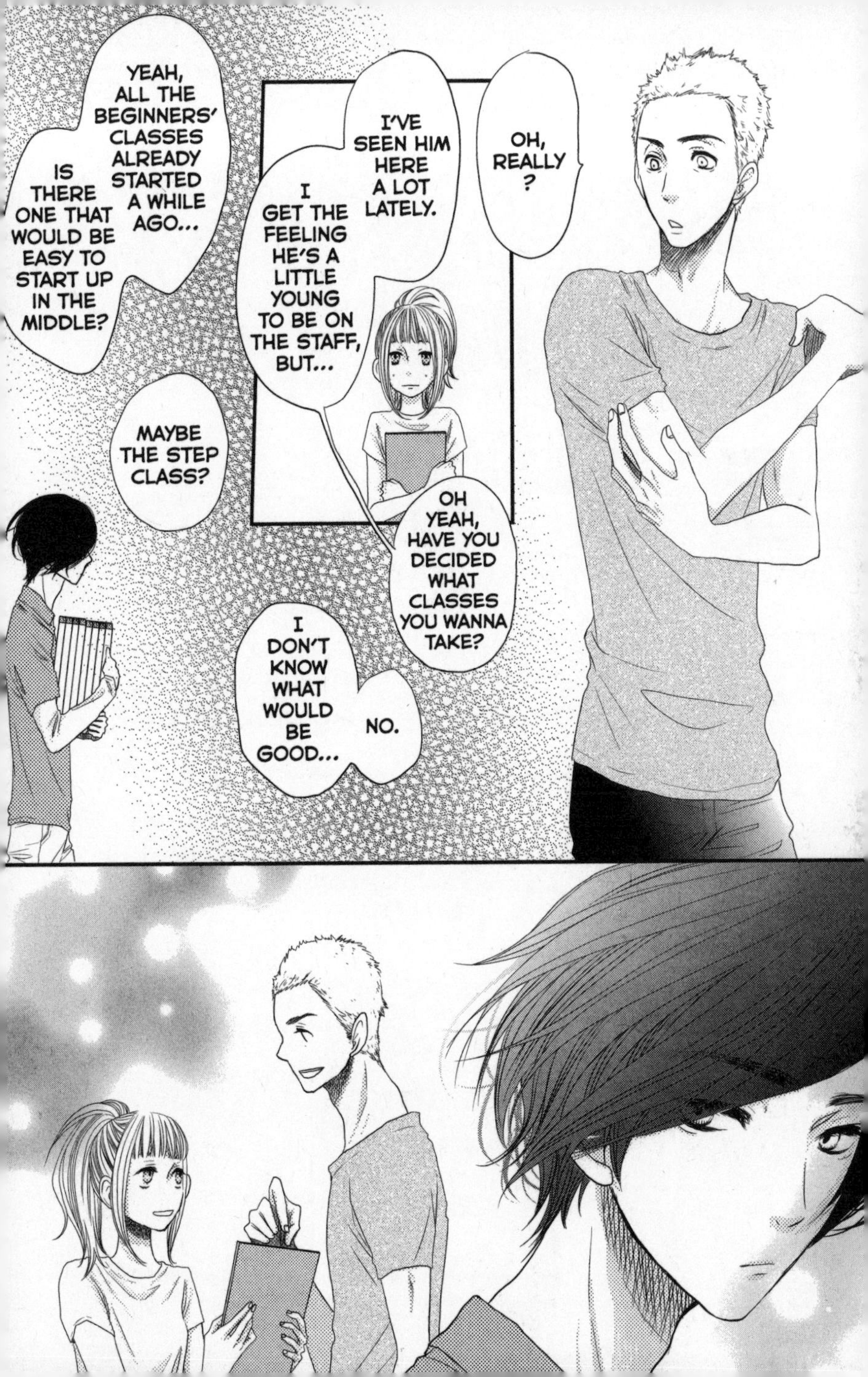
OH, REALLY?
I'VE SEEN HIM HERE A LOT LATELY.
I GET THE FEELING HE'S A LITTLE YOUNG TO BE ON THE STAFF, BUT...
YEAH, ALL THE BEGINNERS' CLASSES ALREADY STARTED A WHILE AGO...
IS THERE ONE THAT WOULD BE EASY TO START UP IN THE MIDDLE?
MAYBE THE STEP CLASS?
OH YEAH, HAVE YOU DECIDED WHAT CLASSES YOU WANNA TAKE?
NO.
I DON'T KNOW WHAT WOULD BE GOOD...

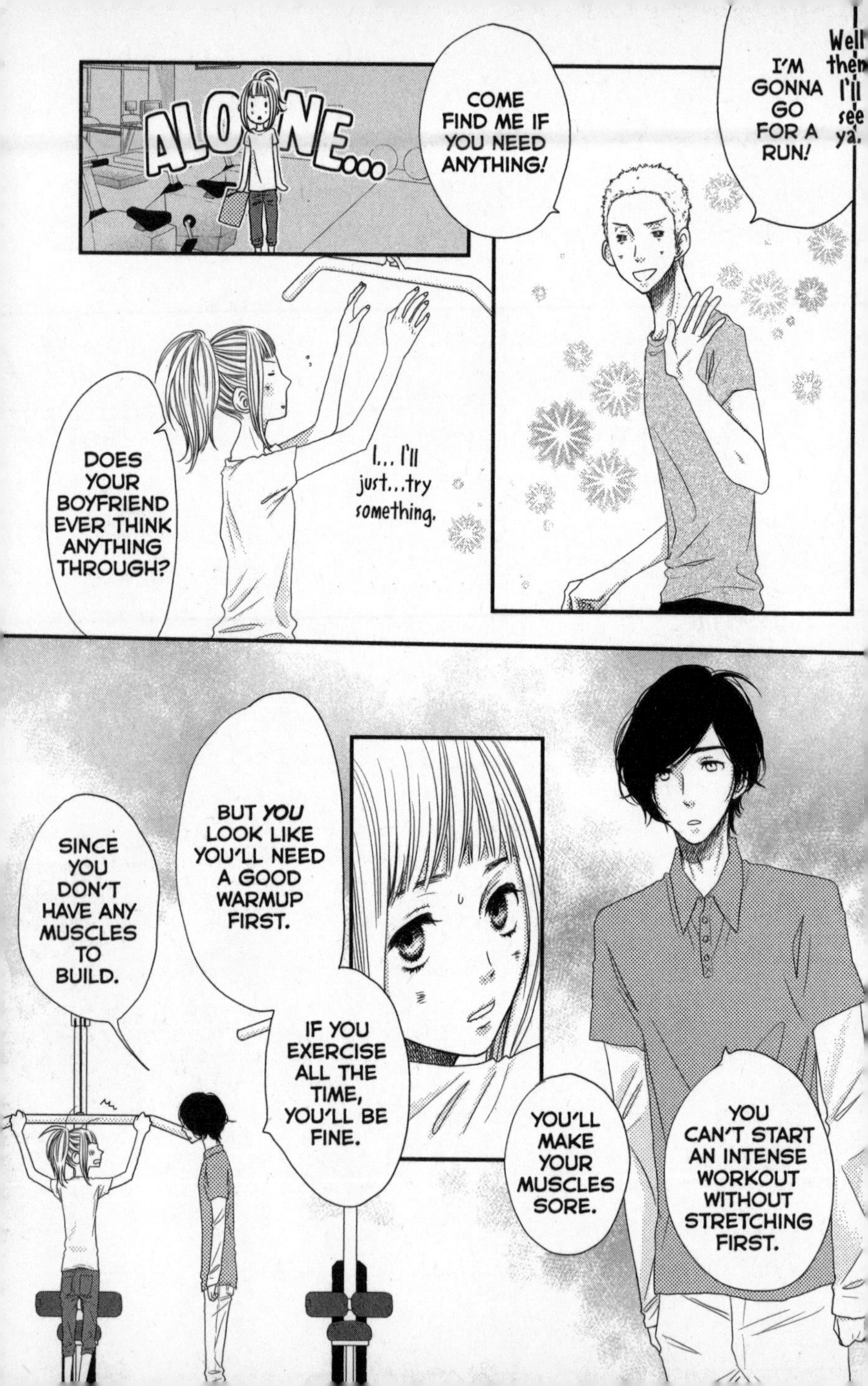
Well then I'll see ya.
I'M GONNA GO FOR A RUN!
COME FIND ME IF YOU NEED ANYTHING!
ALONEooo
I... I'll just...try something.
DOES YOUR BOYFRIEND EVER THINK ANYTHING THROUGH?
YOU CAN'T START AN INTENSE WORKOUT WITHOUT STRETCHING FIRST.
YOU'LL MAKE YOUR MUSCLES SORE.
IF YOU EXERCISE ALL THE TIME, YOU'LL BE FINE.
BUT *YOU* LOOK LIKE YOU'LL NEED A GOOD WARMUP FIRST.
SINCE YOU DON'T HAVE ANY MUSCLES TO BUILD.

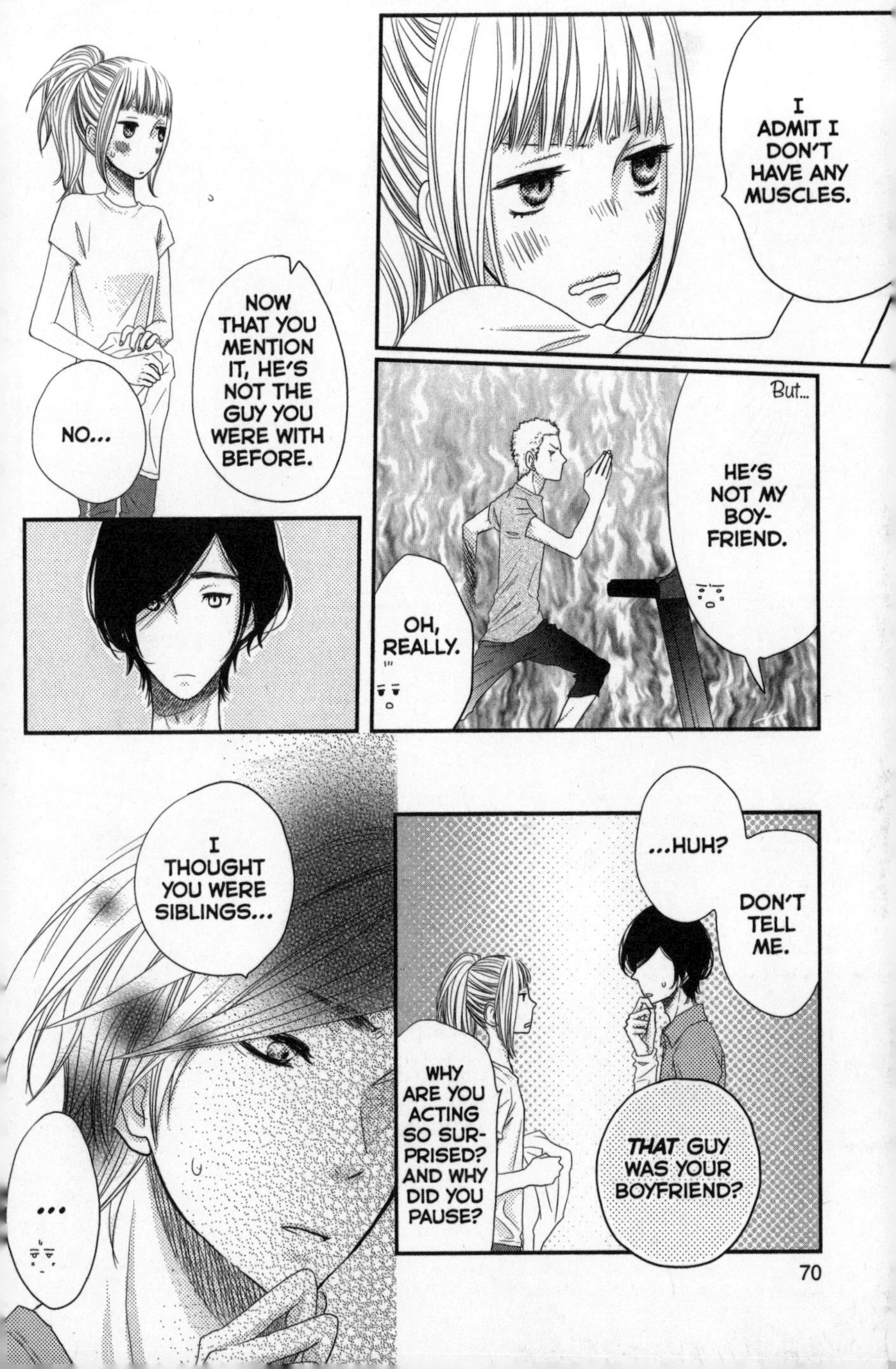
I ADMIT I DON'T HAVE ANY MUSCLES.
But...
HE'S NOT MY BOY-FRIEND.
OH, REALLY.
NOW THAT YOU MENTION IT, HE'S NOT THE GUY YOU WERE WITH BEFORE.
NO...
...HUH?
DON'T TELL ME.
THAT GUY WAS YOUR BOYFRIEND?
WHY ARE YOU ACTING SO SUR-PRISED? AND WHY DID YOU PAUSE?
I THOUGHT YOU WERE SIBLINGS...
...

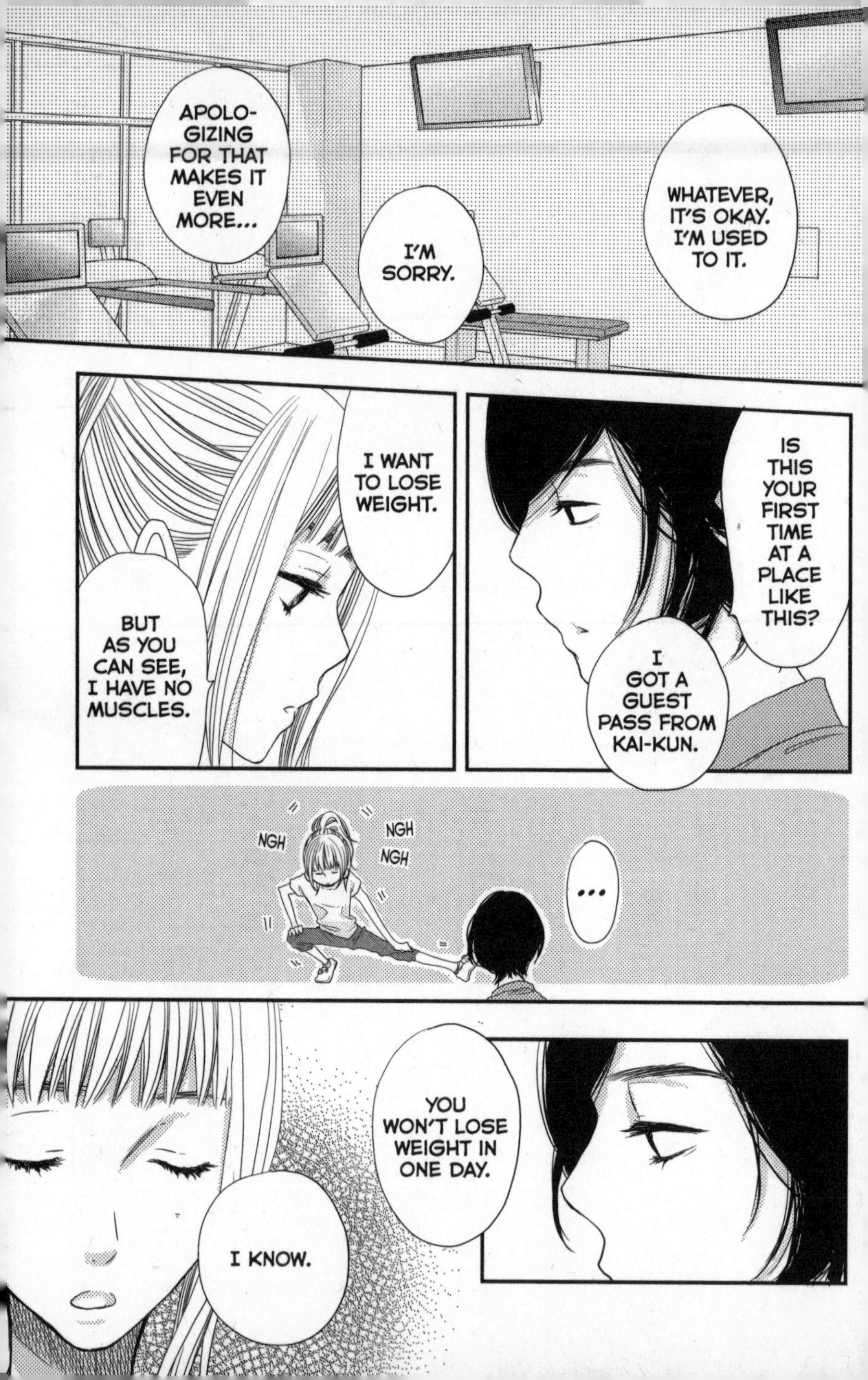
WHATEVER, IT'S OKAY. I'M USED TO IT.
I'M SORRY.
APOLO-GIZING FOR THAT MAKES IT EVEN MORE...
IS THIS YOUR FIRST TIME AT A PLACE LIKE THIS?
I GOT A GUEST PASS FROM KAI-KUN.
I WANT TO LOSE WEIGHT.
BUT AS YOU CAN SEE, I HAVE NO MUSCLES.
NGH
NGH
NGH
...
YOU WON'T LOSE WEIGHT IN ONE DAY.
I KNOW.

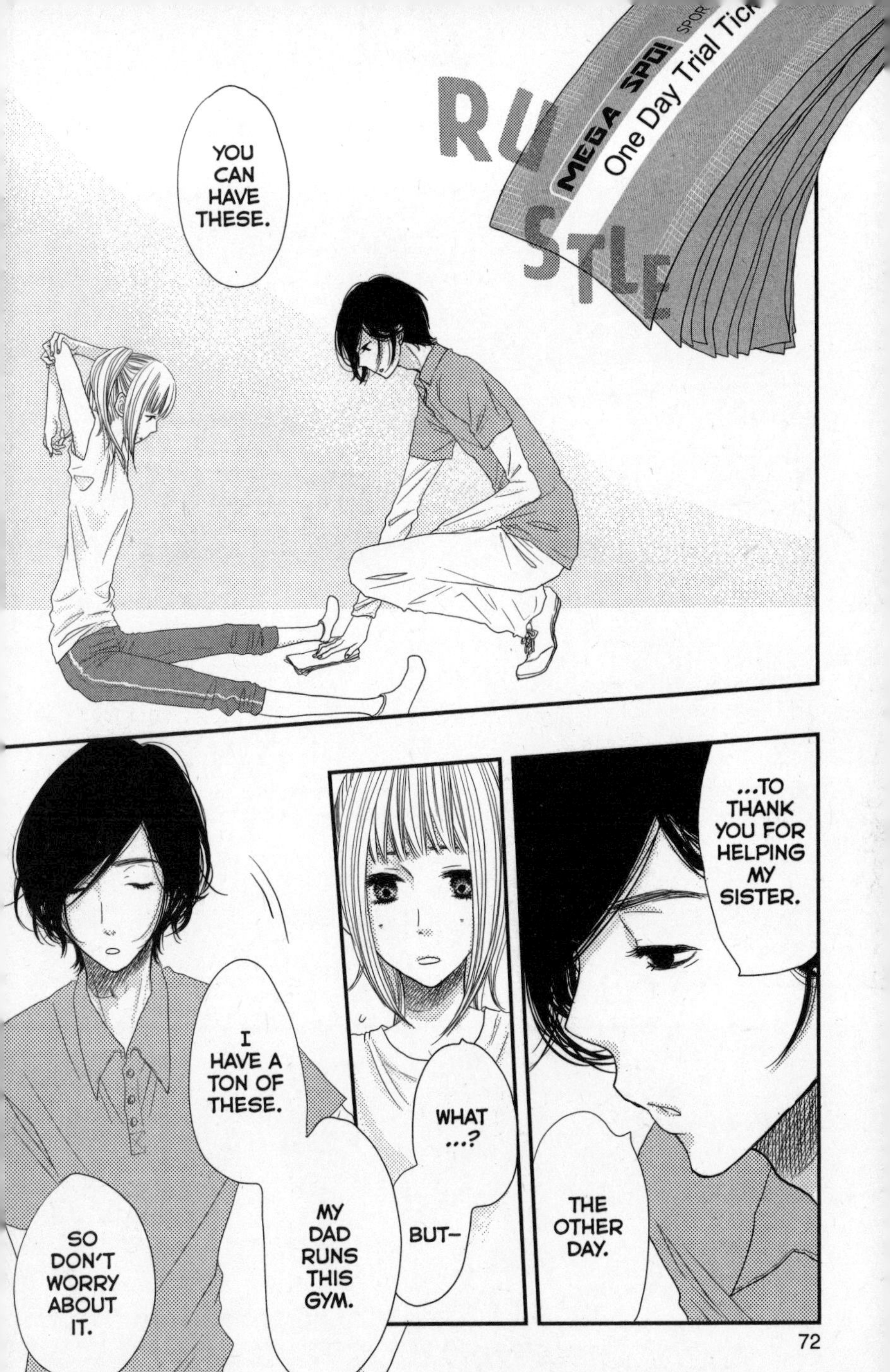
MEGA SPO!
One Day Trial Tick
RUSTLE
YOU CAN HAVE THESE.
...TO THANK YOU FOR HELPING MY SISTER.
THE OTHER DAY.
WHAT ...?
BUT–
I HAVE A TON OF THESE.
MY DAD RUNS THIS GYM.
SO DON'T WORRY ABOUT IT.

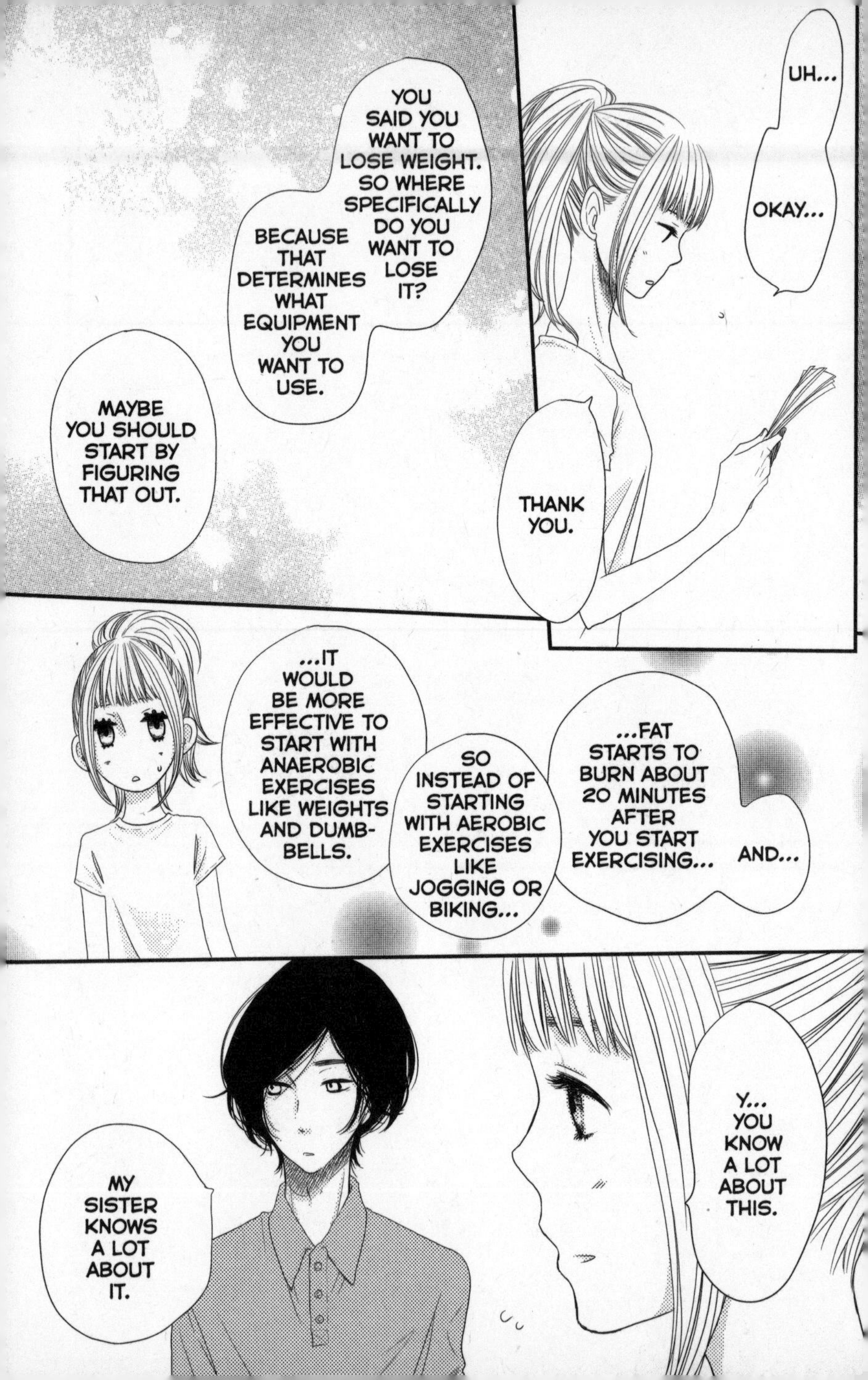
UH...
OKAY...
THANK YOU.
YOU SAID YOU WANT TO LOSE WEIGHT. SO WHERE SPECIFICALLY DO YOU WANT TO LOSE IT?
BECAUSE THAT DETERMINES WHAT EQUIPMENT YOU WANT TO USE.
MAYBE YOU SHOULD START BY FIGURING THAT OUT.
AND...
...FAT STARTS TO BURN ABOUT 20 MINUTES AFTER YOU START EXERCISING...
SO INSTEAD OF STARTING WITH AEROBIC EXERCISES LIKE JOGGING OR BIKING...
...IT WOULD BE MORE EFFECTIVE TO START WITH ANAEROBIC EXERCISES LIKE WEIGHTS AND DUMB-BELLS.
Y... YOU KNOW A LOT ABOUT THIS.
MY SISTER KNOWS A LOT ABOUT IT.

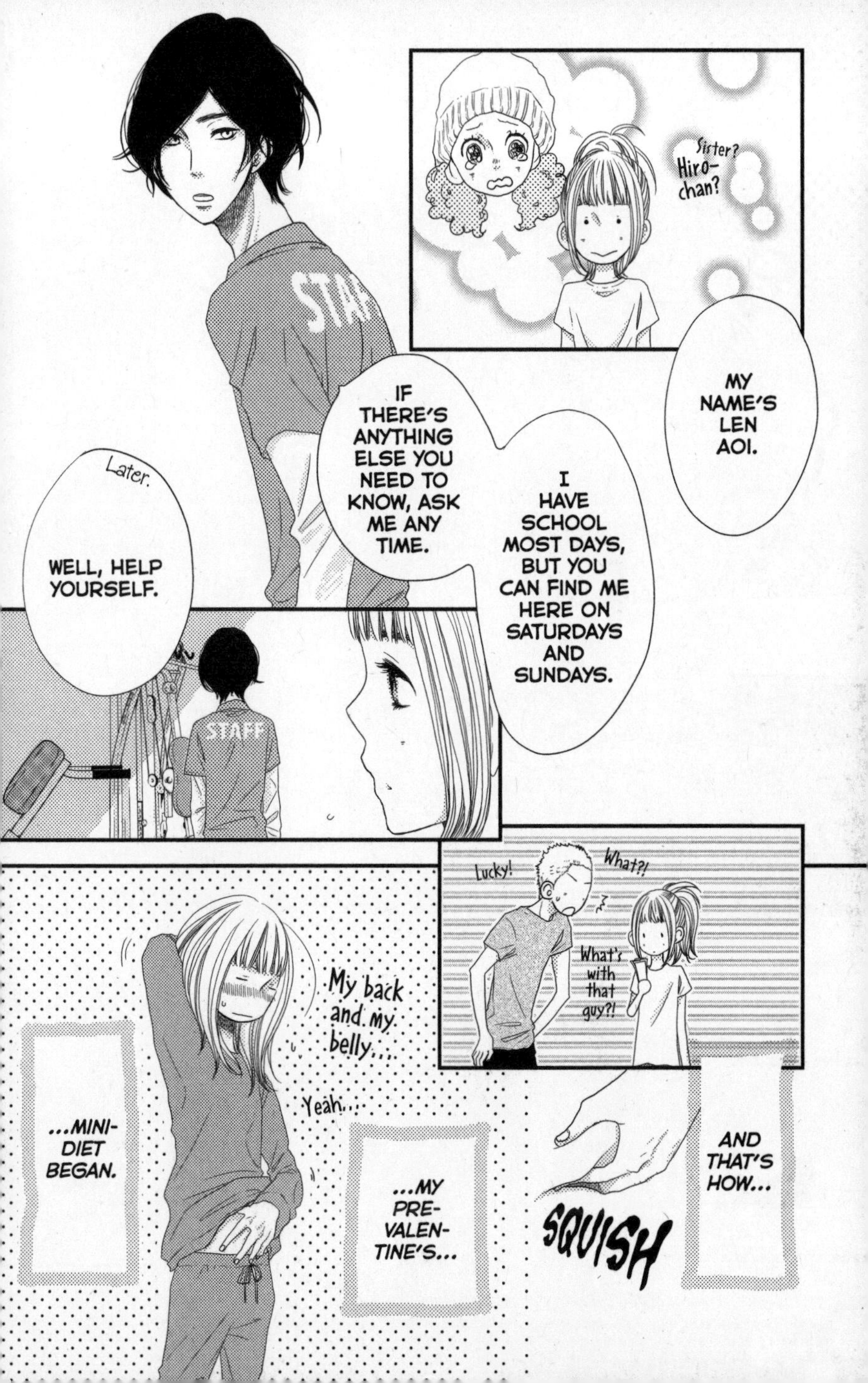
Sister?
Hiro-chan?
MY NAME'S LEN AOI.
I HAVE SCHOOL MOST DAYS, BUT YOU CAN FIND ME HERE ON SATURDAYS AND SUNDAYS.
IF THERE'S ANYTHING ELSE YOU NEED TO KNOW, ASK ME ANY TIME.
Later.
WELL, HELP YOURSELF.
STAFF
STAFF
What?!
Lucky!
What's with that guy?!
AND THAT'S HOW...
SQUISH
...MY PRE-VALENTINE'S...
My back and my belly...
Yeah...
...MINI-DIET BEGAN.

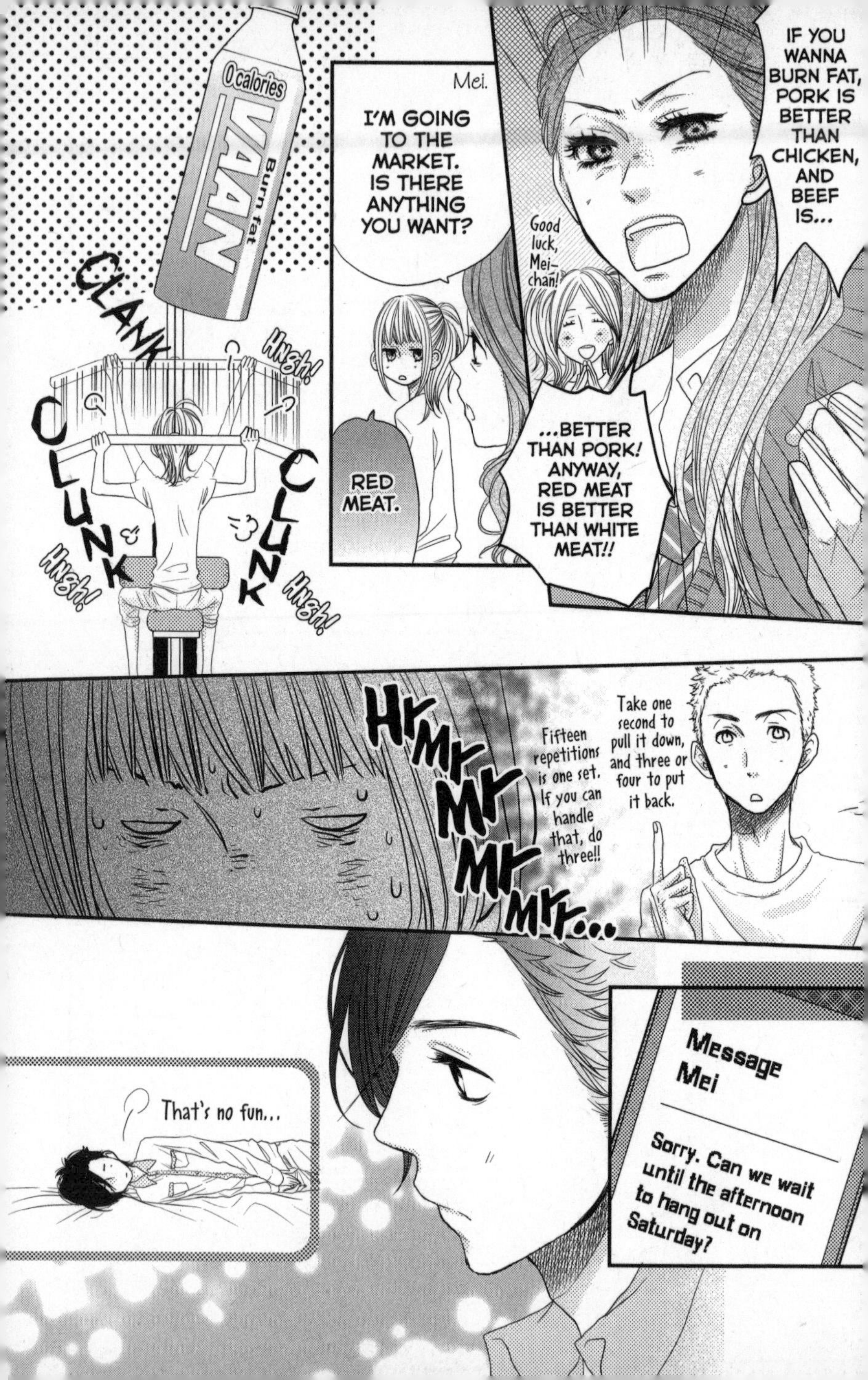
IF YOU WANNA BURN FAT, PORK IS BETTER THAN CHICKEN, AND BEEF IS...
Good luck, Mei-chan!
...BETTER THAN PORK! ANYWAY, RED MEAT IS BETTER THAN WHITE MEAT!!
Mei.
I'M GOING TO THE MARKET. IS THERE ANYTHING YOU WANT?
RED MEAT.
0 calories
VAAN
Burn fat
CLANK
Hngh!
CLUNK
CLUNK
Hngh!
Hngh!
Take one second to pull it down, and three or four to put it back.
Fifteen repetitions is one set. If you can handle that, do three!!
Hrmr mr mr mrr...
Message
Mei
Sorry. Can we wait until the afternoon to hang out on Saturday?
That's no fun...

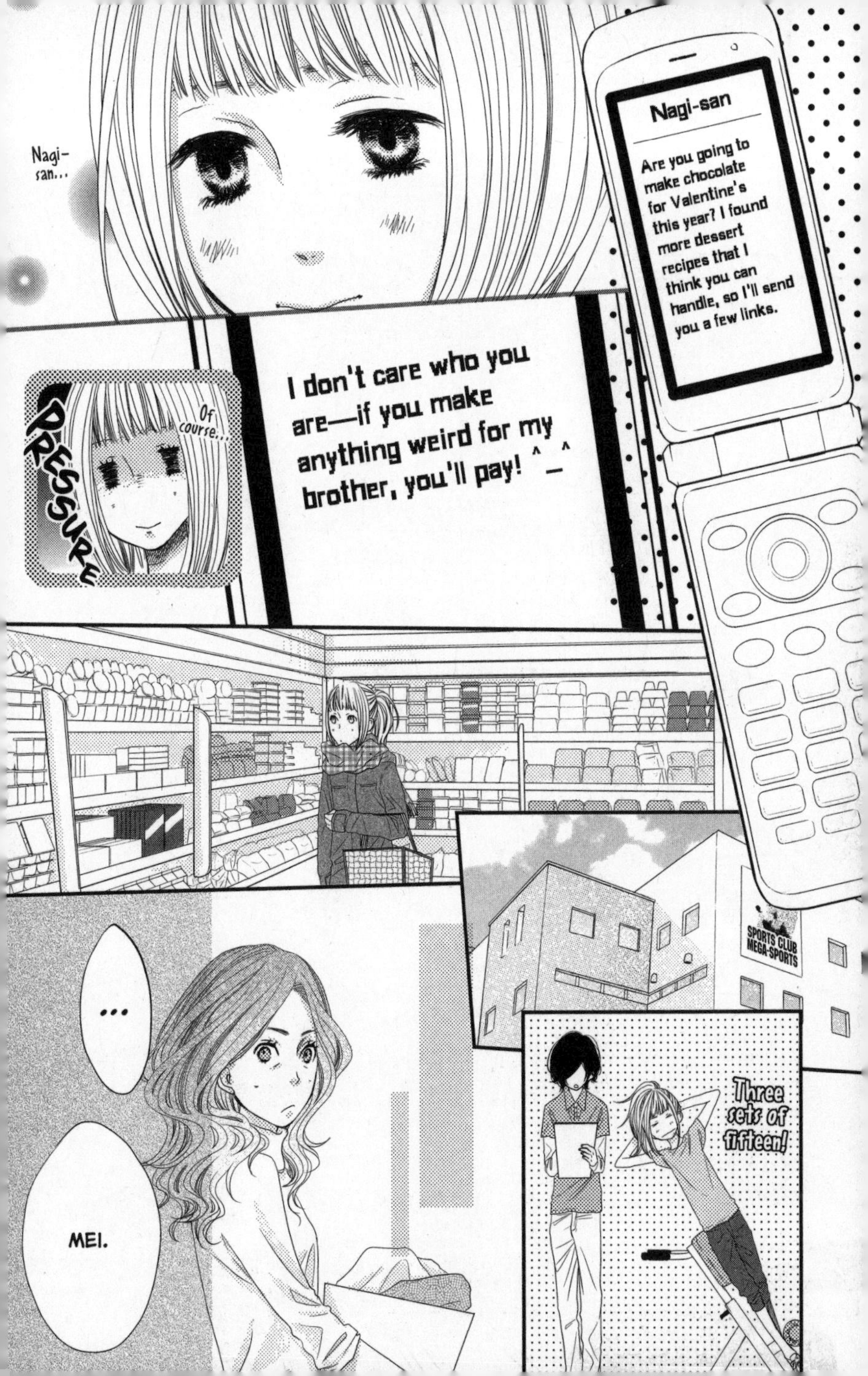
Nagi-san
Are you going to make chocolate for Valentine's this year? I found more dessert recipes that I think you can handle, so I'll send you a few links.
Nagi-san...
I don't care who you are—if you make anything weird for my brother, you'll pay! ^_^
Of course...
PRESSURE
SPORTS CLUB MEGA-SPORTS
Three sets of fifteen!
...
MEI.

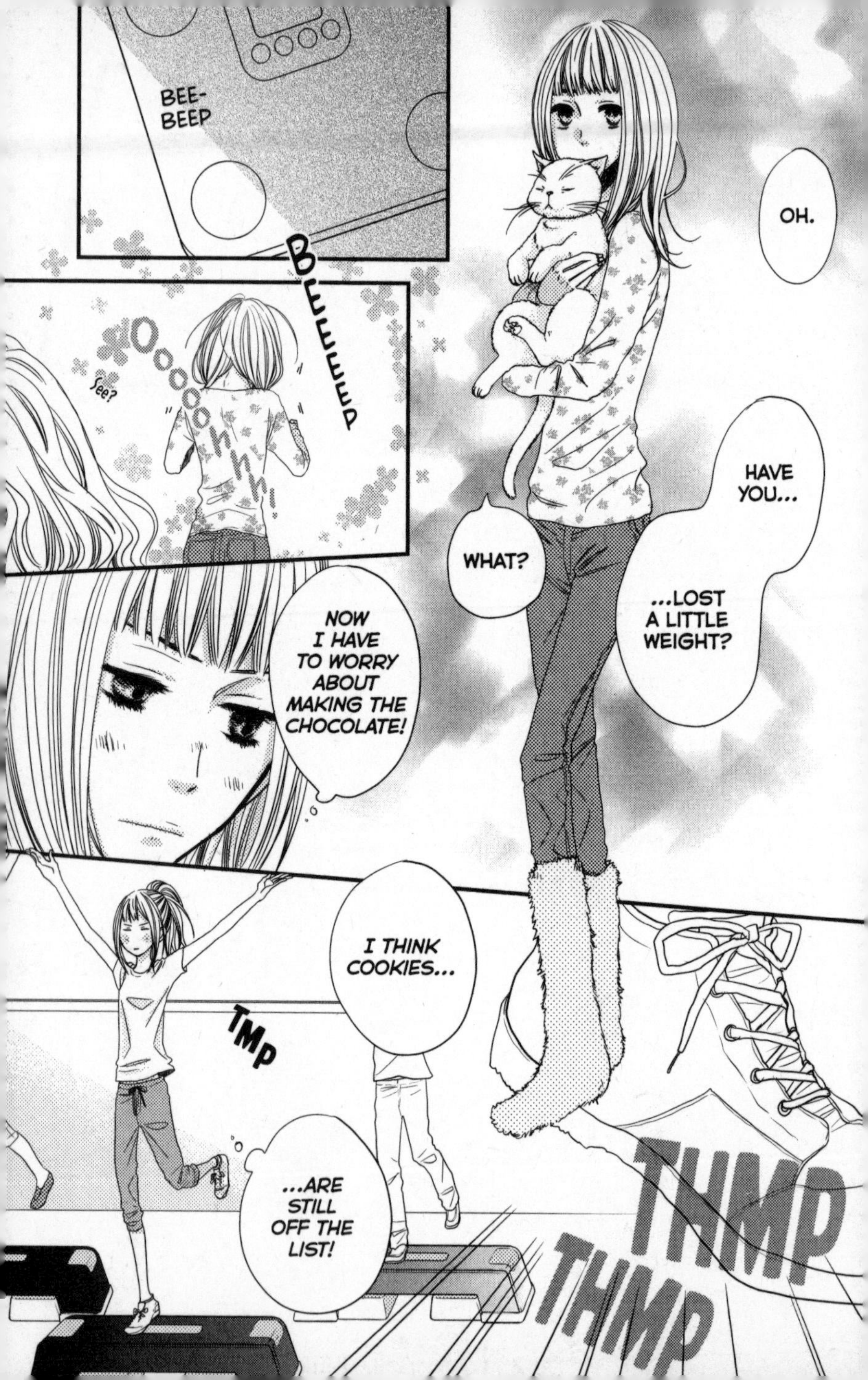
OH.
HAVE YOU...
...LOST A LITTLE WEIGHT?
WHAT?
BEE-BEEP
BEEEEEP
Ooooohhh!
See?
NOW I HAVE TO WORRY ABOUT MAKING THE CHOCOLATE!
THMP
THMP
I THINK COOKIES...
TMP
...ARE STILL OFF THE LIST!

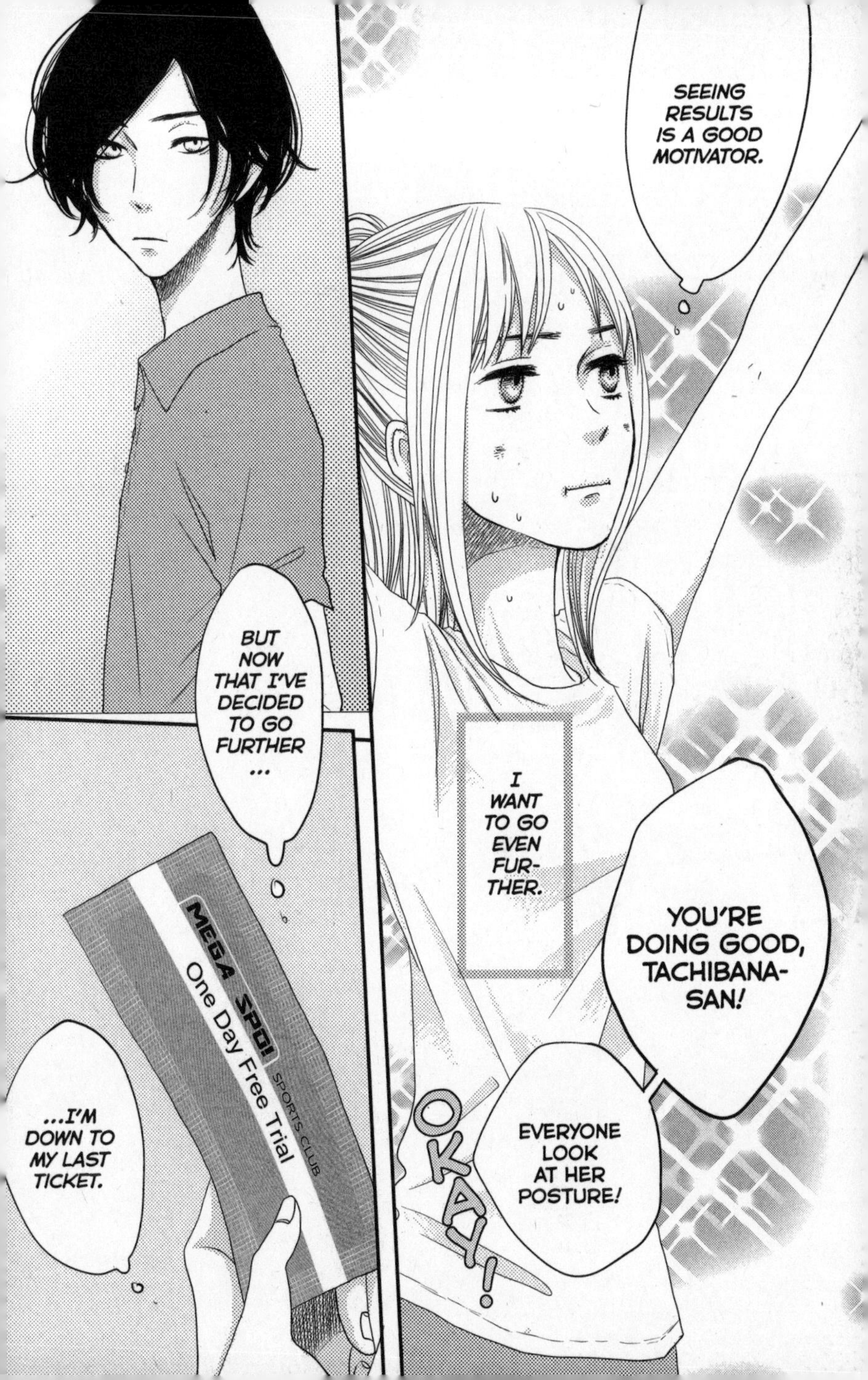
SEEING RESULTS IS A GOOD MOTIVATOR.
I WANT TO GO EVEN FUR-THER.
YOU'RE DOING GOOD, TACHIBANA-SAN!
EVERYONE LOOK AT HER POSTURE!
OKAY!
BUT NOW THAT I'VE DECIDED TO GO FURTHER...
MEGA SPO! SPORTS CLUB
One Day Free Trial
...I'M DOWN TO MY LAST TICKET.

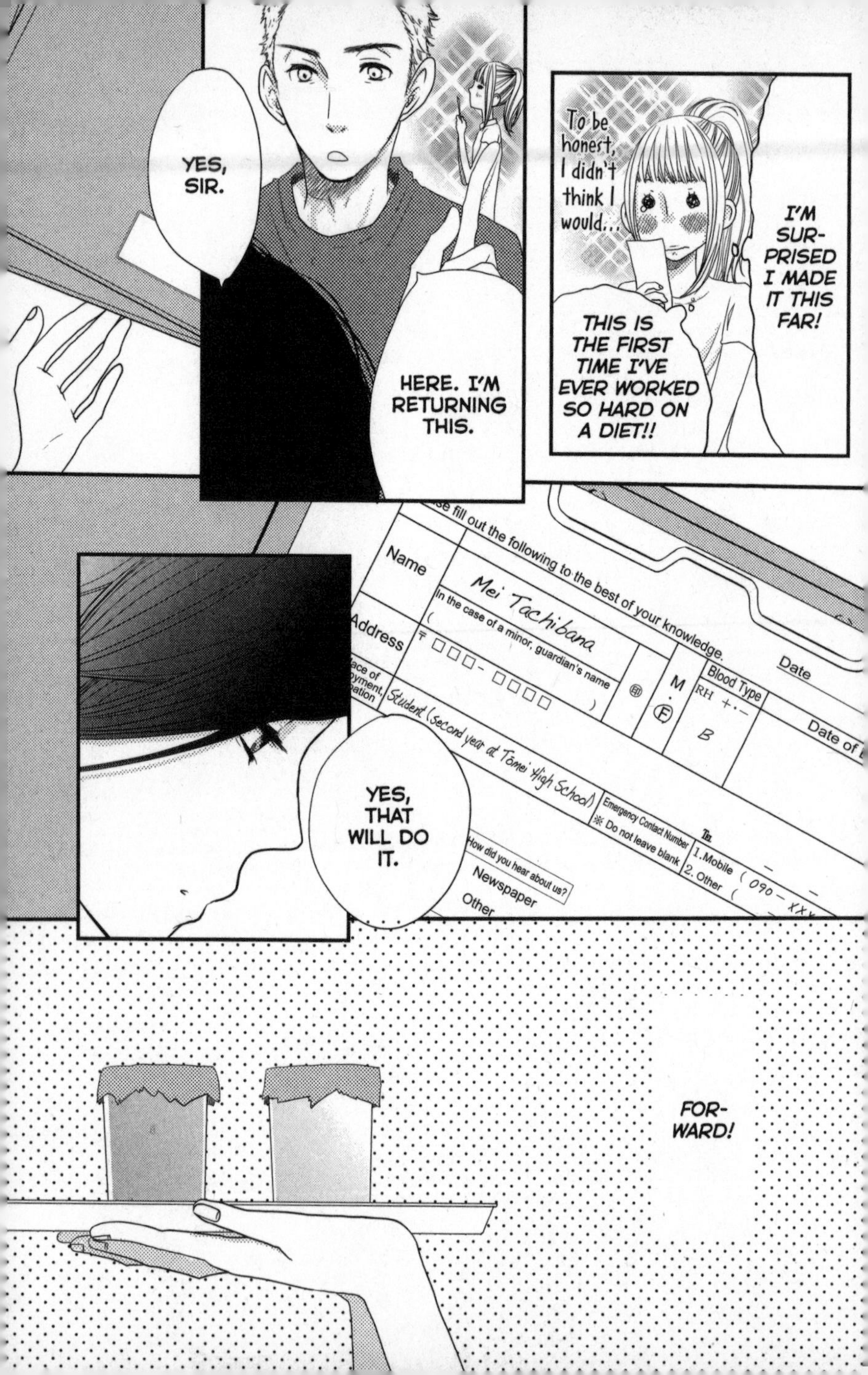
I'M SURPRISED I MADE IT THIS FAR!
To be honest, I didn't think I would...
THIS IS THE FIRST TIME I'VE EVER WORKED SO HARD ON A DIET!!
HERE. I'M RETURNING THIS.
YES, SIR.
...se fill out the following to the best of your knowledge.
Date
Name
Mei Tachibana
In the case of a minor, guardian's name
Address
〒 □□□- □□□□
M
F
Blood Type
RH +・-
B
Date of
Student (second year at Tōmei High School)
Emergency Contact Number
※ Do not leave blank
1. Mobile (090 -
2. Other (
How did you hear about us?
Newspaper
Other
YES, THAT WILL DO IT.
FOR-WARD!

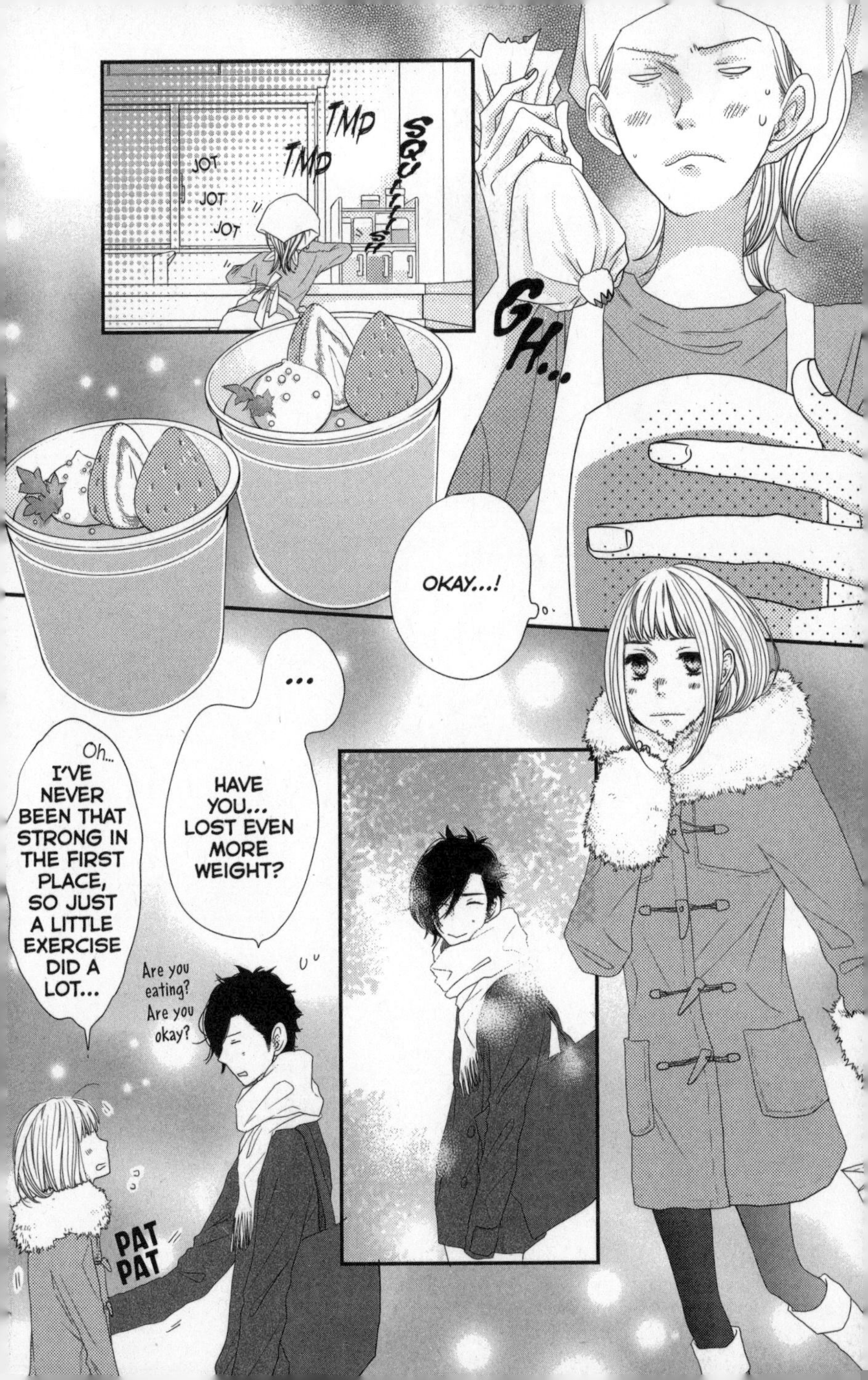
GH...
OKAY...!
TMP
TMP
SQUIIIISH
JOT
JOT
JOT
...
HAVE YOU... LOST EVEN MORE WEIGHT?
Oh...
I'VE NEVER BEEN THAT STRONG IN THE FIRST PLACE, SO JUST A LITTLE EXERCISE DID A LOT...
Are you eating? Are you okay?
PAT PAT

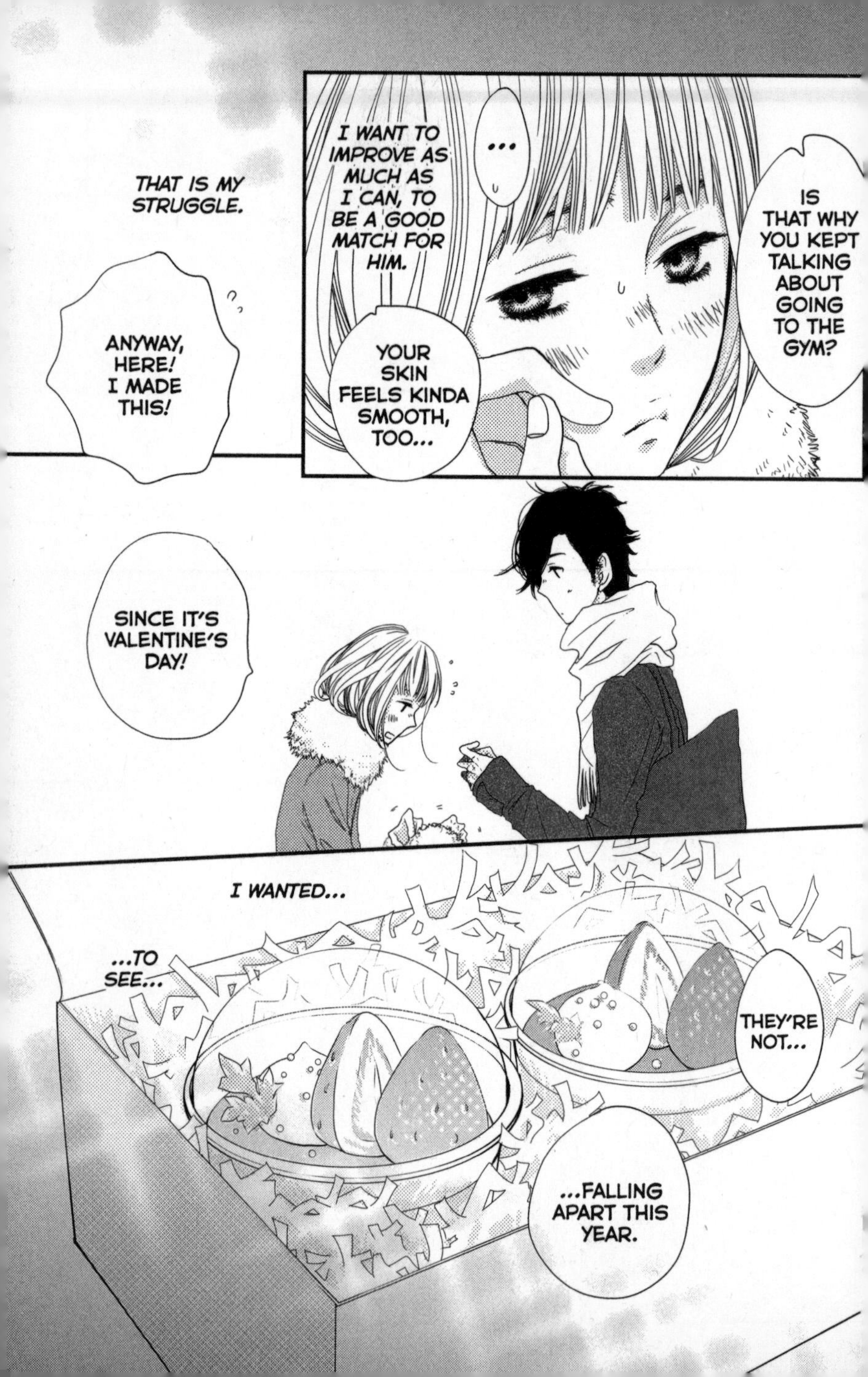
IS THAT WHY YOU KEPT TALKING ABOUT GOING TO THE GYM?
...
I WANT TO IMPROVE AS MUCH AS I CAN, TO BE A GOOD MATCH FOR HIM.
YOUR SKIN FEELS KINDA SMOOTH, TOO...
THAT IS MY STRUGGLE.
ANYWAY, HERE! I MADE THIS!
SINCE IT'S VALENTINE'S DAY!
I WANTED...
...TO SEE...
THEY'RE NOT...
...FALLING APART THIS YEAR.

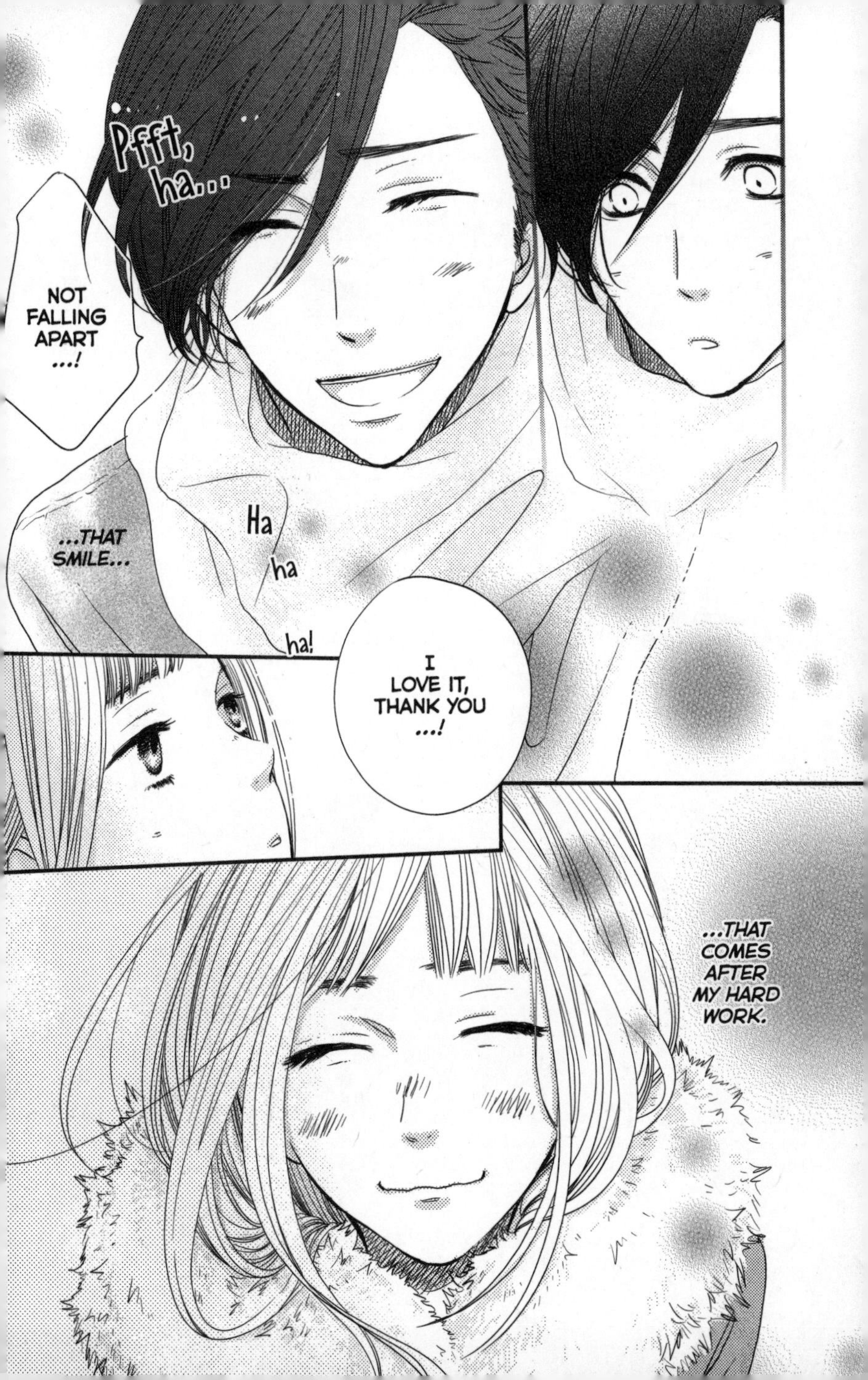
......Pfft, ha...
NOT FALLING APART ...!
Ha ha ha!
...THAT SMILE...
I LOVE IT, THANK YOU ...!
...THAT COMES AFTER MY HARD WORK.

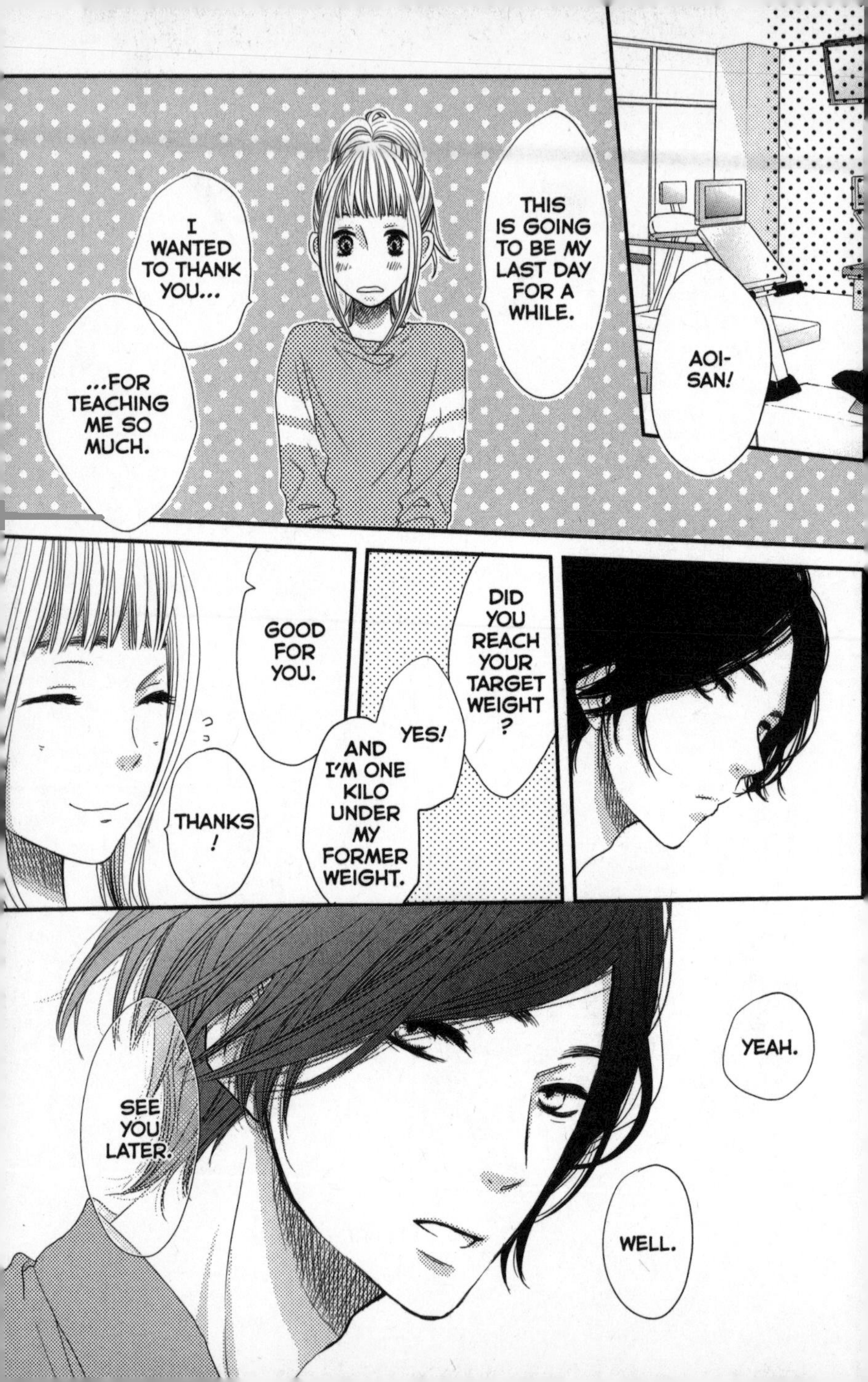
AOI-SAN!
THIS IS GOING TO BE MY LAST DAY FOR A WHILE.
I WANTED TO THANK YOU...
...FOR TEACHING ME SO MUCH.
DID YOU REACH YOUR TARGET WEIGHT?
YES!
AND I'M ONE KILO UNDER MY FORMER WEIGHT.
GOOD FOR YOU.
THANKS!
YEAH.
WELL.
SEE YOU LATER.

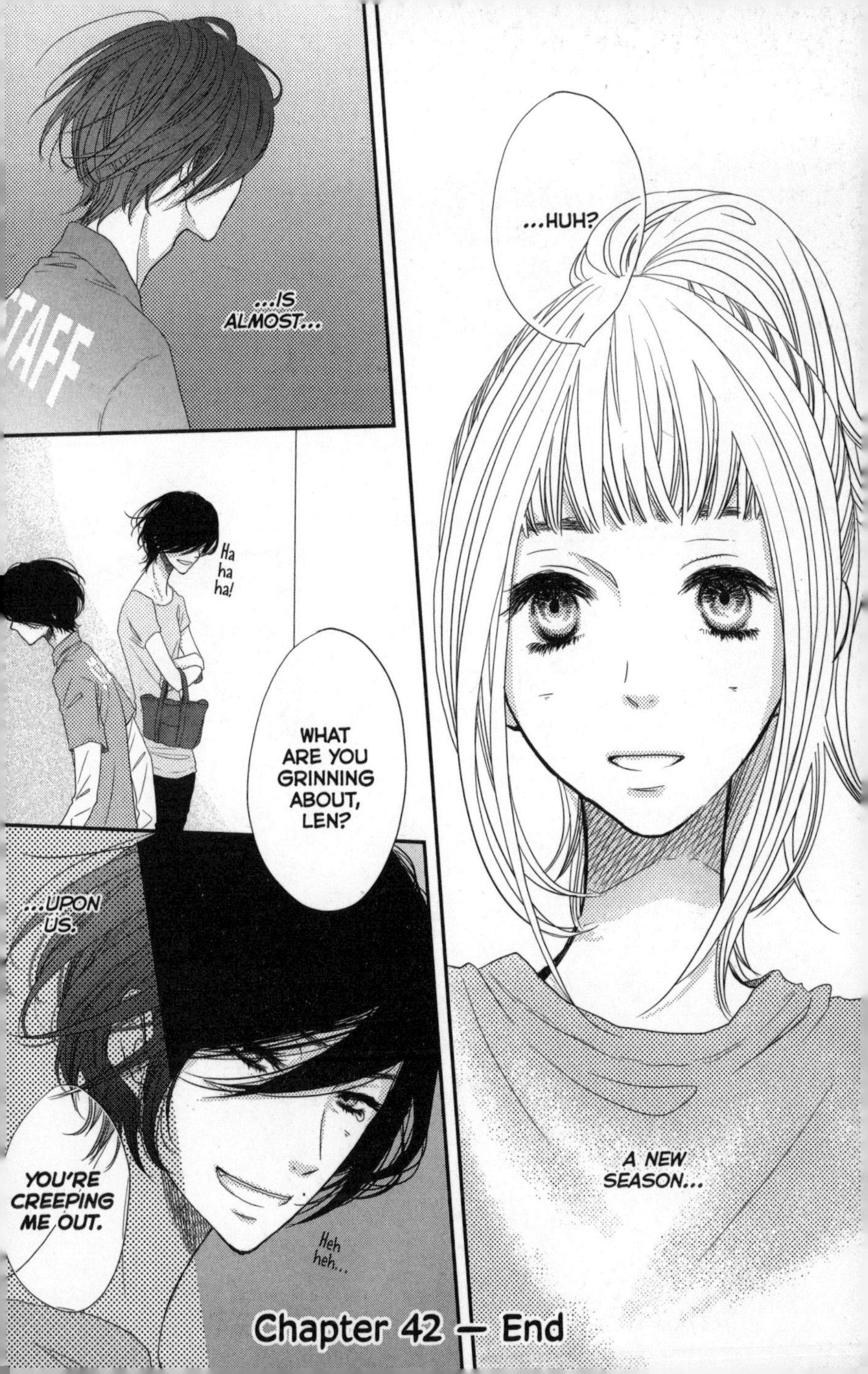
...HUH?
A NEW SEASON...
...IS ALMOST...
WHAT ARE YOU GRINNING ABOUT, LEN?
Ha ha ha!
...UPON US.
YOU'RE CREEPING ME OUT.
Heh heh...
Chapter 42 — End

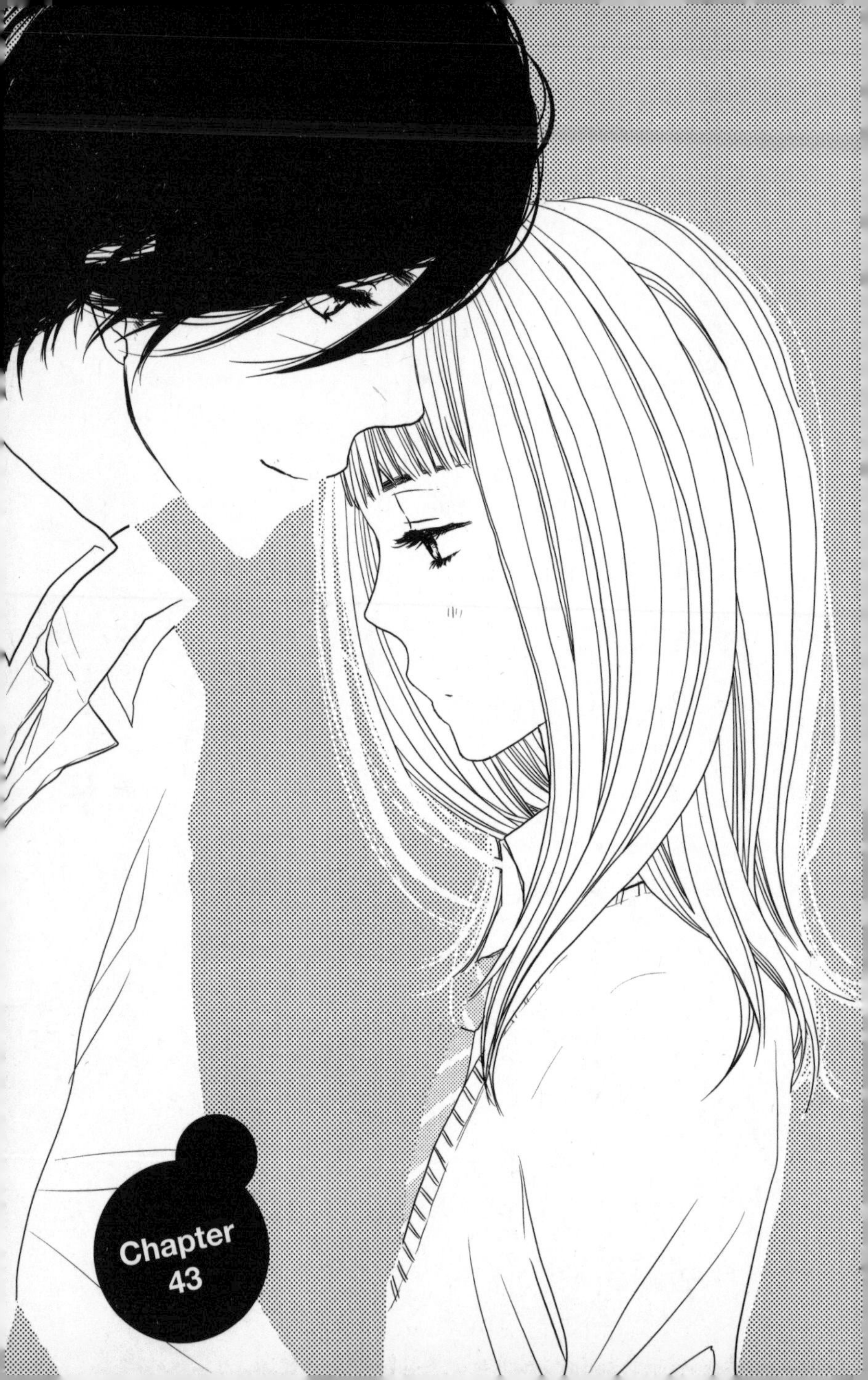
Chapter
43

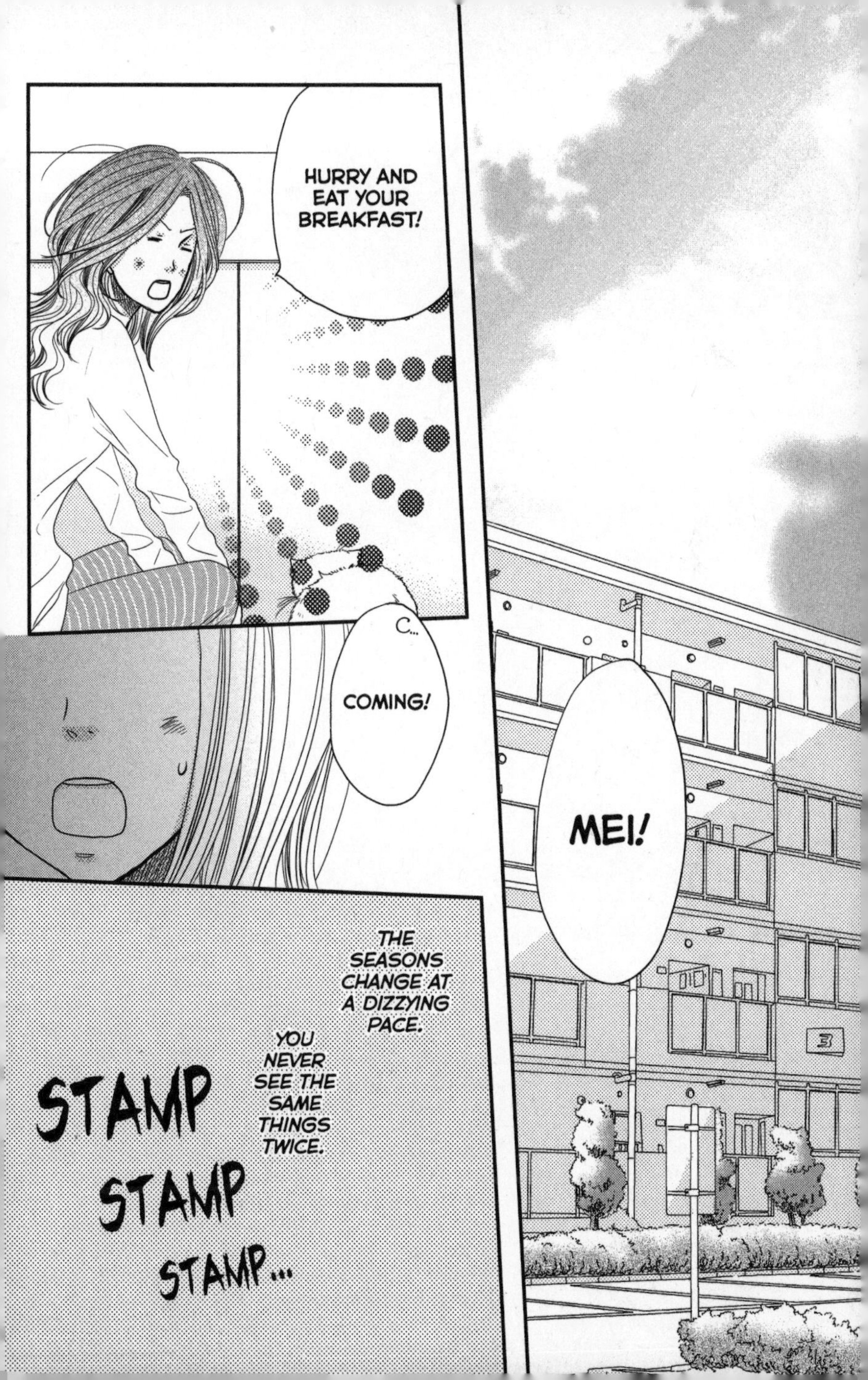
MEI!
HURRY AND EAT YOUR BREAKFAST!
C... COMING!
THE SEASONS CHANGE AT A DIZZYING PACE.
YOU NEVER SEE THE SAME THINGS TWICE.
STAMP STAMP STAMP...

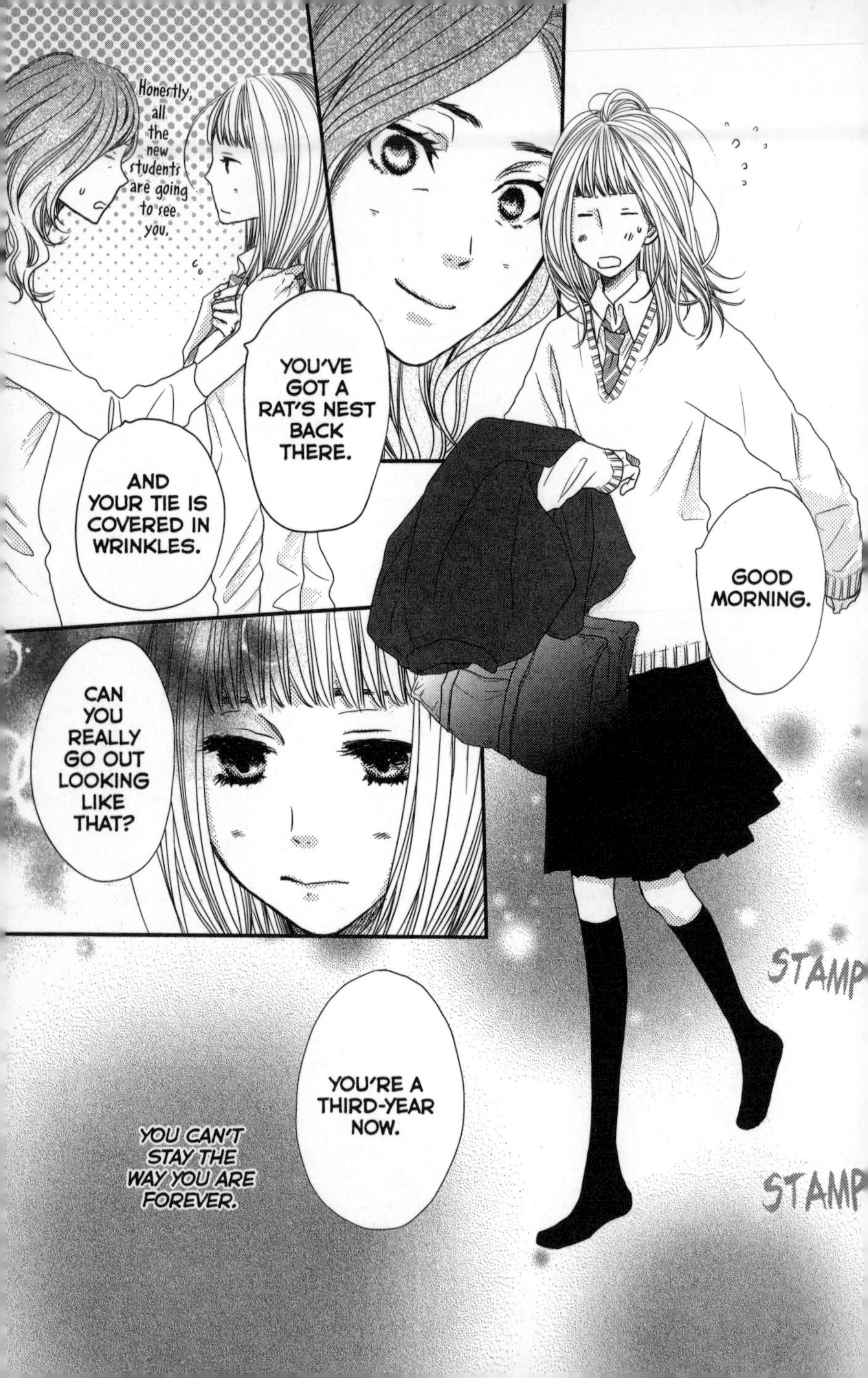
GOOD MORNING.
STAMP
STAMP
YOU'VE GOT A RAT'S NEST BACK THERE.
Honestly, all the new students are going to see you.
AND YOUR TIE IS COVERED IN WRINKLES.
CAN YOU REALLY GO OUT LOOKING LIKE THAT?
YOU'RE A THIRD-YEAR NOW.
YOU CAN'T STAY THE WAY YOU ARE FOREVER.

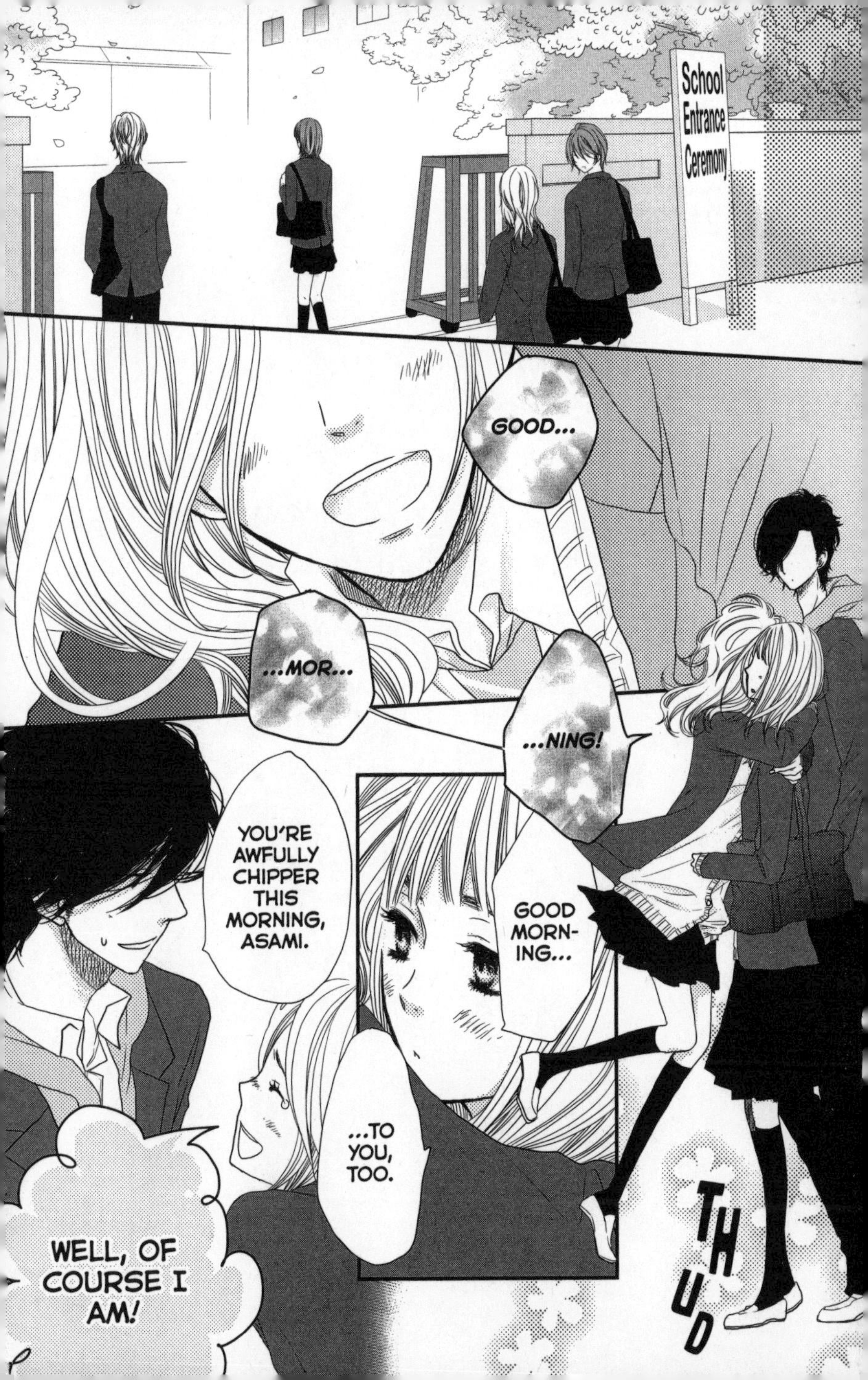
School Entrance Ceremony
GOOD...
...MOR...
...NING!
THUD
GOOD MORNING...
...TO YOU, TOO.
YOU'RE AWFULLY CHIPPER THIS MORNING, ASAMI.
WELL, OF COURSE I AM!

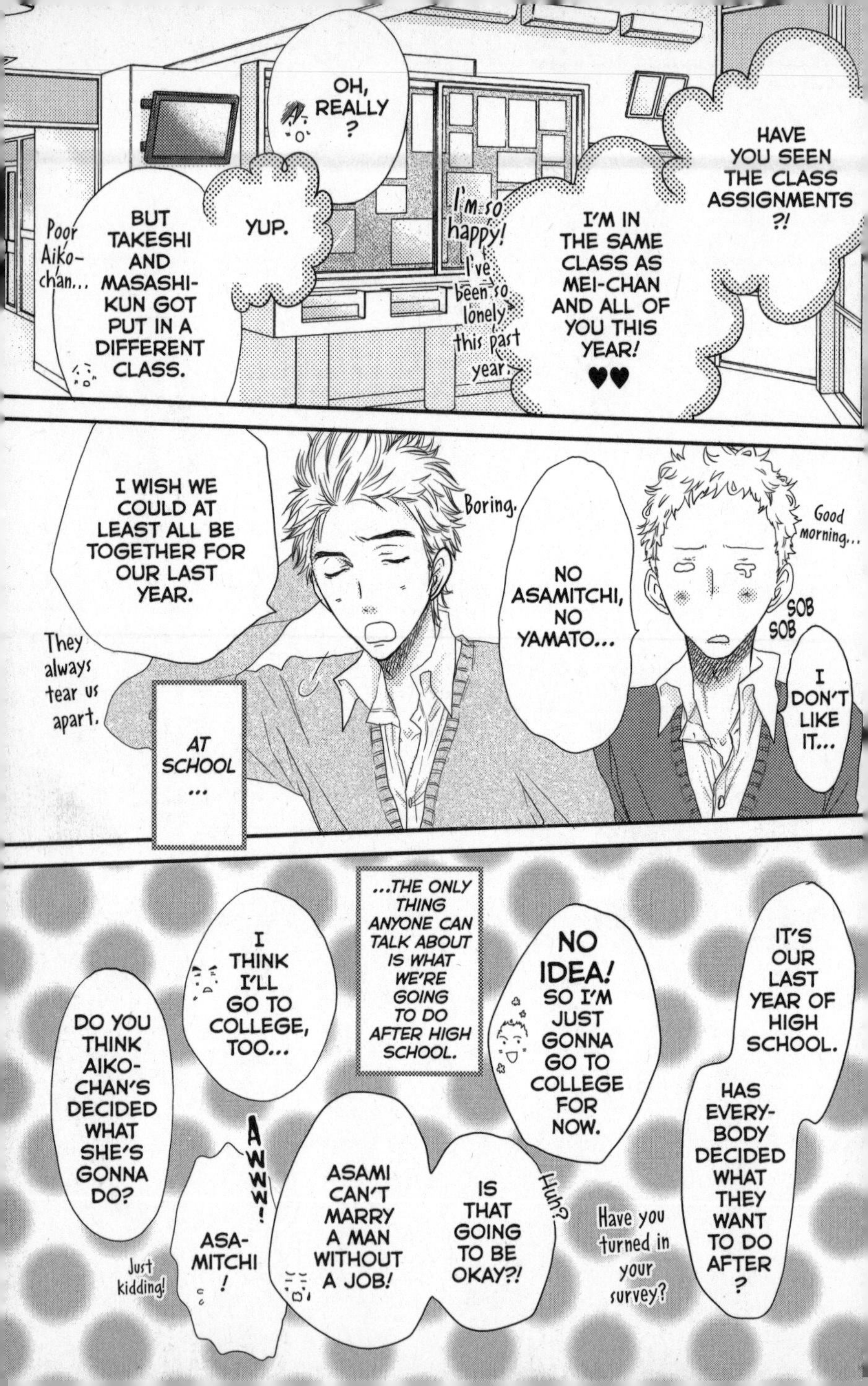

HAVE YOU SEEN THE CLASS ASSIGNMENTS?!
I'M IN THE SAME CLASS AS MEI-CHAN AND ALL OF YOU THIS YEAR! ♥♥
I'm so happy! I've been so lonely this past year.
OH, REALLY?
YUP.
BUT TAKESHI AND MASASHI-KUN GOT PUT IN A DIFFERENT CLASS.
Poor Aiko-chan...
Good morning...
SOB SOB
I DON'T LIKE IT...
NO ASAMITCHI, NO YAMATO...
Boring.
I WISH WE COULD AT LEAST ALL BE TOGETHER FOR OUR LAST YEAR.
They always tear us apart.
AT SCHOOL...
IT'S OUR LAST YEAR OF HIGH SCHOOL.
HAS EVERYBODY DECIDED WHAT THEY WANT TO DO AFTER?
Have you turned in your survey?
NO IDEA! SO I'M JUST GONNA GO TO COLLEGE FOR NOW.
...THE ONLY THING ANYONE CAN TALK ABOUT IS WHAT WE'RE GOING TO DO AFTER HIGH SCHOOL.
Huh?
IS THAT GOING TO BE OKAY?!
I THINK I'LL GO TO COLLEGE, TOO...
ASAMI CAN'T MARRY A MAN WITHOUT A JOB!
AWWW!
ASA-MITCHI!
DO YOU THINK AIKO-CHAN'S DECIDED WHAT SHE'S GONNA DO?
Just kidding!

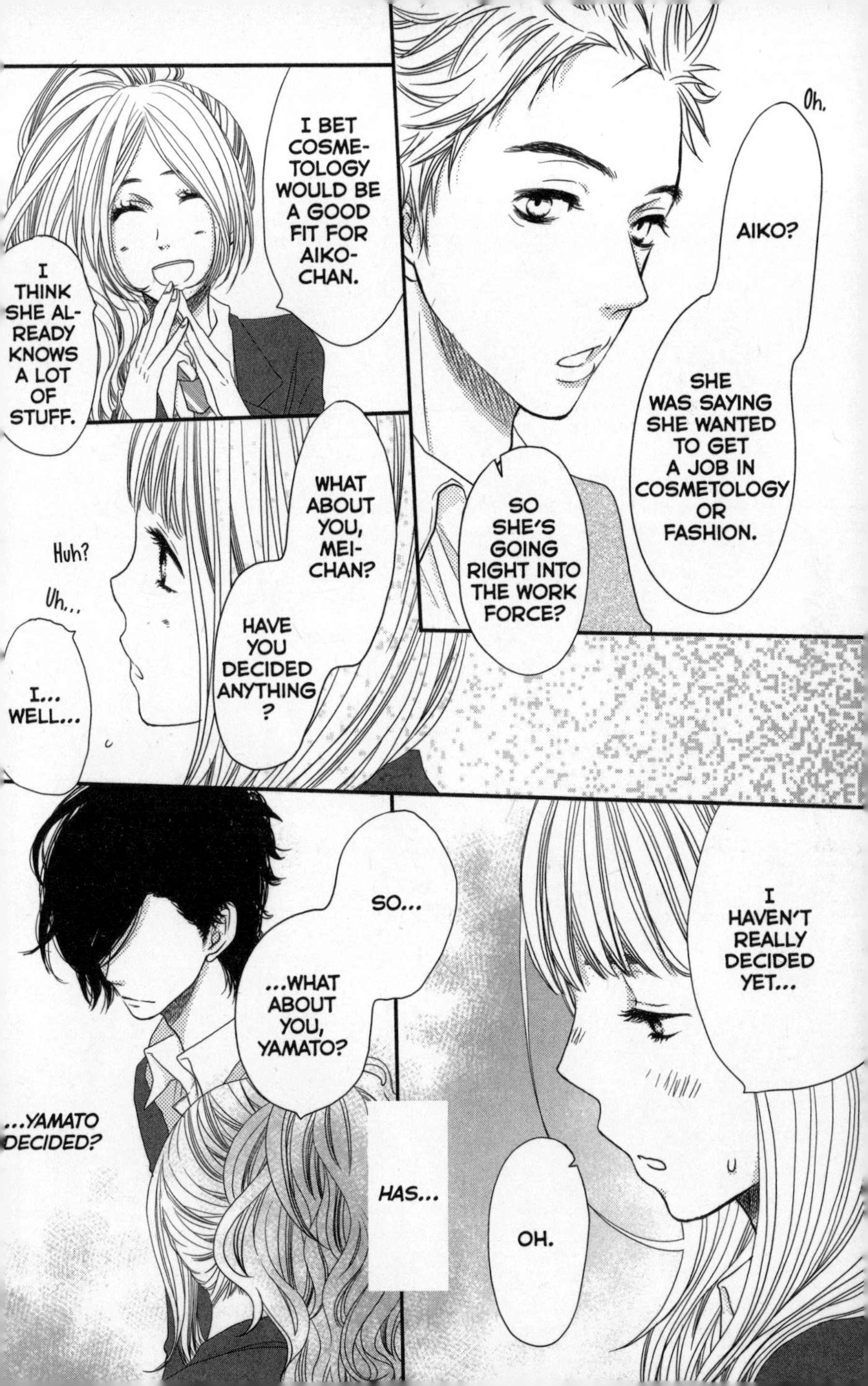
Oh.
AIKO?
SHE WAS SAYING SHE WANTED TO GET A JOB IN COSMETOLOGY OR FASHION.
SO SHE'S GOING RIGHT INTO THE WORK FORCE?
I BET COSMETOLOGY WOULD BE A GOOD FIT FOR AIKO-CHAN.
I THINK SHE ALREADY KNOWS A LOT OF STUFF.
WHAT ABOUT YOU, MEI-CHAN?
HAVE YOU DECIDED ANYTHING?
Huh?
Uh...
I... WELL...
I HAVEN'T REALLY DECIDED YET...
OH.
SO...
...WHAT ABOUT YOU, YAMATO?
HAS...
...YAMATO DECIDED?

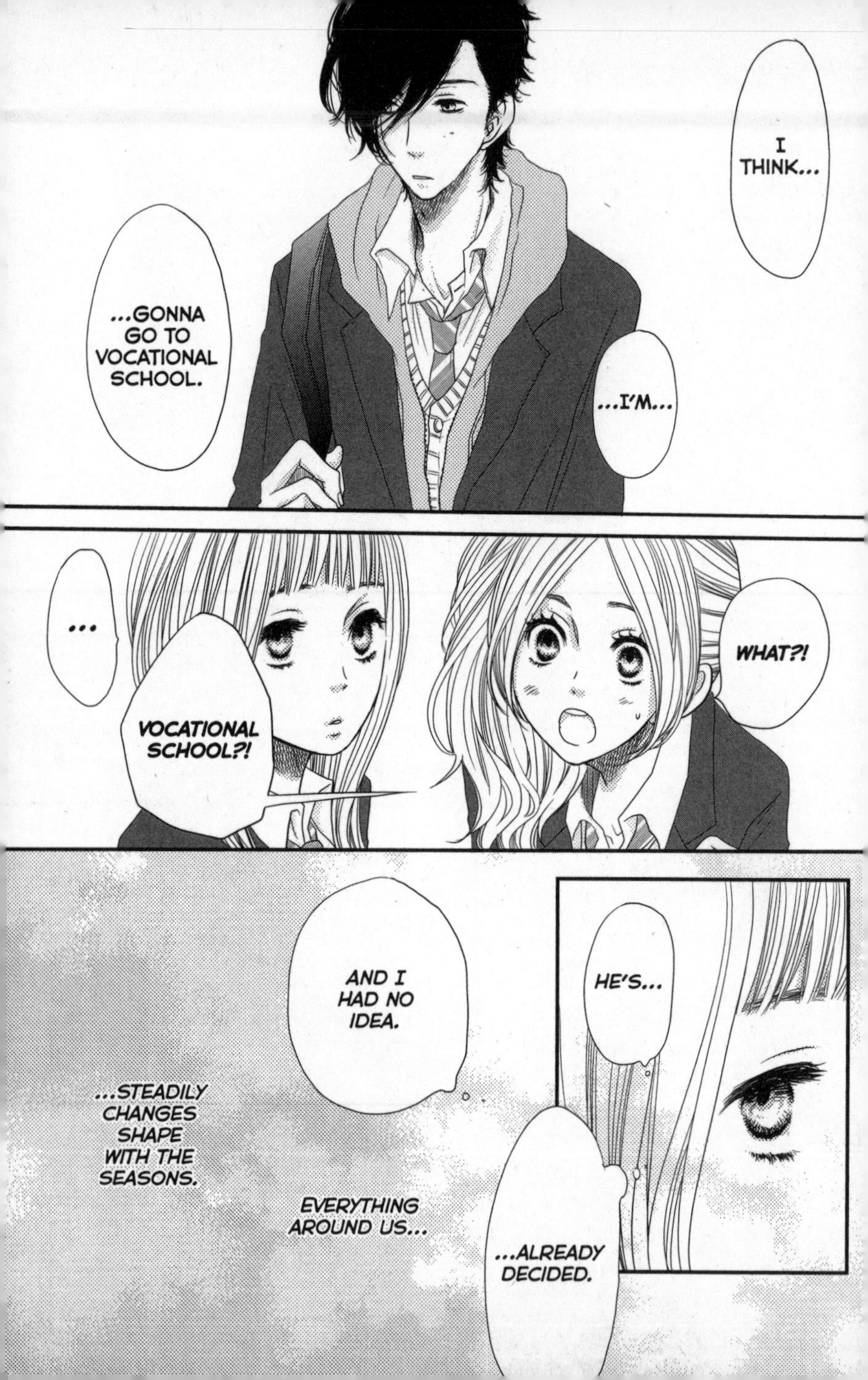
I THINK...
...I'M...
...GONNA GO TO VOCATIONAL SCHOOL.
WHAT?!
VOCATIONAL SCHOOL?!
...
HE'S...
...ALREADY DECIDED.
AND I HAD NO IDEA.
EVERYTHING AROUND US...
...STEADILY CHANGES SHAPE WITH THE SEASONS.

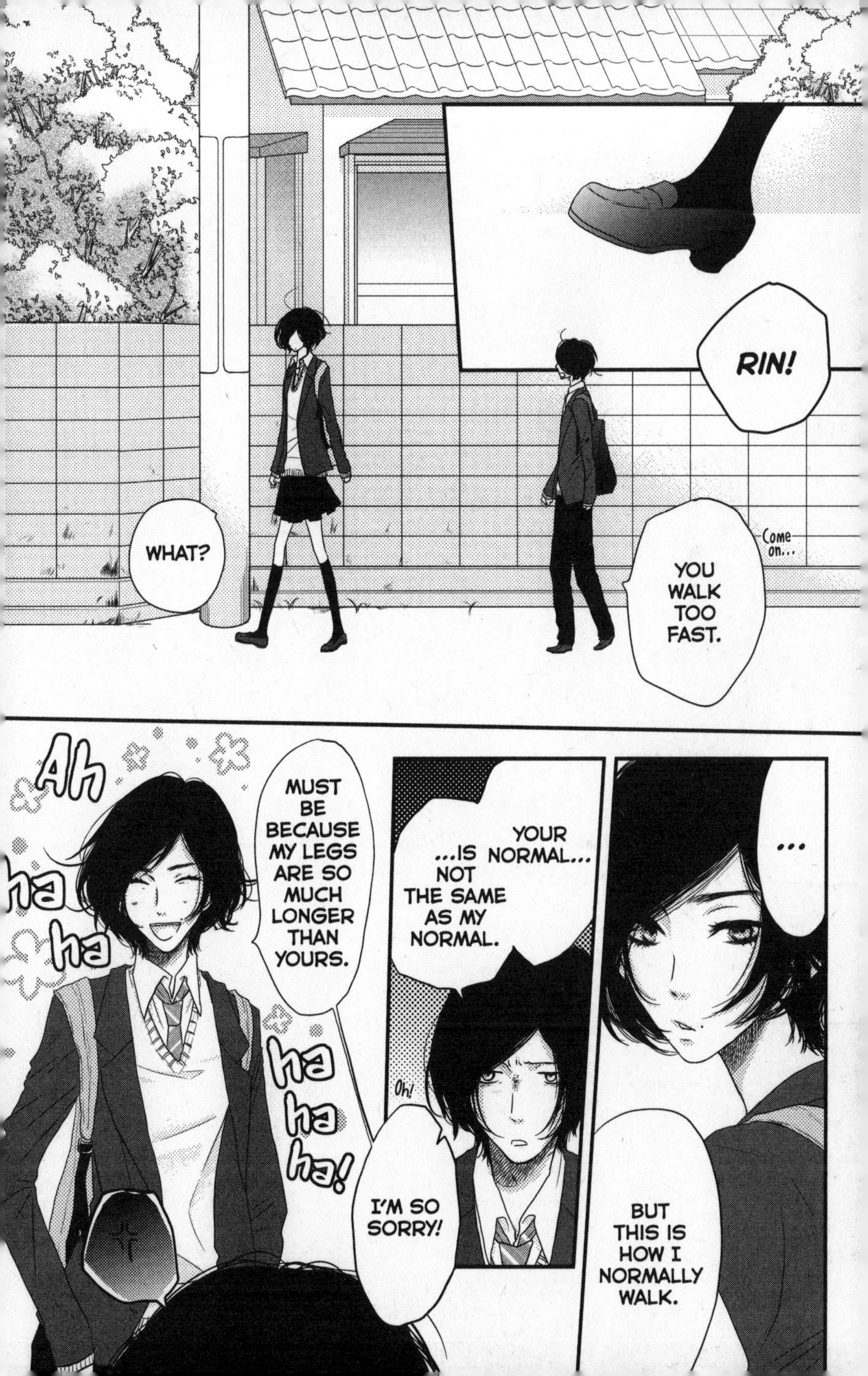
RIN!
Come on...
YOU WALK TOO FAST.
WHAT?
...
BUT THIS IS HOW I NORMALLY WALK.
YOUR NORMAL... ...IS NOT THE SAME AS MY NORMAL.
Oh!
I'M SO SORRY!
Ah ha ha
MUST BE BECAUSE MY LEGS ARE SO MUCH LONGER THAN YOURS.
ha ha ha!

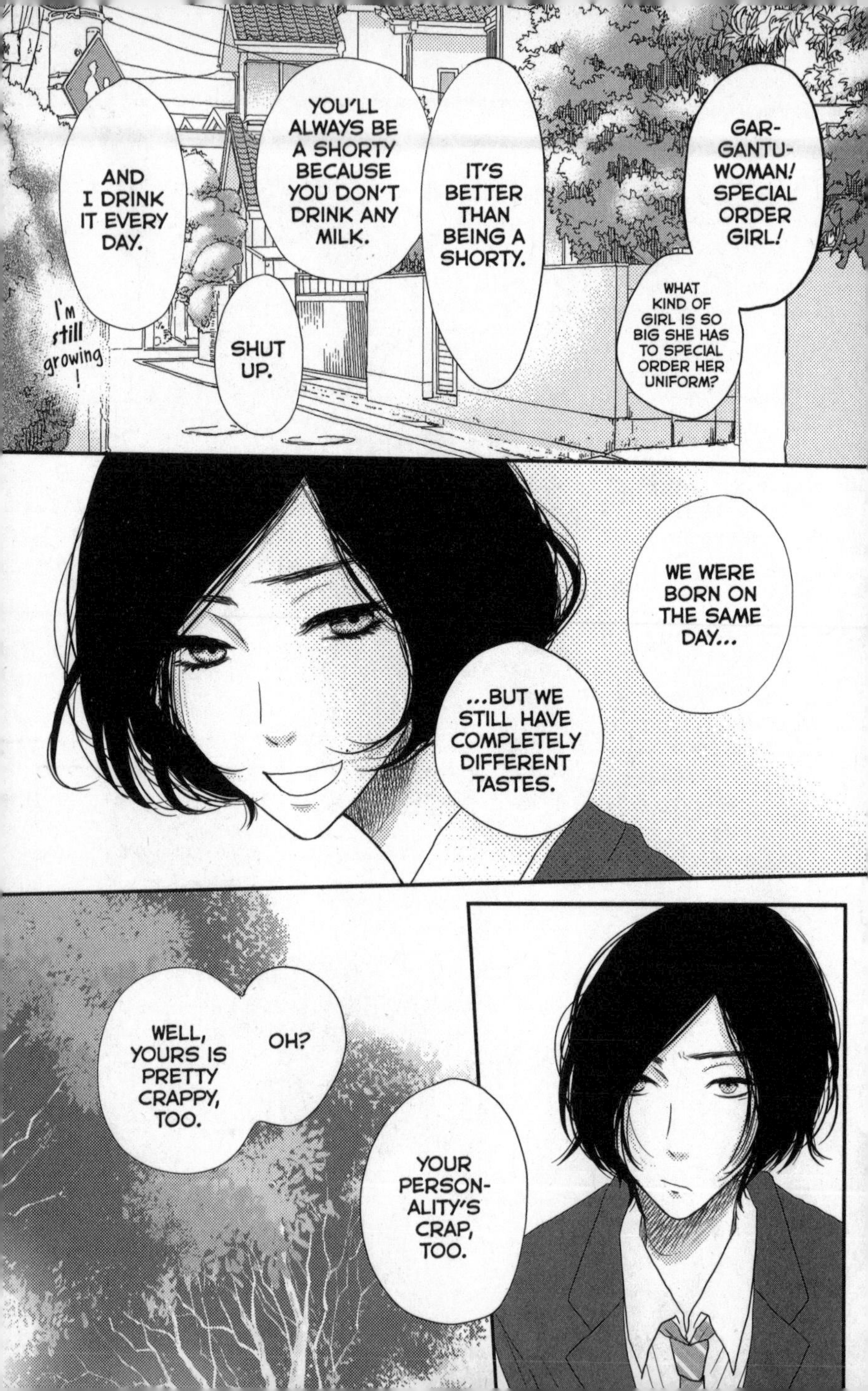
GAR-GANTU-WOMAN! SPECIAL ORDER GIRL!
WHAT KIND OF GIRL IS SO BIG SHE HAS TO SPECIAL ORDER HER UNIFORM?
IT'S BETTER THAN BEING A SHORTY.
YOU'LL ALWAYS BE A SHORTY BECAUSE YOU DON'T DRINK ANY MILK.
SHUT UP.
AND I DRINK IT EVERY DAY.
I'm still growing!
WE WERE BORN ON THE SAME DAY...
...BUT WE STILL HAVE COMPLETELY DIFFERENT TASTES.
YOUR PERSON-ALITY'S CRAP, TOO.
OH?
WELL, YOURS IS PRETTY CRAPPY, TOO.

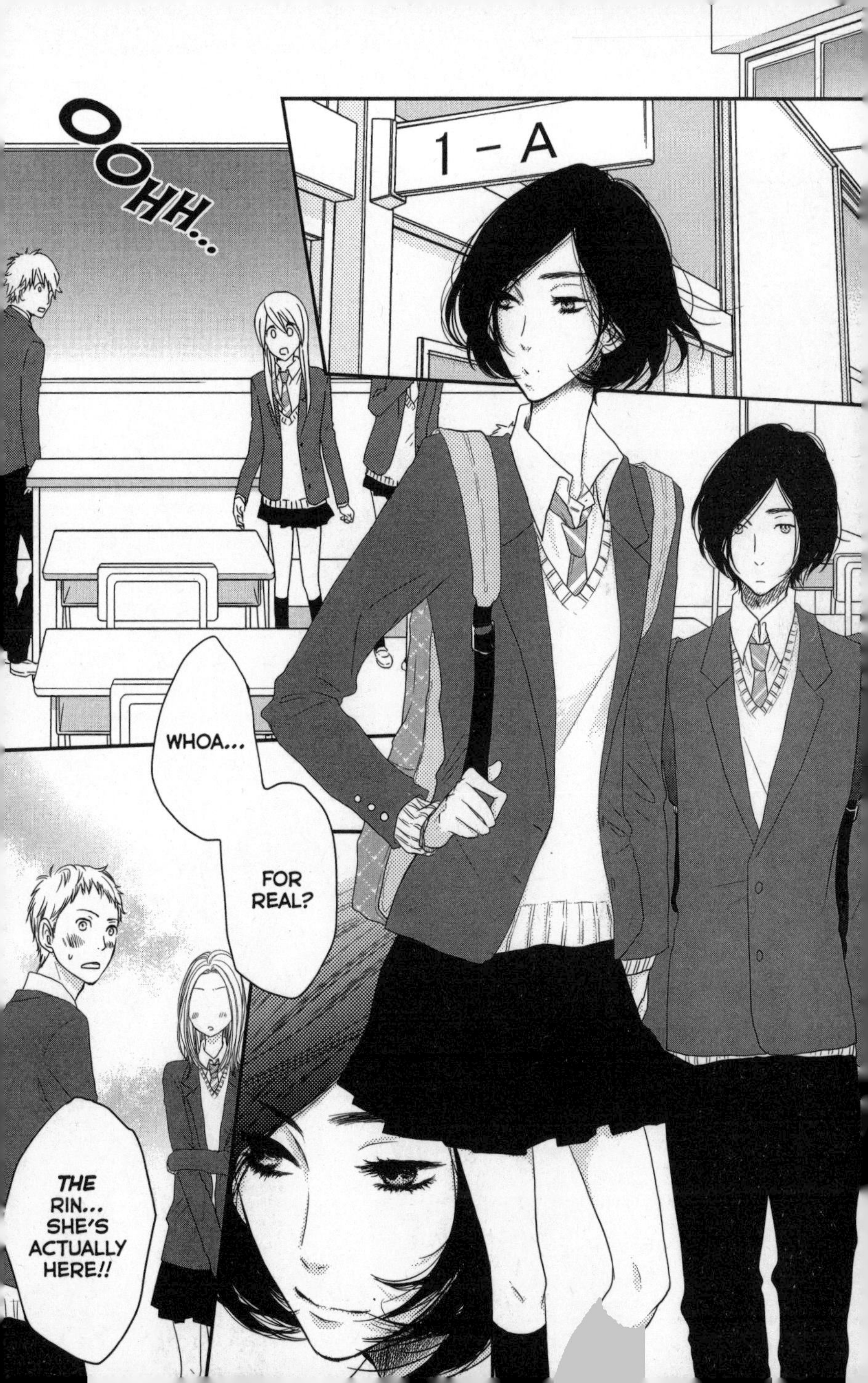
1 – A
OOHH...
WHOA...
FOR REAL?
THE RIN... SHE'S ACTUALLY HERE!!

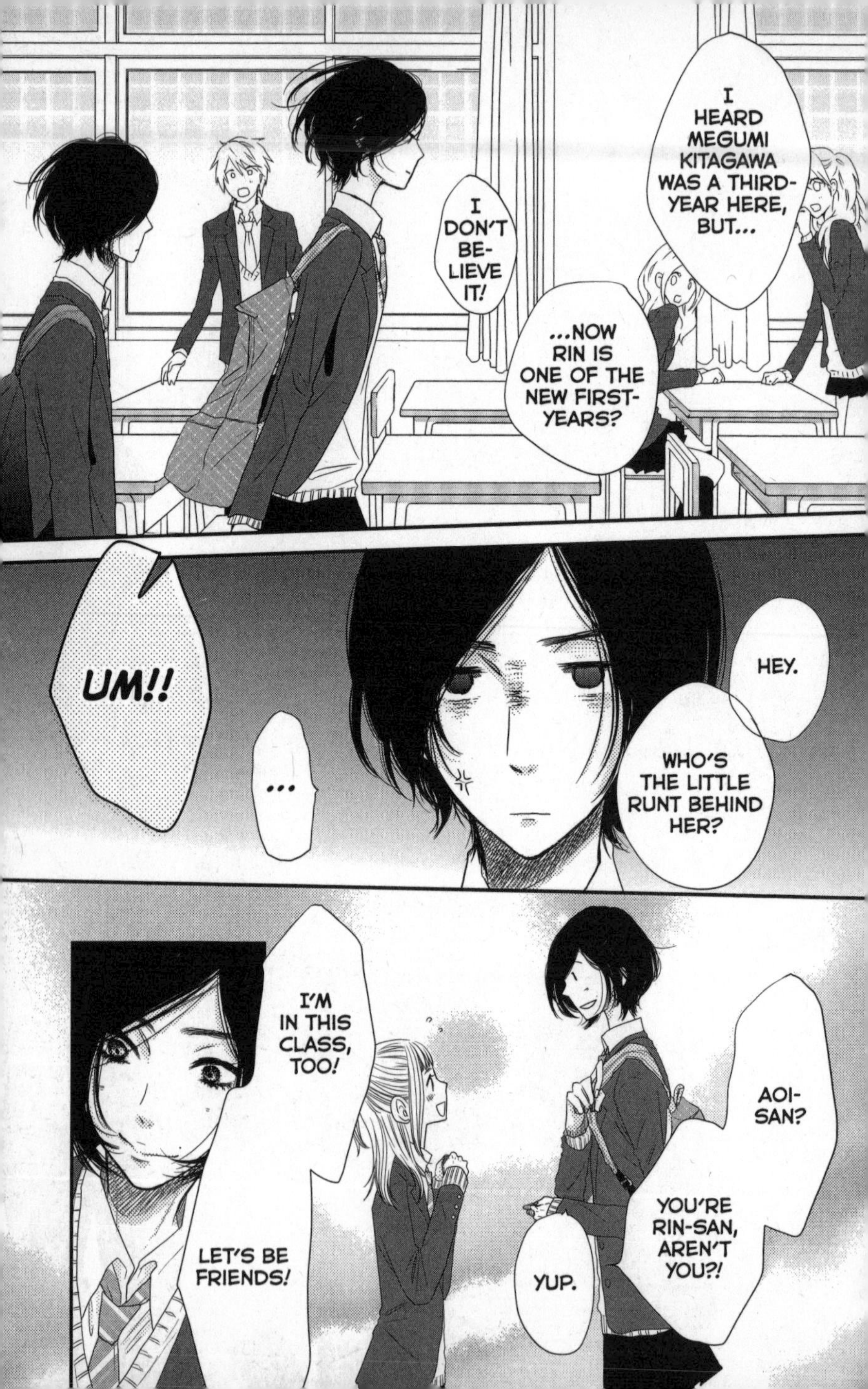
I HEARD MEGUMI KITAGAWA WAS A THIRD-YEAR HERE, BUT...
...NOW RIN IS ONE OF THE NEW FIRST-YEARS?
I DON'T BE-LIEVE IT!
HEY.
WHO'S THE LITTLE RUNT BEHIND HER?
...
UM!!
AOI-SAN?
YOU'RE RIN-SAN, AREN'T YOU?!
YUP.
I'M IN THIS CLASS, TOO!
LET'S BE FRIENDS!

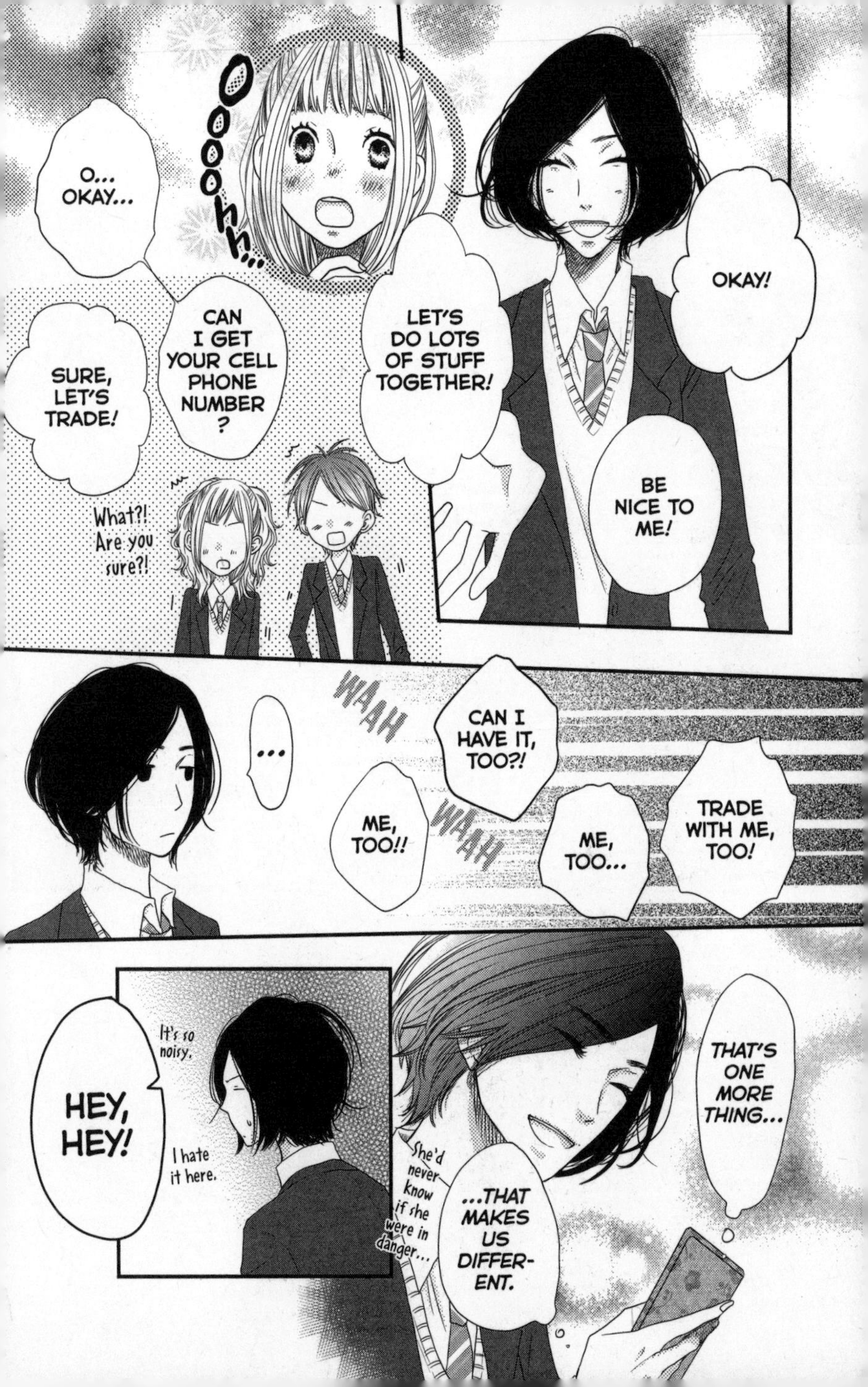
OKAY!
LET'S DO LOTS OF STUFF TOGETHER!
BE NICE TO ME!
O... OKAY...
Oooohh...
CAN I GET YOUR CELL PHONE NUMBER?
SURE, LET'S TRADE!
What?! Are you sure?!
TRADE WITH ME, TOO!
CAN I HAVE IT, TOO?!
ME, TOO...
WAAH
ME, TOO!!
WAAH
...
THAT'S ONE MORE THING...
...THAT MAKES US DIFFER-ENT.
She'd never know if she were in danger...
It's so noisy.
HEY, HEY!
I hate it here.

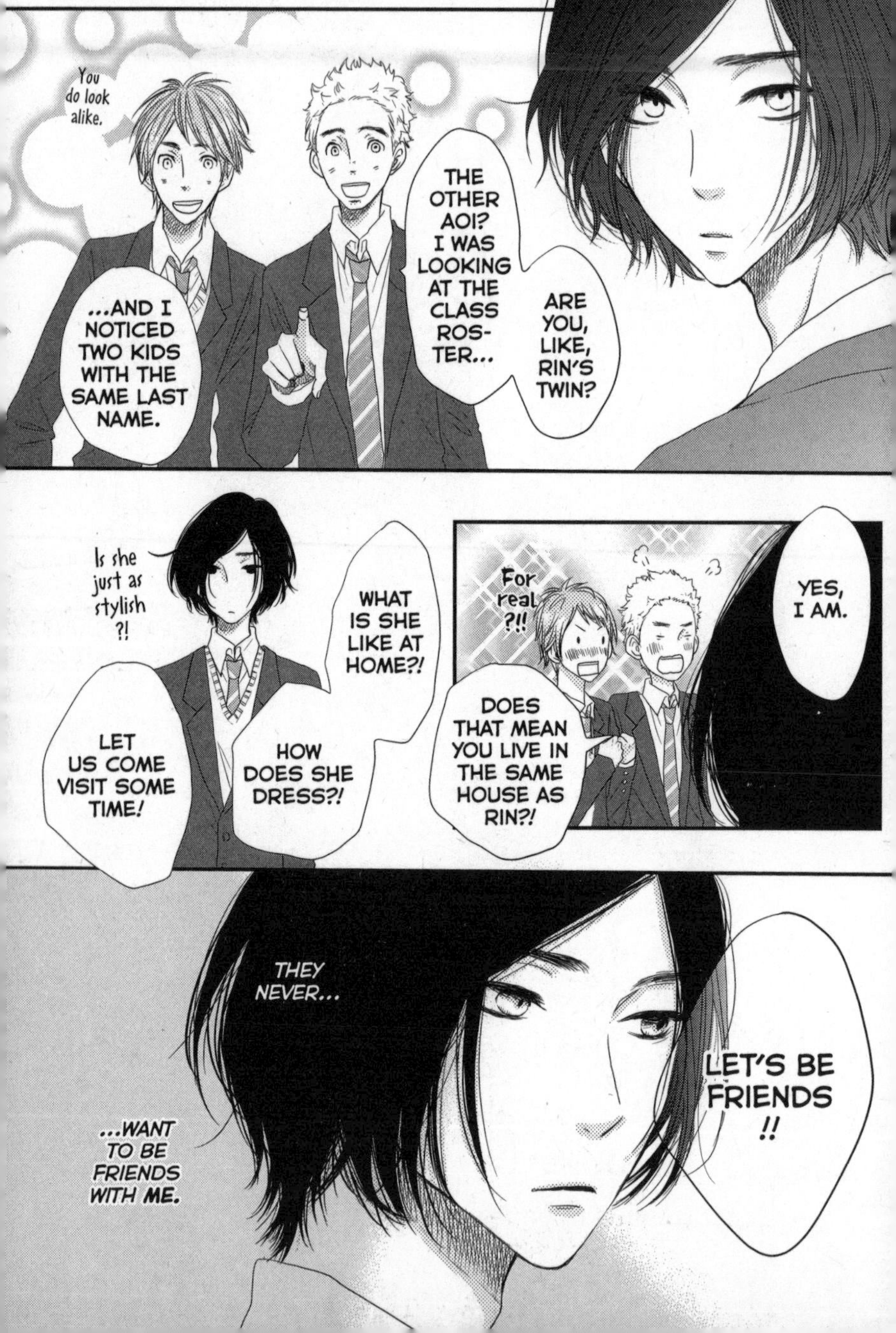
THE OTHER AOI? I WAS LOOKING AT THE CLASS ROSTER...
...AND I NOTICED TWO KIDS WITH THE SAME LAST NAME.
ARE YOU, LIKE, RIN'S TWIN?
You do look alike.
YES, I AM.
For real?!!
DOES THAT MEAN YOU LIVE IN THE SAME HOUSE AS RIN?!
WHAT IS SHE LIKE AT HOME?!
Is she just as stylish?!
HOW DOES SHE DRESS?!
LET US COME VISIT SOME TIME!
LET'S BE FRIENDS!!
THEY NEVER...
...WANT TO BE FRIENDS WITH ME.

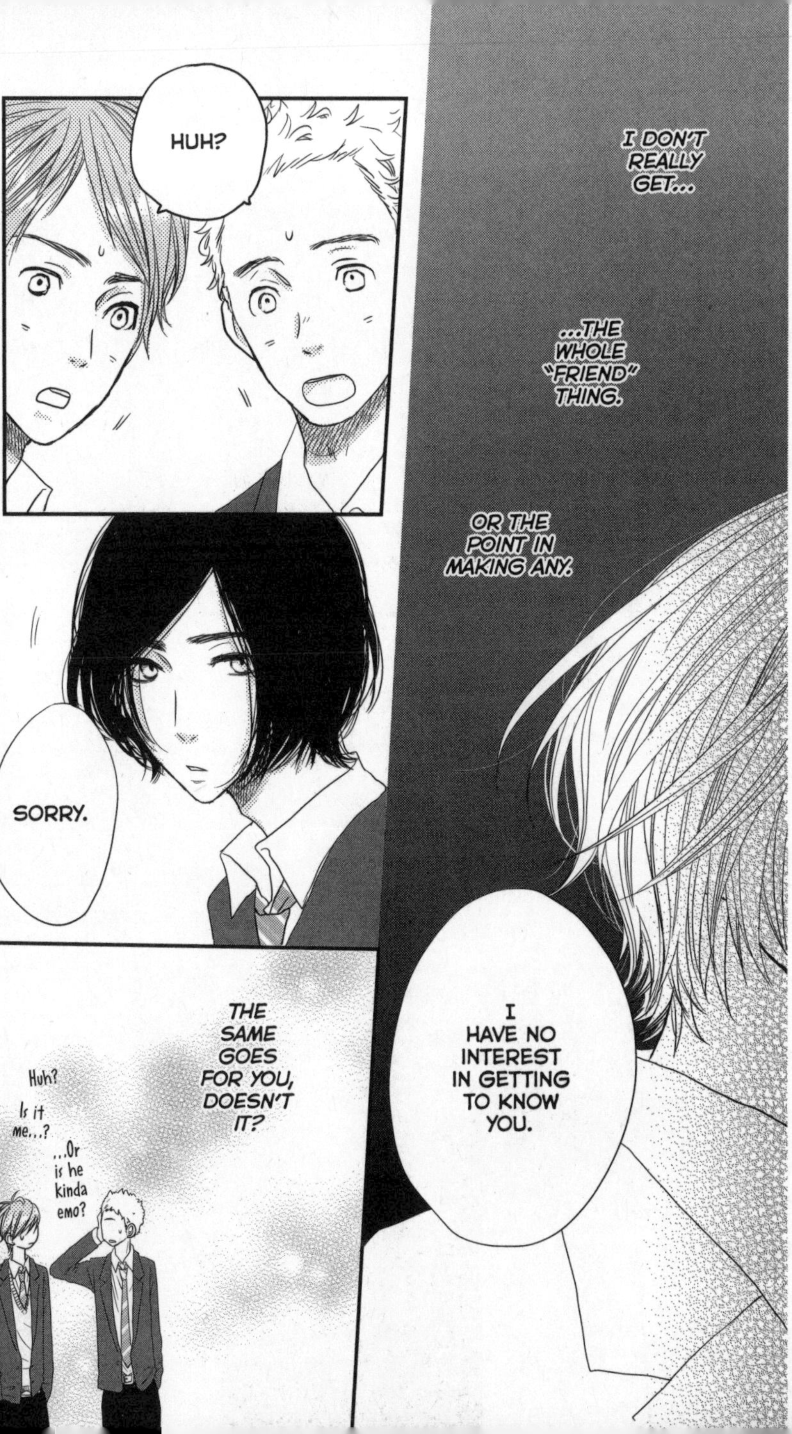
I DON'T REALLY GET...
...THE WHOLE "FRIEND" THING.
OR THE POINT IN MAKING ANY.
I HAVE NO INTEREST IN GETTING TO KNOW YOU.
HUH?
SORRY.
THE SAME GOES FOR YOU, DOESN'T IT?
Huh?
Is it me...?
...Or is he kinda emo?

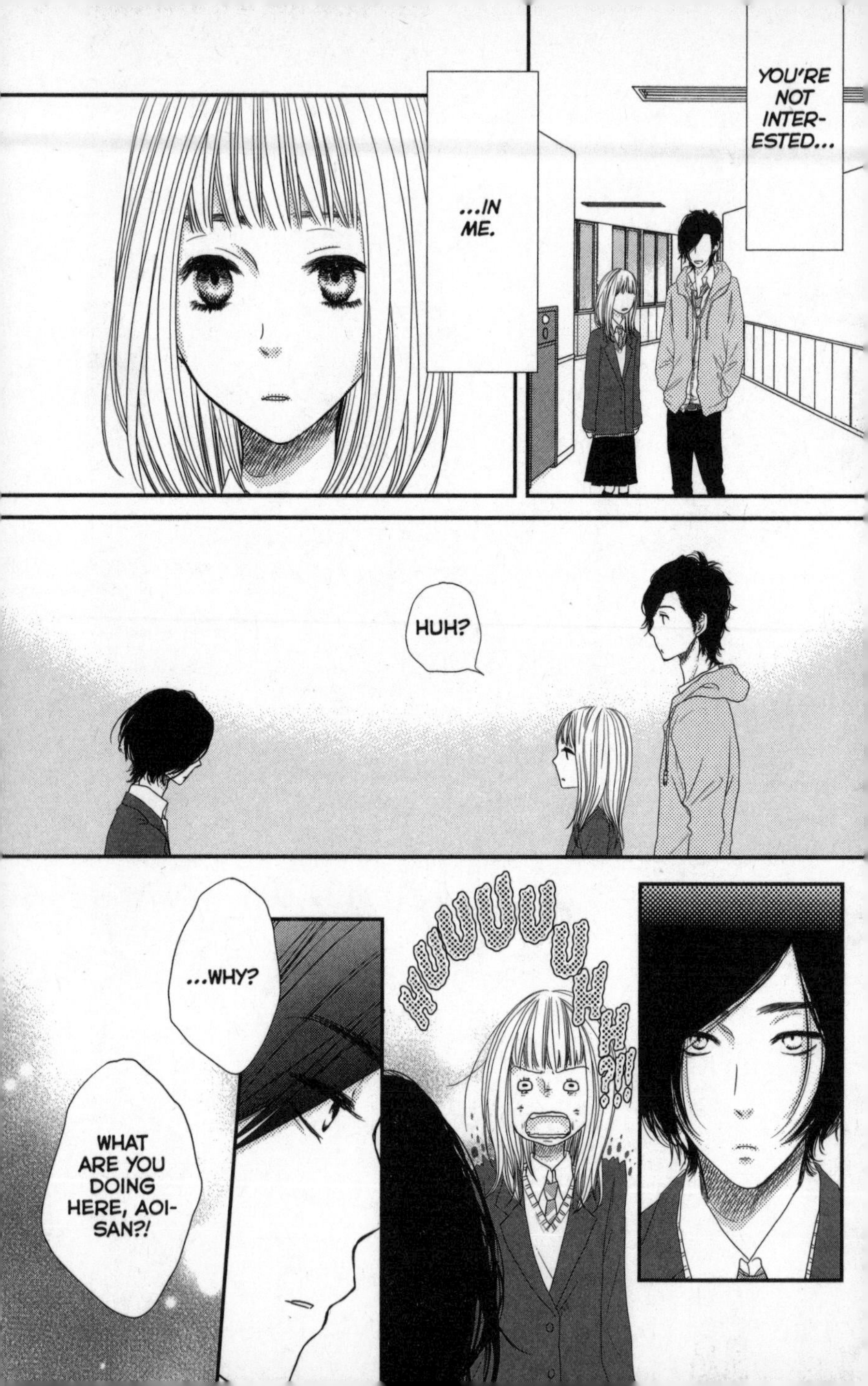
YOU'RE NOT INTER-ESTED...
...IN ME.
HUH?
HUUUUUUHH?!!
...WHY?
WHAT ARE YOU DOING HERE, AOI-SAN?!

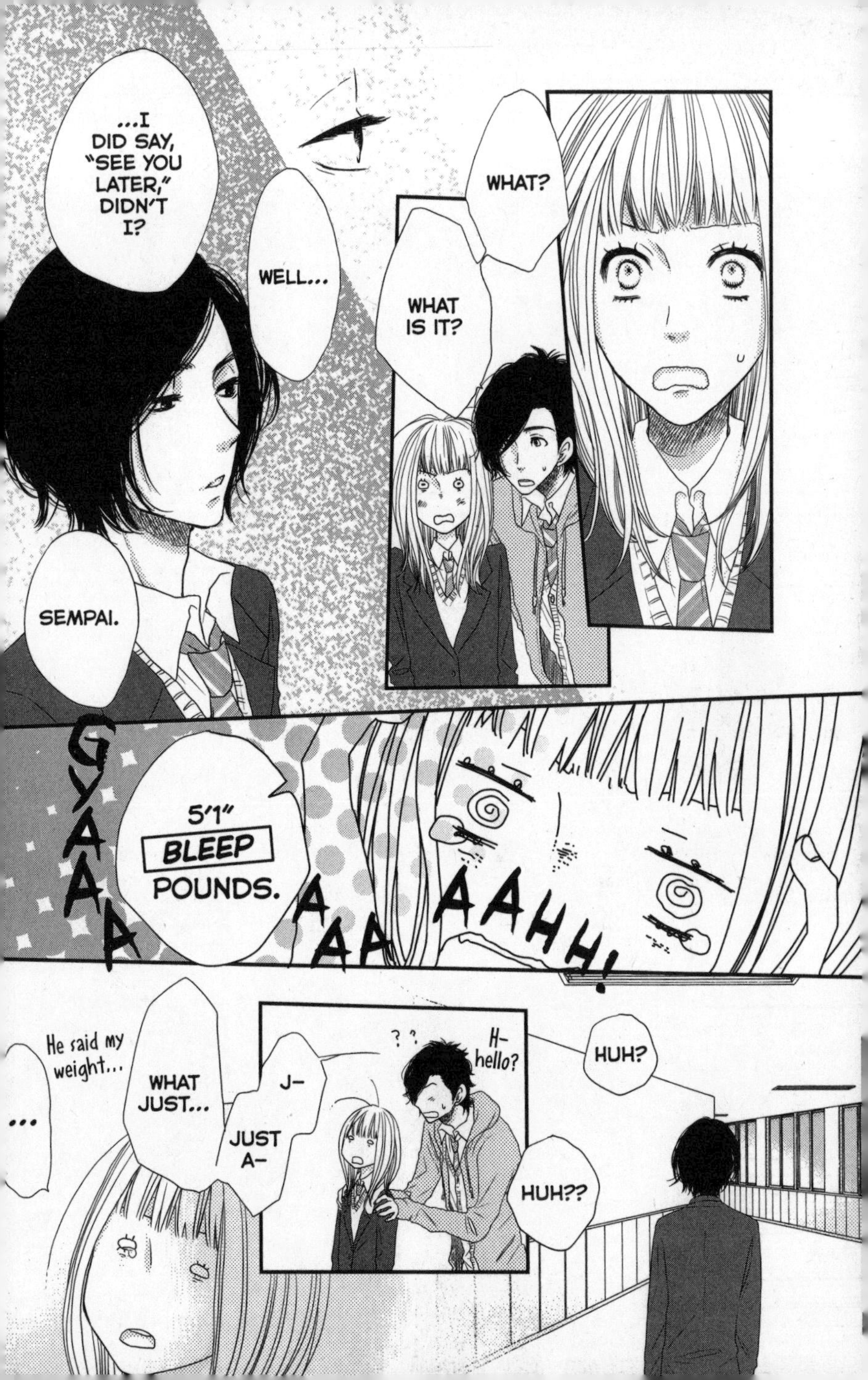
WHAT?
WHAT IS IT?
WELL...
...I DID SAY, "SEE YOU LATER," DIDN'T I?
SEMPAI.
5'1" BLEEP POUNDS.
GYAAAA AAAHH!
HUH?
HUH??
H-hello?
? ?
J-
JUST A-
WHAT JUST...
He said my weight...
...

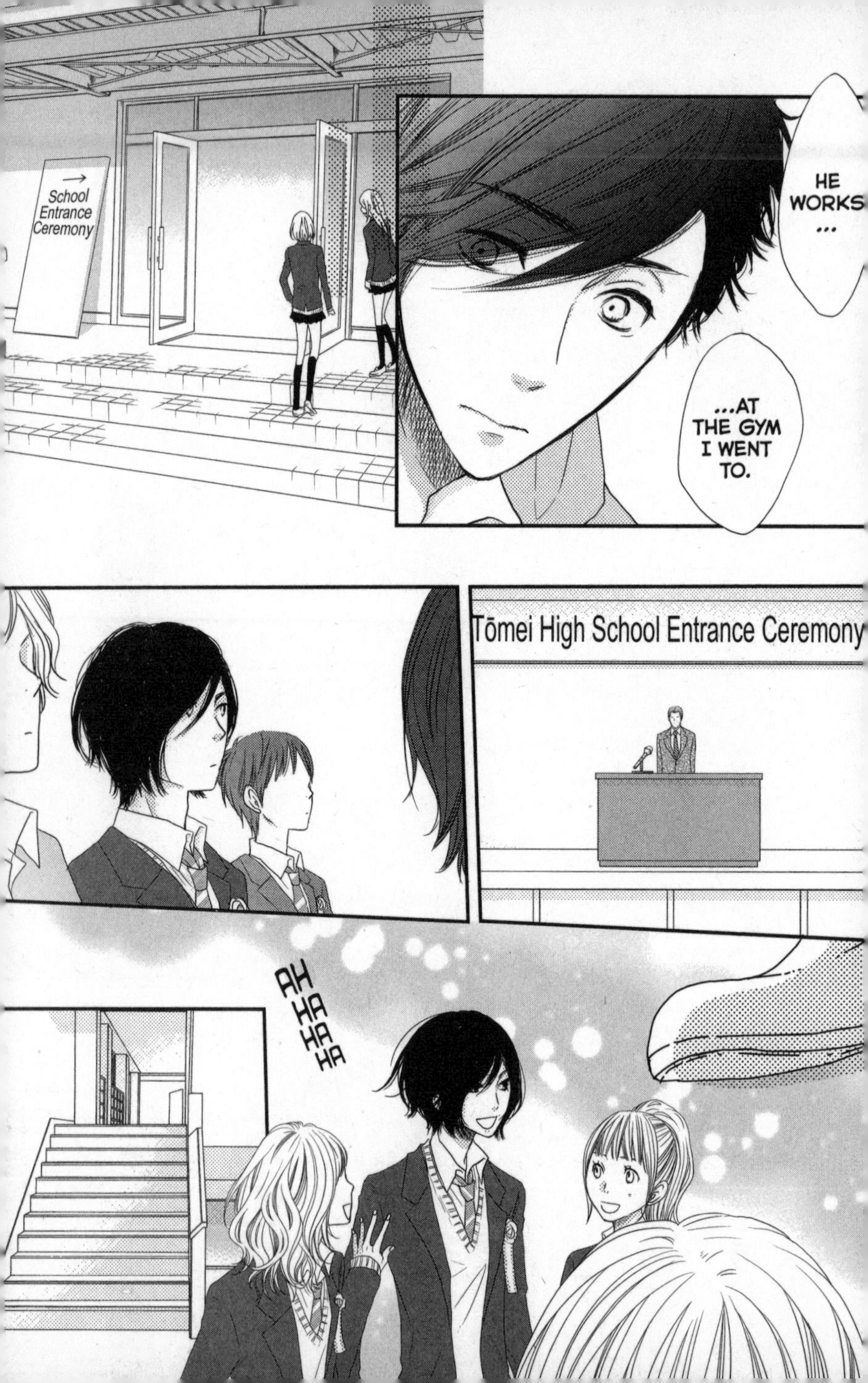
HE WORKS...
...AT THE GYM I WENT TO.
School Entrance Ceremony
Tōmei High School Entrance Ceremony
AH HA HA HA

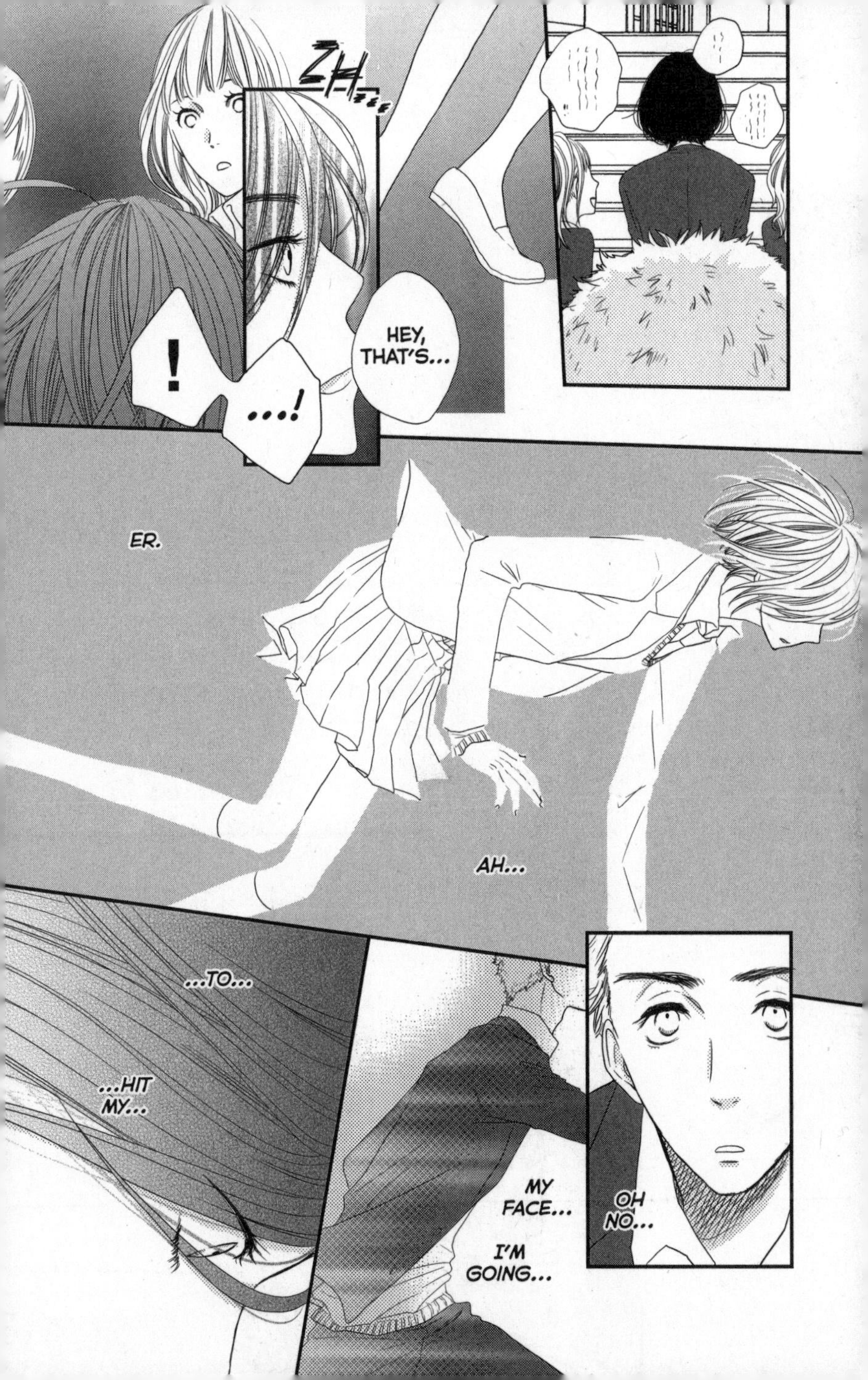
ZH
HEY, THAT'S...
...!
!
ER.
AH...
OH NO...
MY FACE...
I'M GOING...
...TO...
...HIT MY...

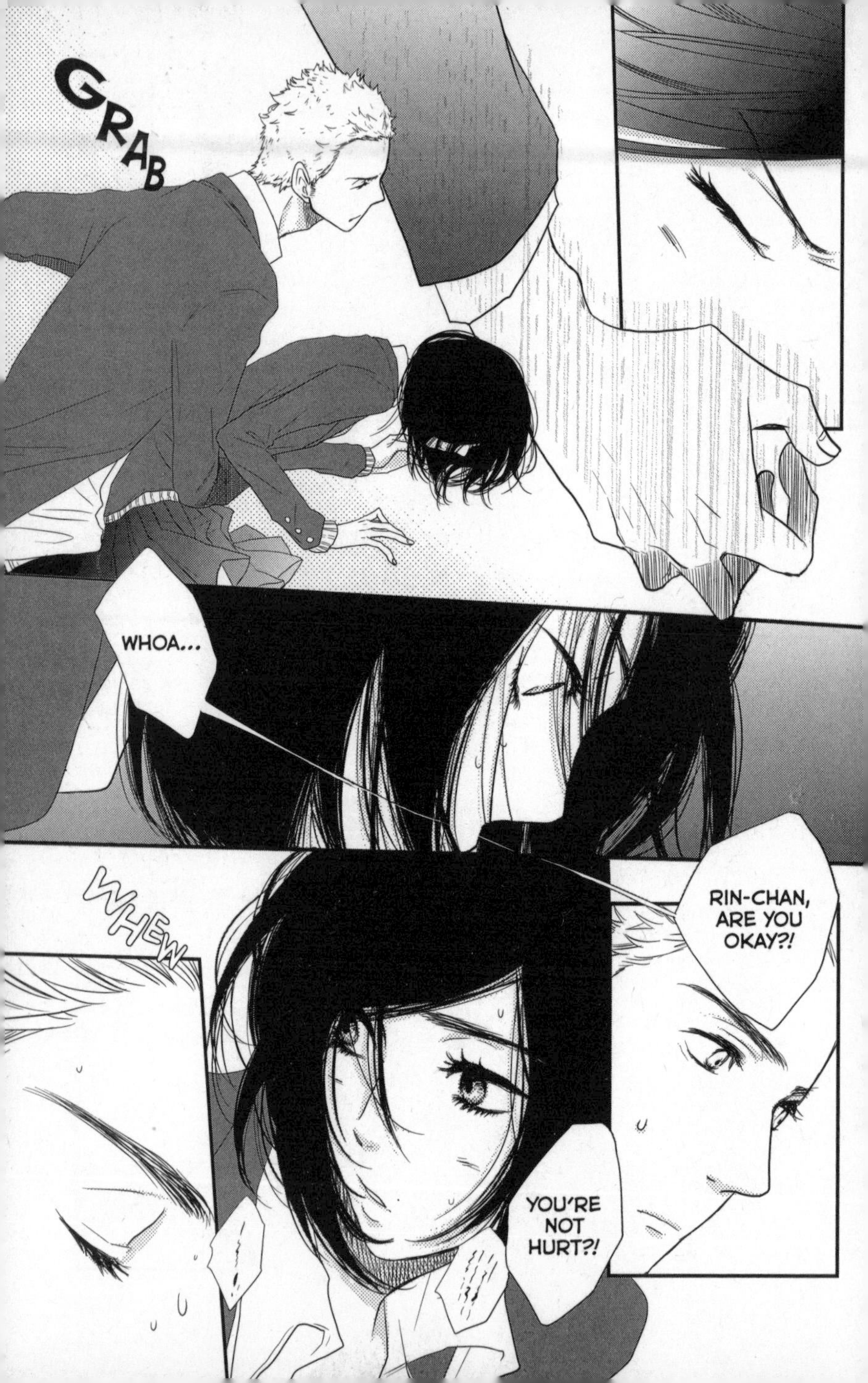
GRAB
WHOA...
RIN-CHAN, ARE YOU OKAY?!
YOU'RE NOT HURT?!
WHEW

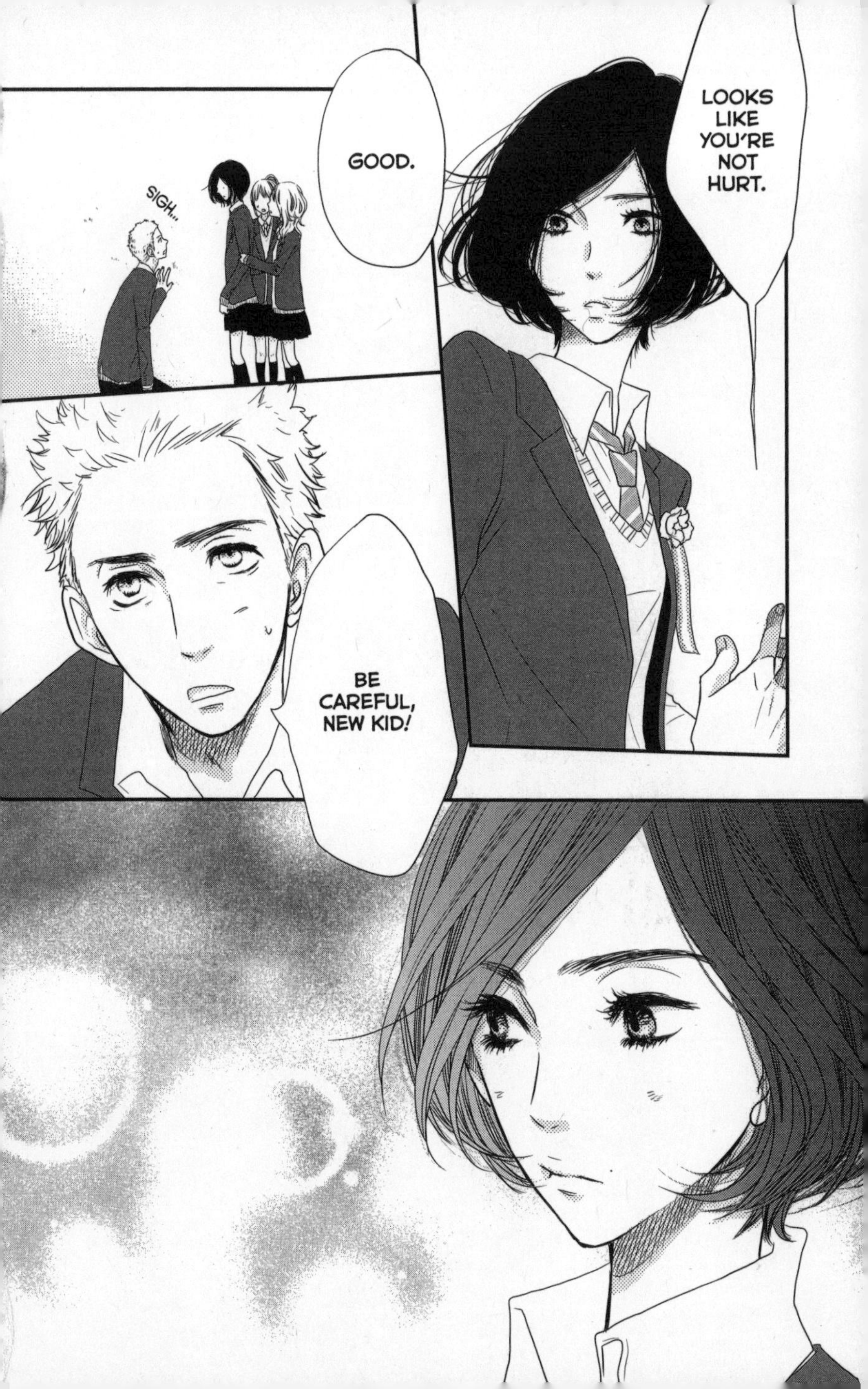
LOOKS LIKE YOU'RE NOT HURT.
GOOD.
SIGH...
BE CAREFUL, NEW KID!

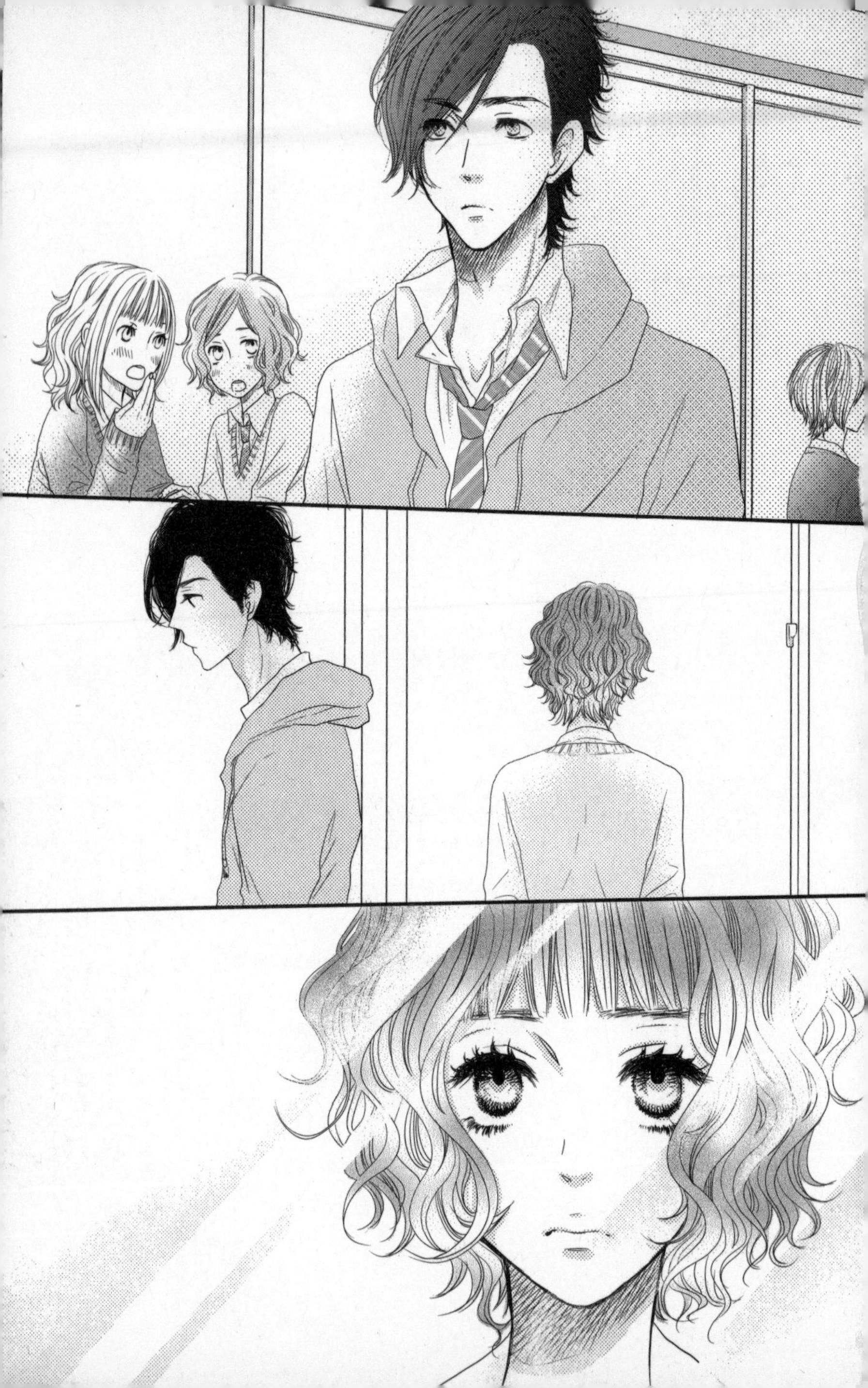

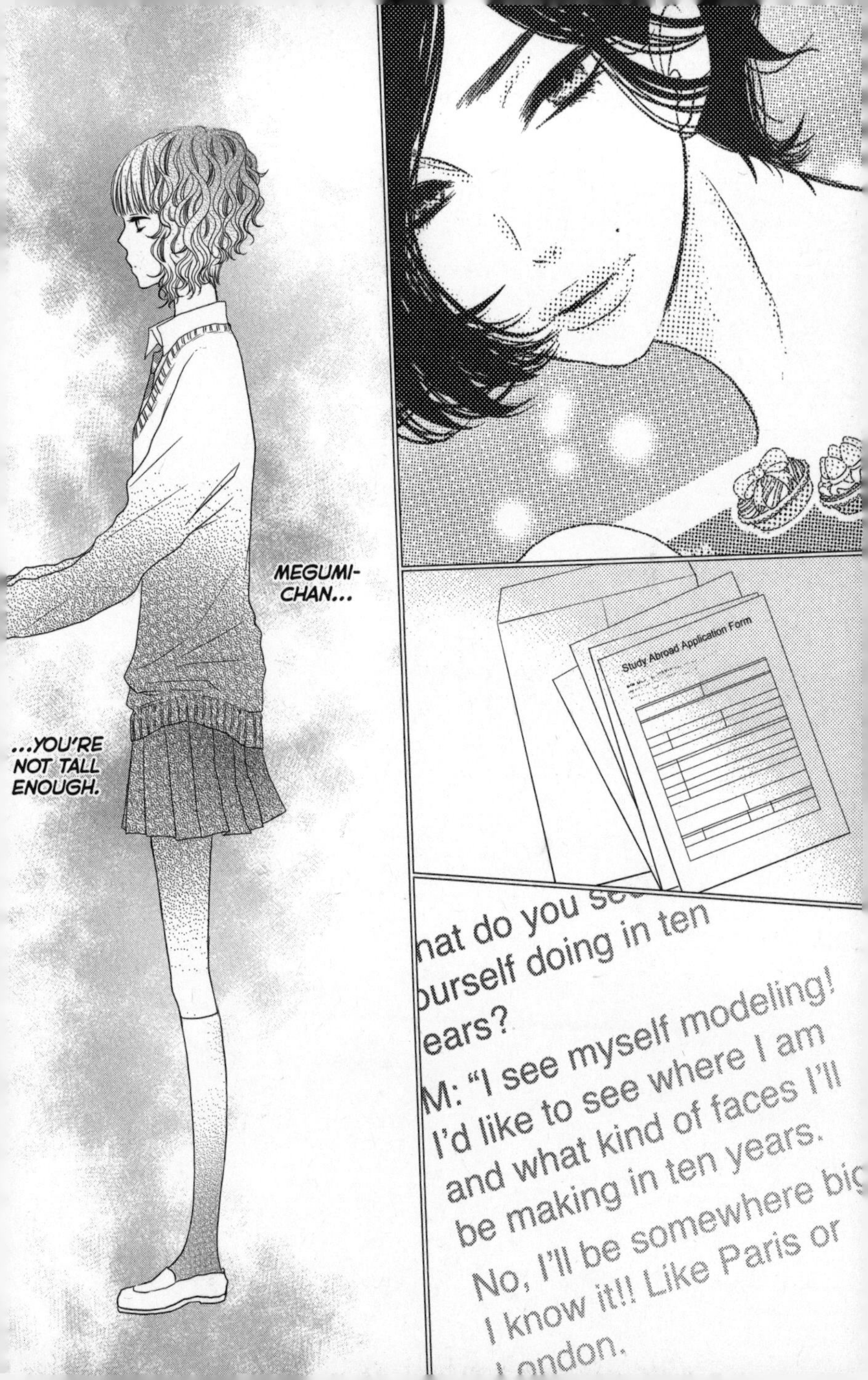
Study Abroad Application Form
hat do you
ourself doing in ten
ears?
M: “I see myself modeling!
I'd like to see where I am
and what kind of faces I'll
be making in ten years.
No, I'll be somewhere
I know it!! Like Paris or
ondon.
MEGUMI-CHAN...
...YOU'RE NOT TALL ENOUGH.

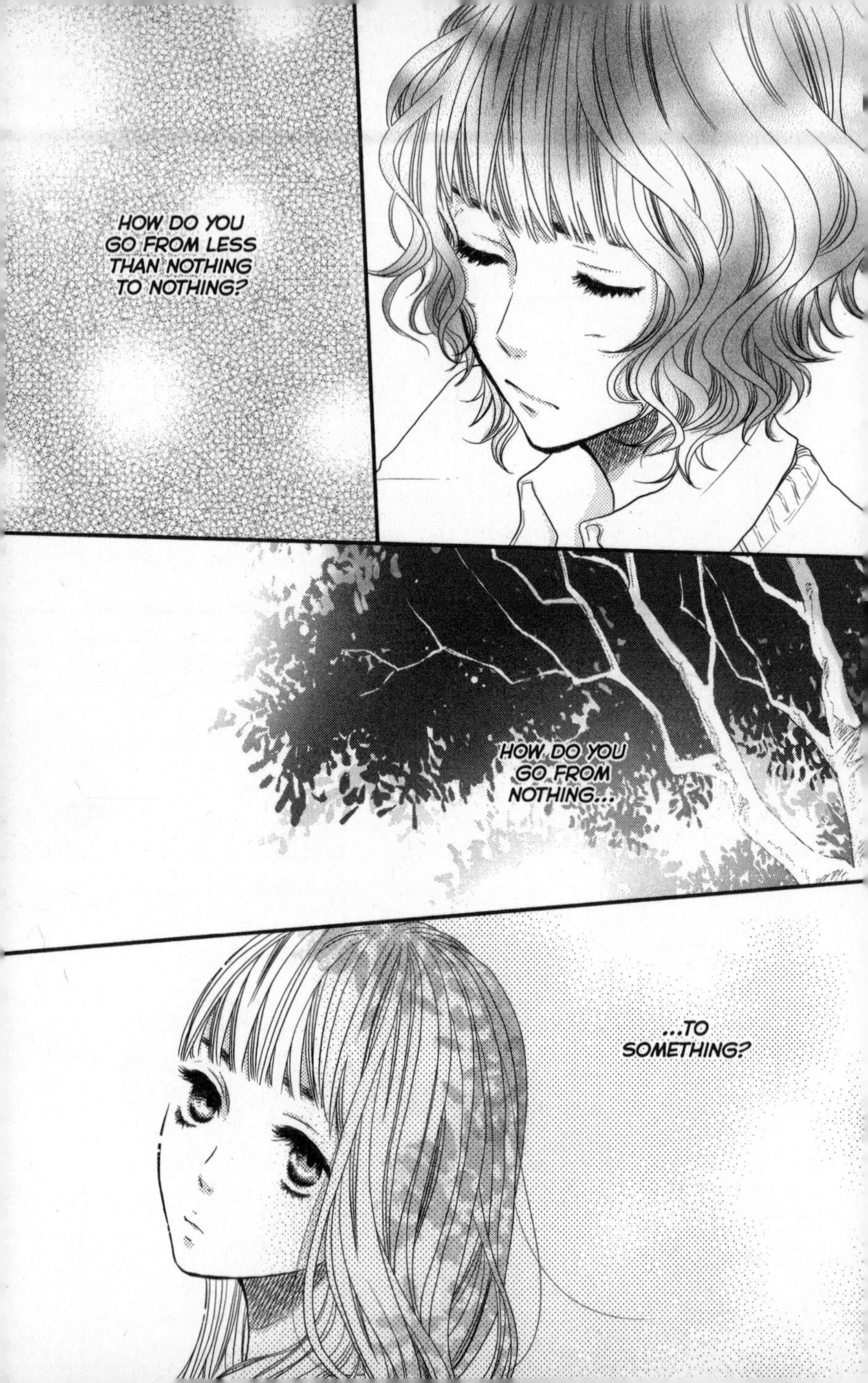
HOW DO YOU GO FROM LESS THAN NOTHING TO NOTHING?
HOW DO YOU GO FROM NOTHING...
...TO SOMETHING?

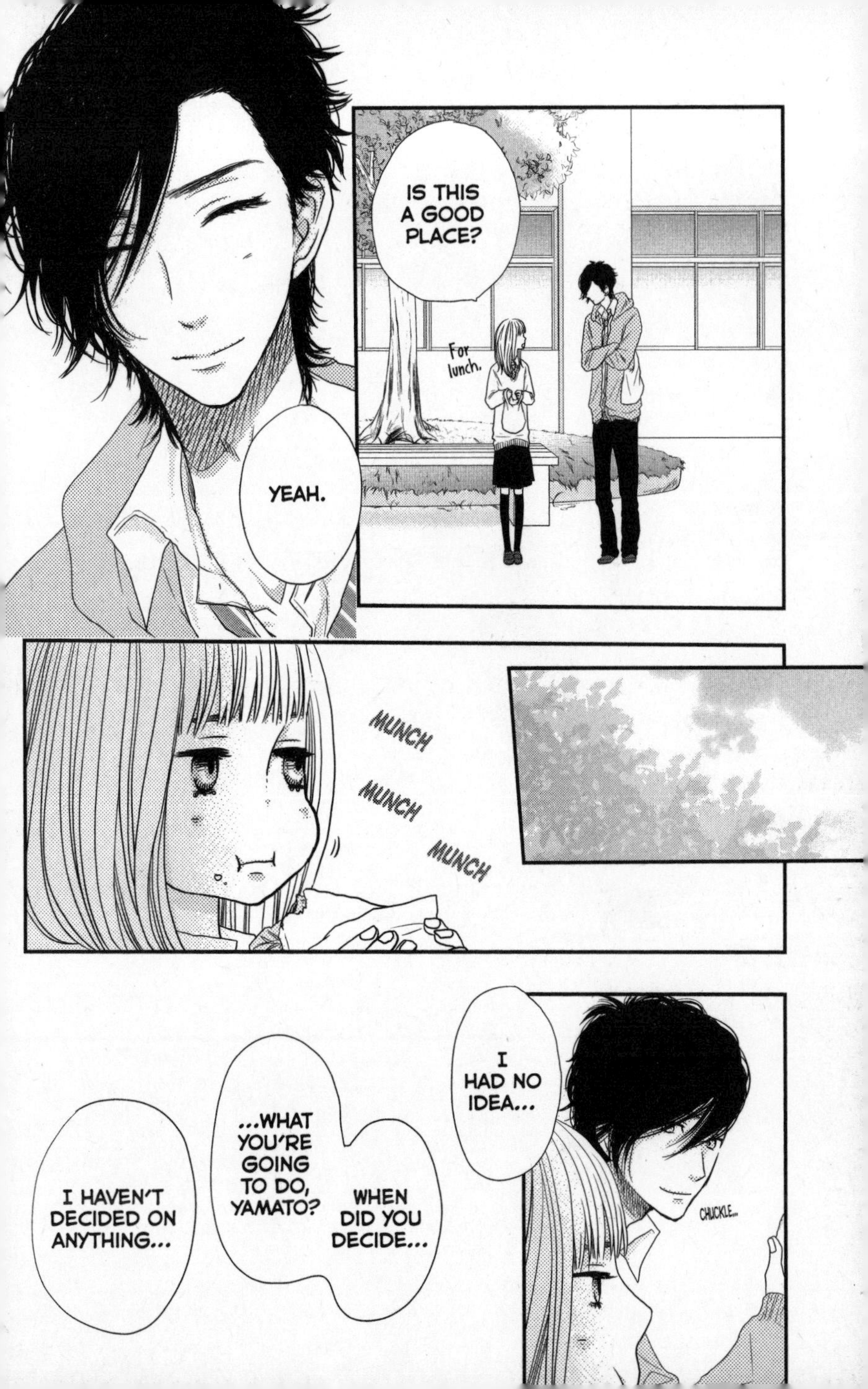
IS THIS A GOOD PLACE?
For lunch.
YEAH.
MUNCH
MUNCH
MUNCH
I HAD NO IDEA...
CHUCKLE...
WHEN DID YOU DECIDE...
...WHAT YOU'RE GOING TO DO, YAMATO?
I HAVEN'T DECIDED ON ANYTHING...

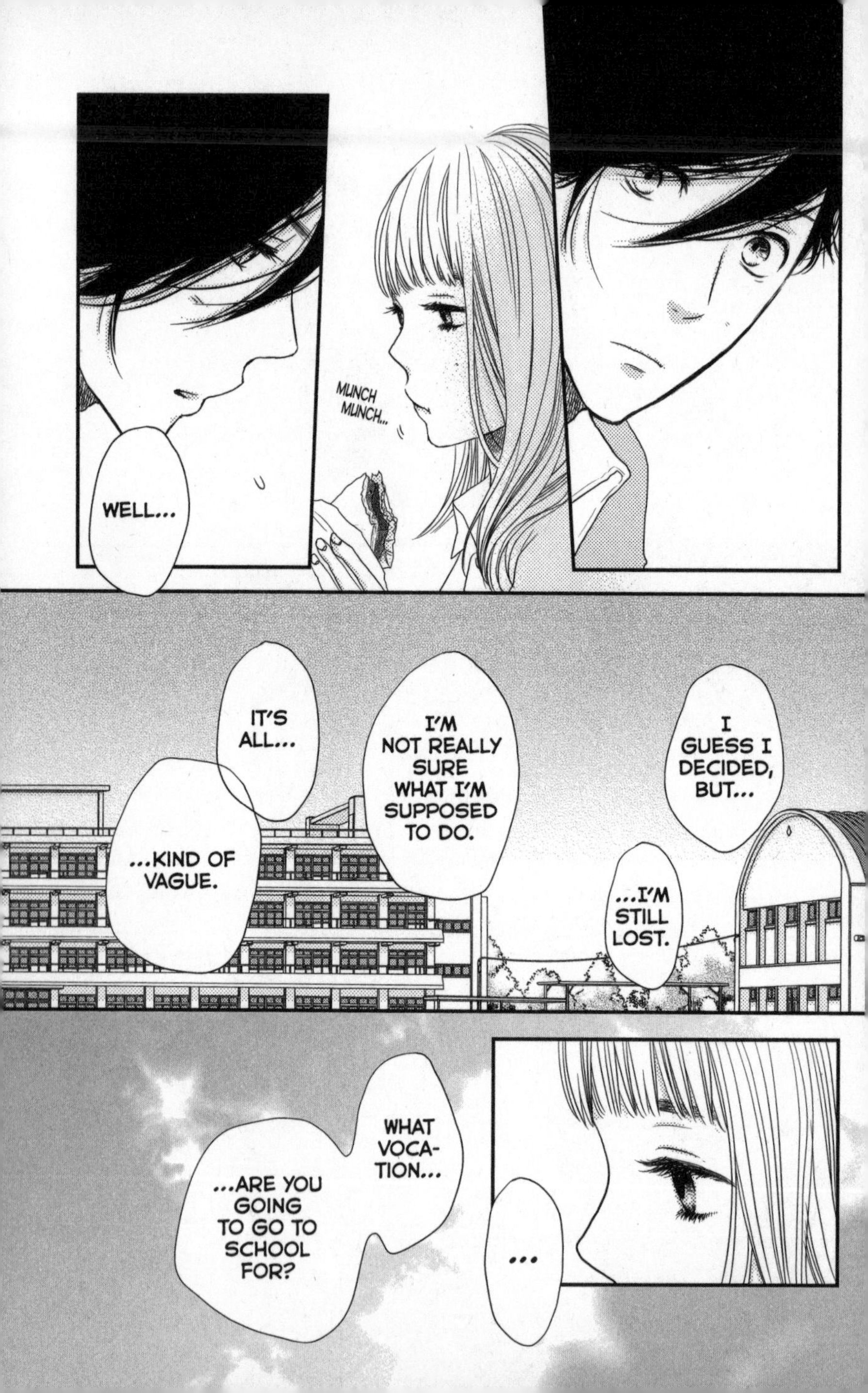
MUNCH MUNCH...
WELL...
I GUESS I DECIDED, BUT...
...I'M STILL LOST.
I'M NOT REALLY SURE WHAT I'M SUPPOSED TO DO.
IT'S ALL...
...KIND OF VAGUE.
...
WHAT VOCATION...
...ARE YOU GOING TO GO TO SCHOOL FOR?

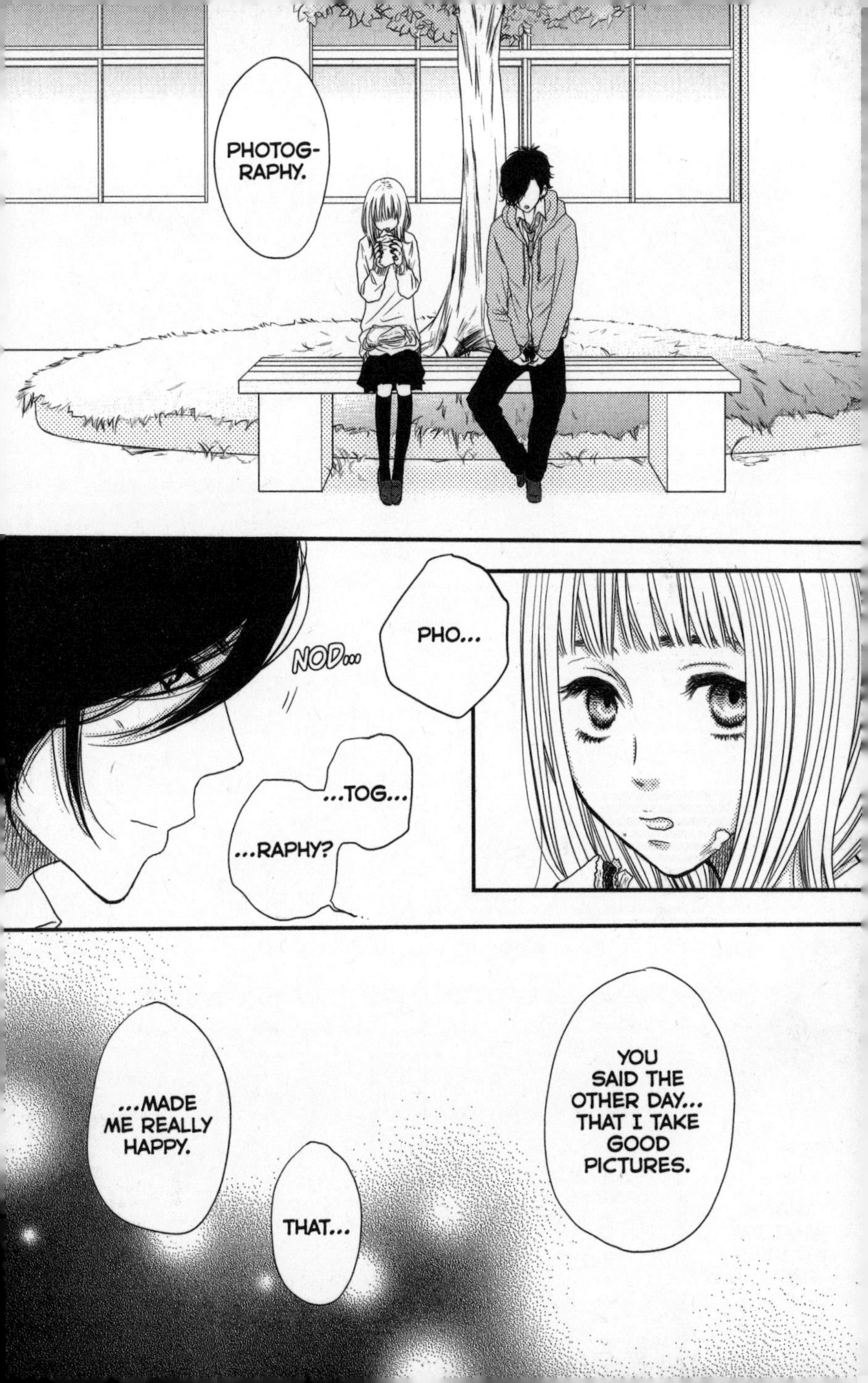
PHOTOG-RAPHY.
PHO...
NOD...
...TOG...
...RAPHY?
YOU SAID THE OTHER DAY... THAT I TAKE GOOD PICTURES.
THAT...
...MADE ME REALLY HAPPY.

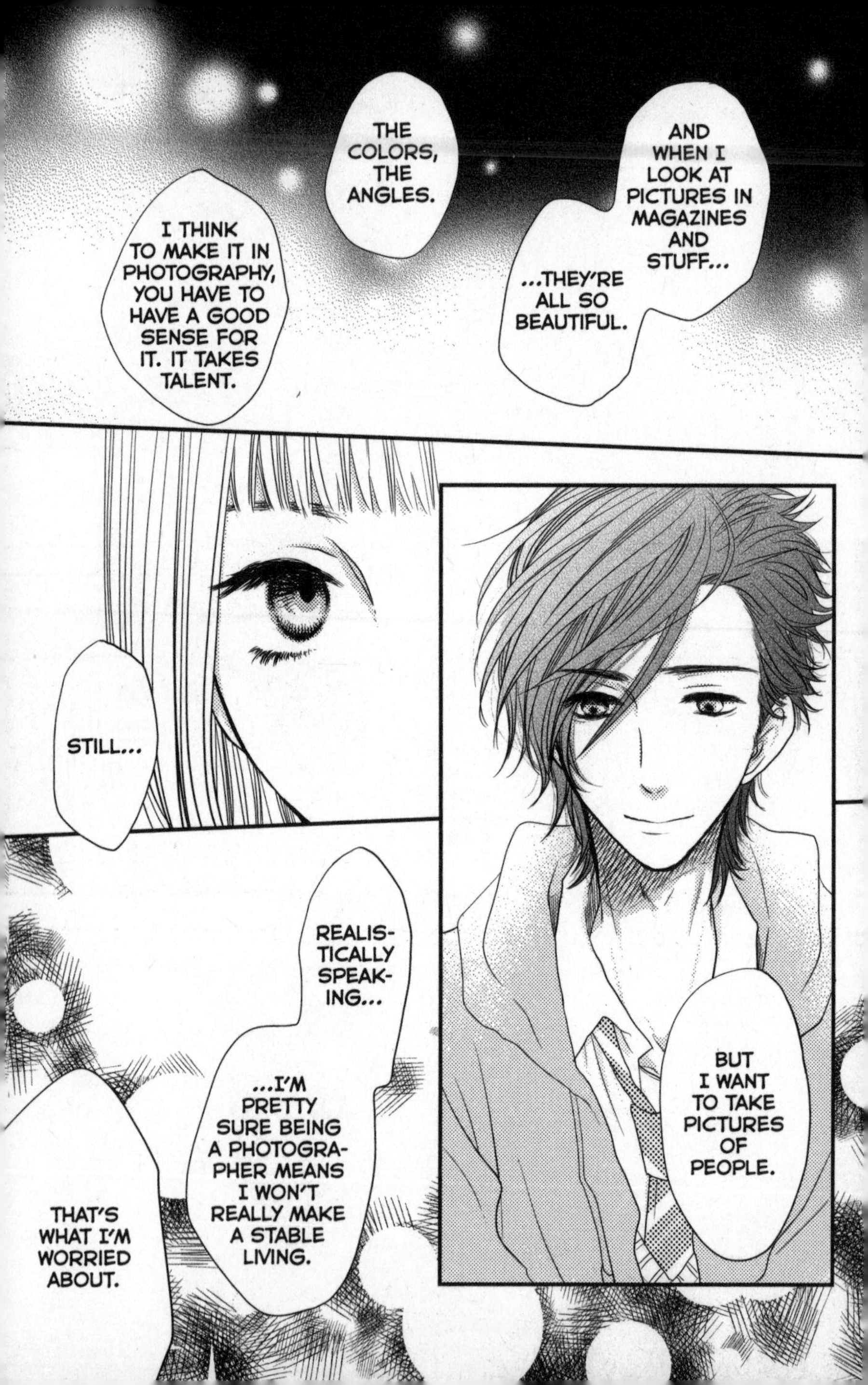
AND WHEN I LOOK AT PICTURES IN MAGAZINES AND STUFF...
...THEY'RE ALL SO BEAUTIFUL.
THE COLORS, THE ANGLES.
I THINK TO MAKE IT IN PHOTOGRAPHY, YOU HAVE TO HAVE A GOOD SENSE FOR IT. IT TAKES TALENT.
BUT I WANT TO TAKE PICTURES OF PEOPLE.
STILL...
REALIS-TICALLY SPEAK-ING...
...I'M PRETTY SURE BEING A PHOTOGRA-PHER MEANS I WON'T REALLY MAKE A STABLE LIVING.
THAT'S WHAT I'M WORRIED ABOUT.

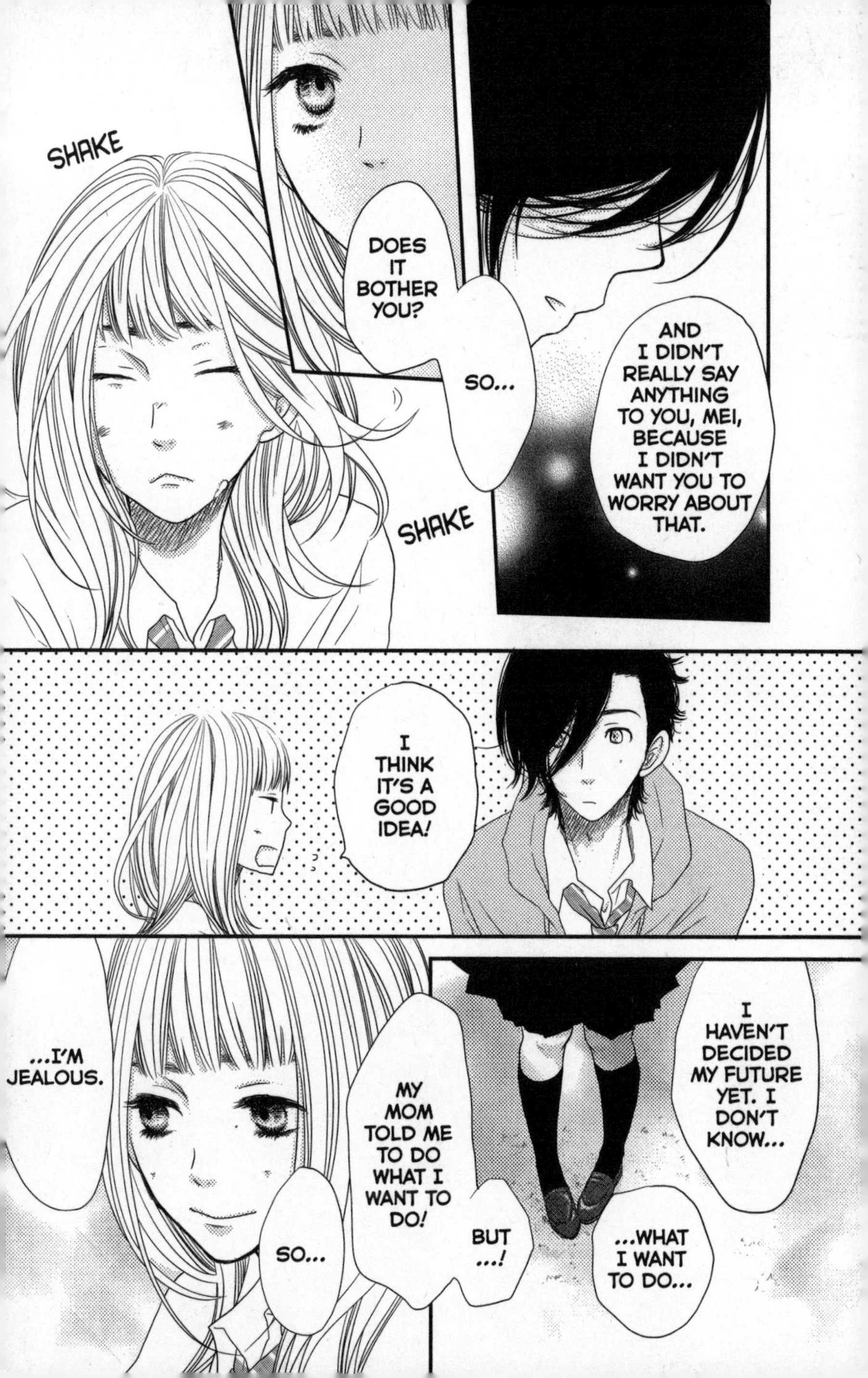
AND I DIDN'T REALLY SAY ANYTHING TO YOU, MEI, BECAUSE I DIDN'T WANT YOU TO WORRY ABOUT THAT.
SO...
DOES IT BOTHER YOU?
SHAKE
SHAKE
I THINK IT'S A GOOD IDEA!
I HAVEN'T DECIDED MY FUTURE YET. I DON'T KNOW...
...WHAT I WANT TO DO...
MY MOM TOLD ME TO DO WHAT I WANT TO DO!
BUT ...!
SO...
...I'M JEALOUS.

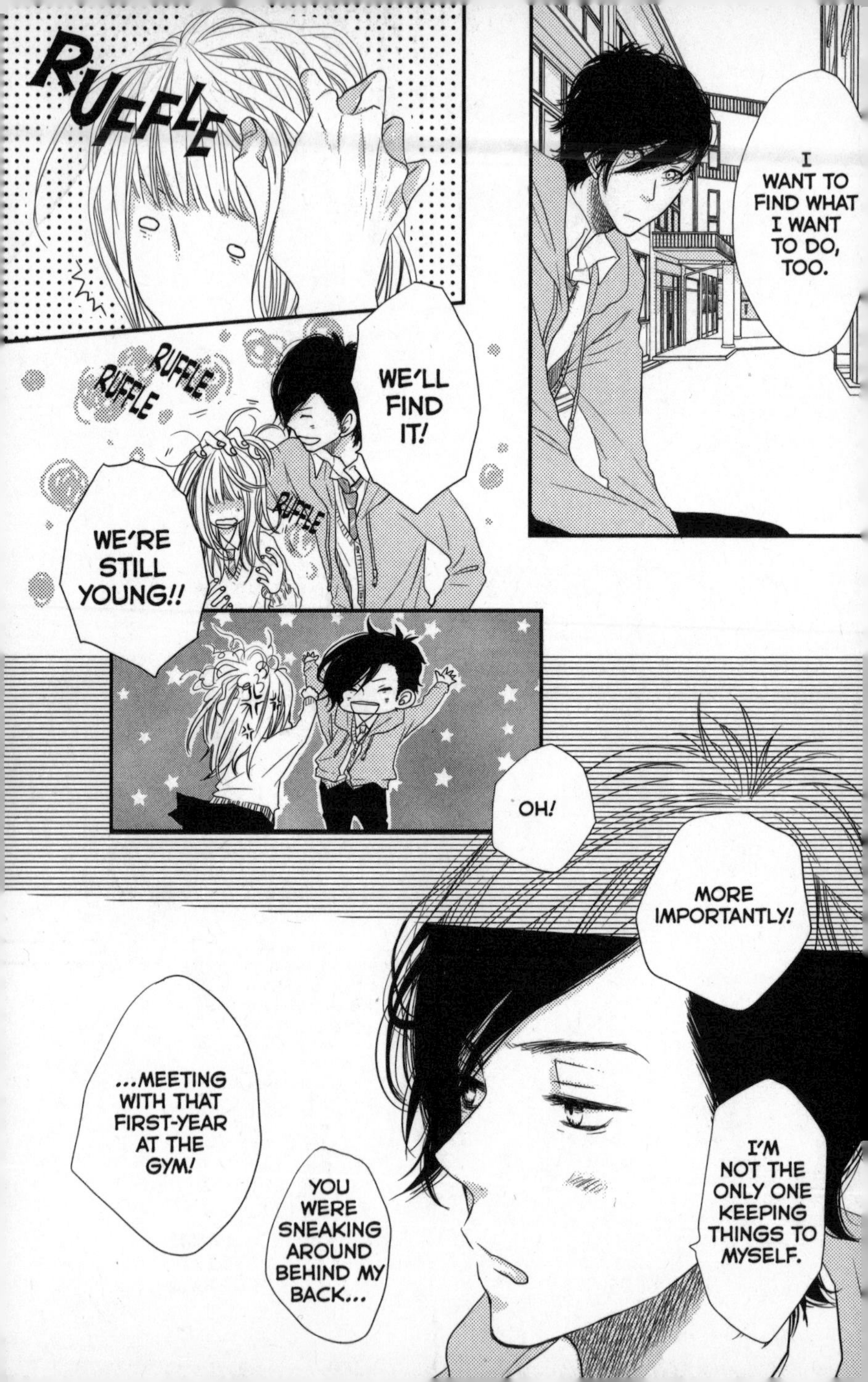
I WANT TO FIND WHAT I WANT TO DO, TOO.
RUFFLE
WE'LL FIND IT!
RUFFLE RUFFLE
RUFFLE
WE'RE STILL YOUNG!!
OH!
MORE IMPORTANTLY!
YOU WERE SNEAKING AROUND BEHIND MY BACK...
...MEETING WITH THAT FIRST-YEAR AT THE GYM!
I'M NOT THE ONLY ONE KEEPING THINGS TO MYSELF.

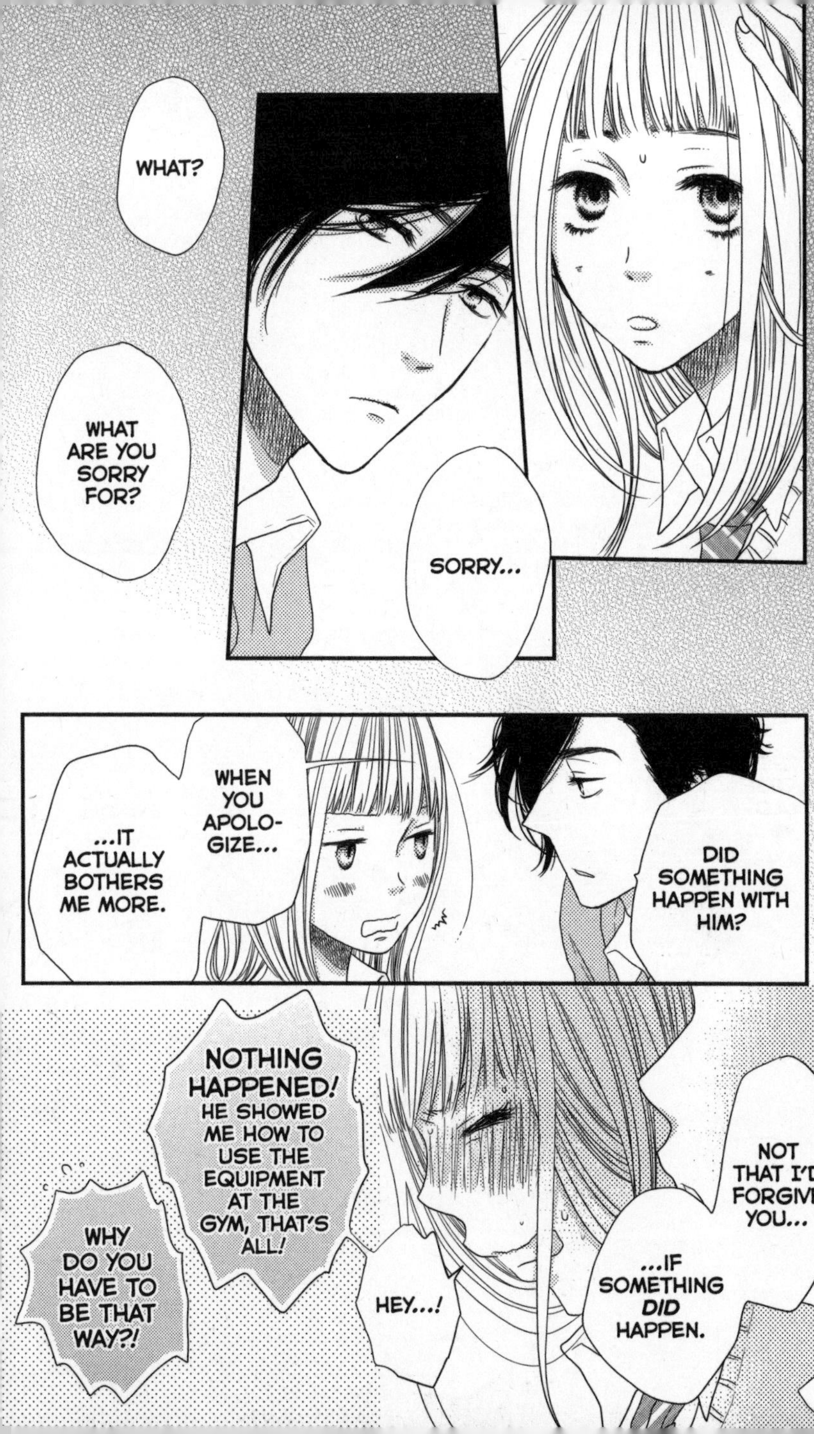
SORRY...
WHAT?
WHAT ARE YOU SORRY FOR?
DID SOMETHING HAPPEN WITH HIM?
WHEN YOU APOLOGIZE...
...IT ACTUALLY BOTHERS ME MORE.
NOT THAT I'D FORGIVE YOU...
...IF SOMETHING *DID* HAPPEN.
HEY...!
NOTHING HAPPENED! HE SHOWED ME HOW TO USE THE EQUIPMENT AT THE GYM, THAT'S ALL!
WHY DO YOU HAVE TO BE THAT WAY?!

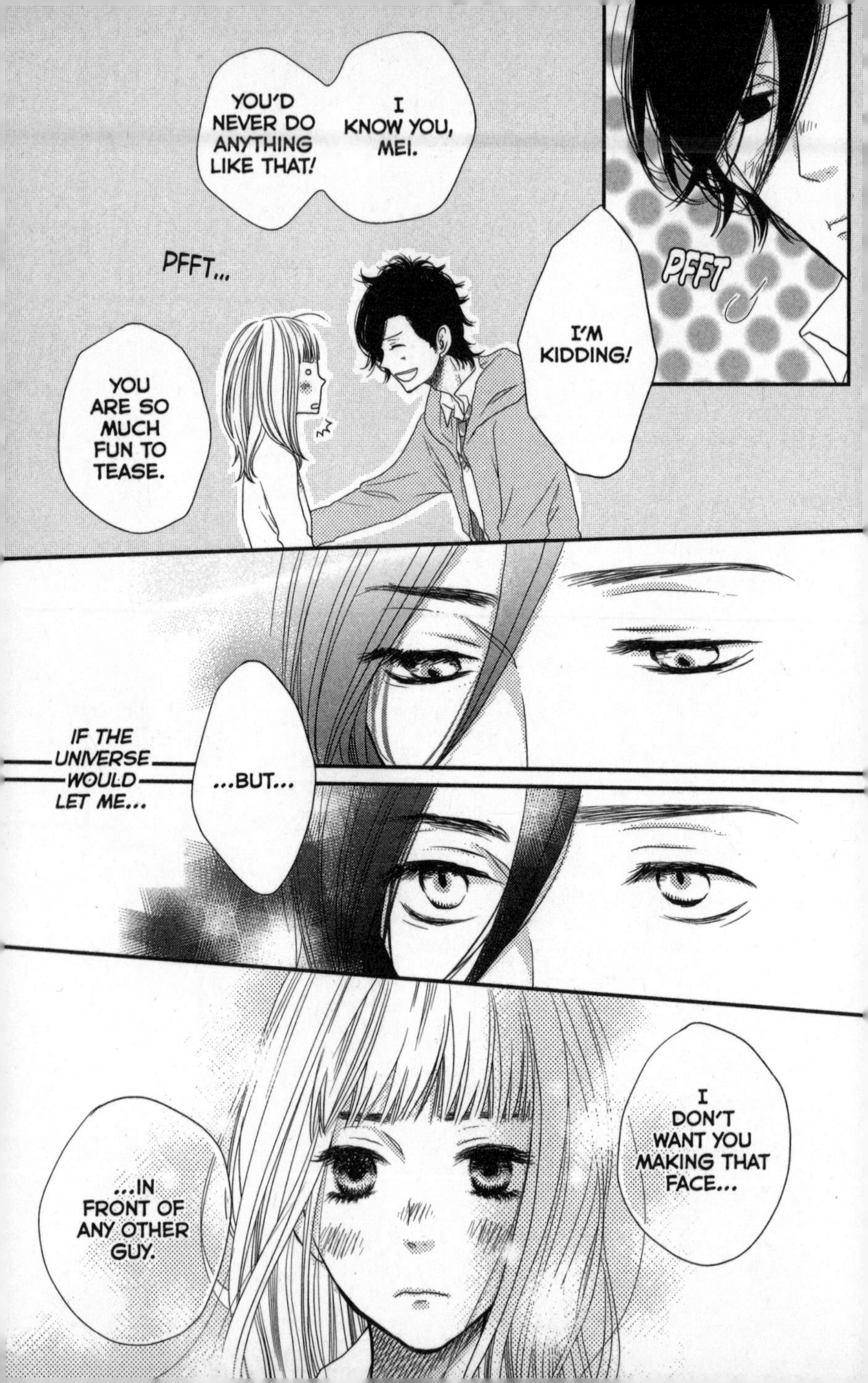
PFFT
I'M KIDDING!
I KNOW YOU, MEI.
YOU'D NEVER DO ANYTHING LIKE THAT!
PFFT...
YOU ARE SO MUCH FUN TO TEASE.
...BUT...
IF THE UNIVERSE WOULD LET ME...
I DON'T WANT YOU MAKING THAT FACE...
...IN FRONT OF ANY OTHER GUY.

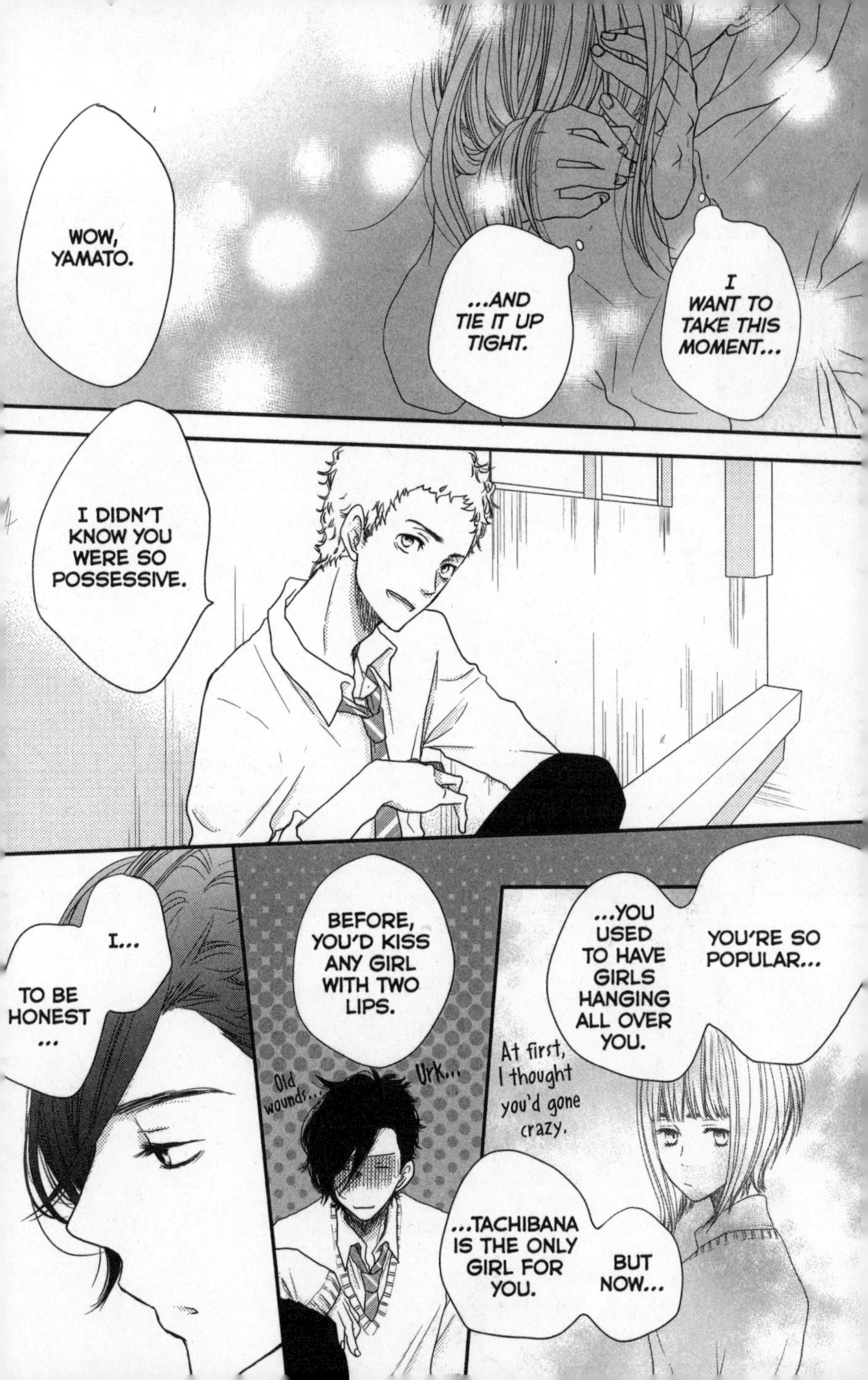
I WANT TO TAKE THIS MOMENT...
...AND TIE IT UP TIGHT.
WOW, YAMATO.
I DIDN'T KNOW YOU WERE SO POSSESSIVE.
YOU'RE SO POPULAR...
...YOU USED TO HAVE GIRLS HANGING ALL OVER YOU.
At first, I thought you'd gone crazy.
BUT NOW...
...TACHIBANA IS THE ONLY GIRL FOR YOU.
BEFORE, YOU'D KISS ANY GIRL WITH TWO LIPS.
Urk...
Old wounds...
I...
TO BE HONEST ...

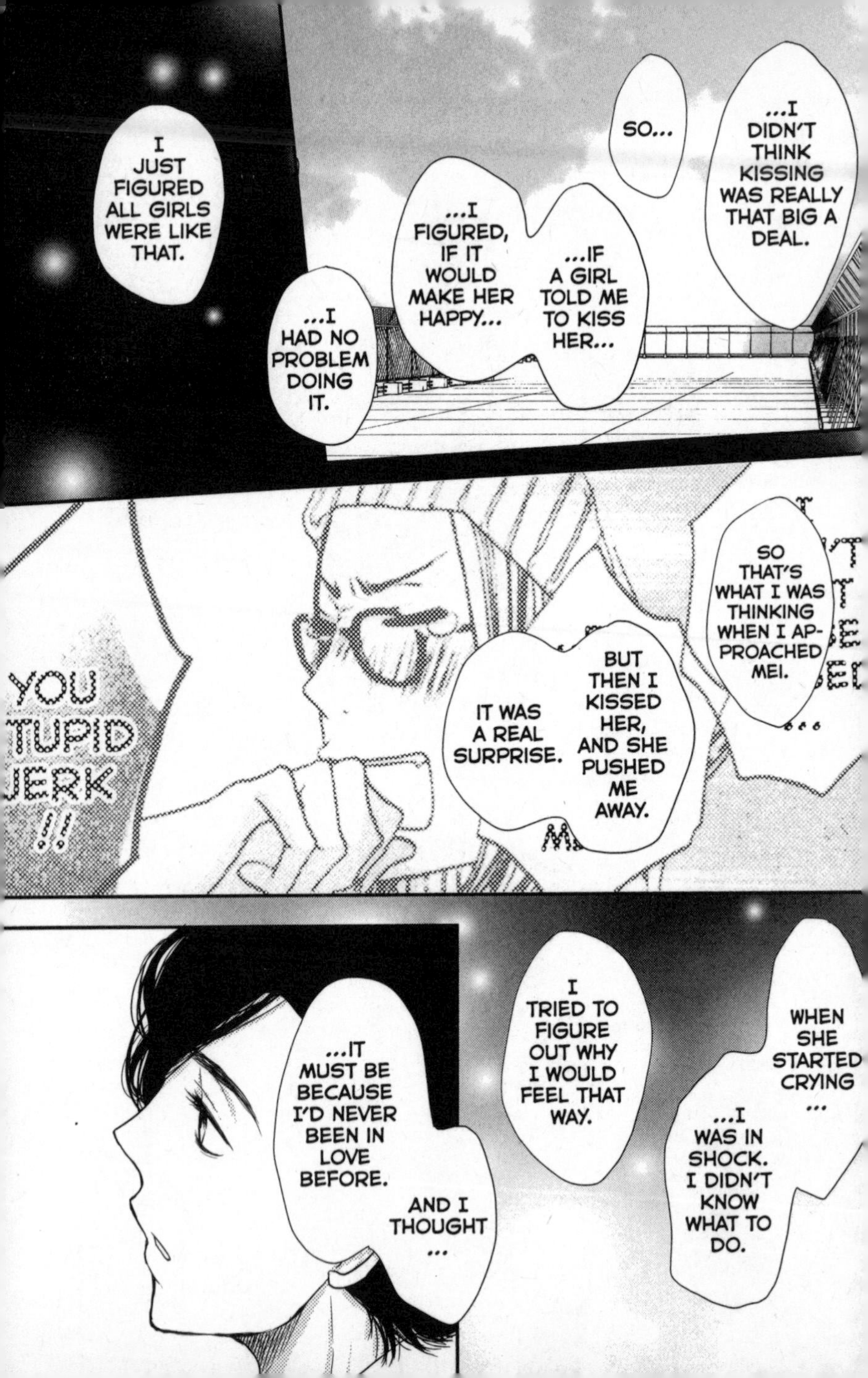
...I DIDN'T THINK KISSING WAS REALLY THAT BIG A DEAL.
SO...
...IF A GIRL TOLD ME TO KISS HER...
...I FIGURED, IF IT WOULD MAKE HER HAPPY...
...I HAD NO PROBLEM DOING IT.
I JUST FIGURED ALL GIRLS WERE LIKE THAT.
SO THAT'S WHAT I WAS THINKING WHEN I AP-PROACHED MEI.
BUT THEN I KISSED HER, AND SHE PUSHED ME AWAY.
IT WAS A REAL SURPRISE.
YOU TUPID JERK !!
WHEN SHE STARTED CRYING...
...I WAS IN SHOCK. I DIDN'T KNOW WHAT TO DO.
I TRIED TO FIGURE OUT WHY I WOULD FEEL THAT WAY.
...IT MUST BE BECAUSE I'D NEVER BEEN IN LOVE BEFORE.
AND I THOUGHT...

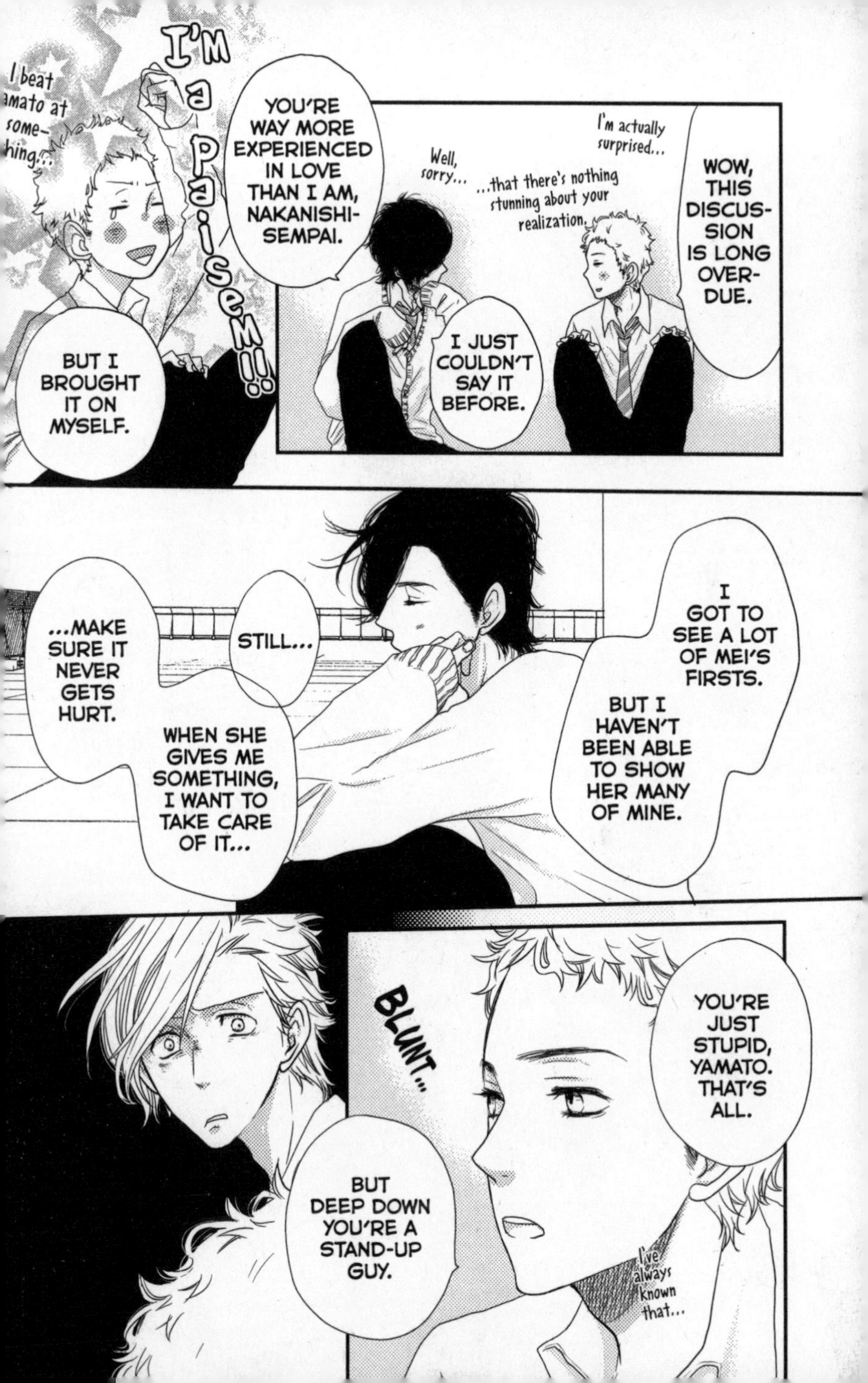
WOW, THIS DISCUSSION IS LONG OVERDUE.
I'm actually surprised...
...that there's nothing stunning about your realization.
Well, sorry...
I JUST COULDN'T SAY IT BEFORE.
YOU'RE WAY MORE EXPERIENCED IN LOVE THAN I AM, NAKANISHI-SEMPAI.
I'M a paisem!!
I beat amato at some-thing...
BUT I BROUGHT IT ON MYSELF.
I GOT TO SEE A LOT OF MEI'S FIRSTS.
BUT I HAVEN'T BEEN ABLE TO SHOW HER MANY OF MINE.
STILL...
WHEN SHE GIVES ME SOMETHING, I WANT TO TAKE CARE OF IT...
...MAKE SURE IT NEVER GETS HURT.
YOU'RE JUST STUPID, YAMATO. THAT'S ALL.
BLUNT...
BUT DEEP DOWN YOU'RE A STAND-UP GUY.
I've always known that...

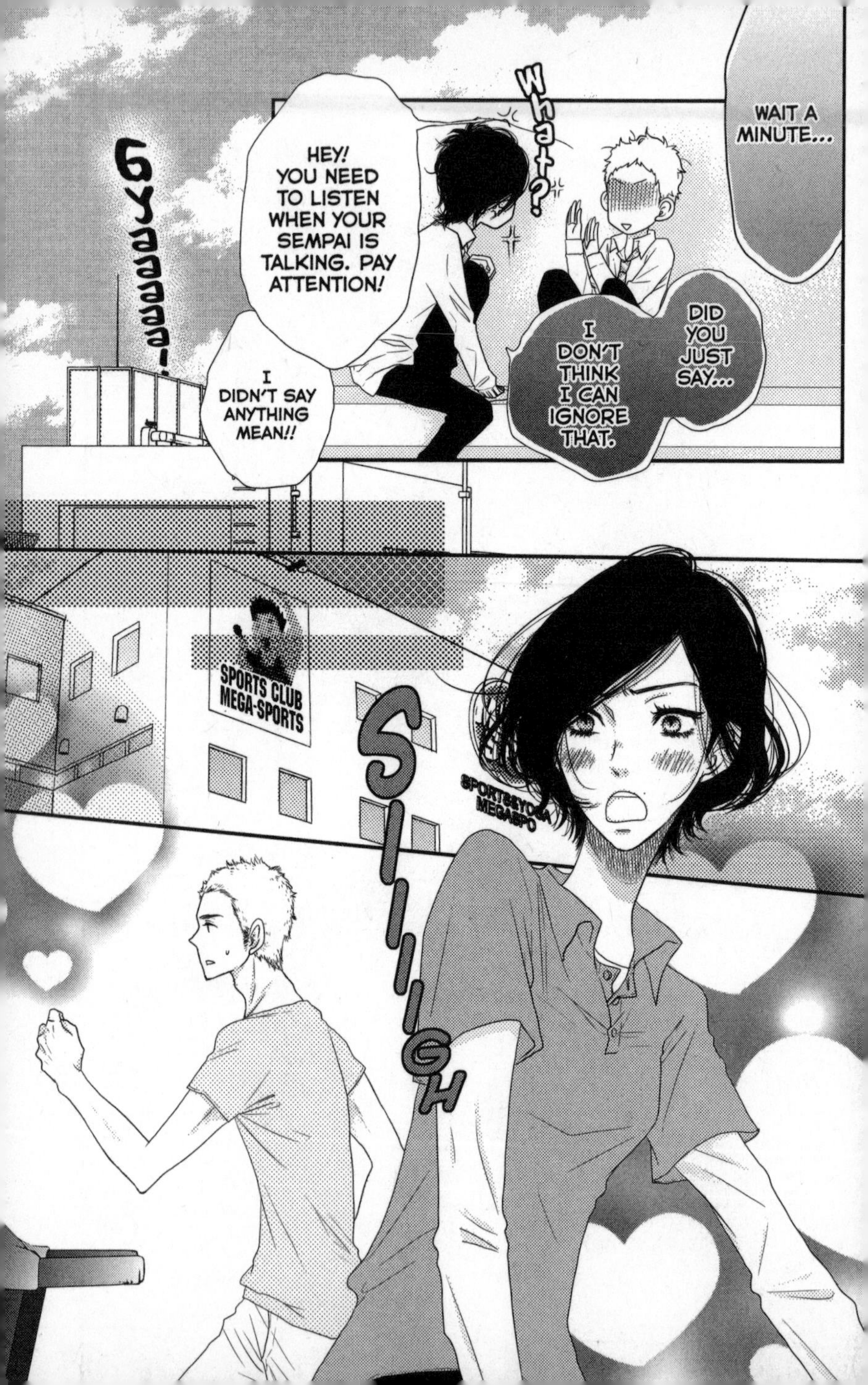
WAIT A MINUTE...
DID YOU JUST SAY...
I DON'T THINK I CAN IGNORE THAT.
What?
HEY! YOU NEED TO LISTEN WHEN YOUR SEMPAI IS TALKING. PAY ATTENTION!
I DIDN'T SAY ANYTHING MEAN!!
Gyaaaaaa!
SPORTS CLUB MEGA-SPORTS
SPORTS&YOGA MEGASPO
SIIIIGH

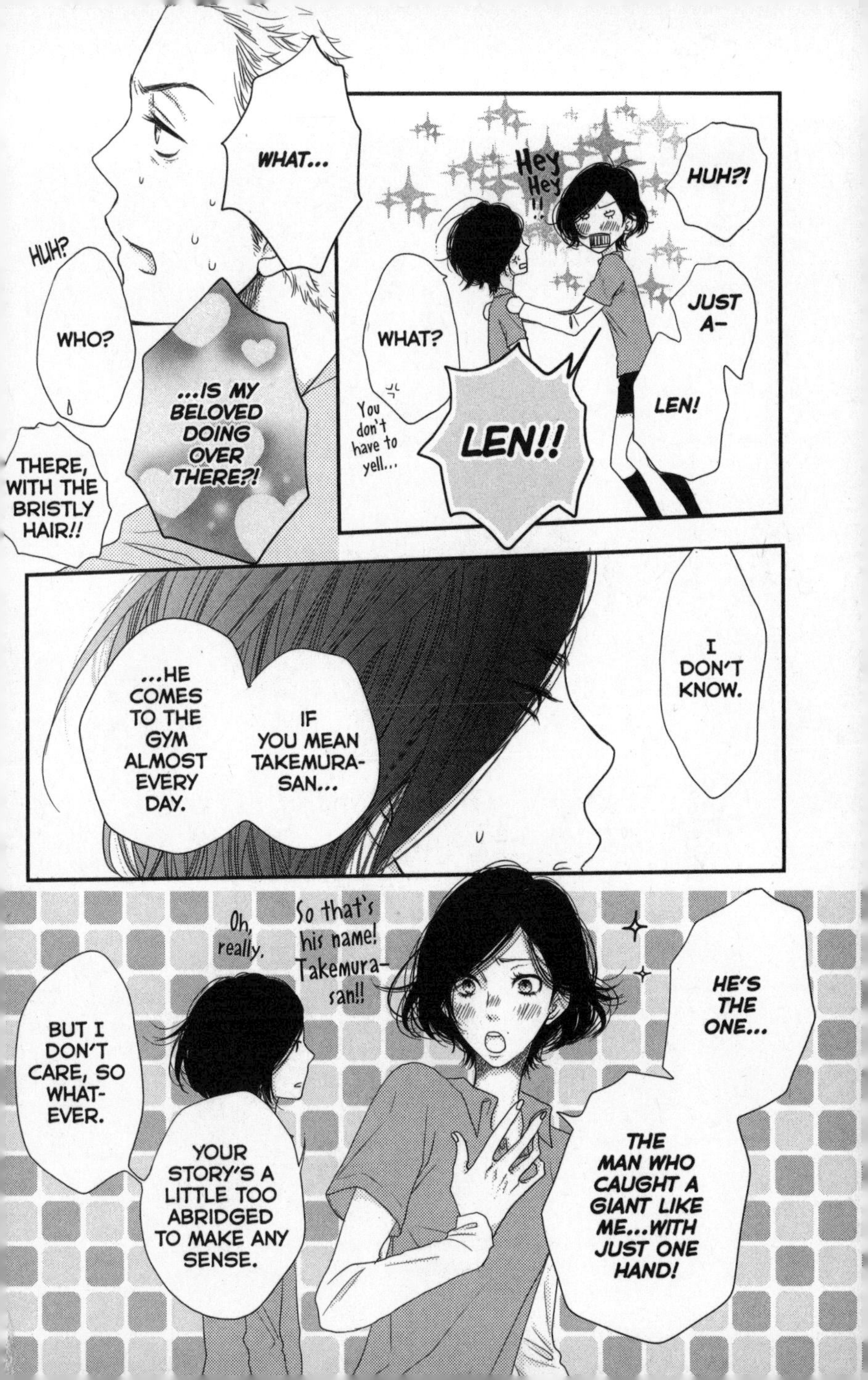
HUH?!
JUST A—
LEN!
Hey Hey !!
LEN!!
WHAT?
You don't have to yell...
WHAT...
...IS MY BELOVED DOING OVER THERE?!
HUH?
WHO?
THERE, WITH THE BRISTLY HAIR!!
I DON'T KNOW.
IF YOU MEAN TAKEMURA-SAN...
...HE COMES TO THE GYM ALMOST EVERY DAY.
HE'S THE ONE...
THE MAN WHO CAUGHT A GIANT LIKE ME...WITH JUST ONE HAND!
So that's his name! Takemura-san!!
Oh, really.
BUT I DON'T CARE, SO WHAT-EVER.
YOUR STORY'S A LITTLE TOO ABRIDGED TO MAKE ANY SENSE.

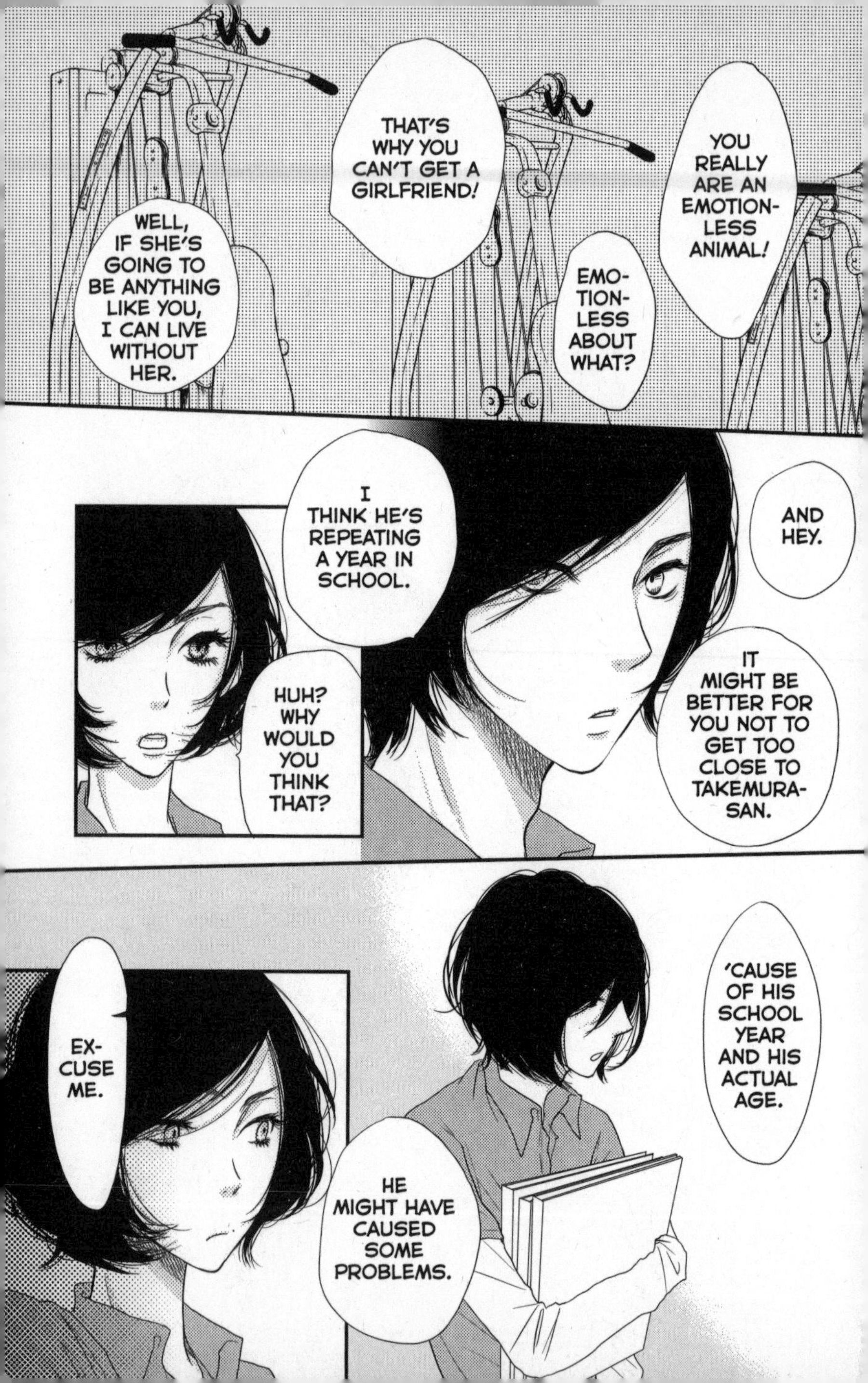
YOU REALLY ARE AN EMOTIONLESS ANIMAL!
EMOTIONLESS ABOUT WHAT?
THAT'S WHY YOU CAN'T GET A GIRLFRIEND!
WELL, IF SHE'S GOING TO BE ANYTHING LIKE YOU, I CAN LIVE WITHOUT HER.
AND HEY.
IT MIGHT BE BETTER FOR YOU NOT TO GET TOO CLOSE TO TAKEMURA-SAN.
HUH? WHY WOULD YOU THINK THAT?
I THINK HE'S REPEATING A YEAR IN SCHOOL.
'CAUSE OF HIS SCHOOL YEAR AND HIS ACTUAL AGE.
HE MIGHT HAVE CAUSED SOME PROBLEMS.
EXCUSE ME.

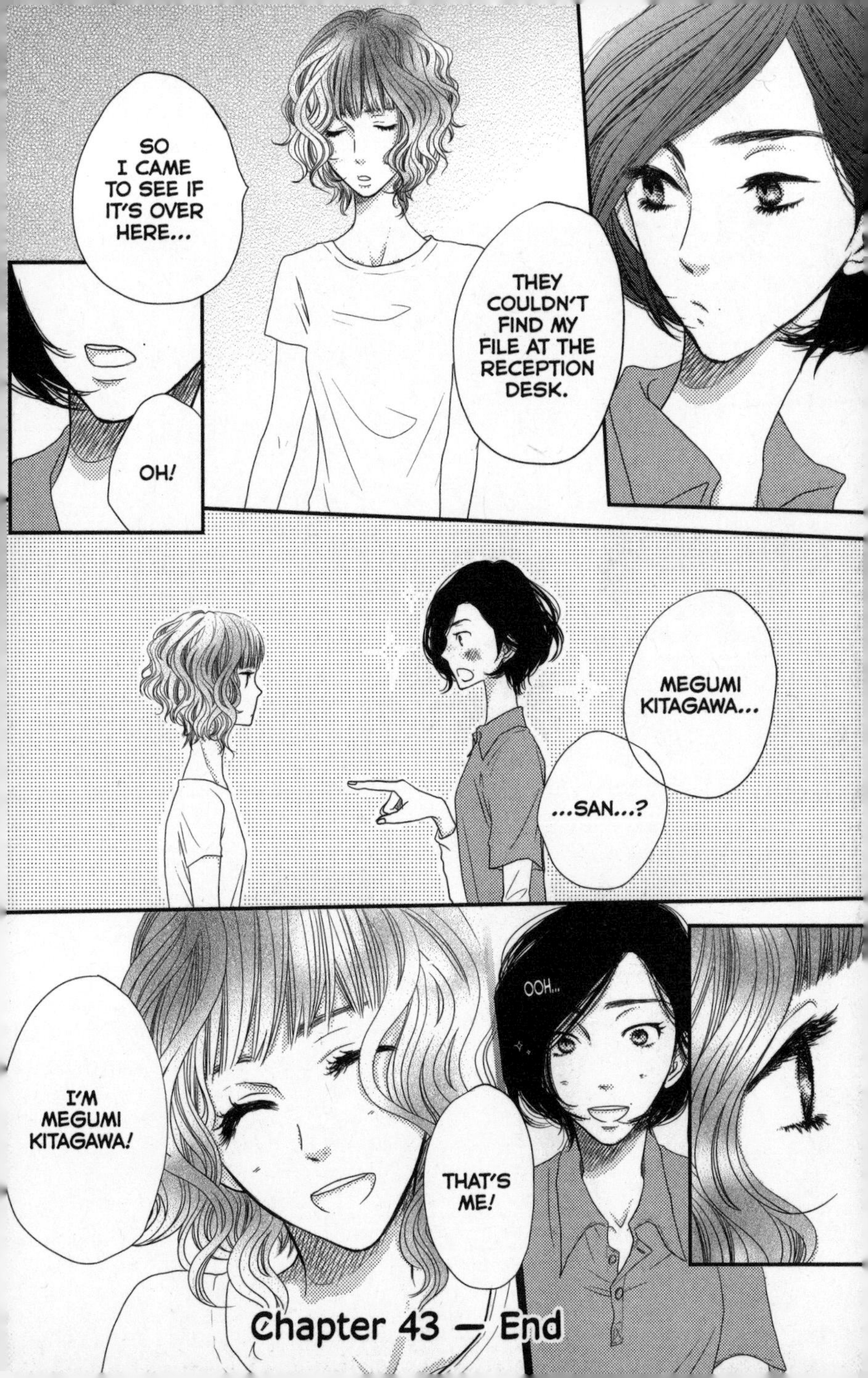
THEY COULDN'T FIND MY FILE AT THE RECEPTION DESK.
SO I CAME TO SEE IF IT'S OVER HERE...
OH!
MEGUMI KITAGAWA...
...SAN...?
OOH...
I'M MEGUMI KITAGAWA!
THAT'S ME!
Chapter 43 — End

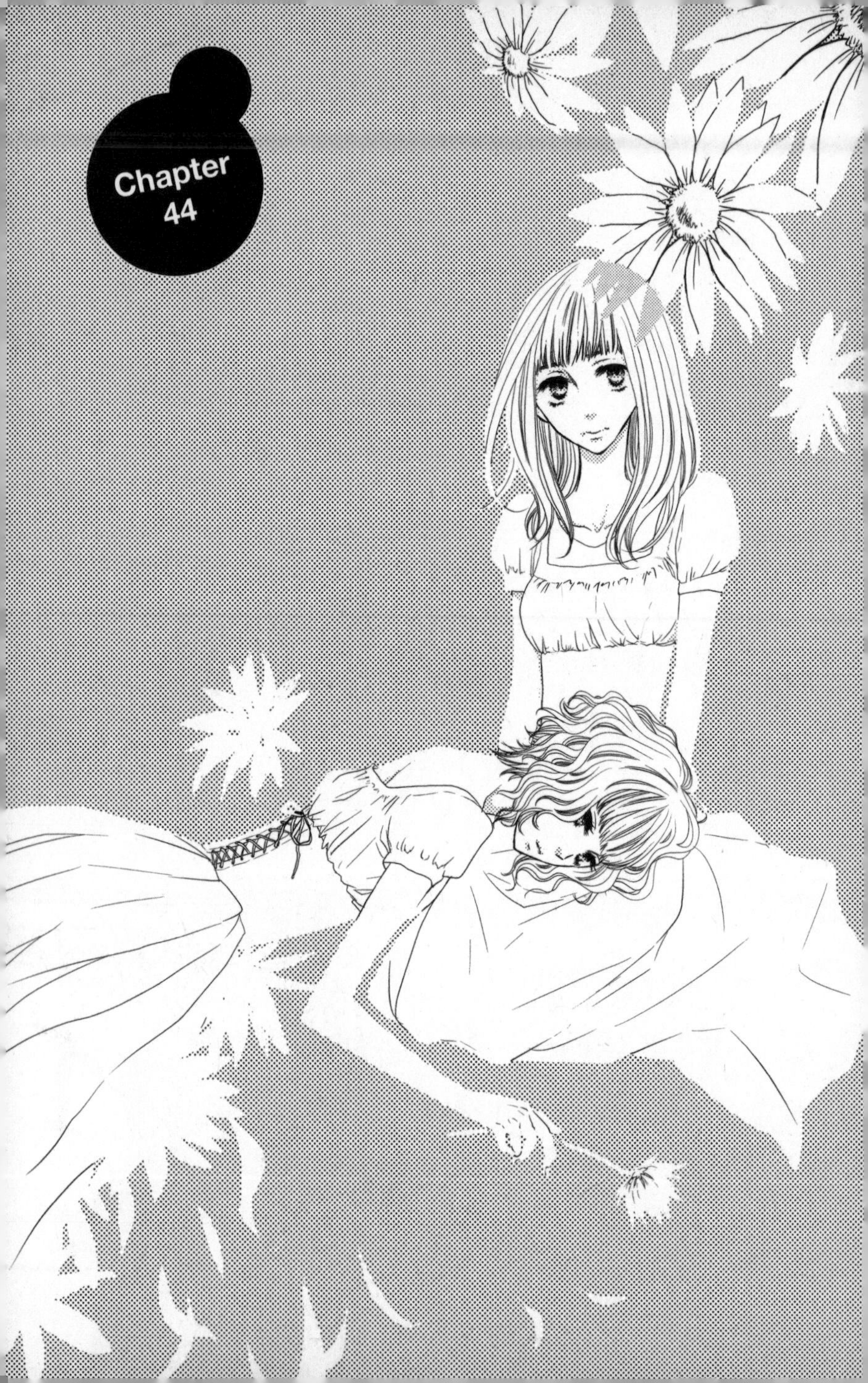
Chapter
44

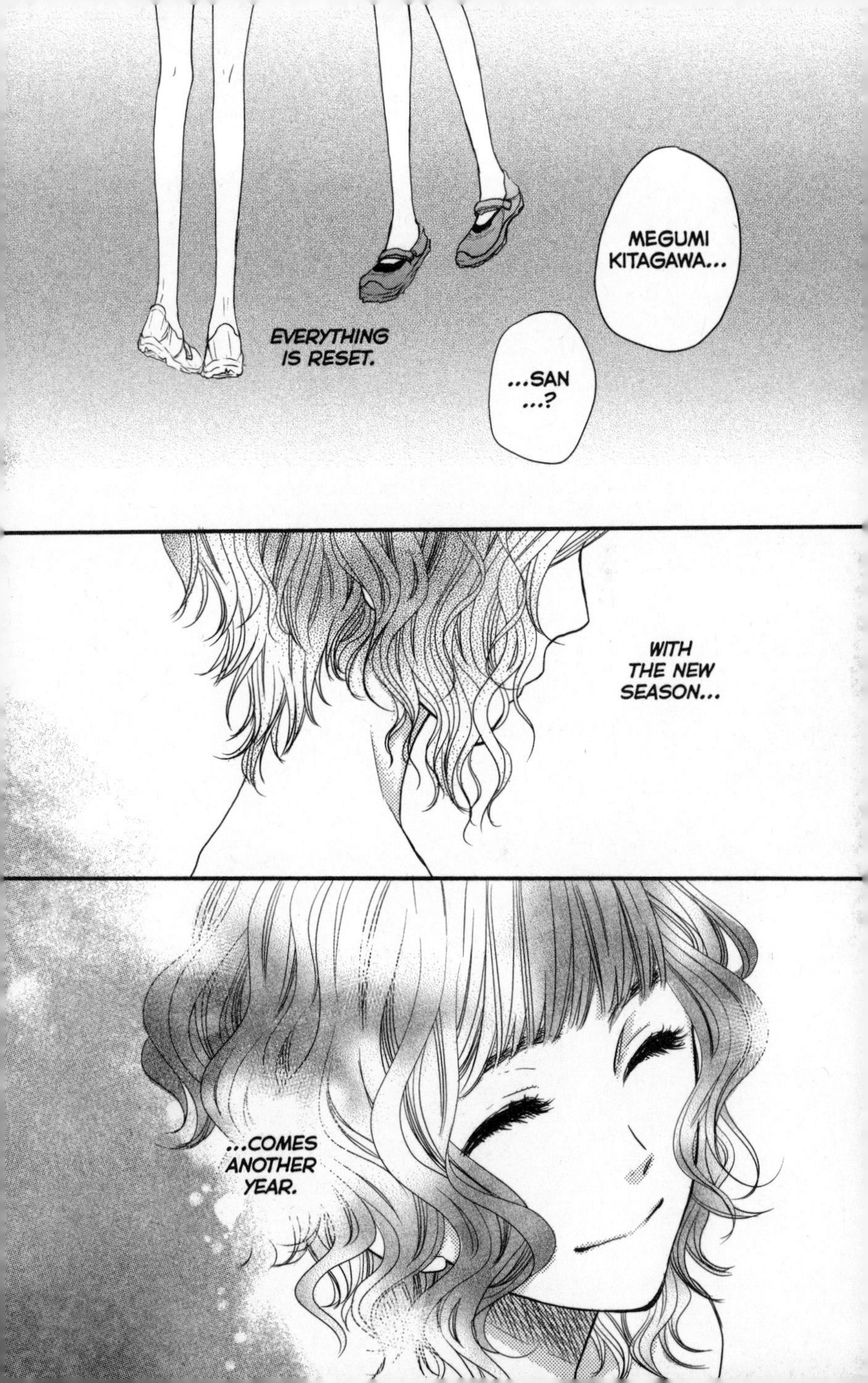
MEGUMI KITAGAWA...
...SAN ...?
EVERYTHING IS RESET.
WITH THE NEW SEASON...
...COMES ANOTHER YEAR.

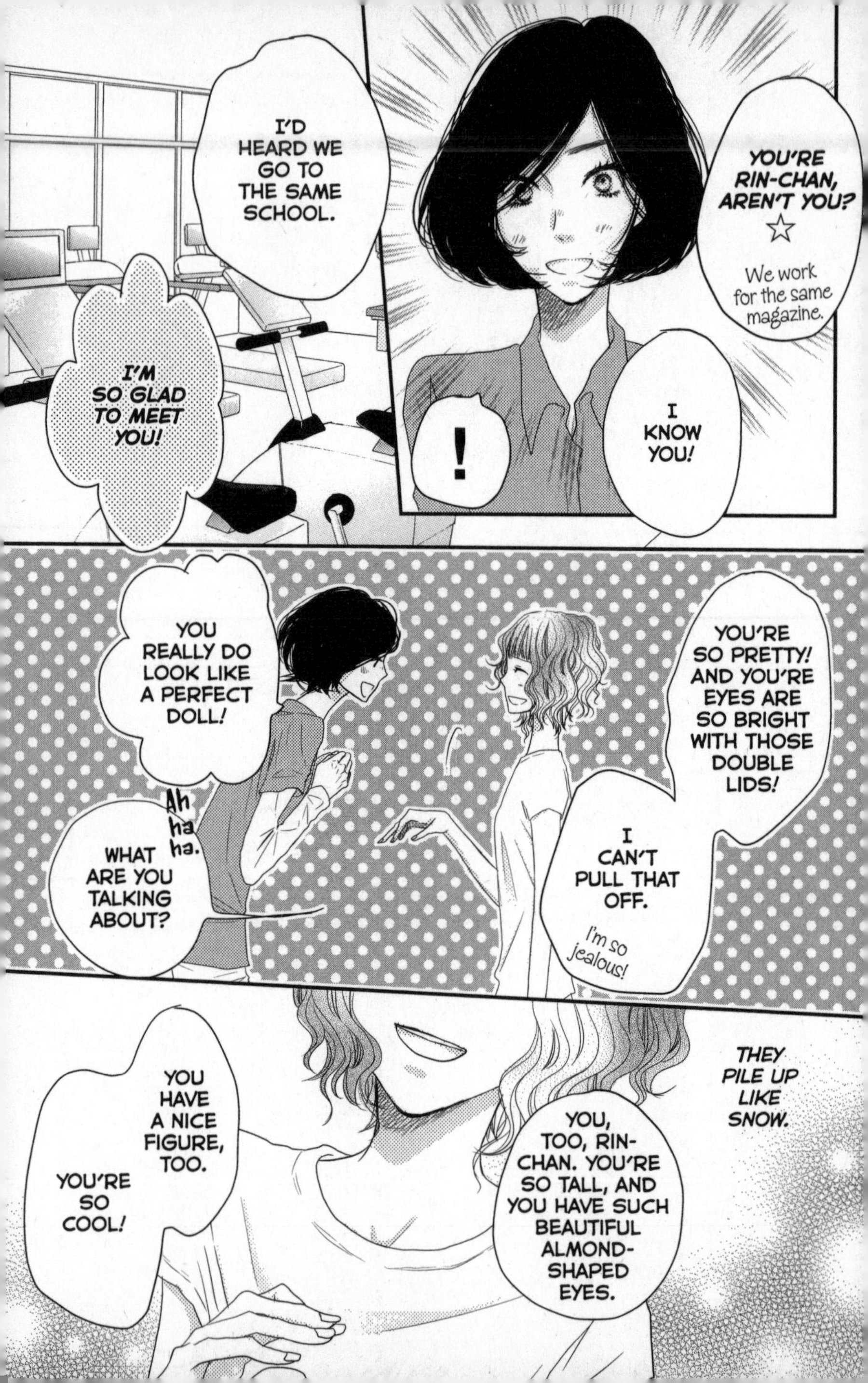
YOU'RE RIN-CHAN, AREN'T YOU? ☆
We work for the same magazine.
I KNOW YOU!
!
I'D HEARD WE GO TO THE SAME SCHOOL.
I'M SO GLAD TO MEET YOU!
YOU'RE SO PRETTY! AND YOU'RE EYES ARE SO BRIGHT WITH THOSE DOUBLE LIDS!
I CAN'T PULL THAT OFF.
I'm so jealous!
YOU REALLY DO LOOK LIKE A PERFECT DOLL!
Ah ha ha.
WHAT ARE YOU TALKING ABOUT?
THEY PILE UP LIKE SNOW.
YOU, TOO, RIN-CHAN. YOU'RE SO TALL, AND YOU HAVE SUCH BEAUTIFUL ALMOND-SHAPED EYES.
YOU HAVE A NICE FIGURE, TOO.
YOU'RE SO COOL!

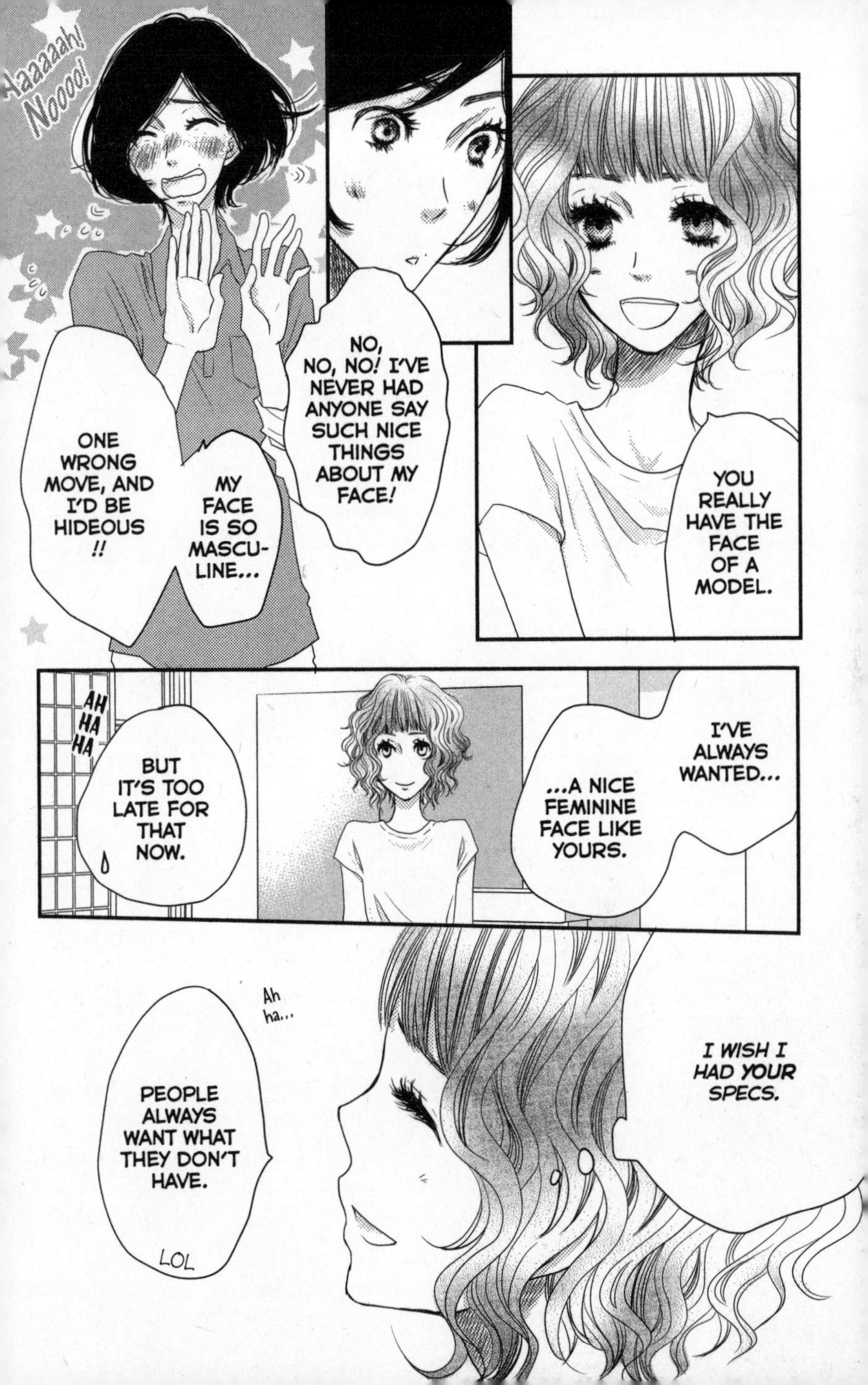
YOU REALLY HAVE THE FACE OF A MODEL.
NO, NO, NO! I'VE NEVER HAD ANYONE SAY SUCH NICE THINGS ABOUT MY FACE!
Haaaaah! Noooo!
MY FACE IS SO MASCU-LINE...
ONE WRONG MOVE, AND I'D BE HIDEOUS !!
I'VE ALWAYS WANTED...
...A NICE FEMININE FACE LIKE YOURS.
AH HA HA
BUT IT'S TOO LATE FOR THAT NOW.
I WISH I HAD YOUR SPECS.
Ah ha...
PEOPLE ALWAYS WANT WHAT THEY DON'T HAVE.
LOL

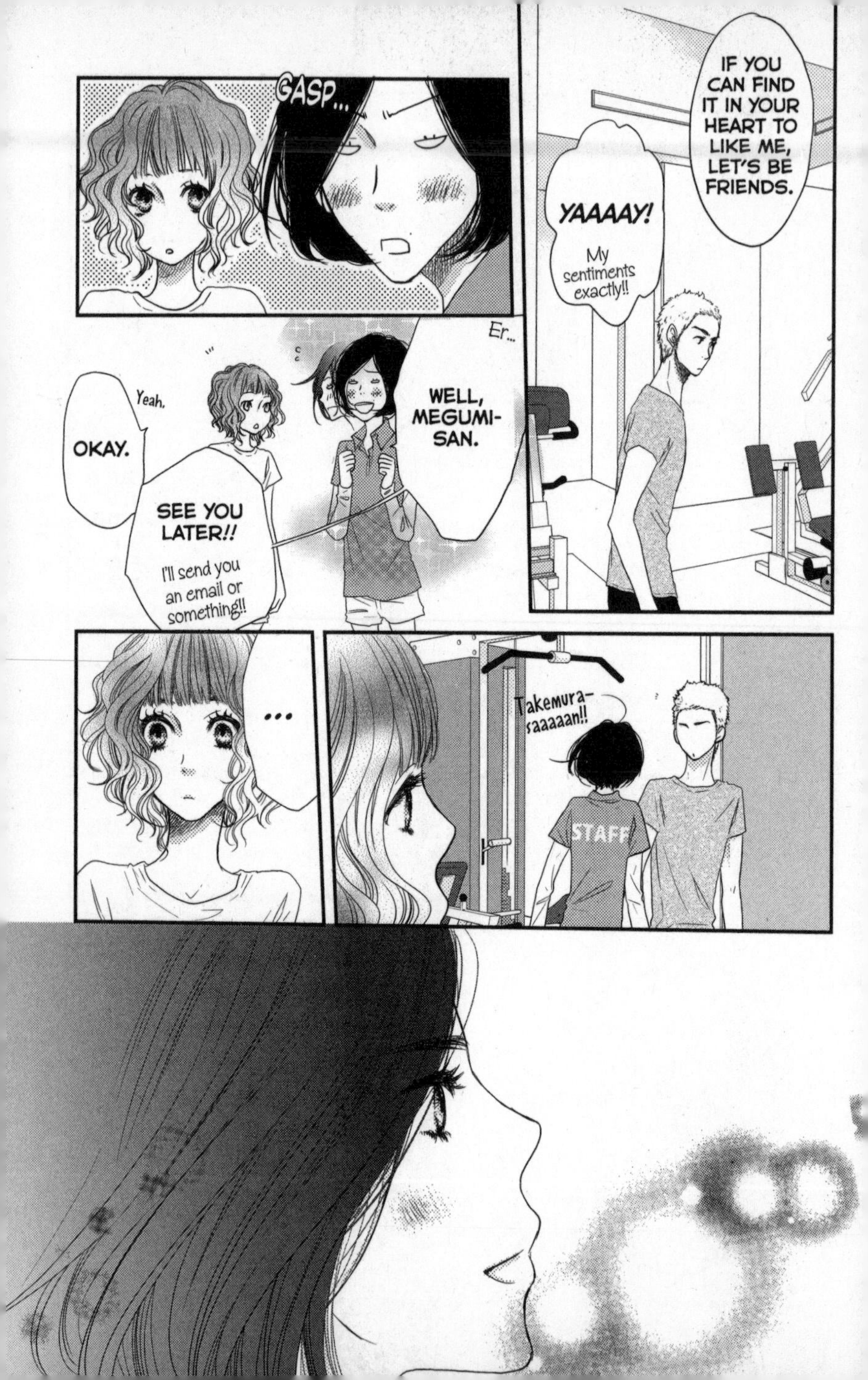
IF YOU CAN FIND IT IN YOUR HEART TO LIKE ME, LET'S BE FRIENDS.
YAAAAY!
My sentiments exactly!!
GASP...
Er...
WELL, MEGUMI-SAN.
Yeah.
OKAY.
SEE YOU LATER!!
I'll send you an email or something!!
Takemura-saaaaan!!
...

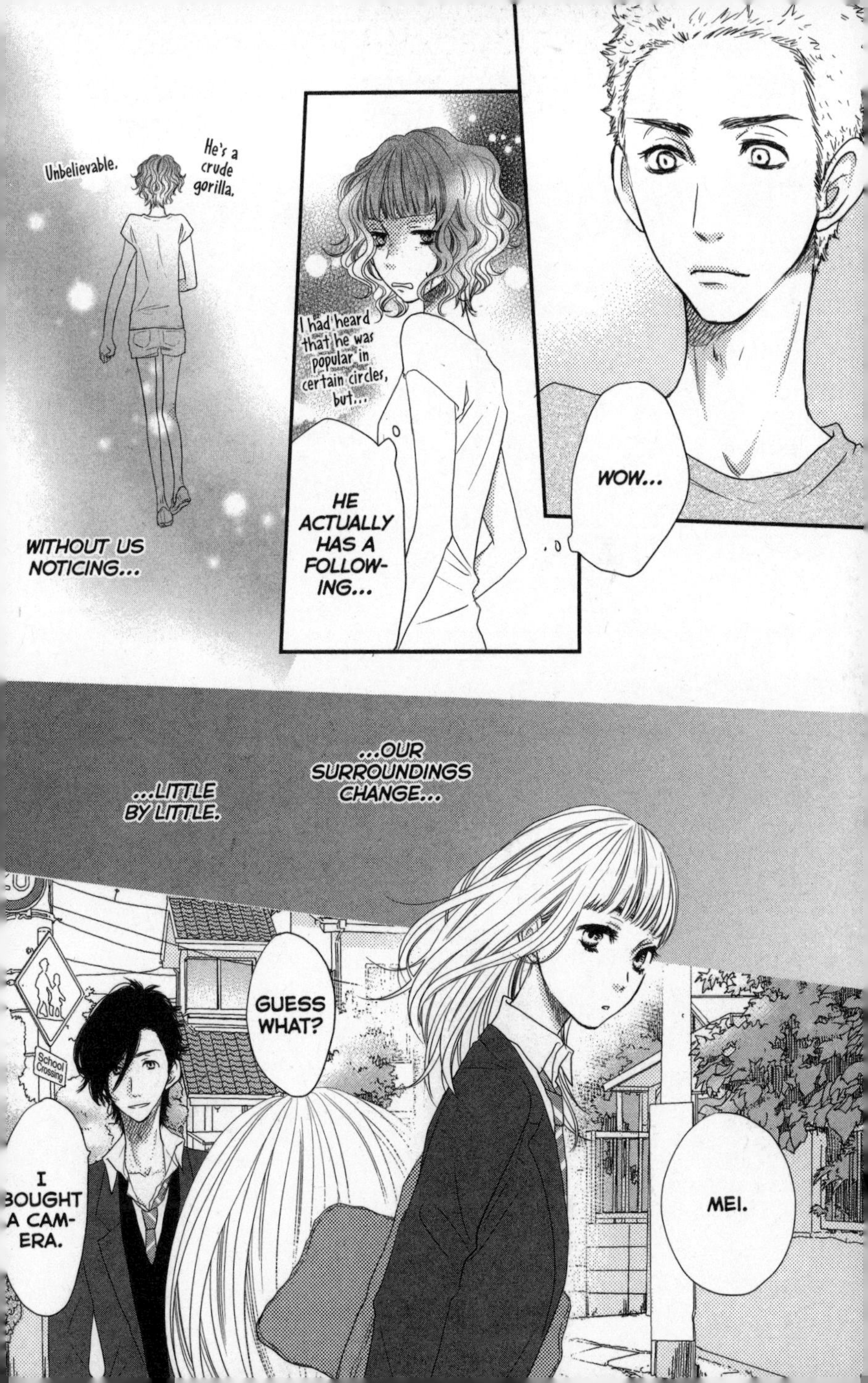
WOW...
I had heard that he was popular in certain circles, but...
HE ACTUALLY HAS A FOLLOWING...
He's a crude gorilla.
Unbelievable.
WITHOUT US NOTICING...
...OUR SURROUNDINGS CHANGE...
...LITTLE BY LITTLE.
School Crossing
MEI.
GUESS WHAT?
I BOUGHT A CAMERA.

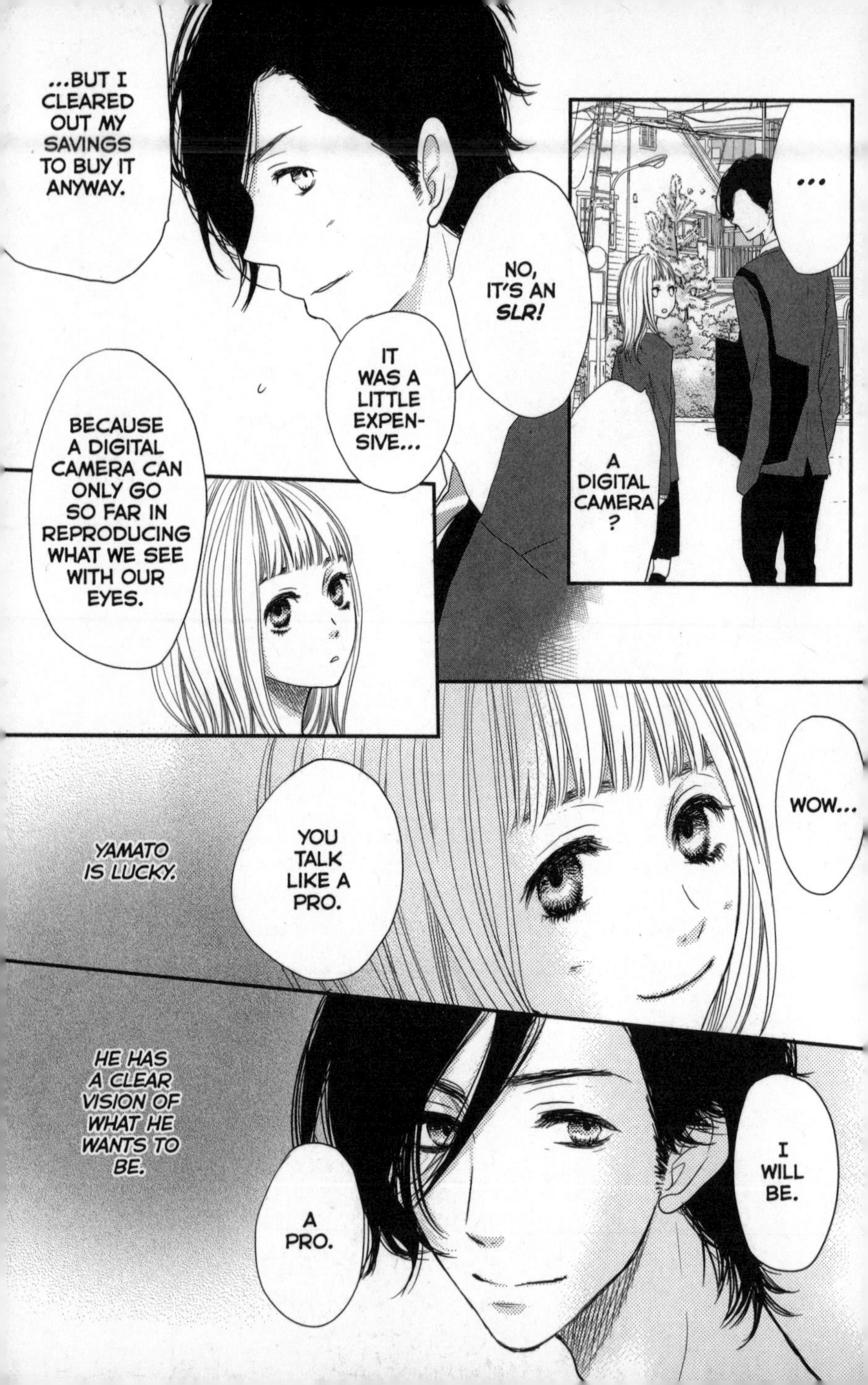
...
A DIGITAL CAMERA?
NO, IT'S AN *SLR!*
IT WAS A LITTLE EXPENSIVE...
...BUT I CLEARED OUT MY SAVINGS TO BUY IT ANYWAY.
BECAUSE A DIGITAL CAMERA CAN ONLY GO SO FAR IN REPRODUCING WHAT WE SEE WITH OUR EYES.
WOW...
YOU TALK LIKE A PRO.
YAMATO IS LUCKY.
I WILL BE.
A PRO.
HE HAS A CLEAR VISION OF WHAT HE WANTS TO BE.

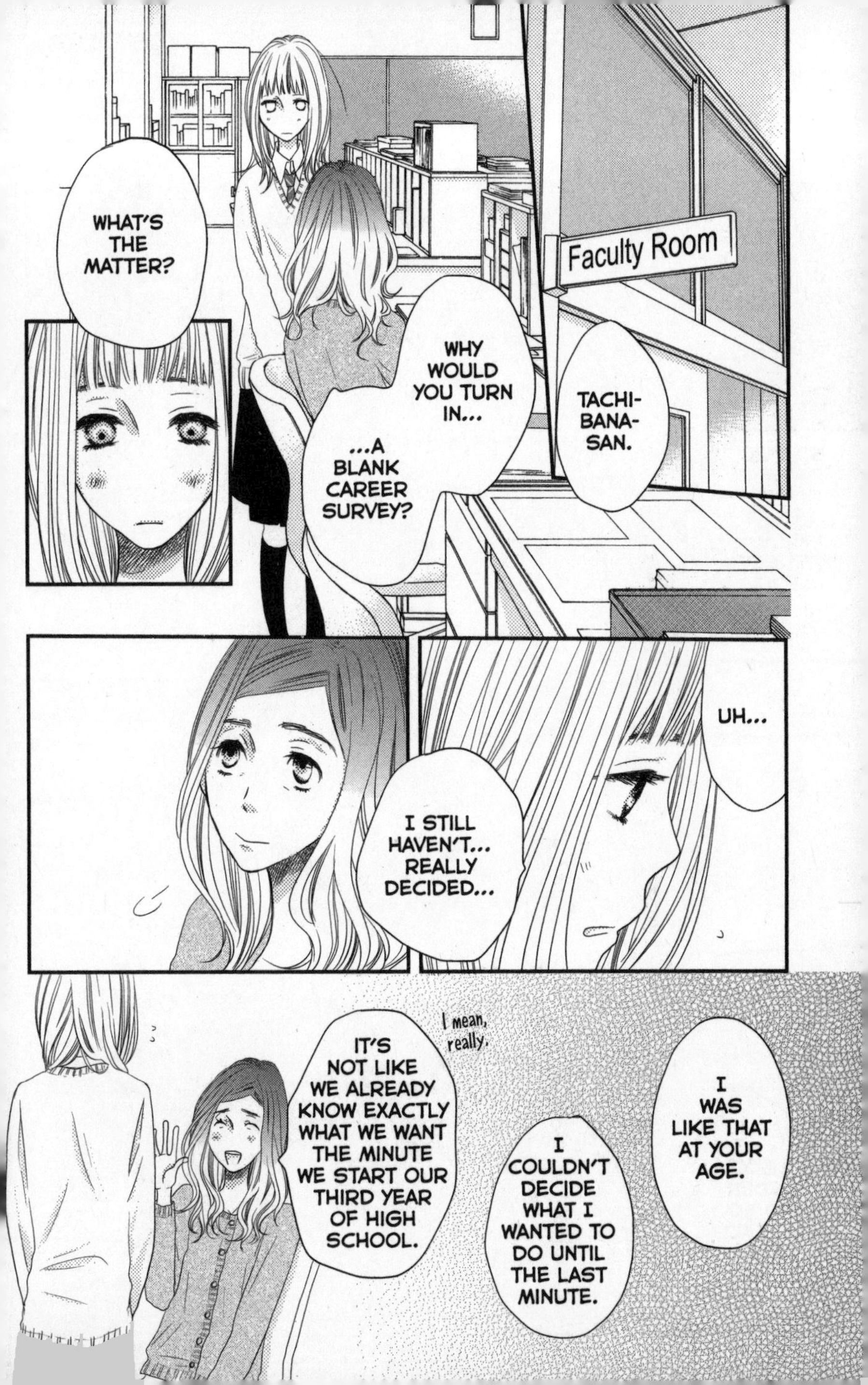
Faculty Room
TACHIBANA-SAN.
WHY WOULD YOU TURN IN...
...A BLANK CAREER SURVEY?
WHAT'S THE MATTER?
UH...
I STILL HAVEN'T... REALLY DECIDED...
I WAS LIKE THAT AT YOUR AGE.
I COULDN'T DECIDE WHAT I WANTED TO DO UNTIL THE LAST MINUTE.
I mean, really.
IT'S NOT LIKE WE ALREADY KNOW EXACTLY WHAT WE WANT THE MINUTE WE START OUR THIRD YEAR OF HIGH SCHOOL.

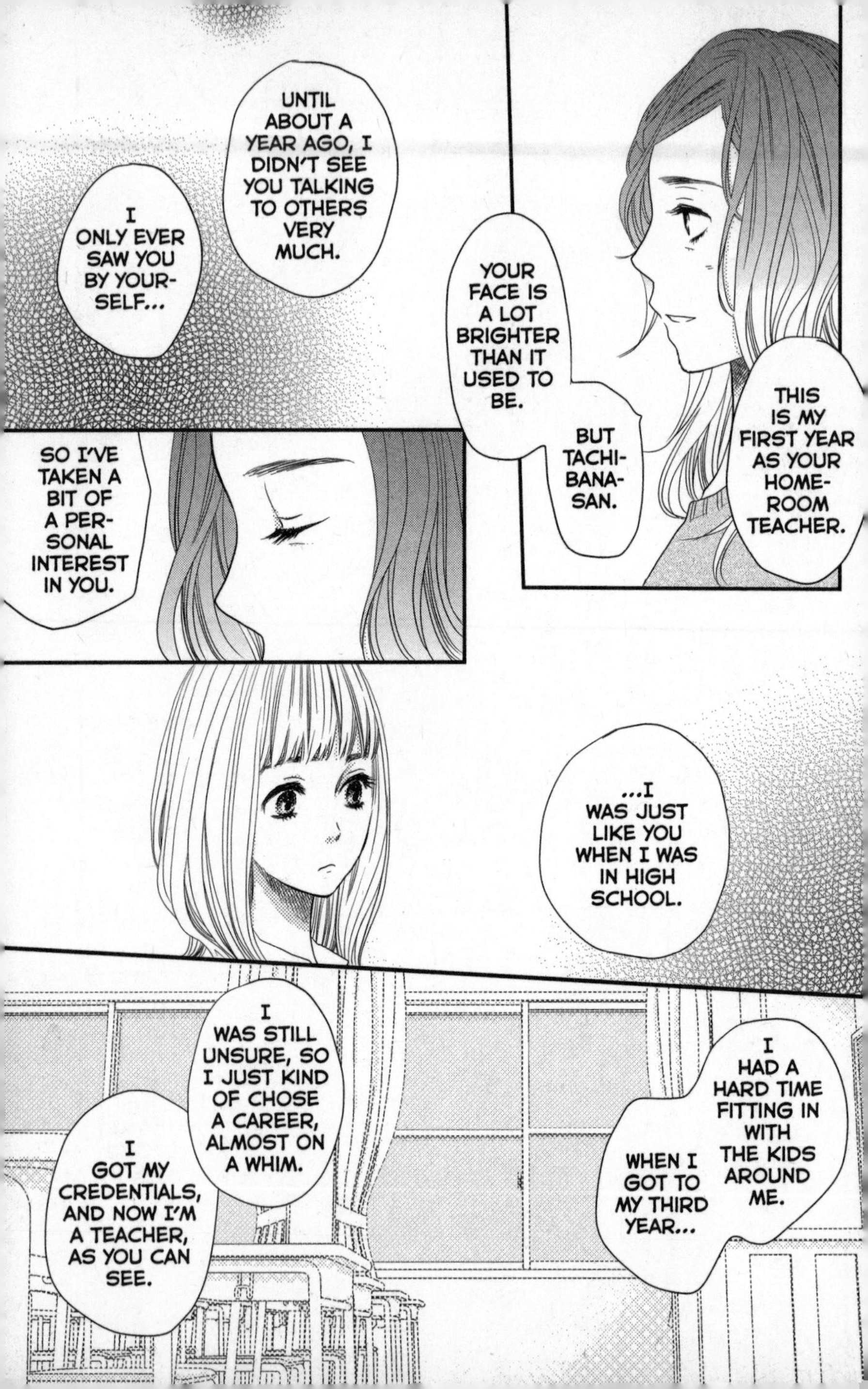
THIS IS MY FIRST YEAR AS YOUR HOMEROOM TEACHER.
BUT TACHIBANA-SAN.
YOUR FACE IS A LOT BRIGHTER THAN IT USED TO BE.
UNTIL ABOUT A YEAR AGO, I DIDN'T SEE YOU TALKING TO OTHERS VERY MUCH.
I ONLY EVER SAW YOU BY YOURSELF...
SO I'VE TAKEN A BIT OF A PERSONAL INTEREST IN YOU.
...I WAS JUST LIKE YOU WHEN I WAS IN HIGH SCHOOL.
I HAD A HARD TIME FITTING IN WITH THE KIDS AROUND ME.
WHEN I GOT TO MY THIRD YEAR...
I WAS STILL UNSURE, SO I JUST KIND OF CHOSE A CAREER, ALMOST ON A WHIM.
I GOT MY CREDENTIALS, AND NOW I'M A TEACHER, AS YOU CAN SEE.

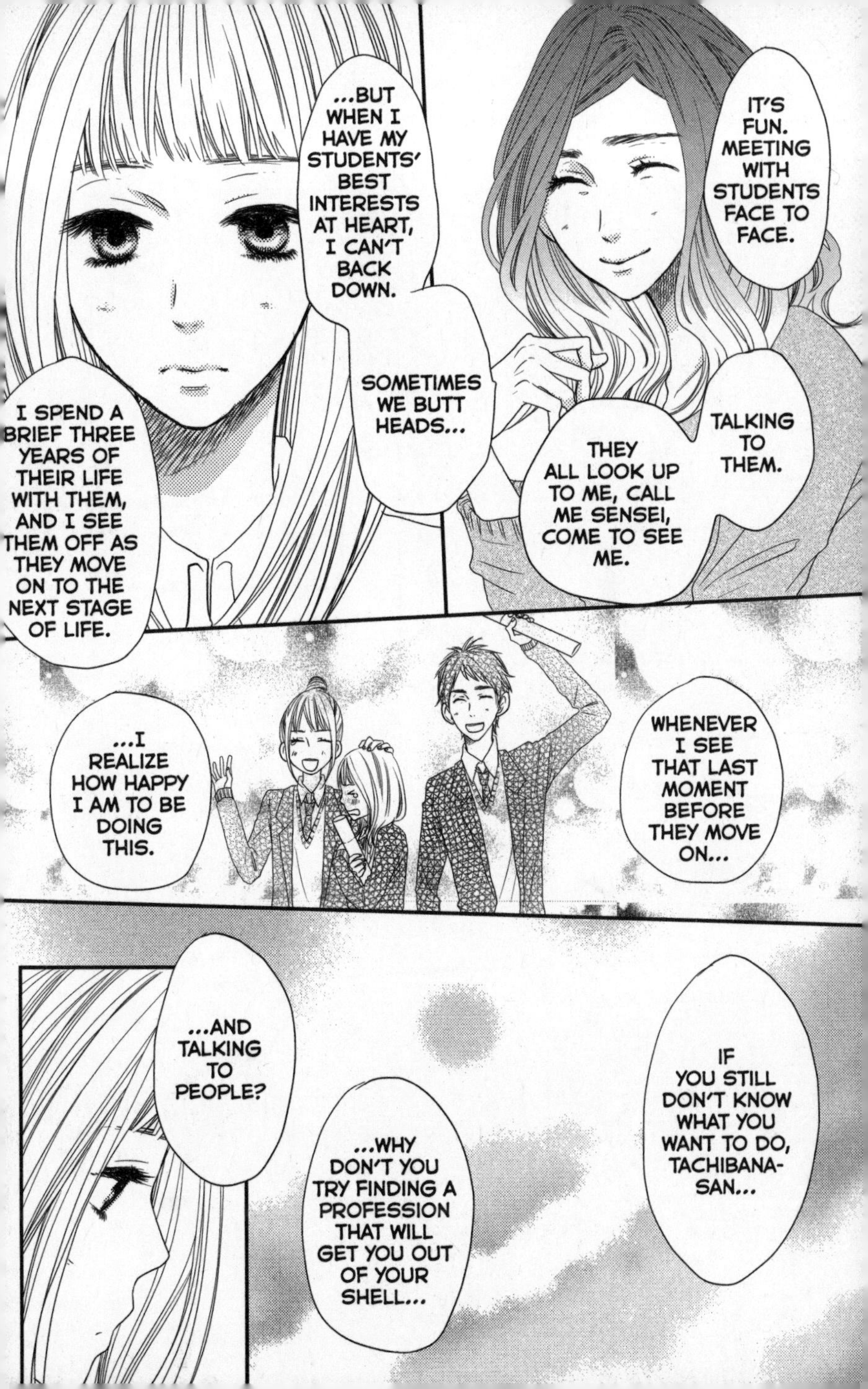
IT'S FUN. MEETING WITH STUDENTS FACE TO FACE.
TALKING TO THEM.
THEY ALL LOOK UP TO ME, CALL ME SENSEI, COME TO SEE ME.
SOMETIMES WE BUTT HEADS...
...BUT WHEN I HAVE MY STUDENTS' BEST INTERESTS AT HEART, I CAN'T BACK DOWN.
I SPEND A BRIEF THREE YEARS OF THEIR LIFE WITH THEM, AND I SEE THEM OFF AS THEY MOVE ON TO THE NEXT STAGE OF LIFE.
WHENEVER I SEE THAT LAST MOMENT BEFORE THEY MOVE ON...
...I REALIZE HOW HAPPY I AM TO BE DOING THIS.
IF YOU STILL DON'T KNOW WHAT YOU WANT TO DO, TACHIBANA-SAN...
...WHY DON'T YOU TRY FINDING A PROFESSION THAT WILL GET YOU OUT OF YOUR SHELL...
...AND TALKING TO PEOPLE?

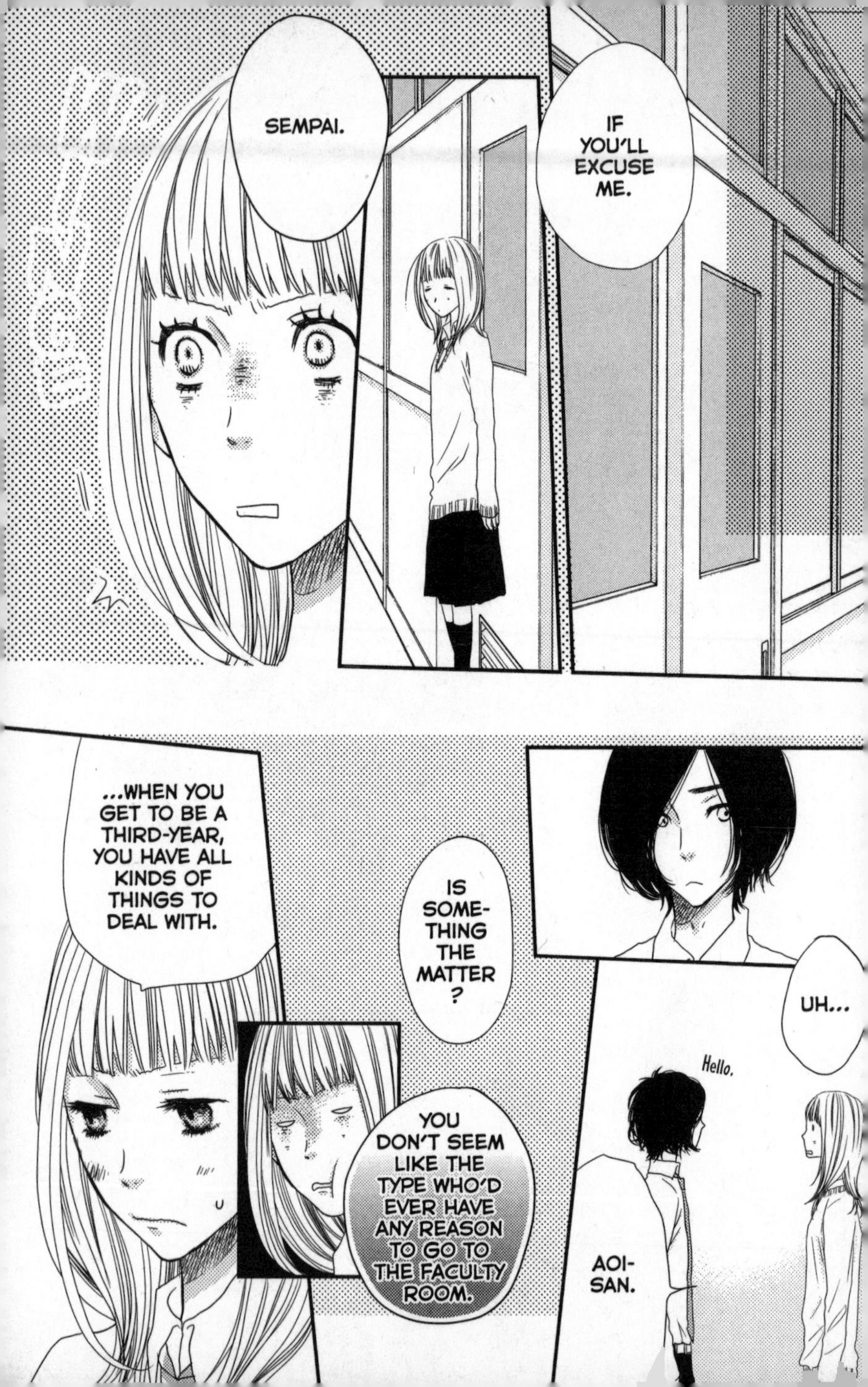
IF YOU'LL EXCUSE ME.
SEMPAI.
Hello.
AOI-SAN.
UH...
IS SOMETHING THE MATTER?
YOU DON'T SEEM LIKE THE TYPE WHO'D EVER HAVE ANY REASON TO GO TO THE FACULTY ROOM.
...WHEN YOU GET TO BE A THIRD-YEAR, YOU HAVE ALL KINDS OF THINGS TO DEAL WITH.

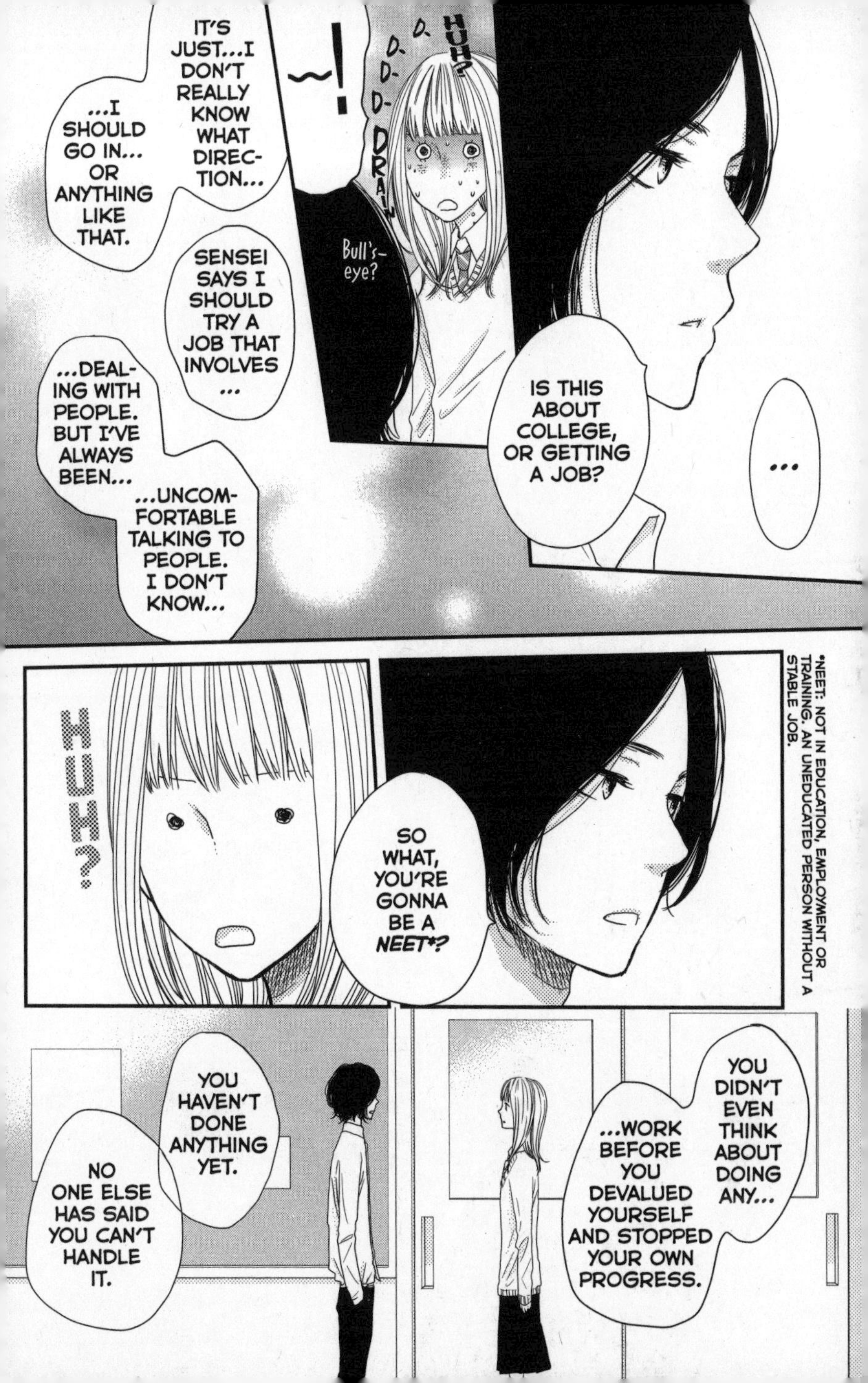
...
IS THIS ABOUT COLLEGE, OR GETTING A JOB?
HUH?
D-D-D-D-D-DRAIN
~!
Bull's-eye?
IT'S JUST...I DON'T REALLY KNOW WHAT DIRECTION...
...I SHOULD GO IN... OR ANYTHING LIKE THAT.
SENSEI SAYS I SHOULD TRY A JOB THAT INVOLVES...
...DEALING WITH PEOPLE. BUT I'VE ALWAYS BEEN...
...UNCOMFORTABLE TALKING TO PEOPLE. I DON'T KNOW...
*NEET: NOT IN EDUCATION, EMPLOYMENT OR TRAINING. AN UNEDUCATED PERSON WITHOUT A STABLE JOB.
SO WHAT, YOU'RE GONNA BE A *NEET**?
HUH?
YOU DIDN'T EVEN THINK ABOUT DOING ANY...
...WORK BEFORE YOU DEVALUED YOURSELF AND STOPPED YOUR OWN PROGRESS.
YOU HAVEN'T DONE ANYTHING YET.
NO ONE ELSE HAS SAID YOU CAN'T HANDLE IT.

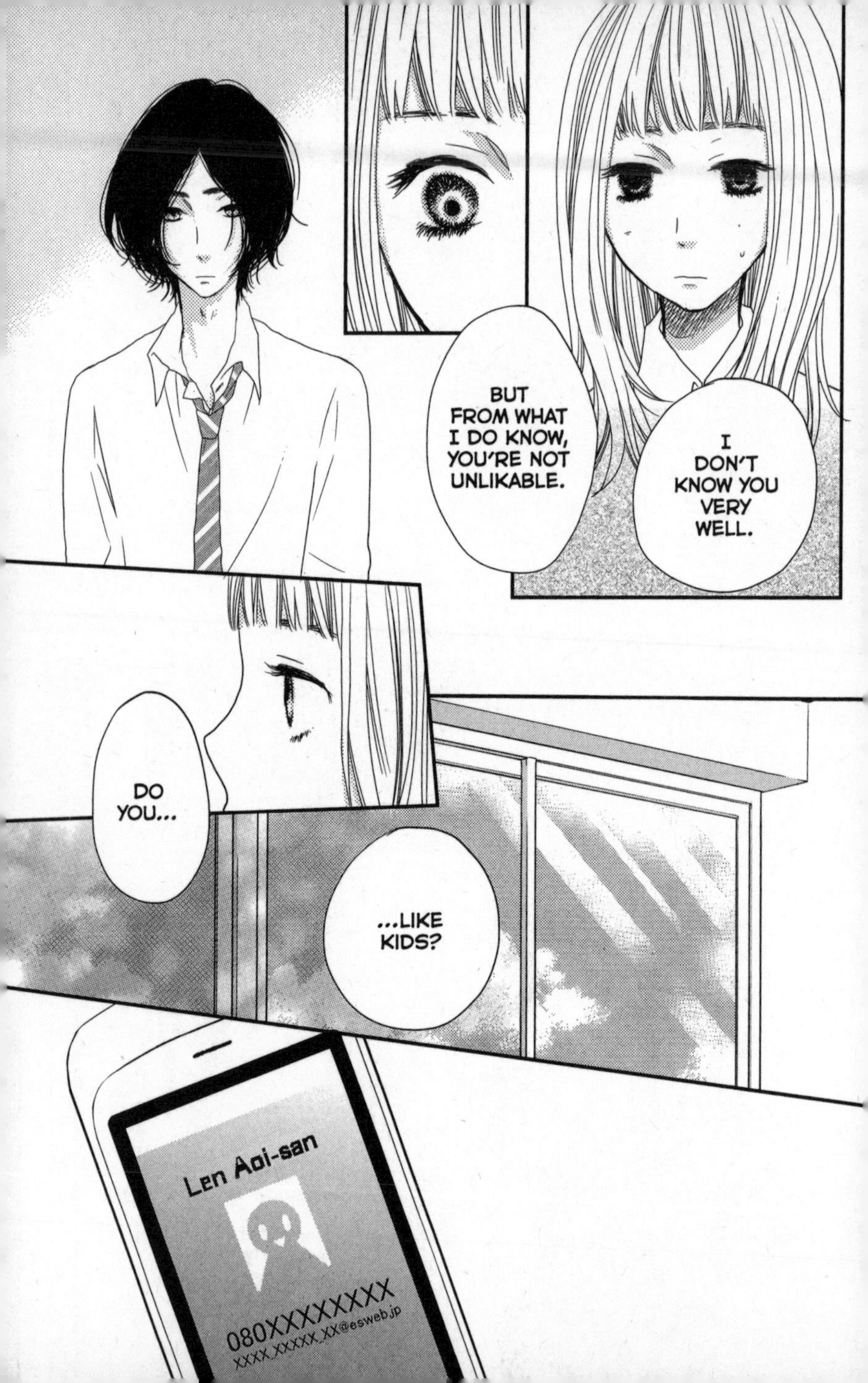
I DON'T KNOW YOU VERY WELL.
BUT FROM WHAT I DO KNOW, YOU'RE NOT UNLIKABLE.
DO YOU...
...LIKE KIDS?
Len Aoi-san
080XXXXXXXX
XXXX_XXXXX_XX@esweb.jp

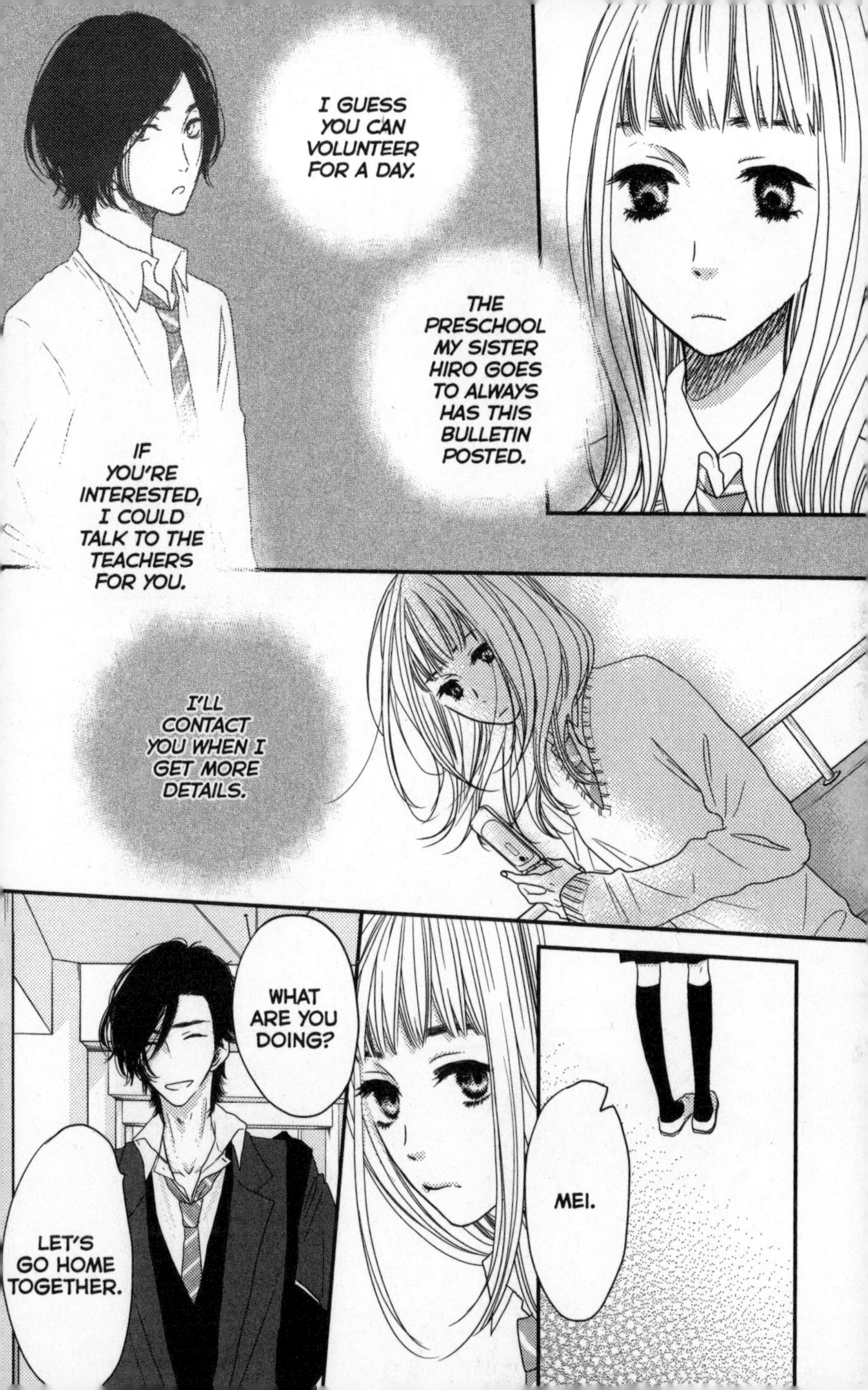
THE PRESCHOOL MY SISTER HIRO GOES TO ALWAYS HAS THIS BULLETIN POSTED.
I GUESS YOU CAN VOLUNTEER FOR A DAY.
IF YOU'RE INTERESTED, I COULD TALK TO THE TEACHERS FOR YOU.
I'LL CONTACT YOU WHEN I GET MORE DETAILS.
MEI.
WHAT ARE YOU DOING?
LET'S GO HOME TOGETHER.

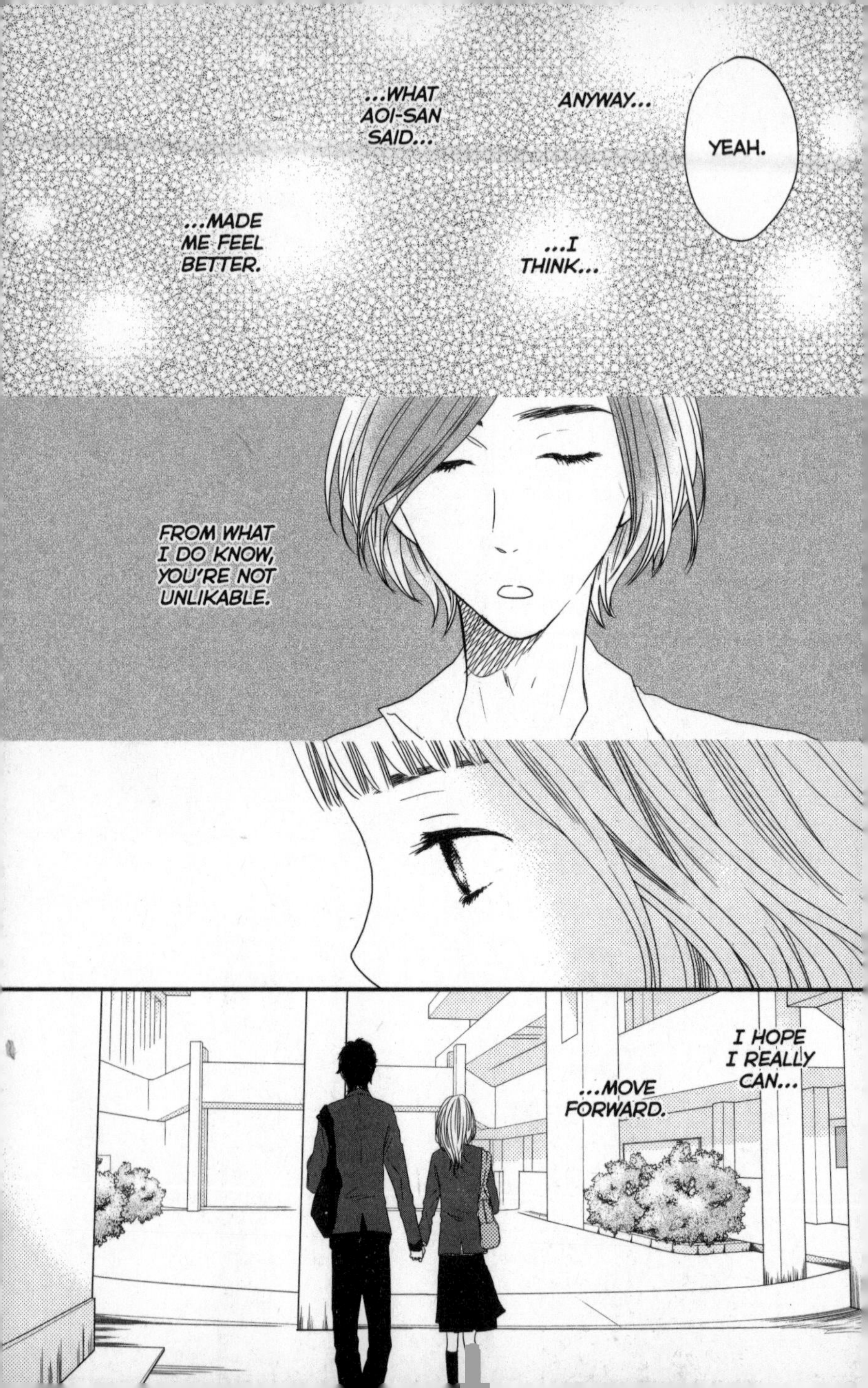
YEAH.
ANYWAY...
...WHAT AOI-SAN SAID...
...I THINK...
...MADE ME FEEL BETTER.
FROM WHAT I DO KNOW, YOU'RE NOT UNLIKABLE.
I HOPE I REALLY CAN...
...MOVE FORWARD.

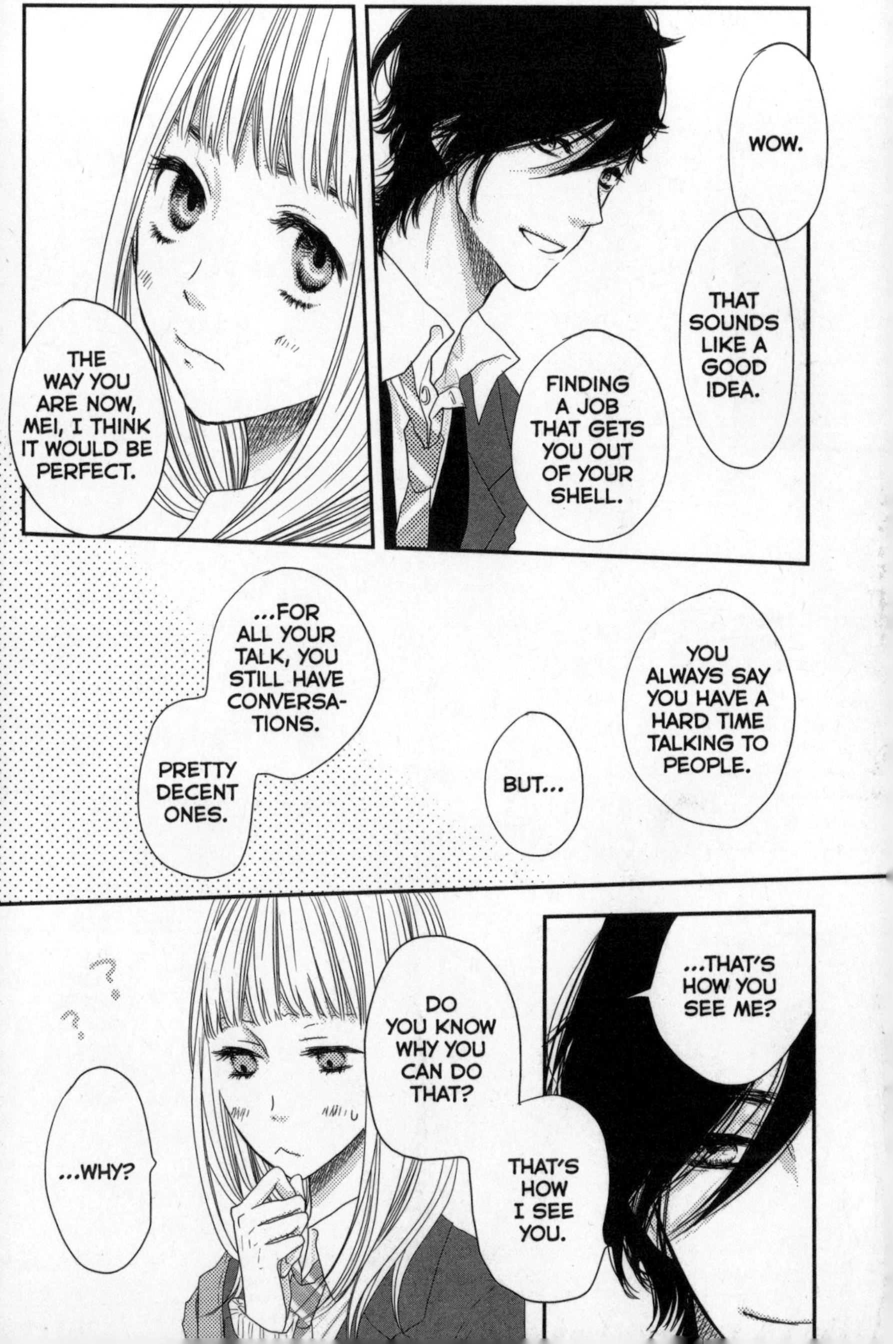
WOW.
THAT SOUNDS LIKE A GOOD IDEA.
FINDING A JOB THAT GETS YOU OUT OF YOUR SHELL.
THE WAY YOU ARE NOW, MEI, I THINK IT WOULD BE PERFECT.
YOU ALWAYS SAY YOU HAVE A HARD TIME TALKING TO PEOPLE.
BUT...
...FOR ALL YOUR TALK, YOU STILL HAVE CONVERSA-TIONS.
PRETTY DECENT ONES.
...THAT'S HOW YOU SEE ME?
DO YOU KNOW WHY YOU CAN DO THAT?
THAT'S HOW I SEE YOU.
...WHY?

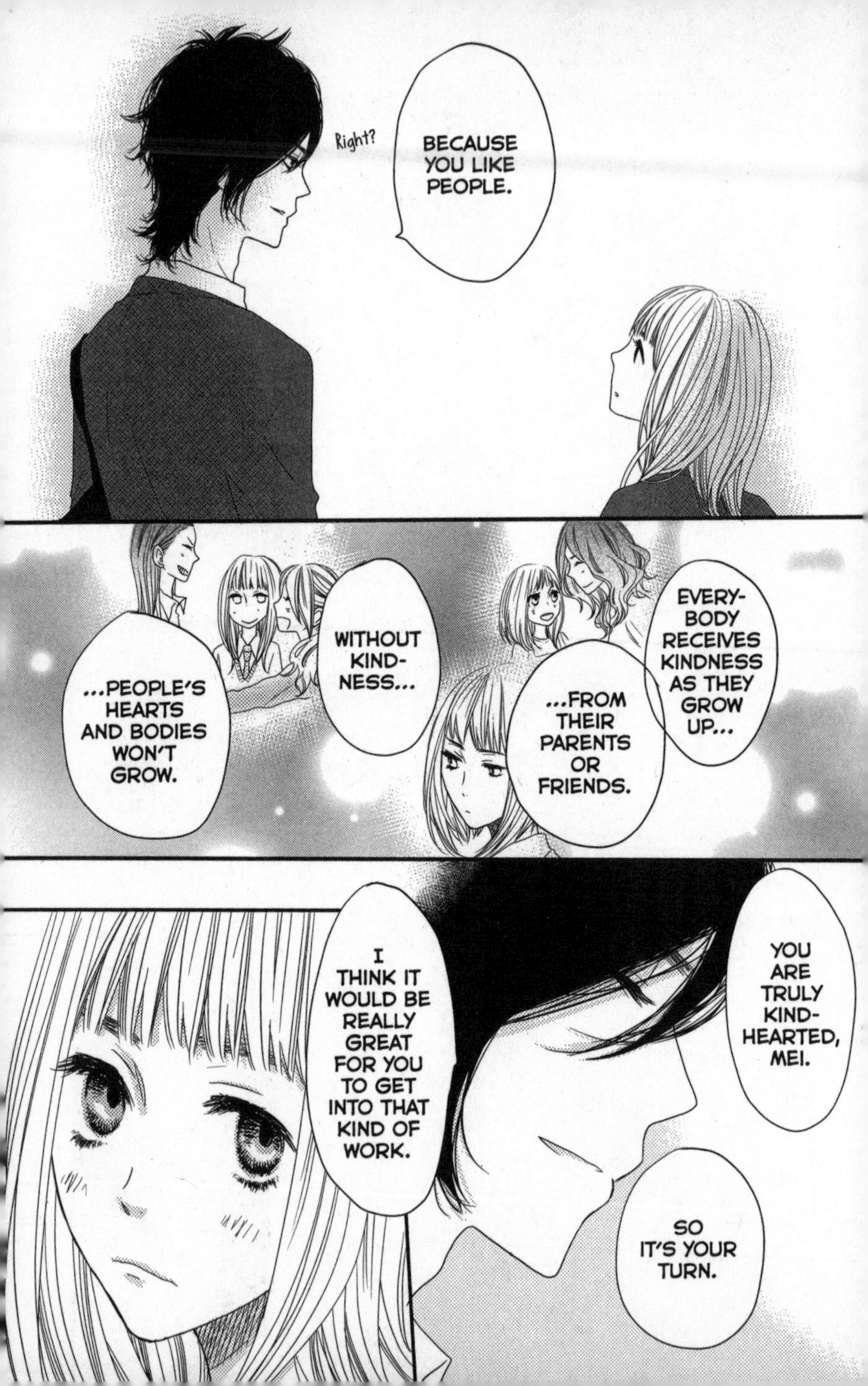
BECAUSE YOU LIKE PEOPLE.
Right?
EVERY-BODY RECEIVES KINDNESS AS THEY GROW UP...
...FROM THEIR PARENTS OR FRIENDS.
WITHOUT KIND-NESS...
...PEOPLE'S HEARTS AND BODIES WON'T GROW.
YOU ARE TRULY KIND-HEARTED, MEI.
SO IT'S YOUR TURN.
I THINK IT WOULD BE REALLY GREAT FOR YOU TO GET INTO THAT KIND OF WORK.

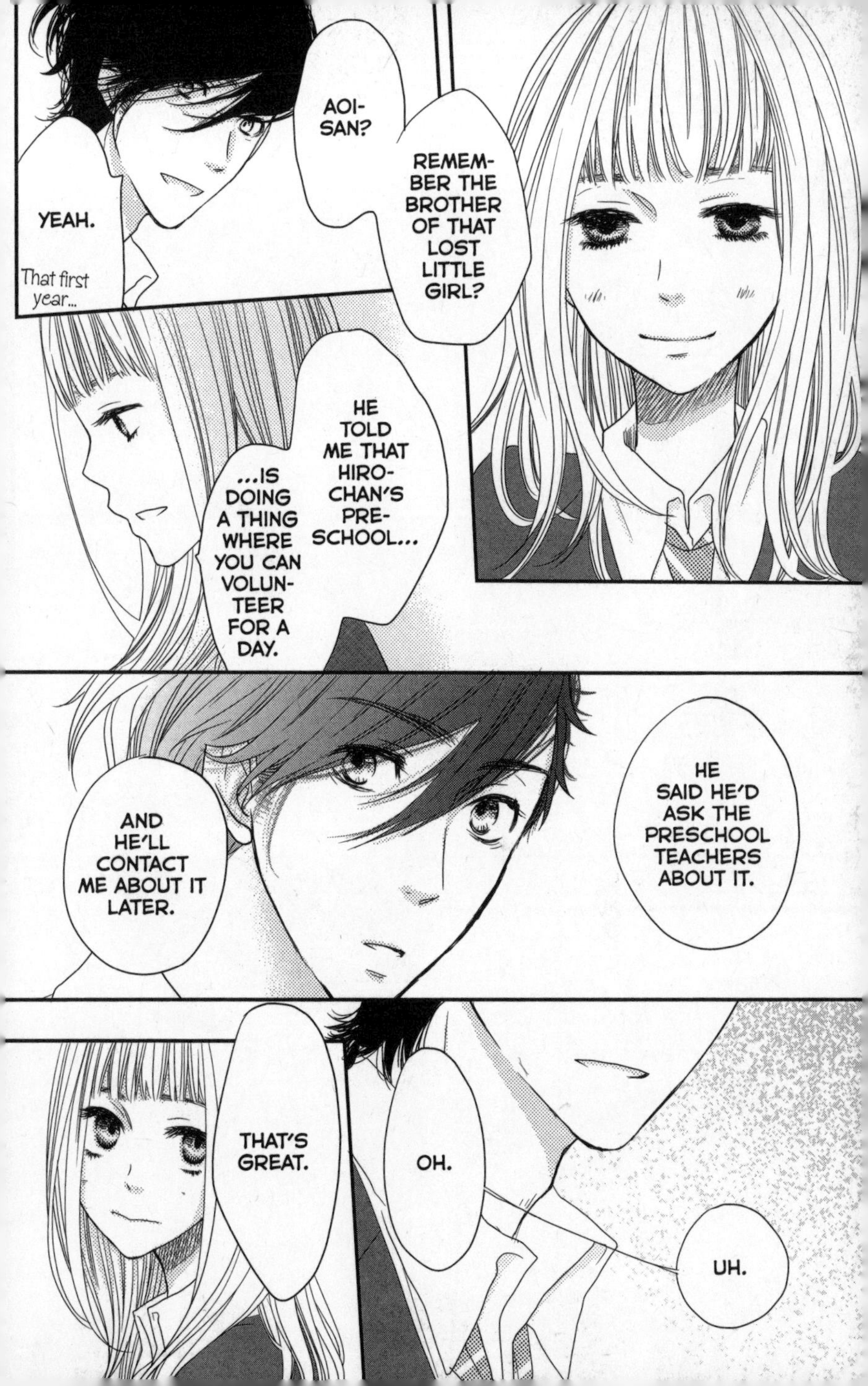
AOI-SAN?
REMEMBER THE BROTHER OF THAT LOST LITTLE GIRL?
YEAH.
That first year...
HE TOLD ME THAT HIRO-CHAN'S PRESCHOOL...
...IS DOING A THING WHERE YOU CAN VOLUNTEER FOR A DAY.
HE SAID HE'D ASK THE PRESCHOOL TEACHERS ABOUT IT.
AND HE'LL CONTACT ME ABOUT IT LATER.
UH.
OH.
THAT'S GREAT.

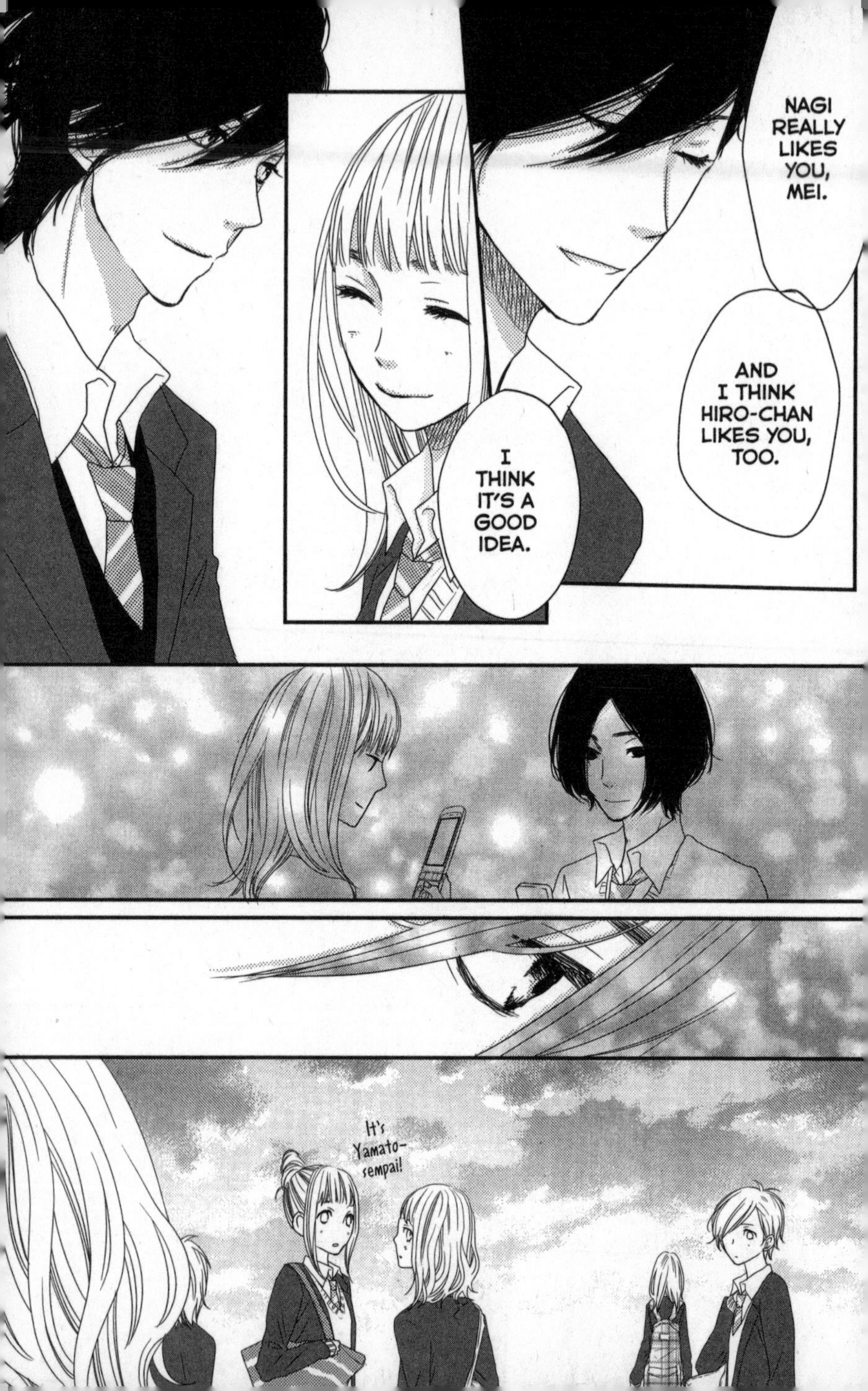
NAGI REALLY LIKES YOU, MEI.
AND I THINK HIRO-CHAN LIKES YOU, TOO.
I THINK IT'S A GOOD IDEA.
It's Yamato-sempai!

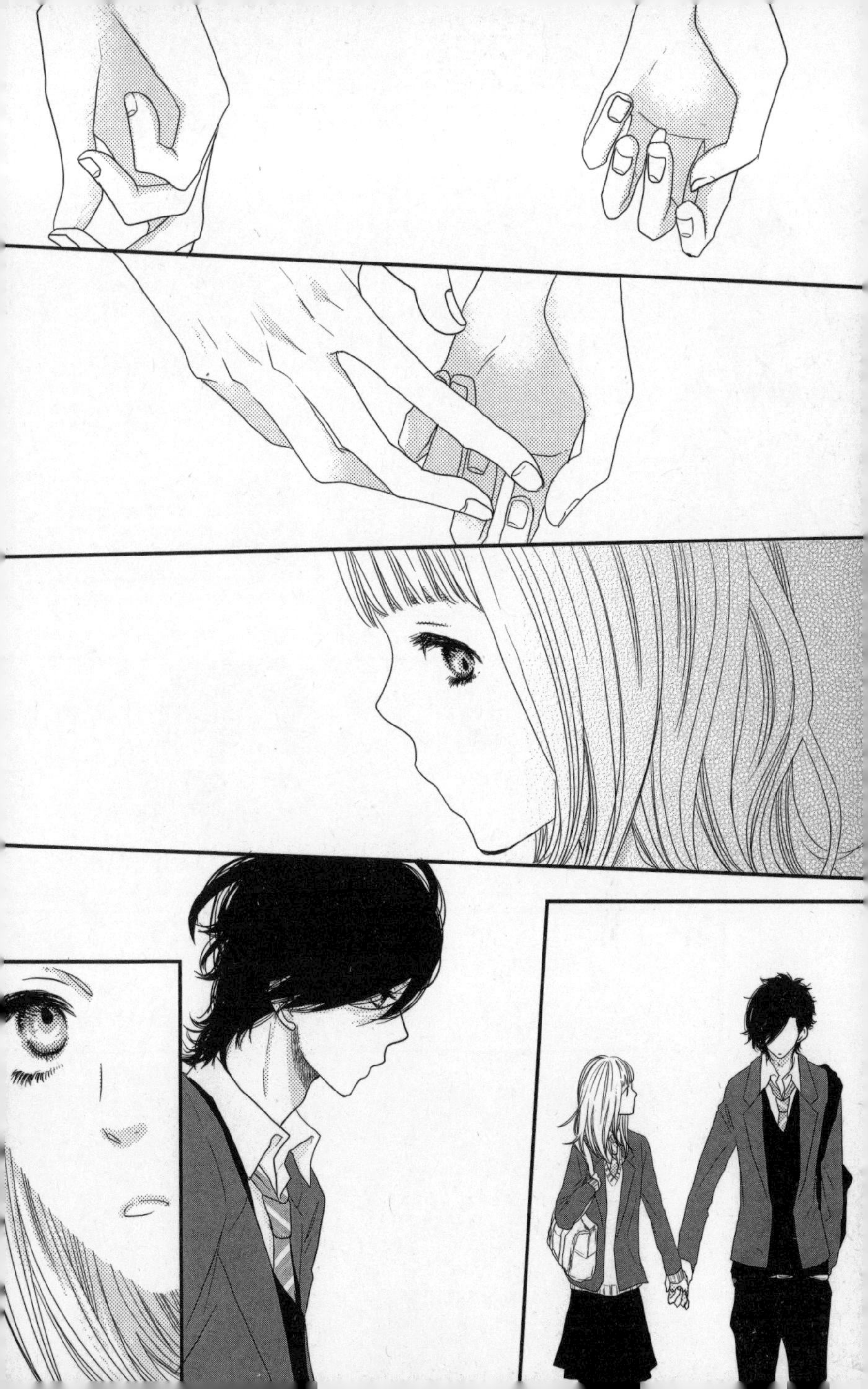

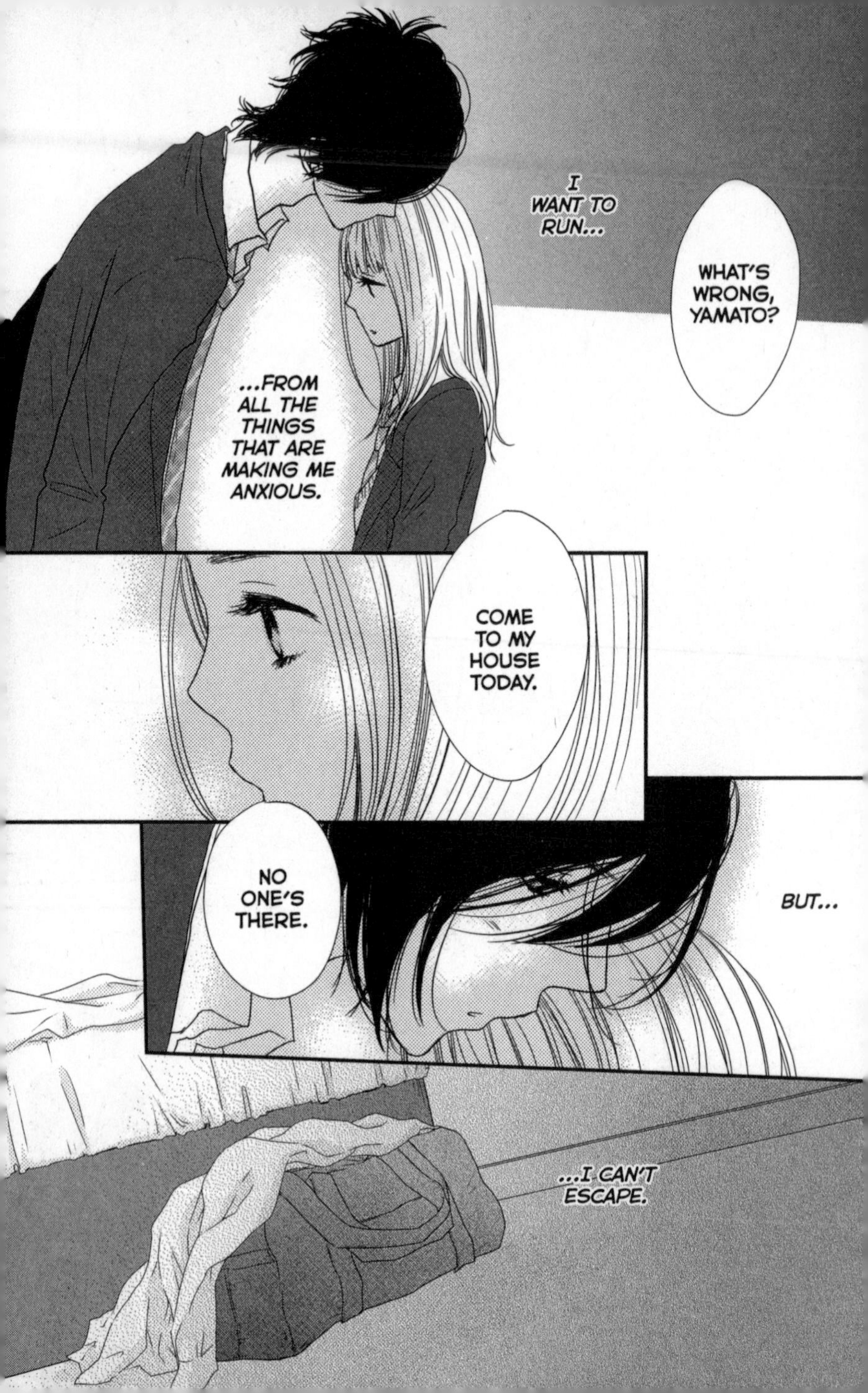
WHAT'S WRONG, YAMATO?
I WANT TO RUN...
...FROM ALL THE THINGS THAT ARE MAKING ME ANXIOUS.
COME TO MY HOUSE TODAY.
NO ONE'S THERE.
BUT...
...I CAN'T ESCAPE.

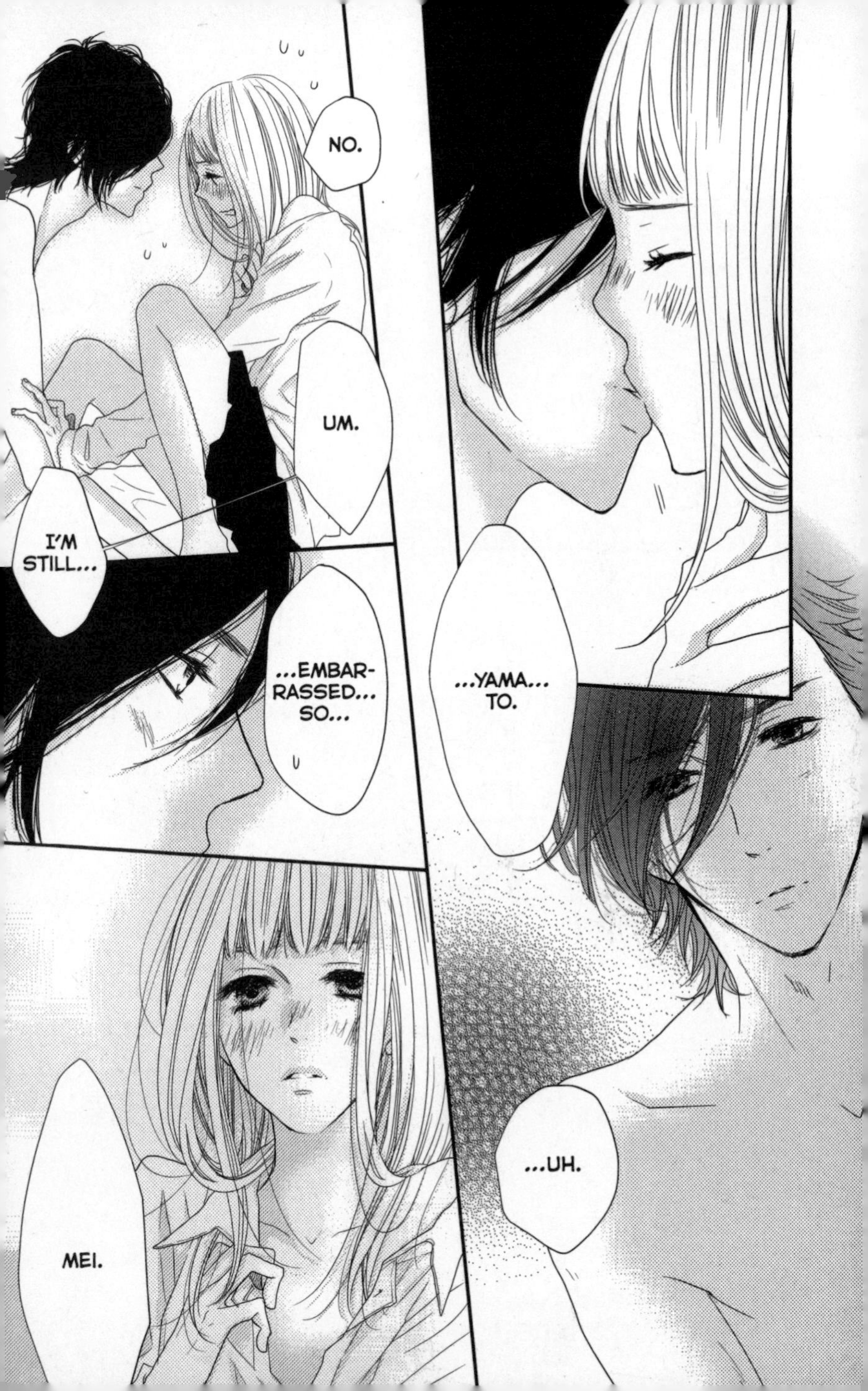
...YAMA... TO.
...UH.
NO.
UM.
I'M STILL...
...EMBAR-RASSED... SO...
MEI.

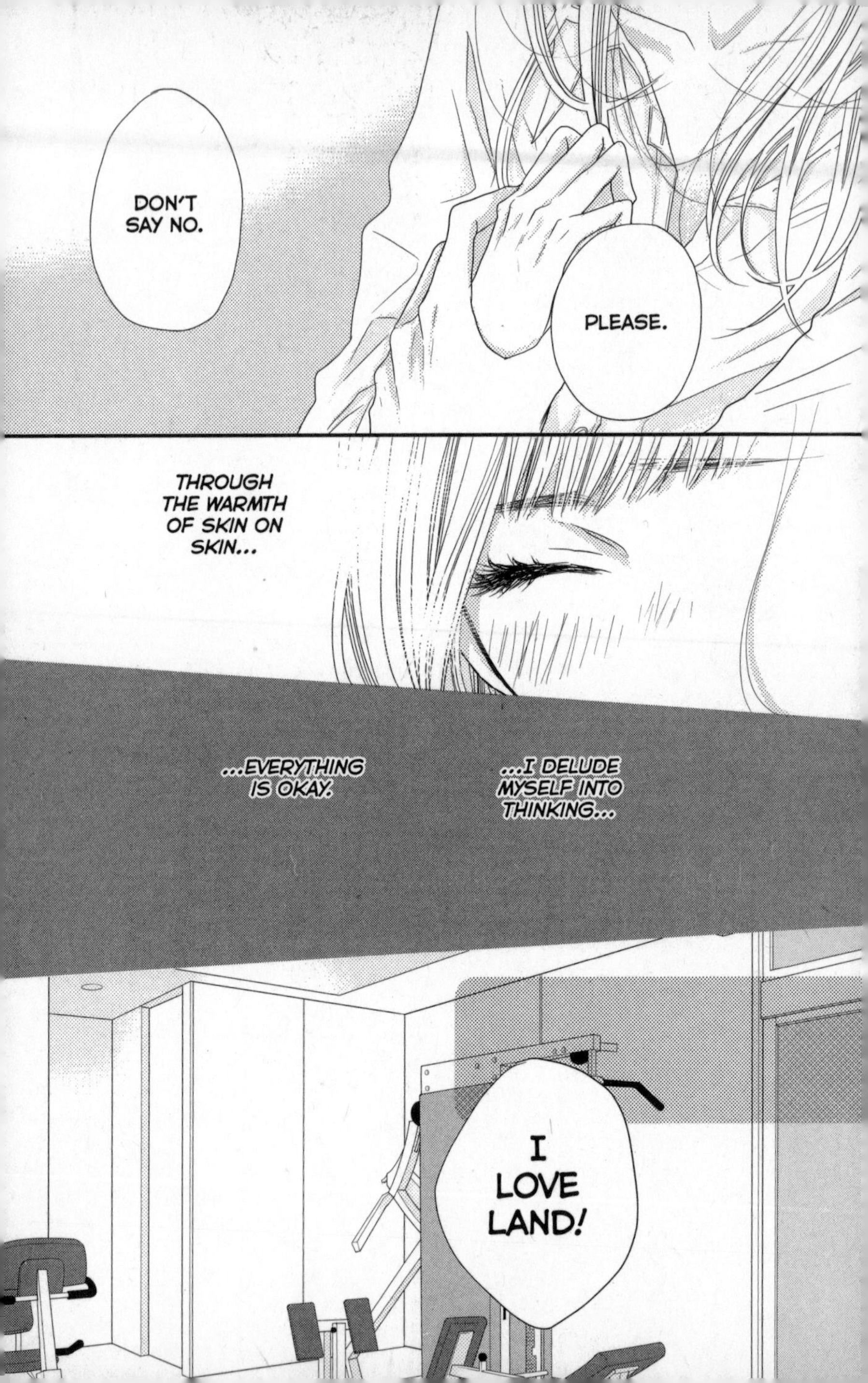
PLEASE.
DON'T SAY NO.
THROUGH THE WARMTH OF SKIN ON SKIN...
...I DELUDE MYSELF INTO THINKING...
...EVERYTHING IS OKAY.
I LOVE LAND!

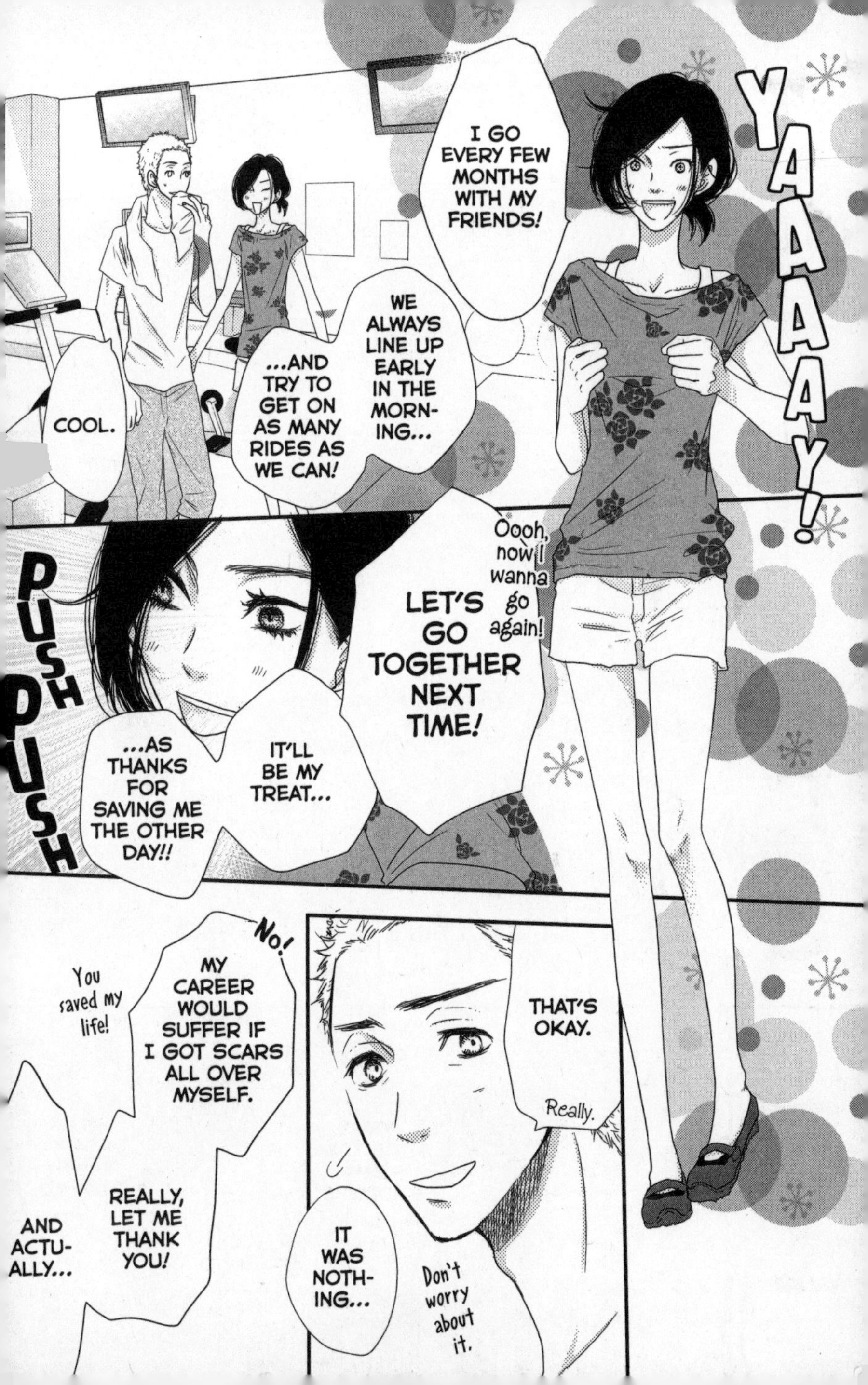
YAAAAY!
I GO EVERY FEW MONTHS WITH MY FRIENDS!
WE ALWAYS LINE UP EARLY IN THE MORNING...
...AND TRY TO GET ON AS MANY RIDES AS WE CAN!
COOL.
Oooh, now I wanna go again!
LET'S GO TOGETHER NEXT TIME!
IT'LL BE MY TREAT...
...AS THANKS FOR SAVING ME THE OTHER DAY!!
PUSH
PUSH
THAT'S OKAY.
Really.
IT WAS NOTHING...
Don't worry about it.
No!
MY CAREER WOULD SUFFER IF I GOT SCARS ALL OVER MYSELF.
You saved my life!
REALLY, LET ME THANK YOU!
AND ACTUALLY...

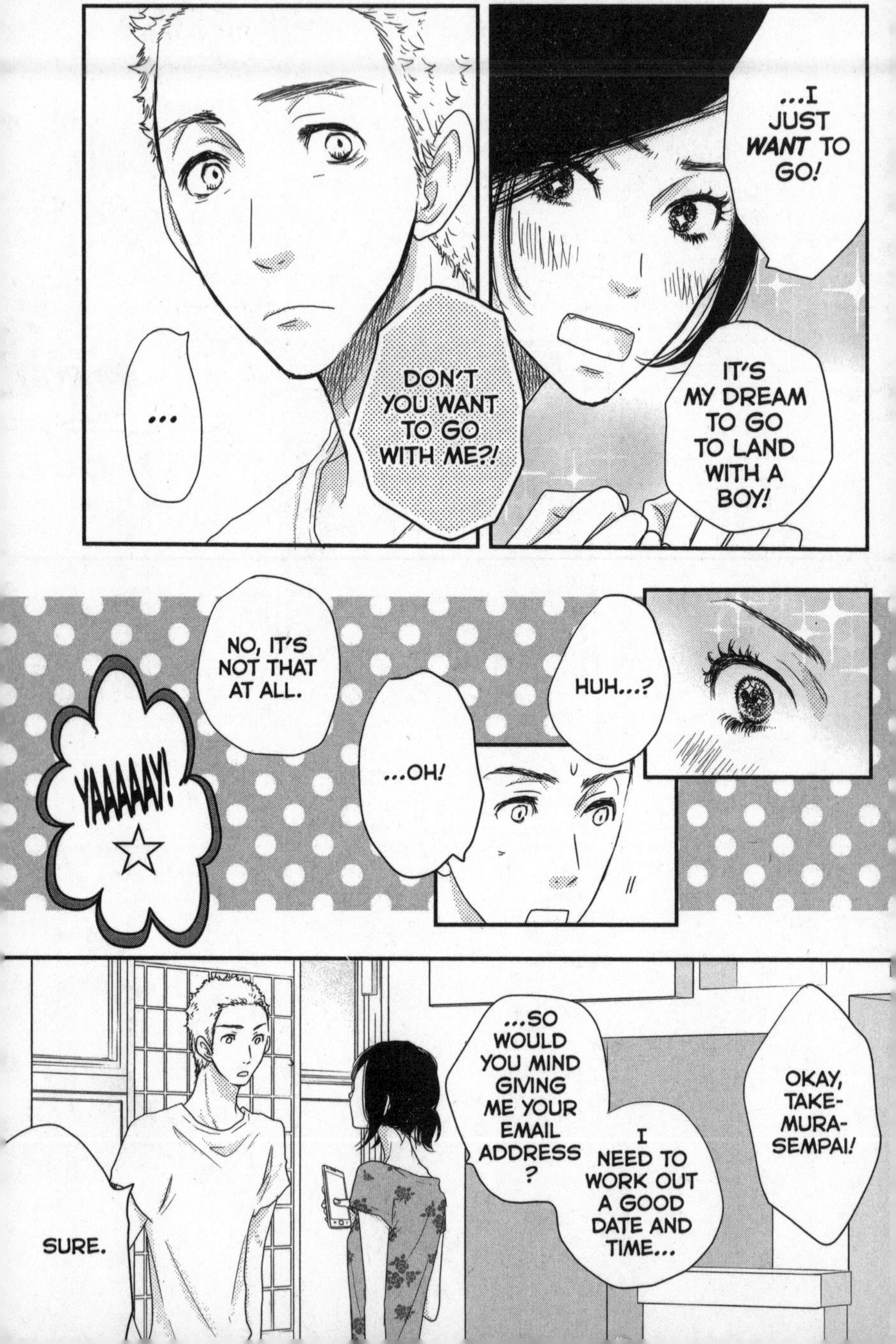
...I JUST *WANT* TO GO!
IT'S MY DREAM TO GO TO LAND WITH A BOY!
DON'T YOU WANT TO GO WITH ME?!
...
HUH...?
...OH!
NO, IT'S NOT THAT AT ALL.
YAAAAAY! ☆
OKAY, TAKE-MURA-SEMPAI!
I NEED TO WORK OUT A GOOD DATE AND TIME...
...SO WOULD YOU MIND GIVING ME YOUR EMAIL ADDRESS?
SURE.

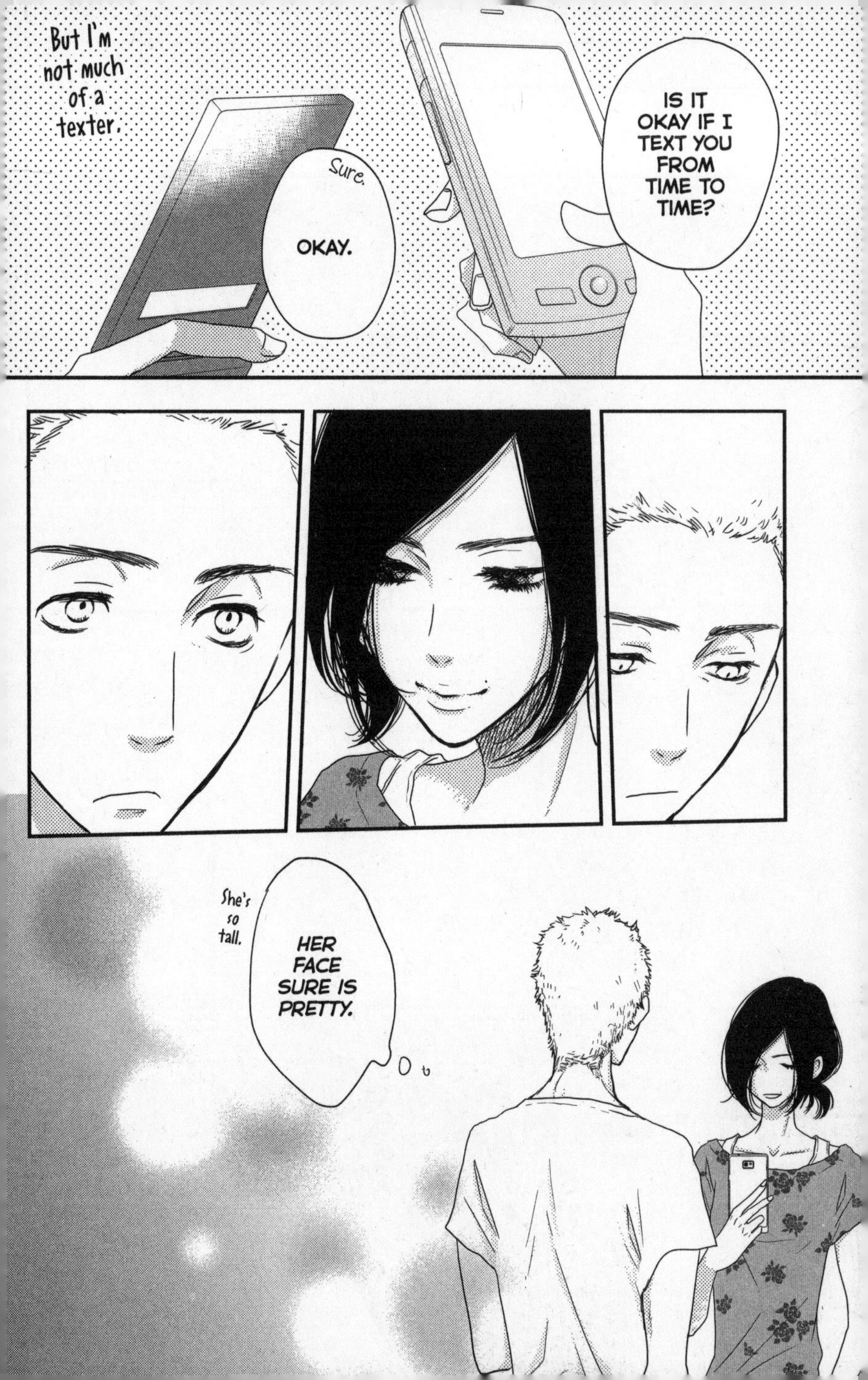
IS IT OKAY IF I TEXT YOU FROM TIME TO TIME?
Sure.
OKAY.
But I'm not much of a texter.
HER FACE SURE IS PRETTY.
She's so tall.

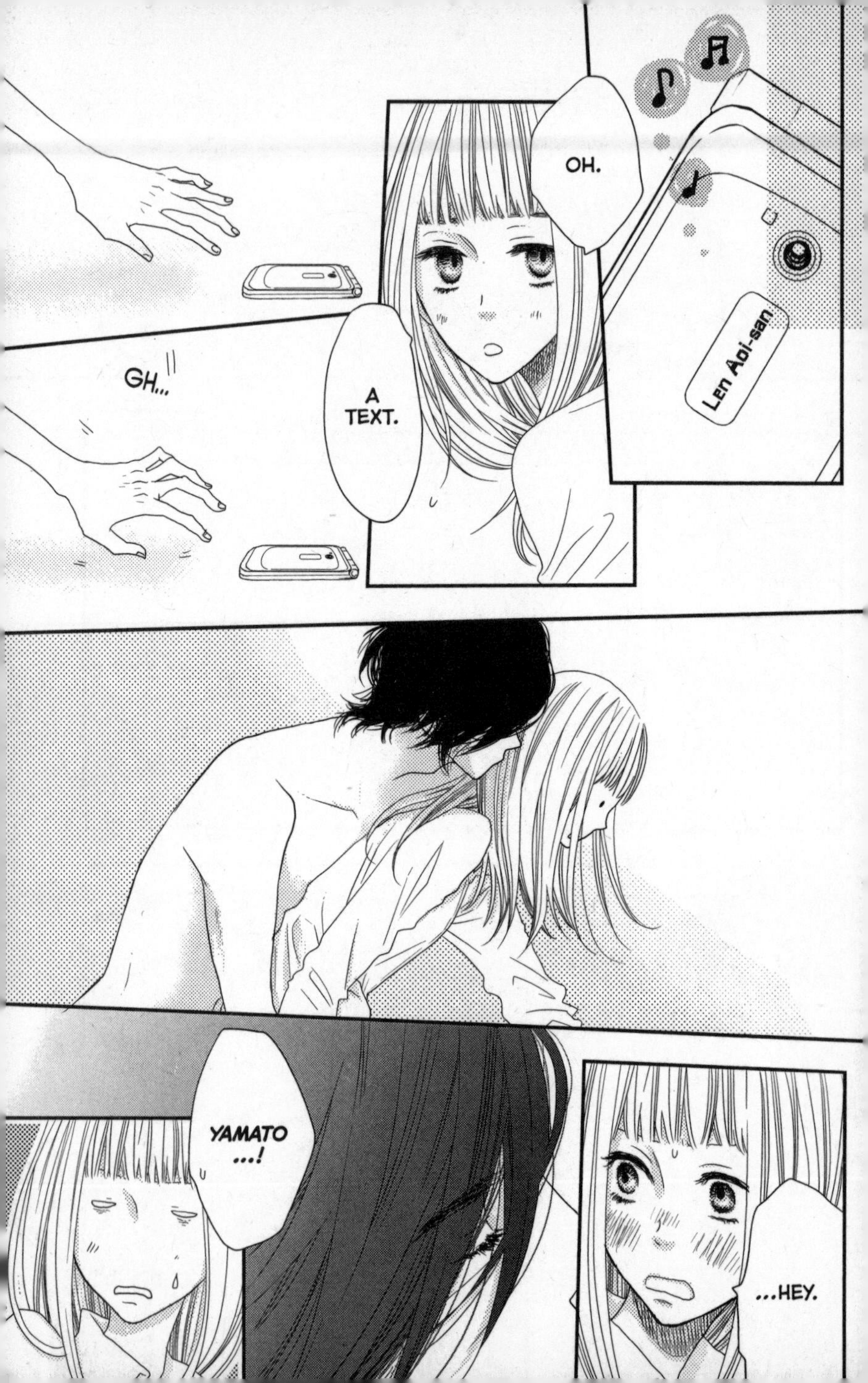
Len Aoi-san
OH.
A TEXT.
GH...
...HEY.
YAMATO ...!

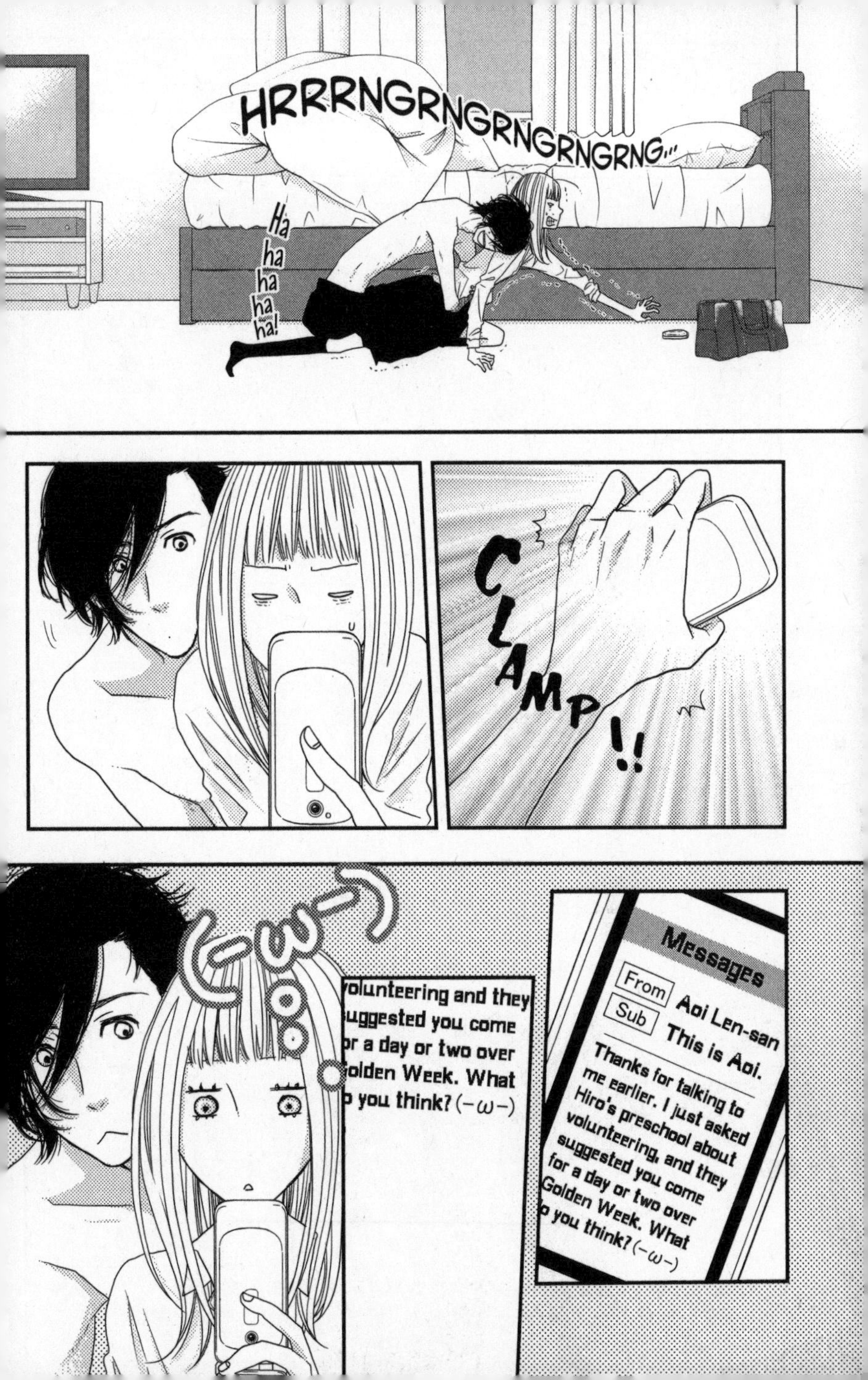
HRRRNGRNGRNGRNGRNG...
Ha ha ha ha ha!
CLAMP!!
Messages
From Aoi Len-san
Sub This is Aoi.
Thanks for talking to me earlier. I just asked Hiro's preschool about volunteering, and they suggested you come for a day or two over Golden Week. What o you think? (−ω−)
(−ω−)
olunteering and they uggested you come r a day or two over olden Week. What o you think? (−ω−)

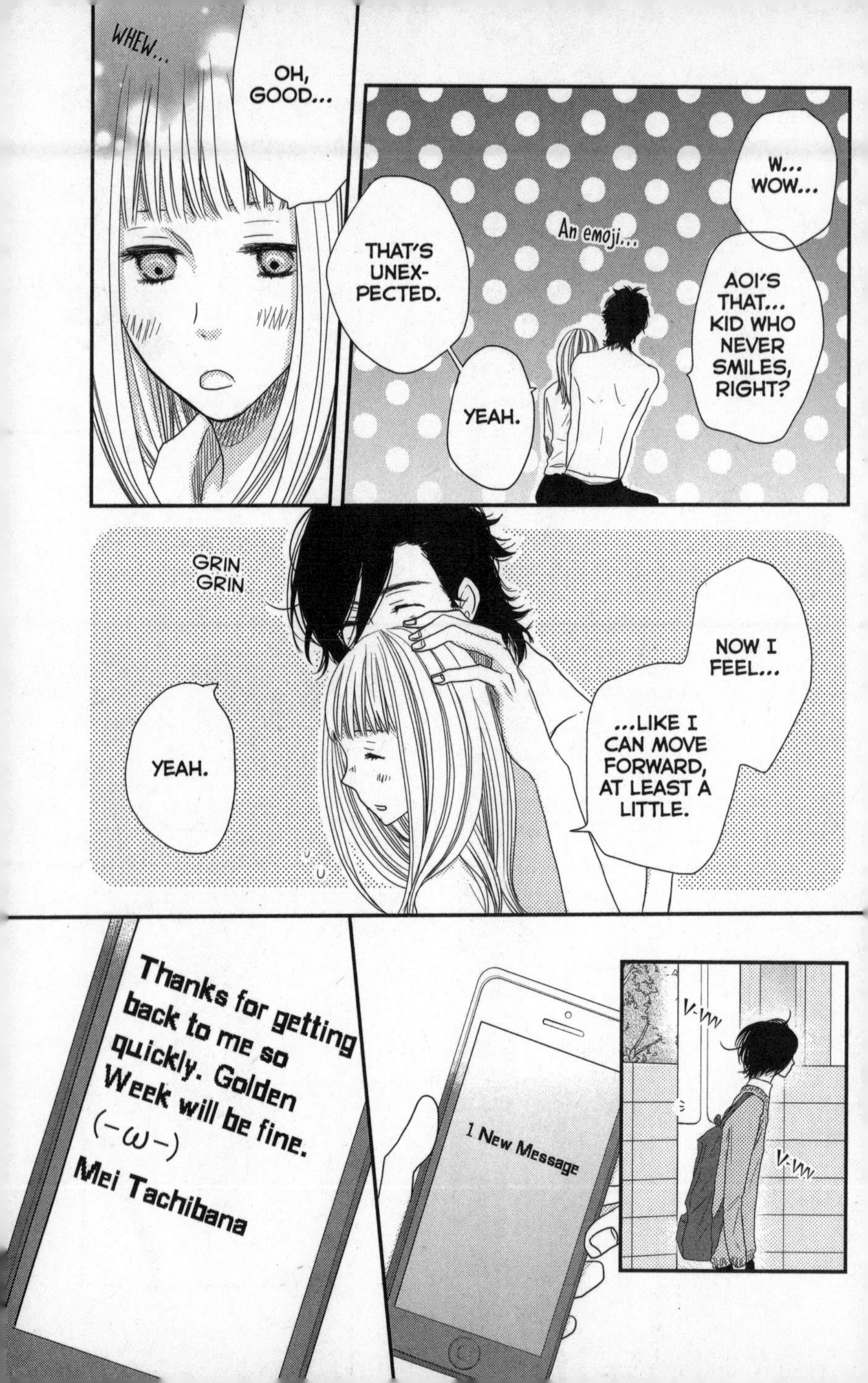
W... WOW...
An emoji...
AOI'S THAT... KID WHO NEVER SMILES, RIGHT?
THAT'S UNEXPECTED.
YEAH.
WHEW...
OH, GOOD...
NOW I FEEL...
...LIKE I CAN MOVE FORWARD, AT LEAST A LITTLE.
GRIN GRIN
YEAH.
V-VV
V-VV
1 New Message
Thanks for getting back to me so quickly. Golden Week will be fine.
(-ω-)
Mei Tachibana

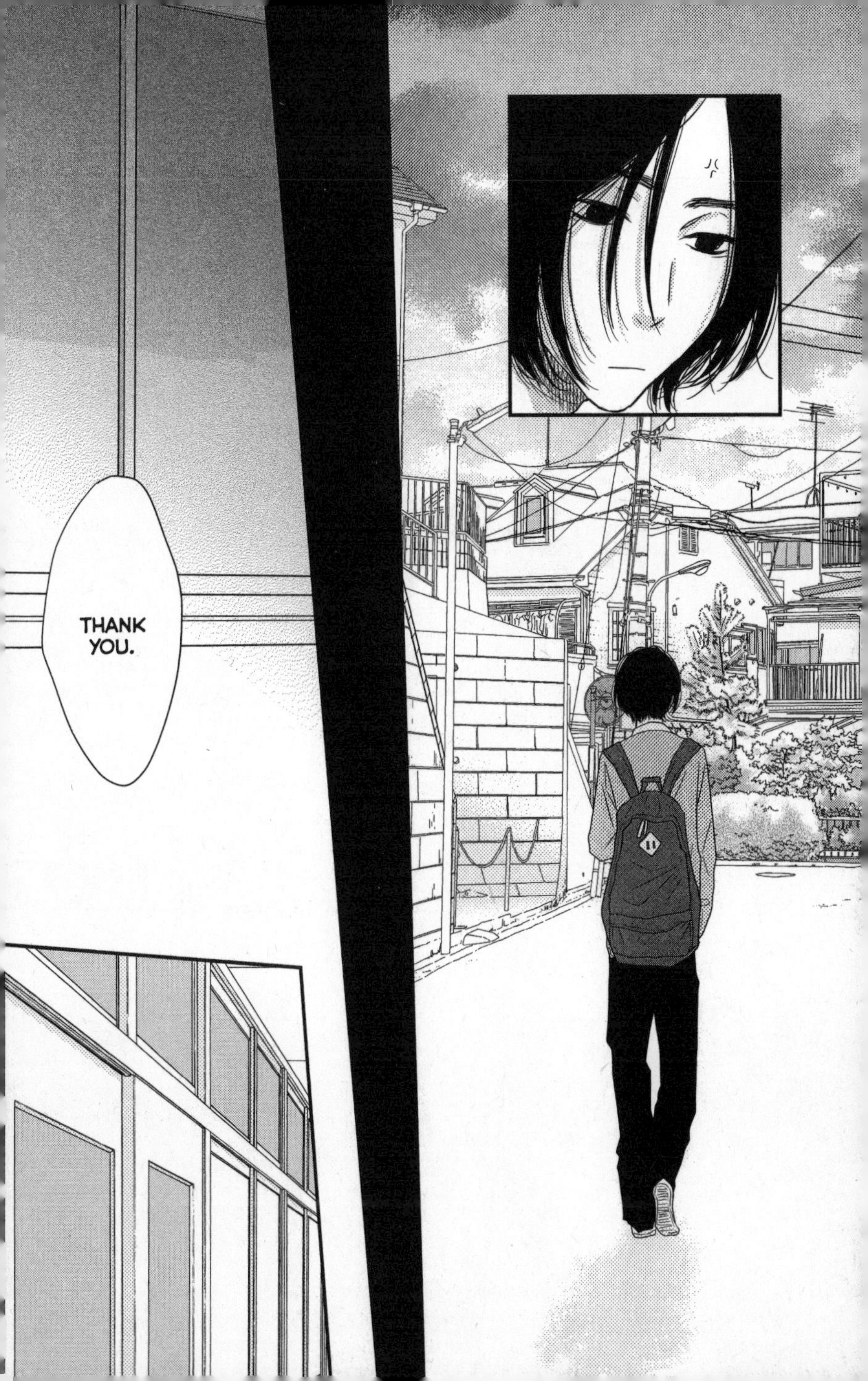
THANK YOU.

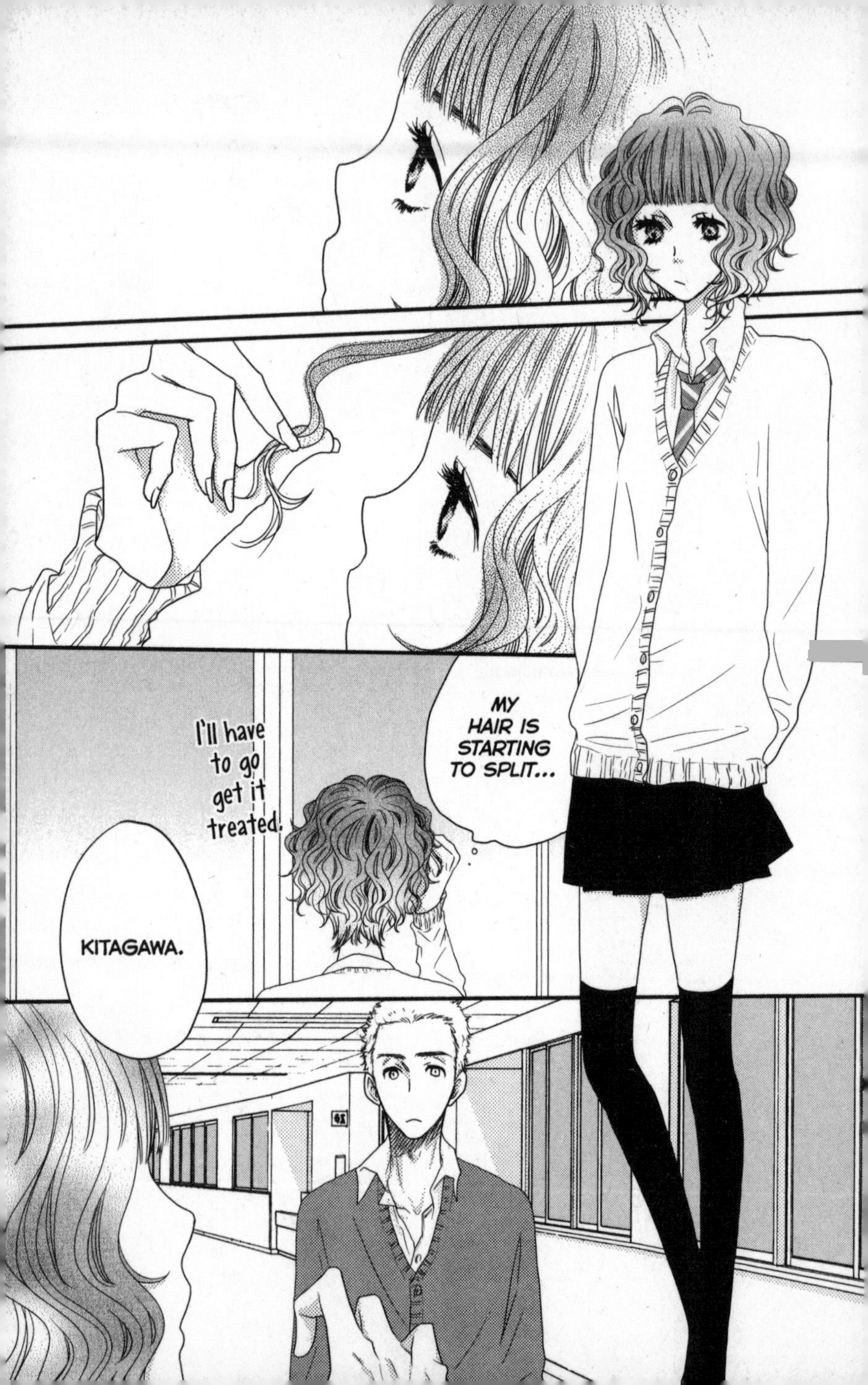
MY HAIR IS STARTING TO SPLIT...
I'll have to go get it treated!
KITAGAWA.

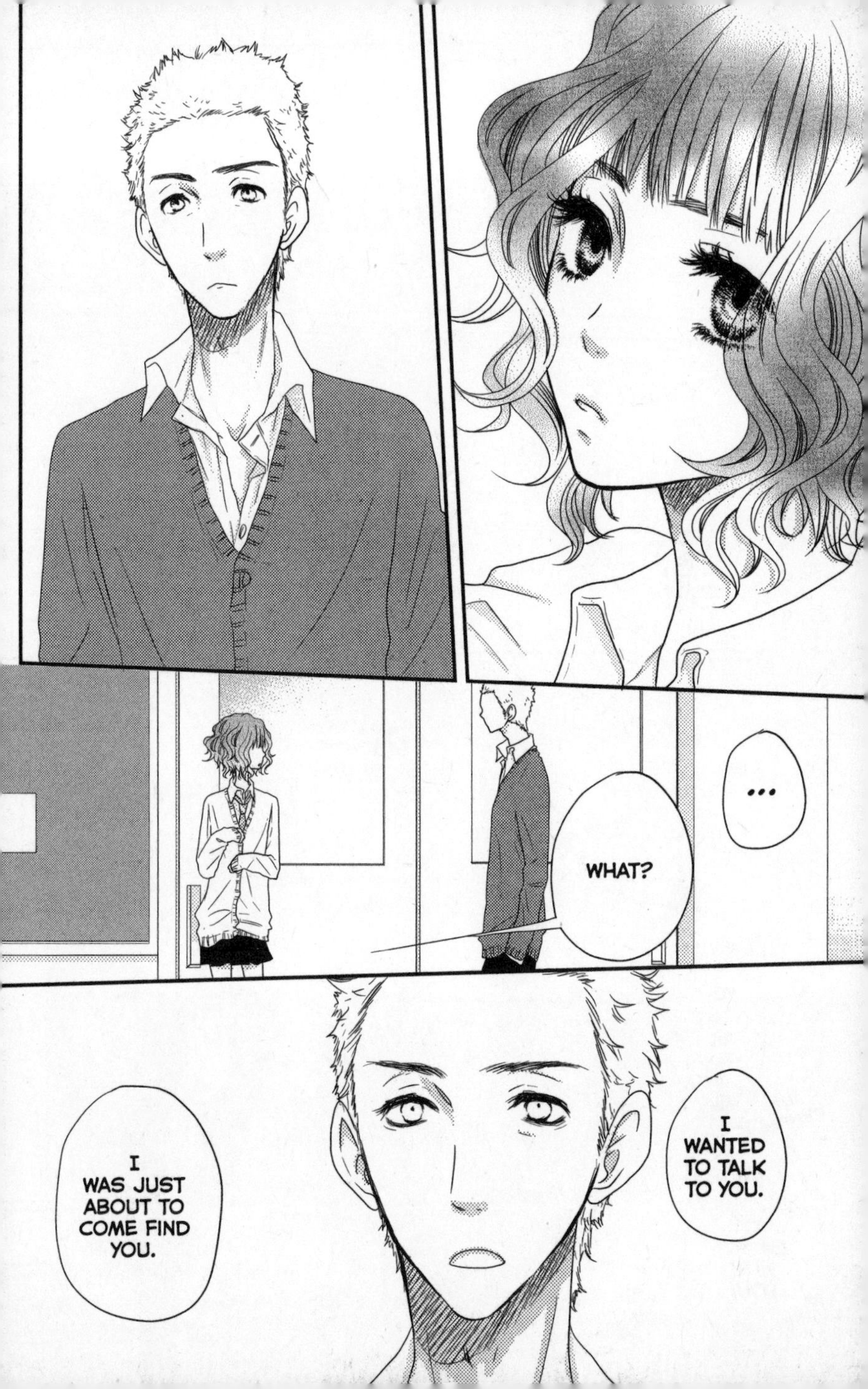
...
WHAT?
I WANTED TO TALK TO YOU.
I WAS JUST ABOUT TO COME FIND YOU.

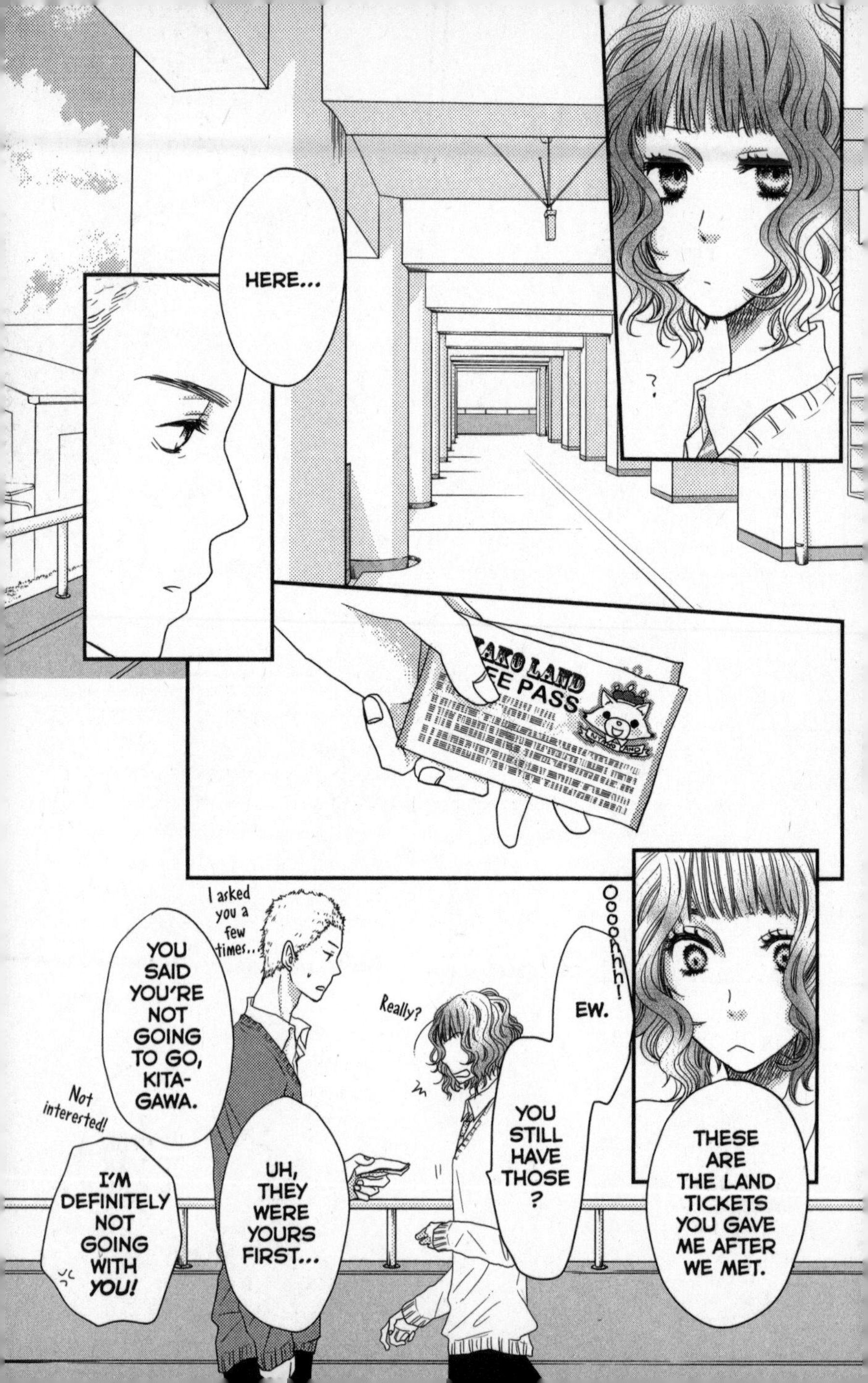
?
HERE...
Oooonhh!
THESE ARE THE LAND TICKETS YOU GAVE ME AFTER WE MET.
EW.
YOU STILL HAVE THOSE?
Really?
UH, THEY WERE YOURS FIRST...
I asked you a few times...
YOU SAID YOU'RE NOT GOING TO GO, KITA-GAWA.
Not interested!
I'M DEFINITELY NOT GOING WITH YOU!

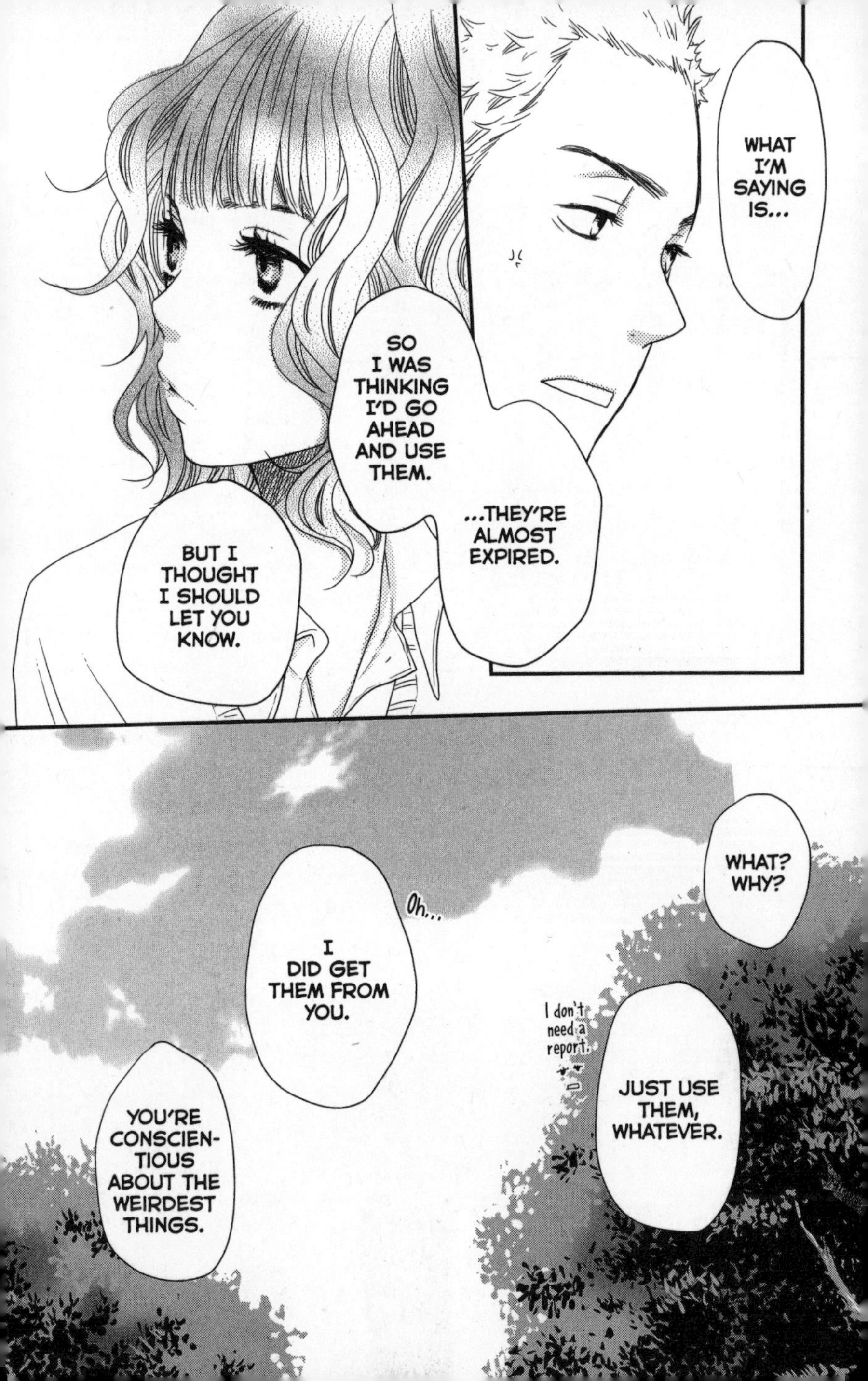
WHAT I'M SAYING IS...
...THEY'RE ALMOST EXPIRED.
SO I WAS THINKING I'D GO AHEAD AND USE THEM.
BUT I THOUGHT I SHOULD LET YOU KNOW.
WHAT? WHY?
I don't need a report.
JUST USE THEM, WHATEVER.
Oh...
I DID GET THEM FROM YOU.
YOU'RE CONSCIEN-TIOUS ABOUT THE WEIRDEST THINGS.

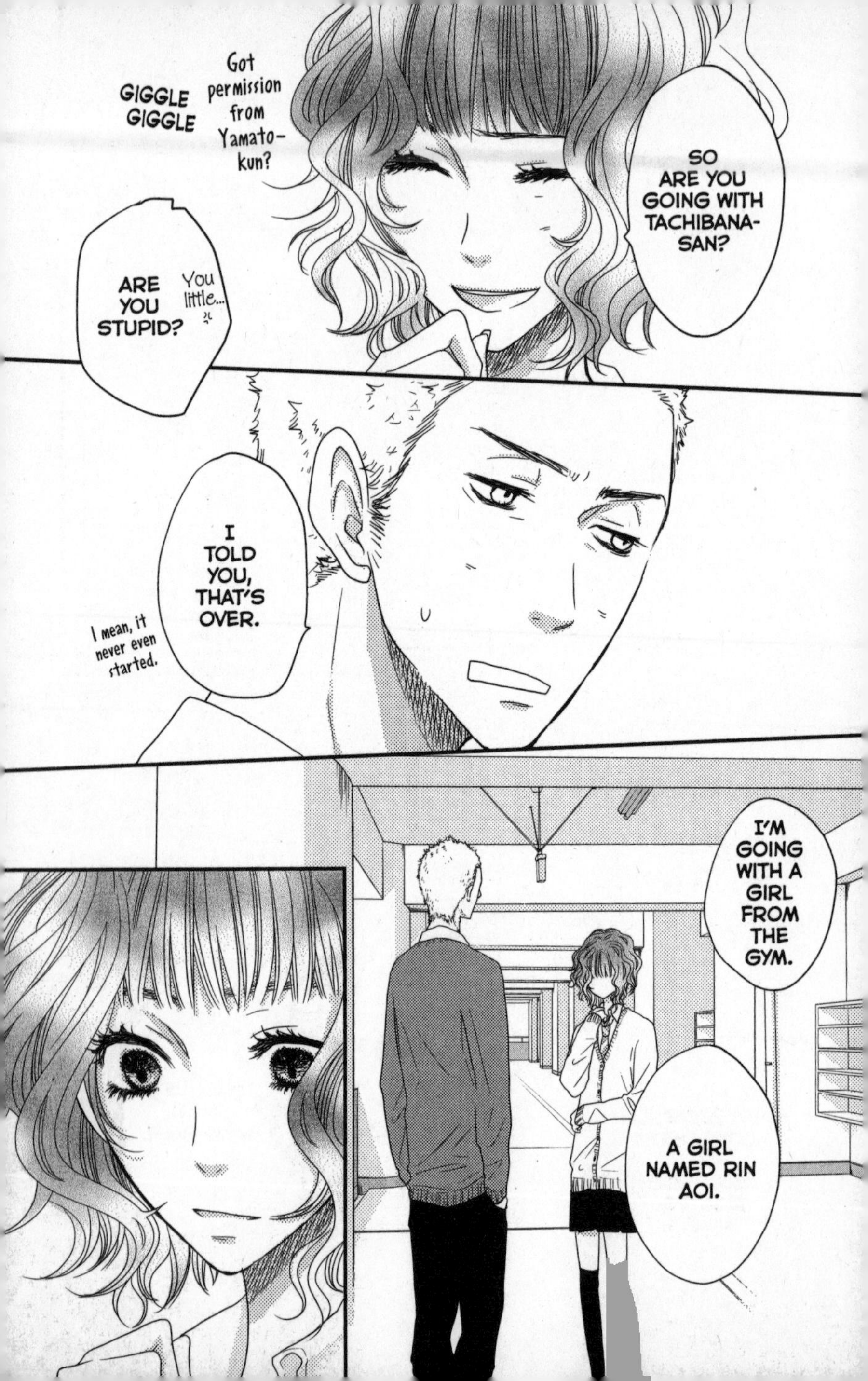
SO ARE YOU GOING WITH TACHIBANA-SAN?
Got permission from Yamato-kun?
GIGGLE GIGGLE
ARE YOU STUPID?
You little...
I TOLD YOU, THAT'S OVER.
I mean, it never even started.
I'M GOING WITH A GIRL FROM THE GYM.
A GIRL NAMED RIN AOI.

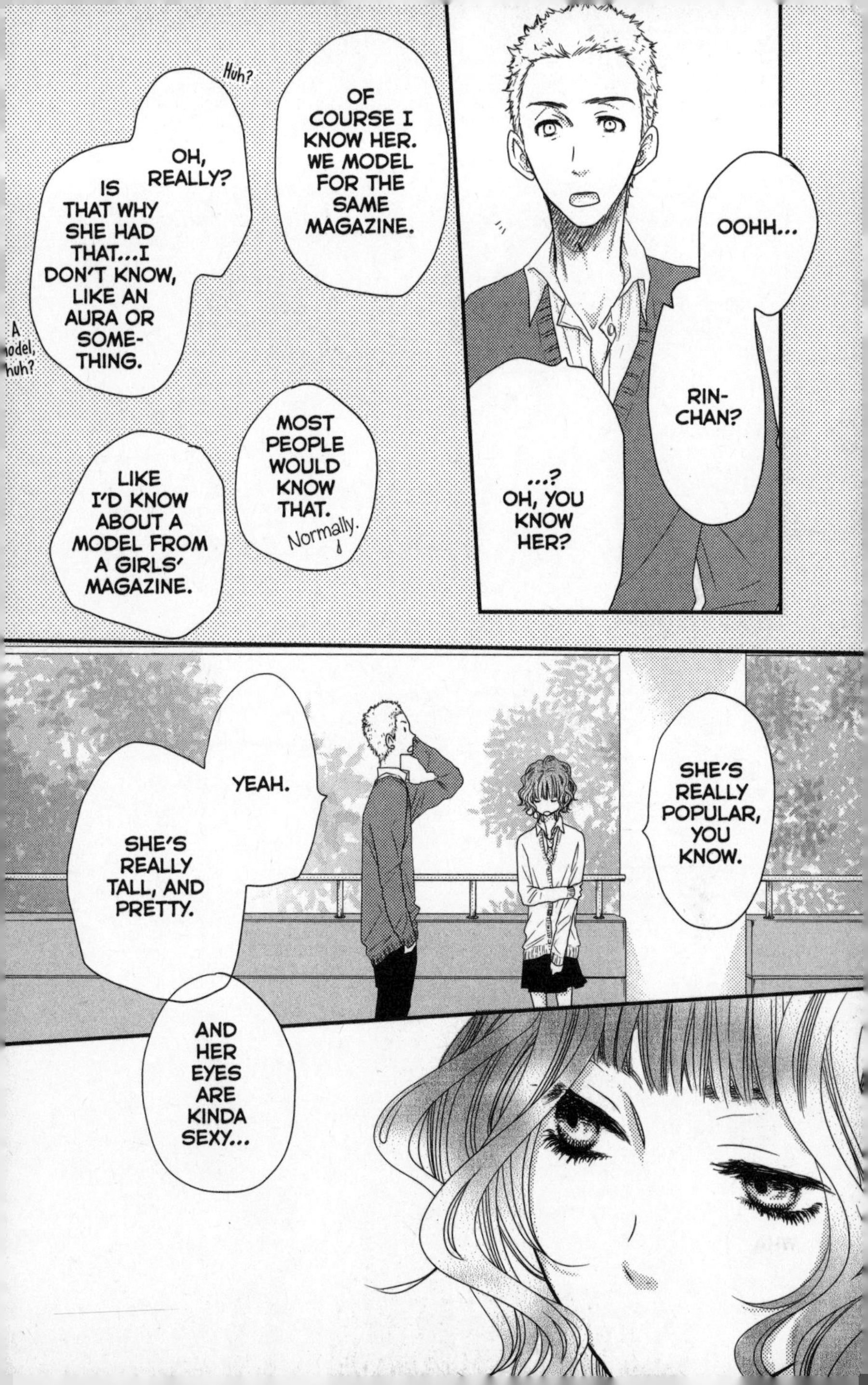
OOHH...
RIN-CHAN?
...? OH, YOU KNOW HER?
OF COURSE I KNOW HER. WE MODEL FOR THE SAME MAGAZINE.
Huh?
OH, REALLY?
IS THAT WHY SHE HAD THAT...I DON'T KNOW, LIKE AN AURA OR SOME-THING.
A odel, huh?
MOST PEOPLE WOULD KNOW THAT.
Normally.
LIKE I'D KNOW ABOUT A MODEL FROM A GIRLS' MAGAZINE.
SHE'S REALLY POPULAR, YOU KNOW.
YEAH.
SHE'S REALLY TALL, AND PRETTY.
AND HER EYES ARE KINDA SEXY...

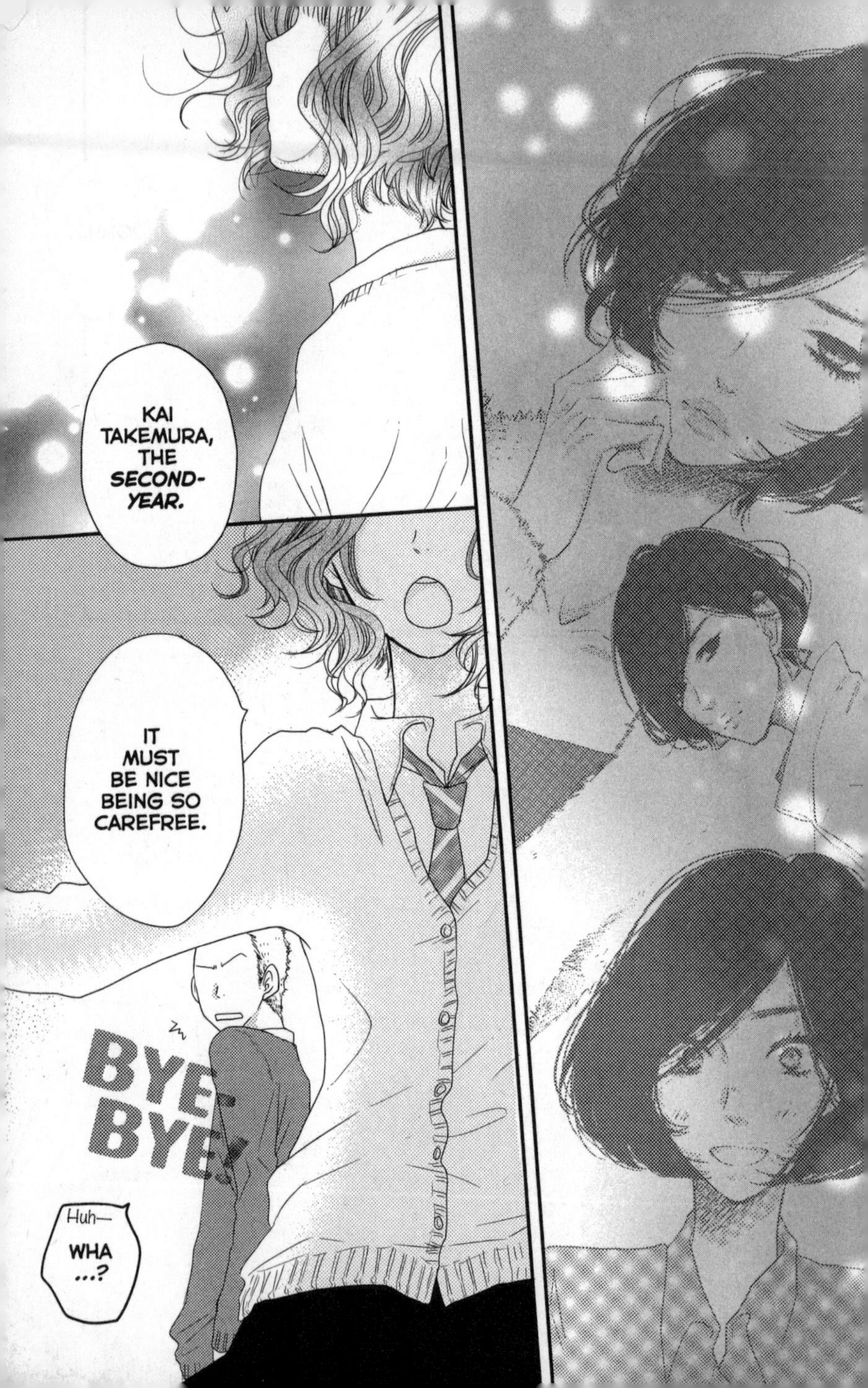
KAI TAKEMURA, THE SECOND-YEAR.
IT MUST BE NICE BEING SO CAREFREE.
BYE-BYE
Huh—
WHA ...?

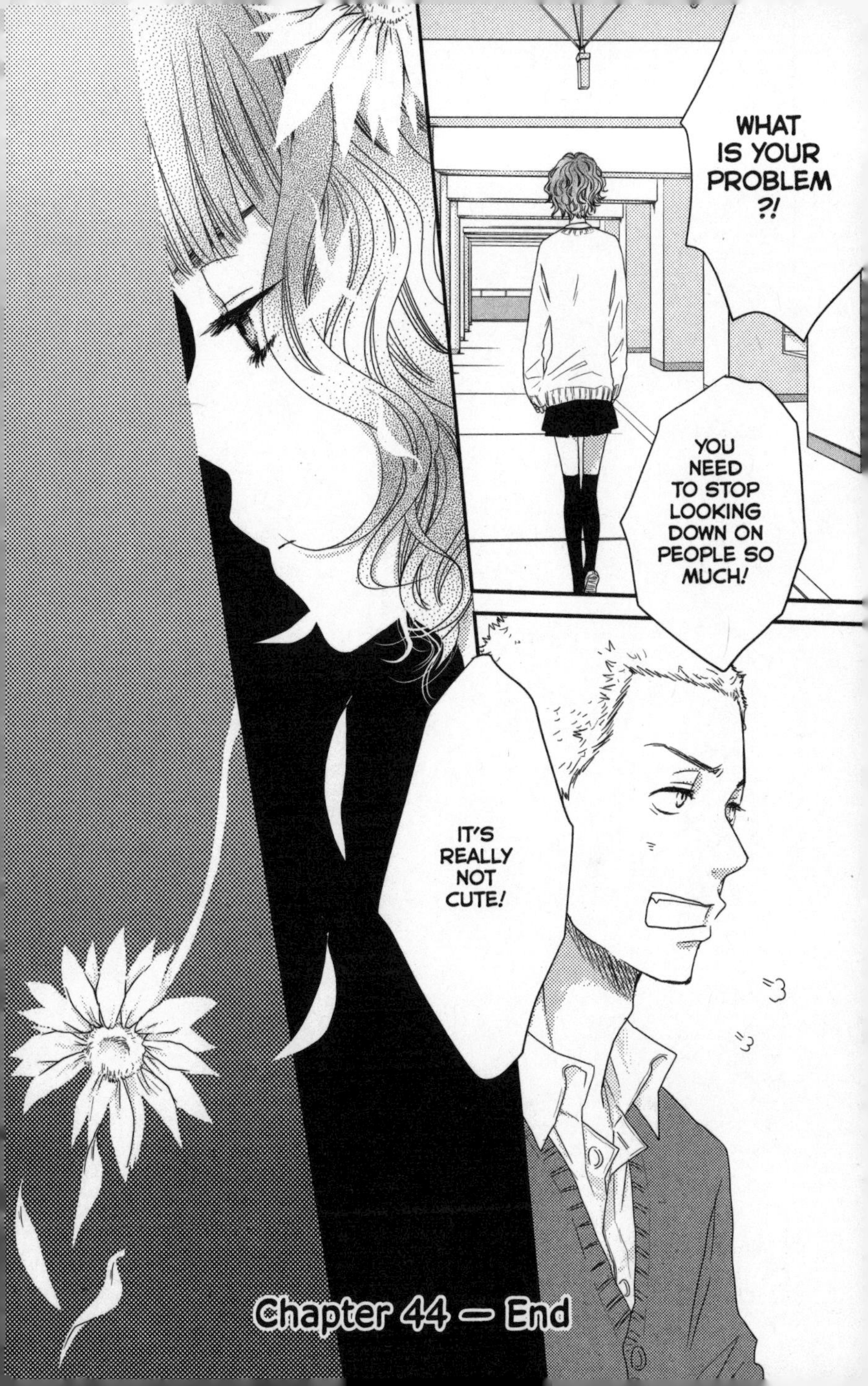
WHAT IS YOUR PROBLEM ?!
YOU NEED TO STOP LOOKING DOWN ON PEOPLE SO MUCH!
IT'S REALLY NOT CUTE!
Chapter 44 — End

Say "I love you".

Hello, I'm Kanae Hazuki. This is volume 11. Mei and Yamato finally slept together in the last volume, and I got an amazing amount of reactions from all of you, so I was really glad I drew it. Now as for this volume...?

It was really nice to have so many people say, "I'm so glad!" "I'm so relieved that they did it," but on the other hand, it definitely puts more pressure on me. I even had people close to me say I could go ahead and end the series now, because what more story is there to tell? It's not good to keep it running long.

But once they do it, is that the end goal? Don't they have more stories to tell after that? Isn't that actually just the beginning for them? I wonder. First of all, I didn't draw this series just because I wanted to hook the main girl up with a hot guy. I wanted to explore how the heroine would think and grow in situations she's never experienced before. Sleeping with the guy she loves is not part of Mei's growth. I went back to the beginning and thought about it. Mei is a third-year in high school. She has to think about her future. And not just Mei, but all the kids around her. This might be the first time I've agonized so much about the future of the characters in my manga.

I went through this period in my life, too, when I was a student. At the time, I really hadn't thought about anything—not for a second—and I never put any real effort into finding a job. Around that time, I would submit my drawings to magazines and I did get some jobs, but I never got paid enough money that you could really call it an income. I really should have been thinking about my future, but I just frivolously thought, "I can live off my art! It'll work out!" My mother watched me the whole time, but she never said anything to me. And then came graduation.

After I graduated, I'd lay around all day like an idiot, thinking, "Every day is a day off! I love this!" Even so, I did occasionally take some manga jobs, but you definitely could not have said I had a secure livelihood. There were a lot of times when even my mother couldn't pay the bills, and I think I made life hard on her. But the only thing she ever said about it was, "As long as I'm alive and kicking, everything will be fine." And back then, I took advantage of the fact that she said that. But when my mother got sick, I realized I couldn't be like that. Reality taught me a hard lesson, and I had to get serious. That's when I started desperately looking for publishers, working at many different places, making lots of work connections, drawing—and with that, I think I managed to make a decent living.

In my case, I realized everything too late, but my mother was very supportive of my art, and she knew that if she tried to tell me what to do, I would only get more stubborn. I think that's why she made it a point not to complain to me much, even if she was concerned on the inside. Thinking back on it now, I also think it would have taken a lot of courage to do what she did. But thanks to her, I was able to pursue my selfish dreams, and now I make a living drawing manga.

To change people's minds, you need to think with them, and give the other person a chance to think, too. People grow by having more time to think. We can grow by thinking. In the end, we're the ones who decide if we rise or fall. No one else can do it for us. And I wanted to give Mei some time to think, too. I want to draw more and more of Mei and her friends' growth. And I want to grow myself so that now, after I've said all this, I won't disappoint.

Thank you for reading this far. I hope we'll meet again next volume.

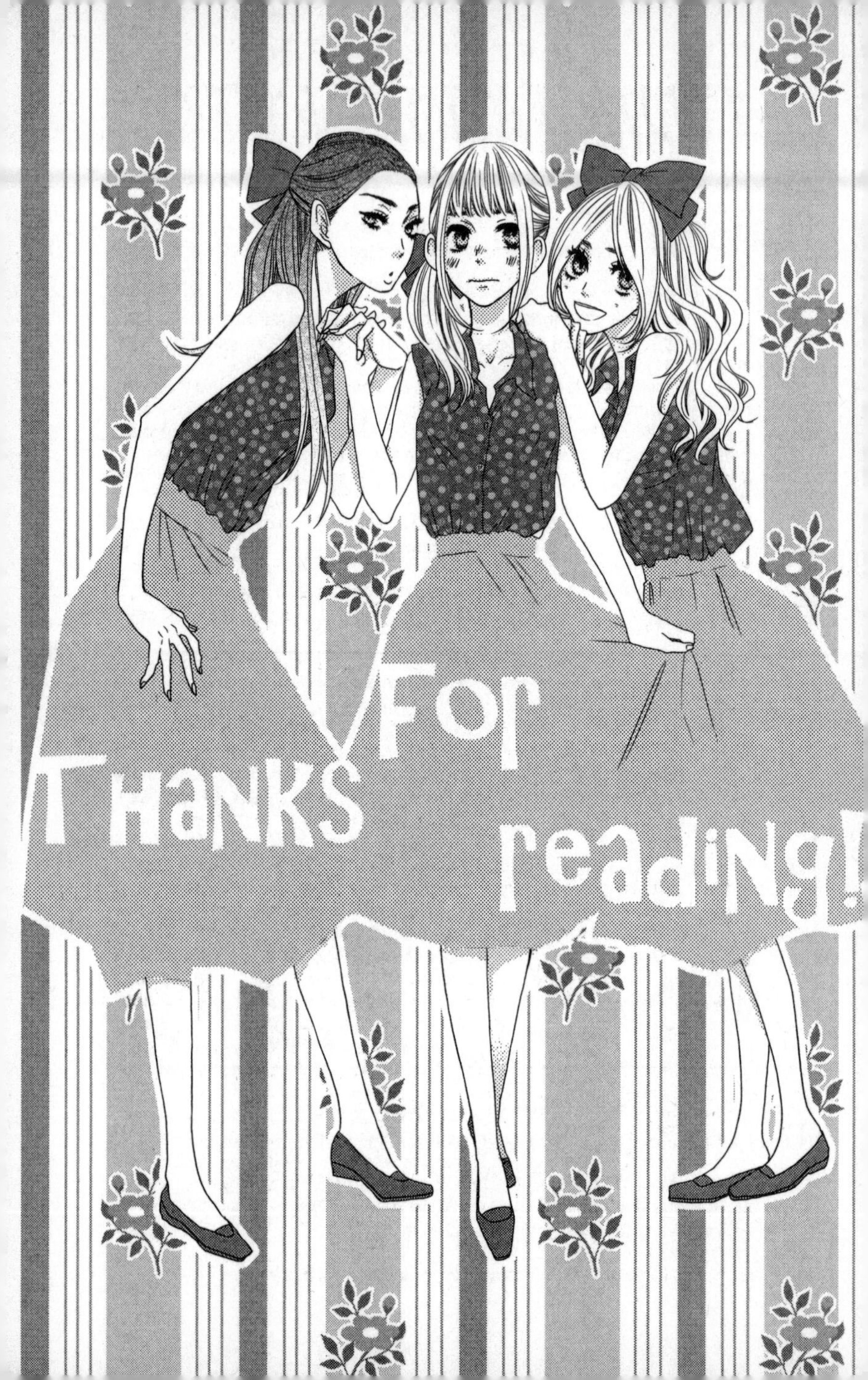
THANKS For reading!!

TRANSLATION NOTES

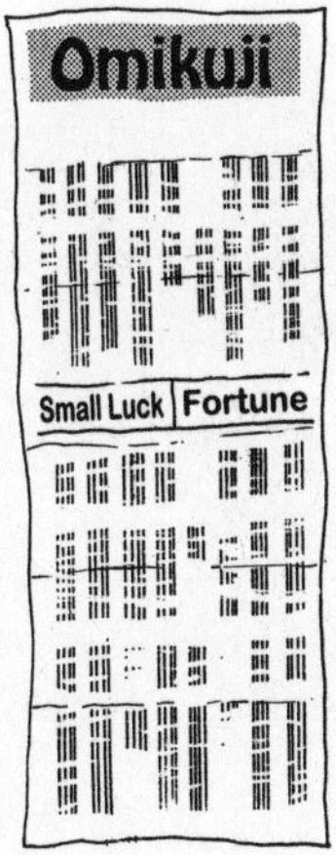
Omikuji
Small Luck
Fortune

Page 7: Omikuji

An *omikuji* is a little strip of paper with a fortune written on it, kind of like what you find in a fortune cookie. This is obtained at Japanese Buddhist and Shinto shrines by making an offering and choosing one at random. Each strip lists the amount of luck the chooser is going to have, ranging from *dai-kichi* (great blessing, great luck), to lesser degrees of luck. They are often obtained during the first temple visit around New Year's Day, so this particular omikuji is probably shown to the readers to let us know that it is now a new year.

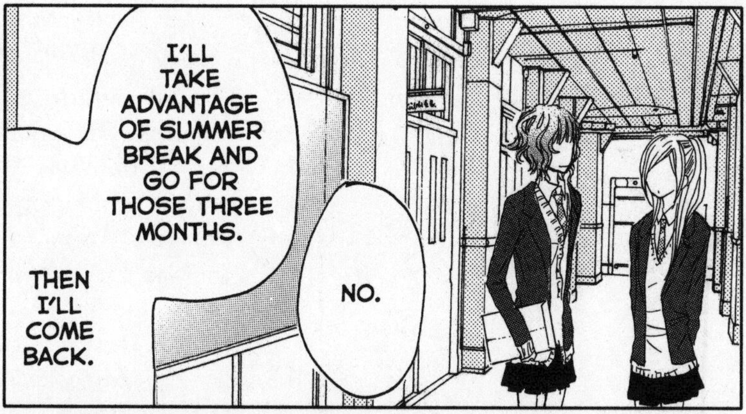
I'LL TAKE ADVANTAGE OF SUMMER BREAK AND GO FOR THOSE THREE MONTHS.
NO.
THEN I'LL COME BACK.

Page 15: Taking advantage of summer break

It may or may not be interesting to note that in Japan, summer vacation is only one month long. Megumi is going to take advantage of that time off to miss as little school as possible, but she will still be missing two months.

Page 16: Ohagi
Also known as *botamochi* or *hagi no mochi, ohagi* is a Japanese treat made from sweet rice packed in a ball and coated with azuki red bean paste.

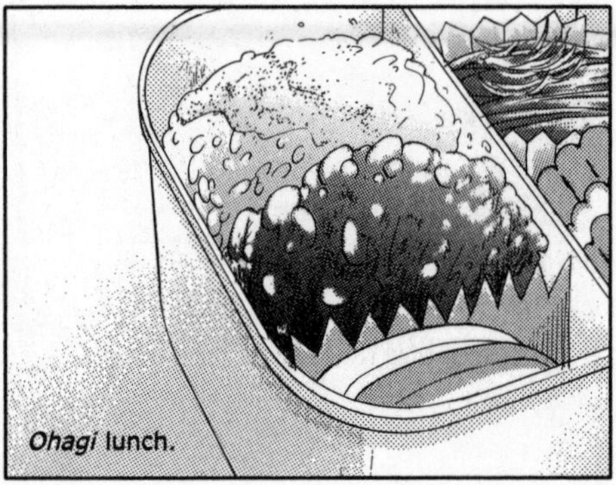
Ohagi lunch.

Page 39: The little girl's oni
Mei is a little shocked when the little girl tries to tell her that she was with her brother *(Onii-chan),* because the beginning of *onii-chan* is *oni.* An *oni,* often translated as "ogre," is a creature from Japanese folklore that can be rather frightening, and this particular little girl doesn't seem like the type you might expect to be hanging out with one.

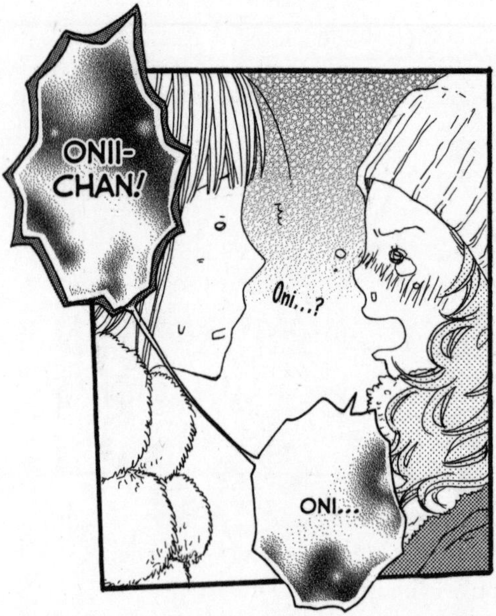
ONII-CHAN!
Oni...?
ONI...

Page 150: Golden Week
Golden Week is the name for the first week in May, when Japan celebrates several holidays all at once. It actually starts on April 29, which is Shōwa Day, the birthday of Emperor Hirohito, who reigned during the Shōwa Era. May 3, 4, and 5 are also holidays.

Messages
From Aoi Len-san
Sub This is Aoi.
Thanks for talking to me earlier. I just asked Hiro's preschool about volunteering, and they suggested you come for a day or two over Golden Week. What do you think? (-ω-)

Say I Love You.

My Little Monster

OPPOSITES ATTRACT...MAYBE?

Haru Yoshida is feared as an unstable and violent "monster." Mizutani Shizuku is a grade-obsessed student with no friends. Fate brings these two together to form the most unlikely pair. Haru firmly believes he's in love with Mizutani and she firmly believes he's insane.

KC KODANSHA COMICS

Say I Love You. volume 11 is a work of fiction. Names, characters, places, and incidents are the products of the author's imagination or are used fictitiously. Any resemblance to actual events, locales, or persons, living or dead, is entirely coincidental.

A Kodansha Comics Trade Paperback Original

Published in the United States by Kodansha Comics, an imprint of Kodansha USA Publishing, LLC, New York.

Publication rights for this English edition arranged through Kodansha Ltd, Tokyo.

First published in Japan in 2013 by Kodansha Ltd., Tokyo as *Sukitte iinayo.* volume 11.

ISBN 978-1-63236-041-0

Printed in the United States of America.

www.kodanshacomics.com

9 8 7 6 5 4 3 2 1
Translation: Alethea and Athena Nibley
Lettering: John Clark
Editing: Ajani Oloye
Kodansha Comics edition cover design by Phil Balsman